Ecologies
of the Heart

Ecologies
of the Heart

EMOTION, BELIEF,

AND THE ENVIRONMENT

E. N. Anderson

Department of Anthropology
University of California, Riverside

New York Oxford | **Oxford University Press** | 1996

Oxford University Press

Oxford   New York
Athens   Auckland   Bangkok   Bombay
Calcutta   Cape Town   Dar es Salaam   Delhi
Florence   Hong Kong   Istanbul   Karachi
Kuala Lumpur   Madras   Madrid   Melbourne
Mexico City   Nairobi   Paris   Singapore
Taipei   Tokyo   Toronto

and associated companies in
Berlin   Ibadan

Copyright © 1996 by Oxford University Press, Inc.

Published by Oxford University Press, Inc.,
198 Madison Avenue, New York, New York 10016

Library of Congress Cataloging-in-Publication Data
Anderson, Eugene N. (Eugene Newton), 1941–
Ecologies of the heart: emotion, belief, and the environment / Eugene N. Anderson.
p.   cm   Includes bibliographical references and indexes.
ISBN 0-19-509010-1
1. Environmental policy.   2. Environmental protection.
3. Human ecology.   4. Environmental sciences—Philosophy.
I. Title.
GE170.A53   1996
363.7—dc20   95-13747

1 3 5 7 9 8 6 4 2

Printed in the United States of America
on acid-free, recycled paper ✖

For the children

Preface

This book looks at how humans process information and how they relate this information to resource management.

I begin by dealing with the question of why people hold beliefs about the environment that seem "counterfactual"—against the facts—to modern scientists. I will show that these beliefs are understandable and have some empirical basis.

I proceed to observe that traditional peoples have often conserved the environment effectively, on the basis of just those "counterfactual," but reasonable, views.

I then point out that there are also, in modern society, counterfactual notions about the environment that *prevent* the sane use of resources, rather than *promote* that goal.

Finally, I offer some suggestions toward a solution to this problem in the modern world. Neither I nor any other person is going to solve the world ecological crisis single-handed, but, on the other hand, the world ecological crisis will not be solved unless we recognize the problem presented by beliefs that are plausible but inadequate.

I am a cultural ecologist—I live by studying the ways in which different groups of people manage the environment. I have lived in fishing communities in Hong Kong, Malaysia, Singapore, Tahiti, and British Columbia, and in a Maya farmtown in the south of Mexico. Having spent most of my life studying fisheries, farms, and forests, I have come to some conclusions about management problems, including difficult ones such as fishery and forest conservation.

The first and most important conclusion is that ecological problems are due to human choice—not to blind forces of technology, and not to such reified value judgments as "greed" or "population explosion."

The second is that human choice is often made on the basis of strong emotions, such as love and hate, as well as more or less dispassionate cost-benefit calculations. The roots of economic action are not unimpassioned.

The third is that human choice, being necessarily made on the basis of what people know, is subject to all the problems of human information processing. People make mistakes. They also set priorities that may be far from those that would guarantee long-term self-interest by any standard.

The fourth is that society must therefore view environmental management as necessarily involving an ethical and moral code backed up by emotional force, but society must also create an economic system that makes ecological sanity economically attractive. This middle ground seems rarely taken. Most analyses of our environmental problems seem almost wholly moral or moralistic (e.g., the spiritual and deep-ecology approaches described by Merchant)[1] or almost wholly economic or technical (e.g., Field).[2]

While my thinking on the subject has been similar to that of others, including Al Gore in his book *Earth in the Balance,* the present book is, however, a very different work. The phenomenon of "simultaneous invention" is common experience for a working scientist, but it is quite a compliment when one is scooped by no less than the vice president of the United States. Vice President Gore leans more toward the moral and less toward the economic side than I do. In this book, I provide studies that are intended to show a range of approaches to thinking about environmental management. After thirty years of working in and around the field of resource management and development—including five years of living with traditional non-Western peoples in their communities—I have had some occasion to see what forces actually influence decisions on the ground.

The title of this book is a conscious play on Gregory Bateson's "ecology of mind."[3] Since Bateson called our attention to the cognitive and emotional sides of ecology, we have learned a great deal more about human behavior. The metaphorical heart—that is, the deep emotional side of humanity—has turned out to be more basic than the metaphorical mind—the conscious, rational actor.

At this point I must specify two assumptions. They are not part of my argument proper, and you, the reader, do not have to accept either one; my argument stands or falls without them. However, they are relevant as guiding principles to my inquiry.

First, I see this book as essentially scientific, and I see science as the pursuit of knowledge. I explicitly use this view to oppose two extreme views that are currently popular: science as a list of Truths (with a capital *T*), and science as an essentially arbitrary social construct. In my view, science slowly accumulates useful observations and synthesizes them with more and more powerful theories. Observations are made to be improved and supplemented. Theories are made to be superseded. Science consists of questions and of means for addressing them—not of absolute truths. This book outlines an approach that may be useful. I hope and trust that it will stimulate enough debate to be itself superseded in a year or two. I do not feel we have the luxury of believing that science or knowledge is essentially arbitrary, a mere social construct. Starvation, disease, and death from pollution are all too real, and we must generate realistic and pragmatic remedies.

Second, an author's views are always somewhat relevant to his or her discussion, and my own views about conservation may be of interest. I am a conservationist and environmental activist committed to long-term or sustainable policies. I am committed to saving species, populations, and ecosystems. I am not, however, a hard-core environmentalist or an animal rights activist. I reserve the right to eat meat and swat mosquitoes. I do not advocate displacing the human inhabitants of the Great Plains. As an anthropologist, I work with humans. I tend toward a utilitarian ethic: the greatest good for the greatest number over the greatest time. However, I see limits to that ethic, as will appear.

Acknowledgments

This book emerged from interaction and discussion with Evelyn Pinkerton, whose dedication to the cause of local management is an unfailing inspiration. I have also benefited particularly deeply from discussion with Sharon Burton (stalwart research assistant and idea source through much of the writing process), Silver Damsen, Leslie Gottesfeld, Eugene Hunn, Bonnie McCay, Robert Netting, two anonymous readers, Joan Bossert (my editor at Oxford University Press), and—of course—my wife, Myra Anderson, whose patient reading greatly improved the manuscript.

Countless others have contributed. Alas, I cannot mention everyone. I have also tried to keep references to a minimum. I hope this does not lead to unfair neglect of anyone, and I apologize sincerely to authors whose relevant work I fail to cite.

As always, I must single out above all my many friends and helpers in the field, especially Chau Hung Fai, Choi Kwok Tai, Ch'ng Tek Liang, Felix Medina Tzuc, and Pastor Valdez and his family. Ultimately, this is their book. They taught me that people around the world have learned to cope with an incredible range of environments, and with difficult—often appallingly difficult—situations.

They taught me more: I learned that people can respond to the hardest and most tragic times with the most brilliant triumphs.

The authentic voice of human ecology is, for me, the blues of John Hurt and of Robert Johnson: pain and agony transmuted into glory that "outshines the sun."

Riverside, California   *E. N. A.*
April 1995

Contents

1. Landscape with Figures 3

2. *Feng-shui:* Ideology and Ecology 15

3. Chinese Nutritional Therapy 28

4. Learning from the Land Otter: Religious Representation of Traditional Resource Management 54

5. Managing the Rainforest: Maya Agriculture in the Town of the Wild Plums 73

6. Needs and Human Nature 85

7. Information Processing: Rational and Irrational Transcended 100

8. Culture: Ecology in a Wider Context 123

9. In and Out of Institutions 135

10. The Disenchanted: Religion as Ecological Control, and Its Modern Fate 160

11. A Summary, and Some Suggestions 174

Notes 185
References 215
Index 235

Ecologies
of the Heart

1

Landscape with Figures

Ah, Love, could you and I with Him conspire
To grasp this sorry scheme of things entire,
How would we shatter it to bits, and then
Remold it closer to the heart's desire!

So wrote Edward Fitzgerald, following (loosely) the Persian of Omar Khayyám. In this quatrain, he captured what may be the most universal and constant yearning of humankind.

Modern psychology has shown what many of us always suspected: humans continually, in the secrecy of their thoughts, do exactly what Fitzgerald wished. The external world is all too refractory, but "the soul is free." Thus, humans often see what they want to see, and believe about it what they wish to believe. The external world may intrude harshly on this process, but people often show a truly instructive ability to shut out reality.

Positive illusions are only one of the ways we distort information. The human brain is a wondrous device—partly because it does not produce a perfect, total representation of what the senses perceive. We are constantly reinterpreting those perceptions in terms of our wants and needs—not only needs for things like food and shelter, but also needs to see the world as hopefully as possible, to see it as simple and comprehensible, and to see it as ultimately manageable. The brain quite literally does shatter perception "to bits, and then remold it closer to the heart's desire."

The world environmental problem is serious, and getting steadily more so. Part of the reason is that humans have seen what they wanted to see and have deliberately blinded themselves to the less desirable consequences of their actions.

The built-in human tendency to see the world through rose-colored glasses has received the name "positive illusions" from social psychologist Shelley Taylor.[1] She points out the advantages of positive illusions. They allow us to face a threatening world. However, positive illusions have their costs. It is, at the best of times, hard to get people to sacrifice short-term interests for long-term benefits. Positive illusions make it even harder.

Such habits of mind lie behind much of the world's pollution, species extinction, deforestation, overfishing, soil erosion, and famine. Political remedies have failed. The vaunted Rio de Janeiro conference of 1992 was disappointing.[2]

Little is being done now to avert the disasters we can predict for tomorrow—depletion of the world's fisheries, new AIDS-like epidemics, worldwide climate changes from the greenhouse effect, and the rest.

Why are we so foolish? We really don't know. Thirty years ago, simple ignorance appeared to account for it. "Ecology" was a little-known word, and the world's environmental problems were known mainly to specialists. Twenty years ago, ignorance was no longer a credible plea, but we could fall back on "shortsighted greed." This too was an inadequate explanation. Even the most shortsighted are often aware that their immediate self-interest is now at stake. Fisheries, grazing lands, and forests, for example, are disappearing so fast that the economic survival of their exploiters is a matter of immediate concern. We are no longer talking about the distant future. Joel Heinen and Roberta Low, after making these points, are driven to postulate instinct: genes drive humans to maximize immediate profit at long-term expense.[3] Yet, as they admit, many societies have succeeded in persuading people to sacrifice immediate goals for long-term or wide-flung interests.

In economic jargon, much of the problem lies in the human tendency to set unrealistic discount rates.[4] Humans seem to value even a very small present good over a very large future good. This is partly due to positive illusions, partly due to other types of mistakes, and partly due to genuine uncertainty about the future. It is also the only truly consistent way to judge ends[5]—for what that's worth.

The most serious environmental problems are, by and large, ones that involve trade-offs between the present and the future, or between a wide, diffuse interest and a specific, intense one. The nature of modern politics makes it very easy for governments to sacrifice a very large but non-immediate interest for a very small but immediate one. Organized lobbies and powerful economic interests win over even the largest and most urgently pressed majorities. The extreme case was presented in Eastern Europe, where governments sacrificed the environment to immediate production. The resulting damage is incalculable. Suffice it to recall Chernobyl, or the Aral Sea catastrophe and the attendant agricultural pollution that raised infant mortality rates to one in ten near that dying lake.[6]

Such governmental neglect of the environment is not a problem of socialism alone. It was blind chance that saved us from our own Chernobyl at Three Mile Island. California's Imperial Valley may yet give us our equivalent of the Aral Sea disaster. The problem is one that is shared by modern capitalism and Communism: a political inability to sacrifice short-term, narrow interests to gain far larger long-term, wide benefits. Modern politics deals with immediate conflicts between groups, frequently groups that are battling over control of resources. Cooperation and long-term vision are squeezed out by the process.

Obviously, the whole environmental issue is a highly emotional one. The classic difference between politics and economics is that politics is about emotion and conflict, economics about sensible and materially productive solutions. This distinction is no longer regarded as valid by economists or political scientists, but it still captures a truth. Politics tends to recast problems that could be solved by common sense into holy wars. In such wars, everyone gets hurt.

Many authorities conclude that we cannot sever scientific issues of ecological management from issues of human emotion and motivation. Conservation biologist David Orr, discussing the teaching of his field, asks, "Why is it so hard to talk about love, the most powerful of human emotions, in relation to science, the most powerful and far-reaching of human activities?"[7] In a wider context, fisheries biologists such as Arthur McEvoy and Donald Ludwig stress the need to consider motivation and political debate in understanding and preventing the decline of fisheries.[8]

The real problem, frequently, is not technology or greed, but human error. The issues are subject to oversimplification and emotional distortion.

We have ample technology to reverse all of today's bad ecological trends without undue economic dislocation. Pollution control and resource management technology have run far ahead of application. The most serious problems—depletion of forests, grazing lands, fish, and topsoil—could be cured simply by saying no.

We also have the ideology. Thoreau coined the term "ecology" a century and a half ago (well before Ernst Haeckel made the word popular), and Charles

Marsh gave "conservation" its modern sense soon after. A hundred years ago, Democratic President Grover Cleveland and Republican President Theodore Roosevelt made resource management a national agenda. Today, most people throughout the world see the problem of poor resource management and want something done. Yet the situation continues to deteriorate.

This is partly because of the particular nature of some of the problems we face. Many resource choices are clear: if pollution is killing people, it should be stopped. More commonly, though, we are dealing with problems of a particularly knotty kind that cannot be solved by ordinary rational calculus, either economic or ethical. These involve trading off a short-term, narrow, but compelling interest against a long-term, diffuse one.

Consider several typical cases.

A factory is polluting the local water supply. Being at the headwaters, it gets pure water. People downstream suffer. The factory owner gets the benefits of his production, while people unrelated to his enterprise pay the costs.

The North Sea herring fishery is depleted by overfishing. This has been known for centuries. In brief respites during the world wars, the herring stocks recovered, but heavy fishing began again as soon as the wars ended. In spite of the fact that every North Sea nation is losing millions of dollars a year by not agreeing to conserve the stocks, no agreement has ever been reached. Each nation is too protective of its own fishermen. Each nation knows that, if it were to curtail its fishing, the other nations would simply expand theirs, and no conservation would take place.

Many Americans faithfully recycle paper. They get nothing from this activity, and it costs time and effort. The benefits to society of any one person's old papers are infinitesimal. Yet, if everyone recycled paper, we would all benefit considerably. Similar is the commuter problem: for any one person to abstain from commuting by private car would be costly to the individual without benefiting society significantly, but if everyone abstained, society would benefit.

In some areas, local peasants are cutting down the last virgin forests of the tropics. (In other areas, the multinational corporations are the cutters, but that is another question.) The plants in these forests have enormous potential value to humanity, but most of that value lies in the future. If the peasants don't cut and farm, they starve to death—in the present. The only possible solution is for humanity as a whole (or its representatives) to pay the peasants to save the forests. Yet, the *known* benefits to individual humans are slight. Perhaps the forests contain the plant that would cure cancer or AIDS—but we don't know. So no one wants to pay.

These cases illustrate four aspects of one problem. The first case is the simplest. The factory owner uses his power to pass on costs as "externalities." As Earl Murphy pointed out long ago in *Governing Nature,* this problem can be solved by giving the downstream users some power to sue or otherwise "specify the costs" on the owner.[9] The problem is that the owner can use his money to influence politicians not to permit any such thing. Such self-sustaining abuse of power is one face of our knotty problem. If the owner would, in fact, lose his competitive advantage and go broke if such legislation were passed, the question gets knottier. A small benefit to water quality would be won at enormous cost to the owner and his employees.

Case two is, of course, a real-world example of Garrett Hardin's "Tragedy of the Commons."[10] An enormous literature has gathered around this question; Hardin's article is said to be the most-cited scientific article of modern times.

Case three is an example of the infinitesimal-effect problem. It is similar to the classic dilemma of the would-be voter: since, in any major election, there is less chance of one vote making the difference than of the voter being run down by a car and killed on the way to the poll, voting in such elections is "irrational."

Case four is another example of the infinitesimal-effect problem. It contrasts a short-term, narrow, but very compelling benefit against a long-term, highly diffuse interest. It also illustrates the problem of uncertainty—of imperfect knowledge—which makes truly rational choice impossible by definition.

Cases of this kind are sometimes called "each-we dilemmas," and such dilemmas are notoriously refractory to rational solutions. Derek Parfit has shown that no logically deduced ethical system, so far, has really handled them adequately.[11] Economists avoid them by the method classically summed up by John Maynard Keynes: "In the long run we are all dead." This statement, "one of the most fatuous ever made" according to Peter Drucker, is—as Drucker and many others point out—all too revealing of modern attitudes toward society and the economy.[12]

However, in fact, people have solved many such problems. Moreover, theories have been advanced that do address the wider issues intelligently.

These dilemmas are often compared to the classic Prisoner's Dilemma of high school philosophy class fame. (The Prisoner's Dilemma involves prisoners who must decide whether to squeal on each other to reduce their sentences.) But these dilemmas are actually much worse. The "PD" is a trivial case of lack of information. Permit information to flow between the prisoners, and the mess can be cleared up. Information does not help to resolve each-we dilemmas. The North Sea nations communicate perfectly well, and they have known precisely what to do about the herring, at least since World War I, and they have chosen not to do it. They have so chosen because of the highly emotional nature of nationalism and nationalist politics. Here, as with the ranchers and loggers, emotionality on all sides has apparently become the block that prevents compromise and thus prevents solving the problem.

There are other problems that are different in structure, but similar in that rational considerations break down in dealing with them. One is Jon Elster's "Sour Grapes" problem: people tend to adjust their hopes to fit their realistic expectations.[13] Surveys show that most people want salaries about 10 percent higher than what they get—no matter how much or how little they get. In conservation, this problem expresses itself in the decline of interest in the environment that sets in among many urban people. They have no realistic hope of getting access to a decent environment, and they have much more immediate concerns to worry about.

Around the world, many societies have dealt with such problems before and found solutions. The solutions are never perfect and never total, but they all have value. At the very least, they show us what factors we have to take into account. This book explores some general questions of how people see the environment and then describes some specific solutions. It grows from practice: from my work in resource management and my experience in conservation politics.

Most people, most of the time, make decisions that are what we usually call "rational" and "sensible." In folk English, these terms refer to decisions that soberly pick the best ways to achieve practical goals, such as obtaining food and shelter. This broadly "practical reason" is the bread and butter of human life.[14] If it were not, we would never have evolved and certainly would have never made it through the Stone Age. Recent attempts to "prove" that all traditional societies are irrational, misguided, "sick," or ecologically foolish are oversimplified, if not simply racist;[15] if they were right, we would not be here, for humanity would have become extinct long ago.

On the other hand, people do a great deal that is less than rational or optimal. We fall in love with outrageous people. We believe in astrology and avoid the thirteenth floor. And we damage the environment—often for no material benefit.

Two centuries ago, David Hume argued in his "Enquiry Concerning the Principle of Morals" that moral behavior—including resource management—can only occur when reason and passions are joined in a search for solutions that work.[16] In the modern world, some conservationists and environmentalists are strictly creatures of passion who overemphasize charismatic megafauna. Others, especially academics, are creatures of reason. They expect people to act on the basis of enlightened, carefully planned self-interest. They are frequently disappointed. Action, especially political action, requires at least some degree of passion.

This book is written from that Humean point of view. Its thesis is that environmental problems are due to a mix of reason and passion, and that solutions must also be such. This perception allows me to explain why some apparently irrational (but not always unreasonable) beliefs serve rational ends in maintaining local environments.

I first studied, in Hong Kong, some beliefs that seemed strange to me. My Chinese friends believed that the hills contained dragons; that the foods they ate were somehow mystically heating or cooling to the body; and that good luck could be attracted by planting trees. I learned that these beliefs were highly useful, in a pragmatic, empirical way—whatever the Western scientist may think of their accuracy. They motivated people to perform actions that were, in anyone's terms, beneficial.

This led me into an attempt to explain inaccurate beliefs in general. Granted that error is ever with us, why do we pick one error rather than another?

Modern psychology provides explanations for error. However, these explanations must be seen in the light of the practical concerns of the peasants. The peasants and fishermen settled on the *most useful* errors. Lacking modern laboratories, they could not learn most of the truths we take for granted, such as the nature of vitamins. They settled not on useless approximations to facts but on useful errors. Moreover, their actual observations were *not* at fault. The Chinese belief in the sanctity of trees, for instance, stemmed from the observed fact that trees around the village *did* produce many utilities. Chinese peasant beliefs in dragons living within hills, mystic qualities of foods, and the enormous spirit force of wolfthorn berries also rest on empirical bases. The errors lay not in their observations, but in their inferences from observation. The wolfthorn berries, for instance, got their reputation because even small amounts of them were seen to build strength in convalescents and invalids. The Chinese could not know, until modern laboratory analyses came along, about the high concentrations of vitamins and minerals that produce these miraculous-seeming results. Spiritual power was a logical inference.

The traditional peoples with whom I have worked have, by necessity, come up with solutions to environmental problems. I have done research mainly among Chinese peasants and fishermen and among native Indian peoples on the West Coast of North America. In these areas, population densities have long been very high, and pressure on the resource base has been a steady, serious fact of life. The prodigal waste of resources seen in a modern open-access fishery was not a possibility. Means had to be found to convince communities and families to economize. In both cases, this was done by a number of psychological strategies. These included representing sound ecological management in strongly religious terms, and developing a view of the environment that stressed specific, concrete bonds between it and the human community. I am not referring to some misty "union with nature," but to specific social codes and institutions.

Every human society that has existed for any length of time has faced the necessity of managing resources for the long term in spite of positive illusions and other natural errors. Even the most dispersed hunter-gatherer group has, at some point, had to deal with overhunting, or competition for resources, or local famine and rationing. It is reasonable, then, that such societies have much to teach us. This is especially true of groups that have maintained high populations over a long time, because they have necessarily had more than their share of hard decisions.

These worldviews are "traditional," but this should not be taken to mean that they are unchanging. The whole point is that they *have* changed. People have learned, over time, better methods of coping. Moreover, some traditions are much newer than others. The Chinese views discussed in chapters 2 and 3 are old—one or two thousand years. Yet, they have not been frozen in time: the Chinese have intensified their land use methods.[17] Some of the Native American ones are much newer. Our own Anglo "traditions" are often newer still. Scottish tartans date from the eighteenth and early nineteenth centuries, old settler lore from the late nineteenth century, much "traditional" folk music from well into the twentieth.[18] This book deals with *beliefs that have been around long enough for long-range consequences to affect them.*

It also deals with the value of many of these beliefs in educating the young and in enforcing moral codes. Rituals and ceremonies typically have this effect. The Maya ceremony of *hanlicol,* "feeding the field," continues to flourish, though some modern Maya have completely reinterpreted its significance. No longer believing that it actually feeds the guardian spirits of the field, they see it as a thanksgiving rite to the Christian God. The lack of change in the ceremony would seem to imply that its main function was not to feed the gods but to bring the living together and involve them emotionally in their fields.

Students of resource management have spent many years living with such groups as the South Chinese, the Alpine peasants of Switzerland,[19] and the

Maya. All these peoples have been on earth long enough to make mistakes, and to alter their courses of action to take account of those failures and improve their management strategies. It is probable that environmental abuse was one of the factors in the fall of Maya civilization. There are now about as many Maya as ever; something valuable has evidently been learned. My goal has been to look for common themes in resource management practices of various cultures. In particular, I have concerned myself with belief systems. I have become particularly fascinated with one kind of belief system: tightly ordered systems that provide very good guides for behavior but are based on assumptions that are incorrect from the point of view of Western science. These systems show how beliefs can be effective. They also show how people make mistakes.

I begin this book by describing some systems of this type. They share the following characteristics:

1. They work.

2. They do not work perfectly; they are brave attempts, not total successes.

3. They are based on a particular kind of logic: an attempt to fit empirical observations into religious cosmology. They thus appear quite strange to the outside observer. However, anyone familiar with local religious beliefs will recognize the logic.

This grounding in local religion is not simply a device to make empirical observation more systematic or "meaningful," although it does provide useful (if dubious) explanations for observed phenomena. It is a device to make conservation a part of the religiously sanctioned ethical code. It is a device to make people aware that misuse of resources has devastating effects—effects that seem like supernatural wrath—while wise use conveys blessings that seem supernaturally good.

Similar cases of constructing resource management as religion so as to bring conservation into divinely sanctioned ethical codes are well described for many societies around the world. Our word "taboo" is borrowed from the Polynesians, who used it, among other things, to protect resources. Overfished reefs, orchards of unripe fruit, or overharvested wild plants and animals would be declared *tabu* or *kapu* until they were ready to harvest again. This has been described in detail for Tikopia and New Zealand by Raymond Firth.[20] Many other authors have remarked on it.[21] Like the Chinese, the Polynesians have sacred groves, and so do the Huastec Maya of Mexico, the Moroccans, and other peoples around the world.[22] The Kayapo Indians of Brazil carefully manage groves of trees, and here too there is religious sanction.[23] Often, as in the Moroccan case, sacred groves preserve forest types that are otherwise extinct. Governments have sometimes taken advantage of religious beliefs in designing conservation plans, as the Tokugawa regime did in Japan.[24]

These cases also show some features of human information processing. In the absence of perfect information, people tend to come up with hopeful and plausible explanations. They seek or invent explanatory models that are consistent with their deeply held beliefs. The vacuum of ignorance is filled with logical extrapolations from conventional wisdom. Thus, Chinese peasants explain landslides as the wrath of the dragon. This type of mistaken inference is not a process confined to peasants. Americans tended to ascribe the downfall of the Communist Party of the Soviet Union to a mass yearning for American-style capitalism. We now realize that ethnic hatreds, political rivalries, pollution, and many other factors had at least as much to do with it.

These case studies lead to questions of how people process information and what are the real ends of human action.

In the modern world, we see a different dynamic: plentiful scientific information about the environment, but woefully inadequate action. No previous culture has ever known so much about the environment. No civilization has ever managed the environment more carelessly. This imbalance led me to a different question: Why do people *not* use the factual knowledge they have, when self-destruction is a clear and obvious danger?

Thus, from explaining certain local belief systems I move on in this book to a consideration of resource management in general, which, in turn, has implications for general theories of human action.

Humans do not see the environment as simply a bunch of stuff lying around waiting to be used. We impose structure on the environment; we love or hate it; we form accurate or misleading beliefs about it. We make pets of some animals, loathe others, and ignore still others. (The same animal—the dog—is petted in America, loathed in Arabia, and ignored in India.) We use resources to satisfy not only our needs for food and shelter, but also our needs for love and security. In trying to understand the environment, we necessarily simplify and distort, and make mistakes accordingly. We get into economic and social binds, where the solution to one problem is itself a problem of a different order. People are creatures of emotion, not creatures of reason. We use reason, but largely as an aid to planning how to reach goals set by instincts and emotions. We plan carefully how to get food, but hunger is not a rational, carefully thought-out thing. We plan how to advance ourselves socially, but the aching need to be loved and accepted is not something we have decided to feel after careful analysis.

Any management strategy that does not take human feelings into account simply will not work. The world ecological crisis results, in part, from the lack of sensitivity of those who propose solutions. All too often, strategies appeal either to a nebulous love of nature or to a narrowly practical economizing expressed in tables of statistics and technical terms. Neither of these appeals works by itself. On the other side of the fence, fear and hate can be direct motives for destroying the environment, on scales ranging from the individual (mentally unstable arsonists) to international (Saddam Hussein's destruction of the Kuwaiti oil fields).

Politics is, by definition, about conflict and about emotion. Above all, it is about mutual accommodation, or lack of it, among people with differing moral codes and different goals. To save the environment in such a world will require, first, that most people develop some form of environmental morality and, second, that the political process accommodates environmental goals. This will not be easy. Expecting everyone to become an environmentalist, let alone to share exactly the same moral code, is unrealistic. Politics will continue to have its debates and its irrationalities. We must somehow save the environment in spite of that.

Humans are not plodding computers, but brilliant approximators. In this world at least, we will never know ultimate truth. What we have always been able to do is have a good enough idea of reality to allow us to survive. We have had to select very carefully—both the "facts" we (partially) know and the ways we represent them to ourselves.

Today, debaters in the environmental management field range from ecologists who wish to depopulate the Great Plains to proponents of the Wise Use Agenda, which advocates unrestrained cutting of forests, grazing of grasslands, and extraction of mineral resources, no matter what the long-term costs are.[25] Views on traditional management vary from those that hold that traditional peoples lived in harmony with nature to the views of Martin Lewis, who argues that traditional peoples were wanton wasters limited only by their simple technology.[26]

It should not surprise anyone that special interests react with anger to attacks on their livelihood. Cattle ranchers, for instance, can hardly be expected to roll over and play dead when faced with environmentalist writings that are emotional and inaccurate.[27] What is surprising is that so much of the public accepts the extreme anti-environmentalist view, rather than coming to a compromise. Sixty-eight percent of Californians, in a recent poll, agreed with the policy of significantly weakening pollution controls to save jobs—number of jobs unspecified.[28] Wise Use Agenda sympathizers now dominate the state legislatures of Oregon and Idaho.[29] Huge rallies against any restrictions on logging have attracted thousands of loggers—though the loggers surely know they are merely guaranteeing their own imminent unemployment.

Thus, it would seem that any solution to the world ecological crisis must have not only economic but also psychological dimensions. The latter have been rather little explored. True, the conservation literature is rich in calls to preserve the beauty of nature, but the actual responses of people to nature are rarely analyzed, and the question is often portrayed as a simple fight between the lovers of nature and the forces of greed. This portrayal does not get us far. Fortunately, the picture is not all so bleak. A number of geographers, anthropologists, and biologists have focused their attention on the wider aspects of human-environment interactions, and especially on the ways people think about the plants, animals, and landscapes among which they live.

2

Feng-shui: *Ideology and Ecology*

My first direct encounter with *feng-shui* came soon after I arrived in Hong Kong in 1965. A new hospital was being built on a hill overlooking Castle Peak Bay, where my family and I lived. The hospital foundations cut deep into the slope. Several old peasants told me, "This is very bad; the construction has cut the dragon's pulse." I learned that the hill had a dragon in it, whose blood circulation had been cut by the foundation trench. This seemed strange to me. I noted it down as a fascinating local belief, and thought no more of it.

Soon afterward, a typhoon dumped two feet of rain on Hong Kong within a few days. The oversteepened, undercut slope failed, and a torrent of mud descended, washing out the hospital foundations and burying a house or two at the hill foot. "See?" said my friends. "This is what happens when you cut the dragon's pulse." A light went on in my head. The Chinese peasants, pragmatic to the core, had described the phenomenon in terms strange to me; but the phenomenon they described was perfectly real. I reflected that the geologists' terms "oversteepening" and "slope failure" were not much more empirically verifiable than the dragon. Any Chinese peasant would find them even stranger than I had found that eminent serpent, since I had already learned from reading that ancient Chinese saw dragons in the scaly, ridged contours of mountain ranges.

As time went on, I learned that I had found more than a different way of talking about obvious facts. Chinese site planning seemed more and more rational. I learned that villages protected the groves of trees that ringed them, because trees attract good influences and also provide shade, firewood, fruit, leafmold, timber, and other goods. I learned that roads to villages were made crooked to discourage evil beings—and that the evil beings included not only demons but also soldiers, government officials, and (other) bandits.

Then came the great floods of June 1966. Traveling around the western New Territories, I quickly saw that every traditional village (sited according to *feng-shui*) was above water and almost every new village was under it. *Feng-shui* teaches that one should put one's house, or village, on a slight slope or rise.

Clearly, *feng-shui* worked. But it also had much that still seemed counter-factual to me: dragons in the hills, tigers in the ridges, veins of subtle circulating force that made some spots energetic in a way I could not understand, and wavelike flows of good and bad luck. Over the years since then, I have come to understand the system as a sophisticated accommodation between empirical knowledge and Chinese traditional cosmology. I have gained great respect for it, and it has become my focal exemplar of a traditional science.

Gary Seaman, ethnologist of Chinese religion, has pointed out that the classical Chinese science of landscape planning is so similar to medicine as to be a part of the same very general system.[1] Medicine deals with the flows of *ch'i* in the body; *feng-shui* deals with the flows of *ch'i* in nature. Veins and channels are seen. The points with good and bad *feng-shui* correspond to acupuncture points. Sometimes the natural world is seen as a society of subtle beings—mystic dragons and tigers in the hills—whose bodies are literally the landscape. Then, *feng-shui* is literally a medicine of these gigantic presences. Even when the resemblance to medicine is more metaphoric, *feng-shui* is part of the same broad attempt to control one's life, health, and welfare by asserting regulatory influence over the circulation of *ch'i*.

Feng-shui means "wind and water," and refers to the science of planning buildings, travelways, and graves such that they will get maximum benefits and minimum damage from the *ch'i* of the cosmos. More specifically, *feng-shui* addresses wind, water, and other natural forces. "Natural forces" in this case include good and bad luck, which are explicitly compared to wind by my Cantonese friends: "You can't see them, but you can feel the effects." Inhabitants of a well-sited home, or descendants of someone buried in a good gravesite, can expect wealth, sons, status, and security to flow to them. However, focally, *feng-shui* involves perfectly practical advice on how to site a house to take maximal advantage of sun, water, and wind. It is a true folk science, as recognized by the first Western observer to comment extensively on it[2] and by many Chinese and Westerners since.[3]

Feng-shui also involves an emotional response to landscapes. Classical landscape paintings are called *shan-shui hua,* "mountain–and–water pictures," in

Chinese. The name is similar enough to *feng-shui* to raise thoughts of connection. Indeed, a landscape painting is intended to bring the viewer into a state of mystical union with the landscape—or at least into a state of intense, focused emotional engagement with it. Some of the *ch'i* of the landscape is captured, transferred, or somehow reinvoked (no one seems clear about this) in the painting, and the viewer experiences this *ch'i*.

Of course, direct experience of the landscape can involve a direct flow of its energies into the viewer. A hiker wandering through a landscape participates directly in its field of subtle forces. Aesthetic experience indicates deep emotional involvement, and that, in turn, could be seen (among some traditional Chinese) as a literal, physical experience of the landscape's *ch'i*.

Moreover, for the folk—the farmers, fishers, and craftspeople—the land was a world of spirit forces. Trees and rocks had their indwelling guardian spirits. Regions and mountains had their gods, as well as dragons. *Feng-shui* managed the interaction between people and these normally invisible beings.

Feng-shui has become mystified, or mystificated, over time, as its experts have elaborated a highly complex and esoteric lore. *Feng-shui* experts had to be called in whenever any new construction or alteration of land or buildings was contemplated. They found it expedient to develop a mystical and esoteric language, preserving trade secrets from possible competitors. Thus *feng-shui* has often been seen by Westerners as a part of religion, or as primarily a social phenomenon.[4] As such, it has been denounced by biased missionaries. The nineteenth-century missionary J. J. M. de Groot, for instance, described it thus: "Feng-shui is a mere chaos of childish absurdities and refined mysticism, cemented together, by sophistic reasonings, into a system, which is in reality a ridiculous caricature of science."[5] This sort of attitude (shared by Eitel, as well as Dore and many others) has discouraged serious attention to *feng-shui* until recently.[6] Not only Westerners but Western-educated Chinese dismissed it as superstition, or, at best, an interesting socio-religious phenomenon.

Today, this attitude is changing. Western[7] and Oriental[8] observers are recognizing that *feng-shui* is fundamentally scientific and has much of value to offer the world. By "science" I mean here a system of empirical observations and pragmatic knowledge, bound together by an overarching theory that is supposed to be naturalistic.

People like de Groot (who, after all, admitted that *feng-shui* looked like science) stressed its mystical or magical nature because its overarching theory, and therefore its deductions, seemed strange to them. Of course, the physics and biology that de Groot learned in nineteenth-century Holland would seem equally strange to us today, and we would even recognize much religious influence on them.

For the purposes of this book, *feng-shui* offers a perfect instance of a folk belief system. It is based on empirical observations; the farther it gets into extrapolating from these, the less accurate it becomes. It is systematized in accord with the dominant schema in Chinese cosmology: the flow of *ch'i* and its association with cosmic beings and channels. Essentially, it involves interpreting experience in the light of what are believed to be the general principles of the cosmos, and therefore systematizing the experience for convenient use.

As anthropologist Edward Hall pointed out, all individuals and all cultures manage space.[9] Moreover, all cultures have some form of site planning[10] and see the landscape in particular ways.[11] China is no exception.[12] Space is a resource, and its allocation and management are a part of human ecology. *Feng-shui* is only a part of the Chinese science and art of relating to landscape. Aesthetics is another part, not by any means totally distinct from *feng-shui*. Religious veneration is related to both, and again is not sharply separated from them, as will appear below.

The Chinese language has no word for "religion"—in the Western sense—and literally cannot express the distinction between managing and venerating the landscape. One must specify on a behavioral level that the geomantic expert is "planning," not "worshiping (*pai*)." Chinese traditional society did not set up a sharp separation between natural and supernatural or between belief and (secular) knowledge. Rather, it stressed the need for humans to put themselves in respectful harmony with whatever existed—the Tao or the winds or the spirits. The behavioral distinction was maintained, however: some beings were *worshiped*. *Feng-shui* experts planned and organized, and only incidentally worshiped. Thus, they are what English must label "scientists," not priests or magicians. I prefer not to call them "geomancers," or to translate *feng-shui* as "geomancy"; that would assimilate them to the frankly magical practices of the Western world,[13] which is wholly misleading.

One of my consultants said that good and evil influences propagate through the world like radio waves, and a well-sited house or grave will pick up the good luck as a radio picks up radio waves. Others talked of the flow of *ch'i*. At some points it concentrates, and these are apt to be fortunate. It flows past other sites, and carries away their fortune, or even brings bad fortune to them. Still others speak of particular conformations or configurations of hills, or of good spirits attracted by particular landmarks. On the whole, the common denominator is concern with the circulation of *ch'i* in the earth, waters and air (in about that order of importance, earth being primary). The arcana of *ch'i* circulation are detailed in Feuchtwang, Lip, and Seaman and need only be touched on here.[14]

Ch'i circulates through subtle channels in the earth. The circulation of water is seen as related in some sense. Water flows along natural lines and contours; *ch'i* behaves similarly, but the lines and contours are less obvious. Wind, too, has its natural lines of flow. Good and bad fortune can follow the channels of any of the three. Locations can be studied with reference to compass points and *ch'i* meridians. A *feng-shui* expert will assess these matters with his compass, an exceedingly elaborate calculating device (one of the most complex achievements of Chinese culture).

There is general agreement, throughout China and Korea, on what constitutes good *feng-shui*. (*Feng-shui* extends to Vietnam and Japan, but there it is becoming a different game.) A good site is protected by hills and streams that surround it almost but not quite completely. A valley ringed by hills and draining through one gap is ideal. The gap, like all entrances, and like officials' thrones, should point south toward the path of the sun. The resemblance of this formation to a womb has not escaped traditional Chinese, Koreans, and modern observers.[15] Equating the macrocosm to the microcosm is a universal and explicit principle.[16] Tombs are also womb-shaped, and the womb-to-tomb correspondence is known to all.

On the other hand, the basic reasons for idealizing a hill-protected site are clearly practical. Such sites are usually safe from the worst effects of storms. Moisture and good alluvial soil are there, held in by the hills. The stream provides water; its outflow gap provides air circulation and sunlight. Such sites were sought out by the pioneer settlers of the American West, without the benefit of *feng-shui*.

If a perfect womb is unavailable, the general principle is that the village should be on a slight slope, surrounded on two or three sides by higher ridges and hills; that it should have a grove of trees upslope, if possible surrounding it on back and sides but not in front; and that it should have a stream at hand. The Green Dragon (the hill behind or left of the village, or otherwise defined on some referent point) should prevail over the White Tiger (the hill extending down on the right as one comes up to the village or whatever point is picked). The more credulous see these as real animals in the landscape; the sophisticated see them as subtle bodies or even purely symbolic ways of talking about particular swirls of *ch'i*. Ideally, two or more streams should meet and pool up in front of the village. Quite apart from providing a mystic womb-gate, this guarantees a reliable water supply. The pool (natural or artificial) is useful for laundry, wallowing water buffalo, and so on.

Trees in front of a house or village make too much shade, especially if—as is normal—the houses face south to the sun; water coming from directly behind or alongside a village, or cutting through it, would carry the village's good fortune away—most obviously by flooding and washing the place out. Also, sanitation and health are maximized: the villages drain well,[17] and wind clears them away rather than blowing masses of dust into them.[18] The village or house should be on the hills' lee side, especially with reference to typhoon winds. The village should face into cool breezes but not into storms. In most of China, this increases the fondness for a southern exposure, for the worst winds come from the dark and cold north. One strives to have a vacant space southwestward, from which pleasant breezes flow.[19]

In the world of rural China, the highest local mountain would receive worship, just as the Chinese state institutionalized the worship of the Five Sacred Mountains. Mountains that were high, rugged, and tree-covered were especially sacred, and typically had monasteries and retreats placed on them. Large old trees were worshiped; in Hong Kong, *Ficus microphylla* (small-leaved banyan) was the most usually venerated species. Dramatic rocks and rock formations were worshipped. Magical qualities were alleged for many springs, streams, points in the sea, and other evidences of flows in nature. Such venerated spots were taken into account in local *feng-shui* readings, just as pagodas and other sacred structures were. Religion is, after all, the manipulation of good; certainly good influences should be captured or directed.

Why are some trees and rocks worshipped? The great philosopher Chuang Chou (ca. fourth century B.C.) tells an ironic little story: He once asked a sacred tree how it had reached such veneration. He dreamed that the tree replied that it had worthless fruit, worthless lumber, and so acrid and stinging a sap that no one dared to bother it. "Thus," said the tree, "I have achieved great age and size, and people respect me." Chuang awoke with the reflection: "All know the use of use, but none know the use of uselessness!" There is some truth in this; trees like the small-leaved banyan grow fast and are not good for much, so they are left alone to mature. Any huge old tree is venerated.

The logic of worshiping such objects is fairly straightforward, as far as my consultants and I understand it, though a *feng-shui* expert would have much more to say. A huge old tree has accumulated more and more *ch'i* during its long life. If it is gnarled, that implies the dynamic twisting, turning, eddying and swirling of truly powerful *ch'i*. Such trees impress even the secular American observer. So do waterfalls and cascades, which are regarded as "power places" (to use a phrase from the anthropological literature) not only by the Chinese but by most other peoples of whom I am aware. So do many vistas and shoreline points. In many of these, one sees water roiling and swirling in the patterns of the gnarled wood grain in an old banyan, and in the patterns of the flames and smoke when a great tree releases its energy by transforming from wood to fire. In general, Chinese folk worshipers, Chinese elite painters, and secular American tourists seem to gravitate to the same spots, and feel the same awe and reverence. The Chinese folk worshipers link it to religion, the painters to a mystical absorption in Beauty and the Tao, and the tourists . . . well, they have their own perceptions. What is truly thought-provoking, and what no one has even begun to explain, is why such places capture our imagination. We do, indeed, feel the awesome power of the cosmos at such spots. Even the ecologically callous Americans protect such wonders as Yosemite and Yellowstone (but build hamburger stands instead of temples).

Dramatic rocks also reveal an especially powerful *ch'i*. In North and West China, where earthquakes are frequent, there is another and far more compelling reason to regard them as power places: one can often feel the earth quite literally move at such points. There, dramatic cliffs and crags are usually markers of earthquake fault traces. The same truth was known to the Indians of California, who venerated such spots because one could feel the actual flow of power in the earth there.[20] Once again, the empirical observations are unimpeachable, and even the theory deduced from them. The earth does have its flows of energy, concentrated and obvious at earthquake points. The modern geologist and the ancient worshiper differ only in how they link and interpret this fact, not in their appreciation of the fact itself.

The Chinese peasant, sacrificing at these sites in hopes of gaining security or some desired good, is usually supplicating. She is not just manipulating a sure, controllable force (as *feng-shui* experts do). Perhaps these apparent oppositions can be resolved by thinking of our attitude to a doctor when we have some curable disease. The doctor represents Science, which can reliably heal. But the doctor, as a human, can give or withhold. We must supplicate—especially if we are short of cash! Similarly, the neighborhood sacred tree has its natural flow of energy, but it can gate that flow, as if it were a personage with at least some form of consciousness.

In Hong Kong, houses are less consistently south-oriented, and the villages are set wherever they are protected from the southeast tradewinds. (Typhoon winds whirl around, so only near-complete surrounds offer much help, but typhoons usually come from the southeast, so villages tend to be sited with a hill range southeast of them.) In Korea, houses face east—toward the dawn and away from the westerly and northwesterly winds that are apparently more annoying there.

The steady flow of wind and water past a site carries wealth and fortune away. Pooling up of air and water means pooling up of wealth and good luck. A house by a lake, river, or sea should be located to look down on currents that meet, and should avoid looking out over a straight reach where currents pass by and away. Straight roads past a village, or—worst of all—pointing directly to it, are dangerous. So, often, is location at a crossroads or junction or between two roads.[21] Here, again, the problems of traffic and unwanted visitors are paramount. Straight water channels pose flood danger, and being downstream on such a channel exposes one to pollution from upstream.[22] Poles and tall buildings can be dangerous. They attract lightning, and wind eddies around tall buildings.[23] Poles provide too dominant and vertical a system and can mean overassertion of the wood element.[24]

The paramount rule, though, is that the house and village should be off the cultivated land—or, if that is impossible, off the most fertile parts of it. The reason for this is obvious, and it is here that even the most devout believer in the dragons and tigers becomes very matter-of-fact in speech. No one has missed the direct bad fortune that accrues from taking land out of cultivation. This is the clearest difference between China and the modern West, where good cultivated land is actually preferred for building, because it is already leveled and cleared! Admittedly, the Chinese have less land per capita, but even the land-rich United States (to say nothing of Europe) is past the point of being able to afford such practices. We simply do not have an adequate ideological and social system, comparable to *feng-shui*, to restrain us.

Within a house, the kitchen is often on the east side, warmed by morning sun but protected from the hot afternoon sun. Bedrooms are kept away from the fire-prone, noisy kitchen.

Finally, the bad effects of too open or exposed a site, or a site otherwise open to evil, can be counteracted by building a pagoda or other tall and more or less holy structure athwart the bad path. This may seem more strictly magical, but pagodas and temples attract many people, and thus wealth, commerce, and activity. Also, the people are usually bent on sacred errands, and thus less apt to rob and steal than the travelers on an open highway.

There is a whole subfield of *feng-shui* devoted to interior design.[25] Here ecology cannot be adduced as an explanation, except insofar as a good interior design provides light and air. However, there is a rationale to the planning of offices and other public spaces. A good *feng-shui* expert will talk learnedly of the Eight Trigrams, the flow of *ch'i,* and much else, but will actually be looking carefully to see how he can rearrange desks to improve lines of flow, separate employees who cannot tolerate each other, and keep people from ponding up at the water cooler or coffee machine. In the Chinese world, until recently, a *feng-shui* expert was involved in the planning and construction of every major building and many minor ones. Moreover, if bad luck followed the inhabitants of a building (if several inhabitants died, for instance), a *feng-shui* expert was consulted to see what could be put right. Remodeling for *feng-shui* reasons was common. In Hong Kong and many other areas of the Chinese sphere, reliance on *feng-shui* experts is still almost universal, and an authoritative, widely known expert commands a high fee.

Significantly, the United States now has several specialists devoted to this art. Chinese who buy houses often massively remodel them to improve the *feng-shui*. This can bring about confrontations with local planning commissions dominated by unsympathetic Anglos. An excellent study of the resulting politics—and the triumph of *feng-shui* in one community—is provided by Mary Elizabeth Crary in a study of San Marino, California, which has been transformed by *feng-shui*. Its house facades are more interesting and diverse as a result.[26]

Feng-shui experts speak in arcane and mystifying language. This is partly because, whether in Los Angeles or in ancient Peking, employees do not like to be manipulated. Those who manipulate them must speak in an esoteric and learned lingo, to impress rather than disturb. Many have surmised that the jargon of *feng-shui* is not only entailed by the cosmology behind it, but also by the need to impress the peasants and to obscure either incompetence or manipulativeness. Most of the surmisers are traditional believers, too; *feng-shui* experts are and always have been viewed with considerable cynicism. General belief in the efficacy of the system does not accompany belief in the efficacy of all its practitioners.

Another subfield applies to graves. The proper grave is located on a hillside, well away from villages, cultivated land, and potential disturbance. In real-world terms, this keeps graves bunched up and, usually, off the cultivated land. A well-sited grave will not wash out or erode away. A grave should be a pleasant place on the third day of the third lunar month, when all traditional Chinese try to visit and picnic at their ancestors' graves. It should overlook a broad prospect of hill slopes, trees, and water. It should have scattered trees—not a dense forest or a barren waste. It should be high up, or somewhat isolated.

Since one component of the deceased soul or soul-complex remains with the body in the grave, the grave must be comfortable—free of waterlogging, termites, rot, and other annoyances. The soil should be light, to weigh lightly on the coffin. The dead are capable of visiting misfortune on their descendants, but—also—the grave serves to focus impersonal good influences or bad ones, and beam them like a searchlight onto the descendants. Freedman and I both found that the mother's grave was more important (at least to most people) than the father's, which is surprising for a patrilineal society.[27] The once-peaceful slope where Sun Yat-sen is believed to have buried his mother has become a jammed cemetery, as Hong Kong residents try to ensure their fortune.

Fortunate and unfortunate sites for graves are a subject for tremendous speculation, divination and controversy. They may even be the focus of conflict. Hugh Baker, historian and ethnographer of Hong Kong, reports a conflict between two lineages who eventually took to sabotaging each other's graves. The conflict climaxed when one lineage actually diverted a sewer into the ancestral tomb of the other, thus wiping out the living rivals through disease and plague.[28]

This brings us to the social significance of *feng-shui*. This aspect is somewhat outside the present focus, and has been discussed in great detail elsewhere.[29] However, it is necessary to point out that *feng-shui* is a major builder of unity within communities. The village will stand together in opposing a new and dangerous road, constructing a new and desirable pagoda, and protecting their sacred grove. They will also stand together in demanding compensation or mitigation from the government when the latter tries to force a major project on them. One bitter government agent told me "*feng-shui* means money," a sentiment common among government planners who find themselves forced to compensate communities. But, as we now know in the West, large government projects are typically very detrimental indeed to local townspeople and farmers. Flooding, pollution, traffic problems and congestion, interference with water supplies, cutting down of valuable trees, driving away of game, and dozens of other damaging effects are universal. Today in the United States, compensation or mitigation is required for the same reasons and under the same circumstances as in the *feng-shui* negotiations of old China.

Feng-shui thus serves as a powerful way for villages to assert control over their lives and organize resistance to outside pressures. This point clearly helps explain why it is so similar to medicine. The dominant traditional medical ideology, as we have seen, gives individuals the means of controlling their lives and resisting disempowerment. *Feng-shui* does exactly the same thing on a community level.

As we have seen in Hugh Baker's story of lineages at war, *feng-shui* can be an almost equally powerful divisive force. However, my very strong sense is that in such cases *feng-shui* is usually an excuse for escalating an already existing conflict. In short, I contend that *feng-shui* actually *builds* and maintains solidarity, but usually only *expresses* conflict. I am certainly aware of conflicts that would not have occurred without *feng-shui*, as when a bullying land-dweller built a latrine in front of the grave of the mother of a fisherman friend of mine.[30] Even here, as I pointed out, the conflict was ultimately about wider and deeper issues.

Yet, there is more. The social functionalists begin and end their discussion of *feng-shui* with its value in maintaining social solidarity.[31] Yet surely that is not all the explanation. *Feng-shui* experts are viewed with cynicism. More to the point: social functions cannot predict anything about *feng-shui*. Every culture in the world has ways of maintaining social solidarity, continuity, respect for the dead, and resistance to social pressure. There is no reason why China should pick this particular way.

Thus, we must invoke the ecological explanation. The breakdown of *feng-shui* in most of the urban Orient provides us with a perfect test case. The dramatic spectacle of the western New Territories in June 1966 was a particularly revealing case, with the old villages standing above water and the new ones mostly awash. But one sees other problems everywhere.[32] South Korea, where once the houses were kept meticulously away from cultivated land, has lost over 15 percent of its farmland to urban sprawl. China has suffered from poorly planned construction; from massive erosion and deforestation following the cutting of *feng-shui* groves; from flooding and pollution. Hong Kong's New Territories have not only suffered from floods and droughts and from loss of trees, but also from extreme scatteration, expense of extending urban services, and chaotic construction. The urban areas have lost aesthetic harmony and become overbuilt to the point of slumminess.

Old Chinese cities were not exactly models of urban design, but they kept the worst problems under some control. And the old Chinese countryside genuinely was a model of design.[33] Long before Ian MacHarg's book *Design with Nature,* the Chinese were experts in listening to the wisdom of the earth in their planning processes.[34]

But *feng-shui* does far more than set guidelines; its real value lies in its ability to act as a powerful motivator of communities to follow the guidelines. In old China, there was no way of *enforcing* rational planning; the folk saying reminds us, "Heaven was high and the Emperor was far away." (After all, we can't enforce rational planning in modern California, with almost a hundred times as high a ratio of officials to population.) *Feng-shui* sold good planning very effectively. All peasants knew that their own future good fortune depended on following its rules. If a peasant was tempted to disregard possible future welfare and choose his own present self-interest, his neighbors would immediately raise the alarm: he was wrecking the community's *feng-shui*.

The proof of the effectiveness of *feng-shui,* both as planning science and as powerful motivating force, is seen in the orderly, tree-rich, well-managed landscape of the more fortunate parts of old China. Erosion in much of North China was beyond anyone's power to stop, and war or rebellion devastated much of the south; but wherever nature and humanity could possibly exist in harmony, they did so.

It was not a perfect harmony. Much of China was ravaged and all of it needed better management.[35] But China in eight thousand years of farming did little or no more damage to its farmland ecology than the United States has in two hundred years. Smil has chronicled the devastating effects of the break-down of the system under Communism: in some areas, as much damage was done in fifty years as in the previous fifty centuries.[36] Feng-shui was not perfectly effective. But compared to the almost total failure of environmental planning in the United States—with its superior scientific establishment and law enforcement capabilities—feng-shui was nothing short of miraculous.

We do not deal, here, with some generalized harmony with nature or some inevitable tendency of Traditional Man and Woman to live in such a pristine and visionary state. We deal with a system that was created precisely to control the greed, shortsightedness, or selfishness of those traditional people, one that in many cases was enforced with a good deal of savagery.

The moral is that there is no substitute for a powerful, institutionalized system that links science with public morality. Science alone, even when far more sophisticated than the humble folk wisdom of feng-shui, cannot have any effect.

Feng-shui was not, however, just an empirical systematization of facts and a religious validation of them. It had its theoretical base in classical Chinese cosmology—modified, again, by common experience. This brings us to the interface of science and religion, so weakly separated at the margins in classical Chinese thought.

By merging into the religious system, feng-shui could partake of the powerful emotional and social forces that religion includes. This is what gave it such power as a sanction and a motivational system. To cut the sacred groves was not just ecological foolishness. It was not even just an antisocial and morally reprehensible act. It was a sacrilege that endangered the entire existence of the community at all levels.

To be sure, a Western scientist might say that accuracy is sometimes sacrificed, along with the pigs that are offered to the gods. To the alien secular observer, it seems as if too cavalier an equation is made between natural energy, human breath, and divine spirit. People are trapped by their own heuristic devices. Trees acquire the qualities of gods and humans. The whole cosmos is personalized, according to the heuristic of thinking of everything as similar to us.

Perhaps, in a sense, our attitudes toward pets and teddy bears, our curses at a refractory automobile, our science fiction extraterrestrials who always act just like Americans, find their parallel in the humanlike trees and rocks of China.

All such rationalizations would miss my central point. Human thought is a dynamic, rather sloppy process; to harness it in the service of wise ecological planning is not easy. The Chinese have succeeded in involving people, emotionally, in their landscape—and then harnessing that emotional involvement, as well as cosmological belief, to motivate people to plan good land use and reasonably sound architectural principles.

The ecological anthropologist Roy Rappaport has argued that much ecological knowledge is coded as religious knowledge, in traditional cultures.[37] In the case of feng-shui, we see his principle illustrated, with the caveat that the situation is not quite so simple (but see chapter 3 of this book). In China, ecological science did not become part of animist religion; instead, religion and ecology fused at their common border. The feng-shui expert with his logico-deductive rules and his elaborate compass came to the same conclusions as the old peasant woman with her sticks of incense and her paper imitations of gold and silver bars. Both saved the trees. Both protected the village from flooding.

Worship and rational planning were two different ways of observing the same facts and principles, not two opposed ways of managing the world. The peasant and the expert, the worshiping system and the feng-shui system mutually supported each other, in the best tradition of Chinese traditional social life. The primal human emotion of awe at natural power is used to drive a religious system. The same perception underlies a scientific cosmology.

In the modern world, as traditional control systems break down, we must find new ways to link the deepest human emotions with institutions that sanction ecological sanity. Feng-shui deserves continued attention.

3

Chinese Nutritional Therapy

C hinese nutritional therapy—the use of food as medicine, to treat illness and physical challenge—provides an ideal ground for studies of how people think about their place in the organic world. Unlike many folk systems of medicine, Chinese nutrition has a long written history. Doctors and food experts have devoted much effort to articulating and systematizing a vast amount of information. Much of the data comes from folk observation—the empirical experience of generations of farmers and workers.

In Chinese medicine, humans as total persons confront a world of plants, animals, and minerals that have varied medical functions. The line between food and medicine does not exist; all foods have some medical significance, and many medicinal herbs are eaten in enough quantity to count as foodstuffs.

Theoretically, there is an infinite number of possible ways of thinking about food and health. The Chinese have constructed a system that represents empirical experience well; fits with their cosmology (the cosmology we have already seen in the preceding chapter); and fits with their views on the individual and society. It is a system that classifies and arranges a great number of facts—statements that are true by the standards of Western laboratory science as well as Chinese experience. It incorporates these truths into a plausible and logical structure, and ties the whole thing to the network of emotions, personal values, and deeply held beliefs that sustain Chinese society. To put it a bit crudely, the system wouldn't sell if it didn't work. But, also, it wouldn't sell if it didn't fit with the rest of the Chinese system of thought and feeling.

In this chapter, I provide a rather thorough account of the traditional Chinese construction of nutritional knowledge. I then show how and why it is logically compelling, given the assumptions of Chinese logic. Finally, I suggest some ways in which it seems to fit well with the Chinese experience of being a person in society.

Cultural ecology concerns itself with all human relationships with the environment. Food is one of the field's main concerns. Foodways provide good examples of demand-driven systems. Foods are produced because people need to eat and want particular foods. The cultural ecologist studies not only food production, but also food consumption.

Thus, I came to study Chinese food.[1] I adopted the "food system" approach widely used in nutritional anthropology, in which production, distribution, and consumption are studied as one system. I found I needed to employ this model in order to work in fisheries development. People were, after all, producing fish for a market. The nature of the market—people's preferences for different types of fish—determined what could be sold.

This led me to investigate Chinese nutritional therapy. Many fish and other food products were produced and sold because they were believed to have medicinal properties. Medical foodways are so important in Chinese culture that they have had important effects on the course of Chinese food production.

Recently, the effects have been disastrous, because many rare species are believed to be medicinally valuable: rhinos are killed for their horn, swiftlets for their edible nests, bears for their gall. Until the last few years, however, Chinese medicinal food use has been a force for ecological good.[2] It has kept the Chinese agricultural system diverse. It has led—and is still leading—to the cultivation of dozens of species, some of which might otherwise have been lost. One hopes that it will continue to serve as an incentive to domestication or preservation. Surely, before the bears run out, someone will take steps to preserve them as a health resource.

Thus, while food consumption may not seem directly related to the ecological mission of this book, it is in fact central. First, food consumption drives food production, and thus affects the whole ecosystem.[3] Second, the logic of Chinese food consumption reveals a great deal about how people think about resources. As such, it is absolutely central to my argument, and necessary for what follows. This chapter may seem long and detailed, but the data simply must be presented with some thoroughness.

Chinese nutritional medicine has its own logic, which is based on a wide and deep empirical knowledge base. Here, as with *feng-shui*, we have a system that has vastly influenced resource management, through a logic that is unique and distinctive.

Chinese medicine is a tradition several thousand years old. It has its general ideological grounding and its separate schools and findings. Put another way, it is an accommodation between an ideology and the experience of millions of Chinese in healing the sick and maintaining strength in the healthy. The Chinese learned many empirical facts—the "natural resources" of information, to be managed like any other resource. This is what psychologists would expect; people relate new information to what they already know, and structure it in terms of their preexisting structures of thought.[4]

China now holds one-fourth of the world's population, yet has only 7 percent of its cropland. Feeding its enormous population has always been an enormous task. Naturally, through millennia of famine and want, the Chinese have learned an inconceivably vast amount about food—how to produce it, how to process it, how to consume it, and how to cope with deficiencies.[5]

Chinese nutritional therapy has relatives worldwide.[6] We shall examine the belief that some foods are heating, others cooling to the body. Most of the world's cultures have beliefs of this kind—often strikingly similar to Chinese beliefs. Thus, the theoretical foundations of Chinese medicine[7] must have some general appeal of plausibility.

As early as the Chou Dynasty (ca. 1100–221 B.C.), the court dietitians were the highest-ranked of the court medical staff. So says the *Chou Li,* the court manual of the Chou. The surviving form of it was heavily reconstructed by the Han Dynasty (206 B.C.–221 A.D.), so we may possibly have a Han courtier's ideal Chou rather than the reality. However, the Han scholars tried hard for accuracy, at least in minor and relatively noncontroversial matters of this sort. The companion work *Li Chi,* in its further accounts of Chou rites, contains much more about food, especially about what dishes are appropriate for what settings: seasonal sacrifices, august banquets, informal entertainments of gentlemen of high or low rank, and so forth. It even specifies appropriate dishes for serving the elderly, and these are easily digestible dishes high in protein, calcium, and iron. The Han Dynasty itself produced a number of medical works, based to some unknown degree on earlier books, that include a considerable amount of sophisticated nutritional knowledge and theory.[8]

There is no question why "China, land of famine"[9] has always put nutrition at the head of the list of medical specializations. Malnutrition was by far the single most important cause of death, killing countless millions directly and weakening countless more so that they died of disease. The Chinese quite properly looked to nutrition in both cases. Moreover, nutrition and its effects were easy to observe in village and family. Herbal medicine probably arose as a handmaiden of nutrition, and has continued to blend into it. The herbals all discuss foods at length. By contrast, the European world focused early on surgery, ranked low by the *Chou Li;* perhaps the Europeans' fondness for war led them to attend more to trauma!

Dominant at this time was a relatively new scientific system, based on the opposition of yang and yin and on the mutual intertransformations of the five elements: water, wood, fire, earth, metal. This system was relatively new at the time, replacing earlier systems that were heavily magical[10] or empirical. The five elements were not like the fixed, perfect elements of ancient Greek thought. In fact, "elements" is a rather arbitrary translation of a word that literally means "goings." (The same word means "street" in some parts of modern China.) Manfred Porkert translated it as "evolutive phases."[11]

We are to understand a dynamic, shifting energy in the universe, whose various manifestations can be conceptualized as woody, metallic, and so on. The same property that makes wood woody makes food sour. Changing according to the laws of cosmic evolution, the energy moves from wood to fire. The same progression is seen when food becomes bitter (scorched-tasting, more or less). Fire produces earth, as wood turns first to flame and then to ash. Similarly, bitter evolves (by some subtle process) into sweet. Earth, smelted, yields metal; sweet yields pungent. Metal collects dew, thus producing water, which is associated with the salt taste (possibly because seawater and salt brines were the Chinese salt sources). The same qualities inform the directions (north is more metallic), the organs of the body, and almost everything else, producing a fivefold classification of the cosmos.

Crosscutting this cycle is the interpenetration of yang and yin, the bright-dry and cool-wet aspects of the universe. Yang and yin do *not* mean, focally, male and female. They are derived from words for the sunny and shady slopes of a hill, as the characters show quite graphically in their early forms. Male sexuality simply involves about twice as much yang as yin energy, female sexuality the reverse.

All these various phases were aspects of *ch'i*. *Ch'i* means, literally, "breath." It does not really mean "energy," but Westerners (myself included) find convenience in so translating it in medical contexts. (But, still, *ch'i shui* means "aerated water," that is, soda pop—not "energized water.") Like the Greek equivalent *pneuma, chi'i* came to refer to a subtle circulating medium. It pervades the cosmos—including that microcosm, the human body. Herein it circulates by subtle channels, the meridians that acupuncturists tap at certain critical points.

Ch'i can be blocked, necessitating medical intervention, since stagnant *ch'i* is devastating to whatever part of the body it may occupy. *Ch'i* can also be depleted; for the Chinese, as for St. Augustine, evil is the privation of good. The flow and quantity of *ch'i* can also be augmented (*pu*), and it was already known that foods high in easily digestible protein augmented health and strength in just the proper way. Indeed, I suspect that we see in the foods proper to old people the ur-form of *ch'i*-strengthening lore.[12]

During the Han Dynasty, there were many debates about this new all-encompassing system. Tung Chung-shu and other Han Confucianists championed it. An older medicine of witches, ghosts, and demons challenged it,[13] as did a still newer, hardheaded rationalism (exemplified by the teachings of Wang Ch'ung) that put little faith in such grand schemes. But it provided a good scientific paradigm: simpler and clearer than other methods of schematizing the world and accounting better for the facts. The old witch-and-demon theories survived but were greatly weakened by attacks from the newer thinkers. Wang Ch'ung's rationalism succeeded in heavily (but far from totally) discrediting the demons, but had little effect on the new theories of *ch'i,* since he proposed nothing better and seems to have believed in a more cautious version of the same sort of theory.

By the sixth century A.D., when T'ao Hung-ching brought out his epochal new editions of the great medical classics, a new influence had come. In T'ao's works we find, for the first time in China, the theory of heating, cooling, wetting, drying, and neutral qualities in foods and medicines. This theory, sometimes known as the "humoral theory" because of similarities to Western humoral medicine, will be described below. Humoral medicine in China was perhaps a local development, but more likely came from the Western world via Central Asia. It fit so happily with yang-yin theory that it must have been adopted easily and rapidly.

Finally, during the same centuries, some foods came to be seen as cleansing (*ch'ing*) to the system. Others seemed to poison it, and still others potentiated poisons or bad *ch'i*. These were both lumped as *tu,* "poisonous or poison-potentiating," or—better—"dangerously strong in potentially harmful force."

T'ao Hung-ching's synthesis of existing medical and nutritional theory was so masterful that no one since his time could do much more than add to it. Medicine developed in orderly fashion during the subsequent dynasties. Only in Sung (960–1280 A.D.) were genuinely new and exciting theories discussed, and they ultimately failed to replace T'ao's great synthesis, though they were not without effect.[14] Even when Western medical lore entered China in modern times, traditional nutritional lore emerged triumphant until well into the twentieth century. The most important reason, I think, was a very simple one:

you stayed healthier if you followed T'ao Hung-ching. As late as the end of the nineteenth century, Western nutritionists either still embraced the heating/cooling theory themselves, or had gone all the way with protein and calories and were advising people not to "waste their money" on fruits and vegetables. Only the discovery of vitamins would finally give the West a better success rate in dealing with malnutrition cases. Even today, Western nutritional science remains rather less developed than, say, surgery. Most of us who have experienced traditional Chinese nutritional therapy believe it still has much to offer.

But there is, of course, more to Chinese nutritional science than that. It incorporated some major errors—statements that were simply empirically wrong. These persisted. Individuals could see that particular drugs failed to act or particular anatomical claims did not fit with common observation of animals; yet they explained away these experiences or regarded them as mere random fluctuations. I have seen this happen many times. Of course, I have seen Western medicine fail on even more occasions, yet Westerners do not doubt the system. Throughout the world, it takes more than random failures to call the framework of medical knowledge into question.

It is possible to look at Chinese medicine either as a storehouse of useful knowledge to add to the world's pool of healing arts, or as a system (a set of texts, if you will) to study in its own right. If you are primarily interested in curing people, you will gravitate toward the first approach—thereby running the risk of ignoring some important aspects of the system itself. If you are primarily interested in the history of science, you will gravitate to the second, thus tending to ignore China's very real contributions to modern international medical practice.

This contrast of approaches informed a classic recent debate, when Paul Unschuld (historian of science) commented from the second position on the monumental work of Joseph Needham (doctor and medical researcher).[15] In a gentlemanly response, Needham agreed to disagree.[16] I humbly propose a union of approaches. With Unschuld, I try to understand the system as a whole. With Needham, I seek to understand it for ultimately practical ends. I believe the system has value in itself and is part of China's lasting contribution—not for its medical accuracy so much as for its value in showing how people structure information.

My experience with Chinese nutritional therapy was largely in the New Territories of Hong Kong, back when they were still quite isolated, rural, and traditional. In the New Territories, until relatively recently, China's old Imperial laws held force in much of civil life. When I did fieldwork in 1965–66, many peasants and fishermen still lived lives that would have been familiar to their ancestors of two thousand years before. I had to hike five miles to reach some villages. By the time of my last prolonged visit in 1974–75, the old lifeways were almost gone, and the old social and physical framework was completely gone, but all older adults remembered traditional society and moved most familiarly in its cultural universe. I was able to observe the close fit between folk theory and folk practice. The Hong Kong variant of Chinese nutritional therapy had much to offer even to modern urban Americans; but it was much more effective in dealing with the realities of peasant life in old South China.

The system, as known to the peasants and fishermen of the New Territories, was based on maintaining a balance of qualities. They were concerned especially about hot and cold, and to a lesser extent dry and wet, assimilated closely to the wider realm of yang and yin. They had much concern with the flow of ch'i, but cared almost nothing for the five elements. Supplementing, cleaning and poison were still very important to them. Closely similar (but not quite identical) folk systems existed elsewhere among South Chinese[17] and among Chinese in America, Australia, and elsewhere. Aspects of the Hong Kong belief system have been excellently described by medical anthropologists, including Linda Koo and Marjorie Topley.[18]

In the New Territories, a generation ago, the fundamental concept of balance overrode all else. Recently I was asked to give a paper on this topic in a panel on balance in Chinese medicine. I followed Paul Unschuld, who contributed a brilliant and exciting paper critiquing Westerners who have overrated the importance of balance in traditional Chinese medicine. As he pointed out, the great Han texts stress dynamism and eschew balance.[19] I had to follow, lamely, with my words on the very real importance of balance to modern Cantonese.

Westerners did not invent the Chinese concern with balance; they got it from the modern Chinese, who have indeed given it a special place not warranted by the Han texts. This is, in part, a result of Western influence many centuries ago, especially in the form of the humoral system. It is also part of a development within Chinese society. Symptoms are not seen as labels of a particular insult so much as markers of something wrong with the body's equilibrium or dynamic balance. This does not mean that there is no external insult, but rather that the body was not able to cope with it, or that it destabilized the body and the imbalance has to be corrected.

Western medicine was seen by my friends as being directed toward the insult; Chinese medicine was directed toward fixing the body itself.[20] Thus the Cantonese could, and did, combine both for maximal effect, focusing on balance—in the body as a whole or in some particular organ's field of influence within it. (The Chinese terms translated "heart," "kidney," "liver," and so on actually refer to functional subsystems of the bodily system of organs and *ch'i* flow. They refer focally to networks of functions, centered on the organs named, but extending throughout the body.)

When my friends on the waterfront of Castle Peak Bay, Hong Kong, talked about health and illness, they rarely strayed long from the idea of balance. The simple Chinese word is *p'ing*, which originally referred to the dynamic, sensitive balance maintained by the beam of a weighing scale. Often, in discussing health, the term was expanded to *ho p'ing*, "harmony and balance" or "harmonious balance." A healthy person can be described as a *p'ing jen*. Closely related concepts include the idea of center or median (*chung*) and the idea of maintaining a harmonious, unobstructed, unrushed flow of *ch'i*, activity, blood, and life in general. The concept of balance in the western New Territories of Hong Kong, as in classical Chinese tradition, was clearly a dynamic one: the fragile stability of the beam, or even of the spinning top, rather than the solid stability of a rock. Maintaining *ho p'ing* in life was an ongoing process. Every day brought its disturbances: sudden heat or cold, a stressful event, an attack by wind (literal or medically metaphoric), a snack that was too rich.

Richard Currier, drawing on his research in Mexico and on the theories of George Foster, argued that such attention to balance in medicine serves as a metaphor for attention to balance in society.[21] Groups especially concerned about maintaining social harmony should be similarly concerned about harmony within the human body. For the Chinese this is certainly true. The concepts of balance and harmony are expressly used in discourse about social life and about the relationships of humanity to the cosmos, and they have been so used for several thousand years. For instance, a wedding or other joyous social occasion is a "hot" event,[22] just as ginger and pepper are "hot" foods, and as such can be stressful to the system if not balanced by cool, restful times.

P'ing, he, ho p'ing, and *p'ing ho* are terms that are all commonly used. They tend to merge into each other. My friends would report that they meant more or less the same thing, but not quite. Harmony refers to things working together and working right. Balance refers to the aspects of a thing being in correct proportion, and the thing itself being centered, able to rest without instability. Harmony is thus more active and implies the presence and action of various forces or entities; balance is a property inherent in systems. Each can be seen as a special case of the other (it depends on how broadly one wishes to define one's system), and the two naturally co-occur. *P'ing-an*, "balance and security," is the Chinese word for "peace." *Ho p'ing* implies the ideal situation for any system. The resemblance of this and subsequent axioms to systems theory is not coincidental. The folk system is part of the tradition that, formalized as administrative theory in the Chou Dynasty, became one of the ancestors of modern systems theory.[23]

In medicine, balance is most important to maintain between the forces of yin and yang. The dynamic interplay of these forces is basic to human life and to the cosmos. For the people of Castle Peak Bay, the question of balance and harmony came up most frequently in regard to nutrition. Indeed, almost every question of health became first and last a question about food.

In folk nutritional science, balance was most commonly used to refer to the "neutral" point in the humoral system. Foods were coded as heating or cooling, and, less saliently, as wet or dry. Those that were perfectly balanced between heating, cooling, wetting, and drying were referred to as *p'ing* or *ho p'ing*. Our word "neutral" is not a true translation; these foods were not lacking in the forces of heat, coolness, wet, and dry, but had all of them to the ideal degree, so that they balanced each other correctly. The most perfectly balanced food, defining the set point, was ordinary boiled rice, *fan*. Foods of similar whitish color, moderate caloric value, nonirritating quality, and major dietary importance were also balanced: white-fleshed fish, noodles, potatoes, many steamed breads, and the like. Insofar as foods deviated from this, they were classified as increasingly heating or cooling.[24] Sickness almost always resulted from, or involved, some degree of imbalance between these qualities. Balance was restored by appropriate diet therapy. Menus had to be planned to balance the meal; for example, if fat pork (heating) was served, there should be watercress or carrots or cabbage in soup (cooling).

The heating/cooling dimension is far more important in Chinese medicine and nutrition than the wetting/drying one. The latter is almost undocumented. Cantonese of Hong Kong believed that shrimps and similar crustaceans were heating and wetting (and thus made venereal disease worse). Coffee and roasted peanuts were heating and drying, because they irritated the throat. Nothing was cooling and wetting or cooling and drying. The vast majority of foods, then, were evaluated only on the heating/cooling dimension.

Foods that were high in calories and cooked by intense heat were the focal heating foods. These included anything fried; anything baked for any great length of time; anything greasy. Spices that English also labels "hot"—chili, black pepper, ginger—were heating in proportion to their pungency. Alcohol was hot. The higher the calorie levels and the spicier the taste, the more heating was the food. Some other foods were considered heating because of their "hot colors": red beans, for instance. Green beans were cooling, white beans neutral.

Cooling foods were those that were sour, watery, low-calorie, and cool-colored. The focal cooling foods were thus green, leafy vegetables and the green-fleshed large radish (which does not have a "hot" taste). The more sour and watery the vegetable, the more cooling it was. Black tea was heating because it brews to a red color; green tea was cooling. Some foods gave mixed signals: oranges, plums, and tomatoes are a hot color but are watery and sour. About these, people disagreed. There was continual debate and adjustment. Many people, for instance, separated "cold" foods from "cooling" ones; this is a classical distinction that has been debated for centuries.

These codings were based on observed physical responses to food. Feasts—which featured greasy, spicy food, with alcohol—led to indigestion and hangover, pathological conditions easily cured by avoiding the foods in question for a day or so, and eating soothing foods like rice and vegetables. Scurvy is also a "hot" condition, involving sores, dry, flaky skin, rashes, and other burnlike symptoms. Green vegetables cure it. Conversely, a diet of rice and vegetables is apt to lead to thinness, pallor, wasting away, low body temperature, and the like. In Western terms, we would diagnose lack of protein, available iron, and other minerals. Chinese would diagnose too much cold and not enough heat. So heating foods, specifically meat and highly nutritious plant foods like wolfthorn berries, were eaten. They worked. Heating foods of this kind are also eaten for convalescence, recovery from childbirth, and other situations in which rebuilding strength through good protein and mineral nutrition is desirable.

Individual differences that we would explain by "allergies" were explained by differences in basic nature. Some people are basically hotter or cooler than others. They have to eat differently. Some foods that are cooling for most people are heating for a few—these are mostly cases of allergy rash. Conversely, heating foods may cause diarrhea (a cold condition) in a few susceptible people.

I have shown elsewhere that the Chinese did the best they could to make empirical observations comprehensible by a simple scheme.[25] Carol Laderman has confirmed this line of thinking by demonstrating the same for the closely related Malay system of folk nutrition.[26]

Some form of the hot/cold belief system is found in most of the world's cultures, and was obviously invented independently on several occasions. There is much evidence for its existence in the pre-Columbian civilizations of the Americas, for instance. This is obviously due to the fact that sick people usually do show excess heat (fever) or cold (chills). No one can miss the association. Observations of the therapeutic effects of certain foods follow naturally.[27] The heating/cooling belief existed throughout Europe until well into the twentieth century.

In short, we have here a case in which human information processing leads naturally to a particular scheme that is simple, memorable and effective. It is "wrong" by the standards of modern biomedical science, but it is "right" for the pragmatic peasants who use it.

In addition, foods could have value as *pu p'in:* "supplementing" or "patching" foods.[28] The very name implies restoring a balanced condition, though these are seen as strengthening foods more than as restorers of balance. Other foods were used to clean the system, restoring harmony by eliminating bad things that had entered. A standard herbal and nourishing preparation was *ch'ing-pu-liang,* "cleansing, supplementing, and cooling," a mixture of herbs and seeds made into a soup used for those purposes.

In preparing medicines, ingredients such as licorice were introduced to harmonize the other ingredients, producing a balanced system. This led to maximal good effect and minimal side-effects. Cooking served as a model: some ingredients without much flavor were introduced to bind the main ingredients, producing a single dish with a proper balance of flavors rather than a bunch of disparate ingredients lying together in the pot. These last examples showed that *ho p'ing* is not solely a matter of regulating an existing system. It includes actually creating a system from its component parts, or creating a functional system from a nonfunctioning one.

Other medical practices within the traditional Chinese therapeutic universe were also seen as restoring balance, harmony, and proper function to the human system. This extended to the essentially psychological (in Western terms) practices of the spirit mediums (*wu shih* and other categories), of whom there were many in the area. They did much that was far from harmonious—driving away or exorcising ghosts, casting lots, going into ecstatic trances, slashing themselves with swords. Yet, in practice, their treatments consisted of prescribing medicines, performing ceremonies to restore lost components of the souls, calming agitation and stress, and making soothing statements to their clients. One favorite statement was: "Some people have been saying bad things about you, but you are really a good person. Those other people just have some badness in their hearts. Don't pay attention to them and you will be all right." I heard this line many times in spirit medium performances.

The practices of the spirit mediums and other fairly fixed formulas stressed the value of social harmony. In the eyes of both the mediums and the patients, social imbalance and disharmony were specifically pathogenic, causing genuine physical distress. They had to be treated, if only by telling the victim to rise above them.

Ideally, the disharmony itself would be cured. Indeed, local grassroots leaders were described as restorers of balance and harmony, just as curers were.

Leaders healed the body politic in the same general way that curers healed the body physical. Harmony with the gods, spirits, ghosts, and natural world was also necessary. Driving ghosts away from a patient can be seen as restoring harmony between human and ghost realms, rather than as a statement of total war between those realms. Giving deliberate or unintended offense to a supernatural being was a common cause of illness.

Offending the natural landscape could lead to its indwelling spirits visiting one with illness. The similarity of tapping into *feng-shui* channels and acupuncture, for instance, was known to several of my informants. The forces of the cosmos must be properly in balance, in relationship to the individual and the community, at any given time and place. Without that, ill luck and ill health follow. The other principal forms of folk medicine in Castle Peak Bay—herbal therapy, exercise, massage, and physical therapy—also operated from a model of restoring balance. Even the rather dramatic and painful techniques were thought to harmonize the *ch'i*. These included hard massage, coin-rubbing—raising a bruise by rubbing or pinching with a coin—and moxibustion, which involved burning cones of powdered sagebrush on the bare skin to leave a serious blistered welt. By contrast, "Western" medicine (international bio-medicine) was seen as usually involved with specifically fixing injuries or exterminating invading pathogens, rather than as restoring a global personal balance to the individual.

The major forms of medicine at Castle Peak Bay were diet therapy (largely a home matter), herbal treatment (largely in the hands of Chinese doctors and pharmacists), and spiritual medicine (practiced by spirit mediums). These overlapped; the gods, speaking through their mediums, routinely prescribed homey herb and food remedies in cases of soul loss, witchcraft, and divine vengeance. The contrast between "naturalistic" and "personalistic" medicine was not very meaningful to Castle Peak Bay people. Indeed, spirit mediums seemed to specialize in naturalizing the personalistic. Exercise, massage, and rest were other harmonizing modalities. Only Western medicine was seen as based on a really different paradigm. (Acupuncture, so dear to the hearts of Western devotees of Chinese medicine, was rarely utilized by Castle Peak Bay individuals.) Medicine was supposed to give not just freedom from disease, but a long and vigorous life. Only a moderate, harmonized life could be prolonged.

However, it is not enough to say that the people of rural Hong Kong were simply following ancient tradition. Cantonese folk culture is extremely different from China's elite culture, let alone the elite culture of Chou. Paul Unschuld has quite correctly pointed out that Chinese medicine has many rhetorics.[29] It includes passages as militaristic as modern American popular writings about the immune system. It includes many strong charges to avoid, prevent, repel, dispel, and evade. It includes many theories of sickness that are quite separate from the concept of balance. Indeed, all these various other theories and modes of discourse are present in Cantonese folk tradition as well.

Yet, they are not only reduced in relative importance (vis-à-vis the classical medical tradition), they are often simply subsumed under the balance-and-harmony rhetoric. They are incorporated into that overarching view, at a lower level. One must explain why this particular net of concepts was so enthusiastically adopted. My friends stressed balance and harmony in health more than the orthodox Chinese medical traditions do, just as in social matters they stressed them even more than orthodox Confucian traditions do. Other concepts of great importance in classical writings were of no interest to the Hong Kong villagers; for instance, they were vaguely aware of the fivefold correspondence doctrine but did not take it very seriously. They had greatly overgeneralized and overextended one part of ancient tradition (that relating to balance and harmony) at the expense of much else (five phases, ch'i flow specifics, the apotropaic language cited above, acupuncture, and more).

Following Currier's theory, one would expect to find that this focus on medical harmony implied that social harmony was an extreme, indeed transcendent, value to the villagers. This is, indeed, the case. It is the highest good. When I sought out definitions of the word "good" as applied to individual and social life, discussions invariably turned to the maintenance of social harmony or good relations. Here the related words include kuan-hsi, "mutual goodwill" with a sense of "mutual responsibility," and kan-ch'ing, which means "sentiment" with a sense of "wanting to help and be helped by someone." A "good person" was one who could create and maintain harmony through these and other means of networking.[30] John Young, in a book about Castle Peak Bay's neighboring market town Yun Long, provides a superb account of these matters.[31] A healthy person was one who maintained a comparable internal state. Once again, the microcosm and the macrocosm function according to the same rules.

Currier's theory implies a corollary: such societies have particular problems with social order. Specifically, Currier finds that balance is stressed in societies that are strongly hierarchic, with a powerful, traditional hierarchy that is strongly represented in the ideology. Here Currier grounds his ideas in George Foster's hypothesis of the "image of limited good" in peasant societies. Foster points out that peasants, living in a frequently static economic order, see human kindness and other virtues as limited in quantity, like land and wealth.[32] They work to make the best of what they have, and to reduce tension or the appearance of tension. Here again China fits the pattern.

In particular, this allows us to differentiate such societies from others with different overarching, fundamental tenets of proper living. The Northwest Coast Indians maximize power, including healing power.[33] Americans, indefatigable competitive individualists, tend to see illnesses as invasions that must be fought off[34] (though Americans, too, have a concept of "balanced diet"; the Cantonese stress on nutrition and the American stress on "germs" clearly have much to do with the relative roles of balance versus defensiveness in the respective rhetorics).

Strongly and stably hierarchic societies could be expected to have such a focus on harmony simply as a result of ideology generated by the elites. One could see the whole belief as simply a way that elites persuade ordinary people to stay calm and amiable. Yet we find that the villagers and fishermen of the South China coast are among the most independent people in China, with a long history of rebelliousness and regionalism, and are quite aware of the importance of ideology in such matters. They do not adopt ideas lightly. They are, in fact, far too aware of the role of ideas to adopt the idea of balance and harmony unless it did in fact promote good health and also produce social benefits to both individuals and communities.

Some biological benefits of the ideology of balance are clear. Dietary excesses, excesses of activity or sloth, exposure to too much sun or too much cold, sexual excesses, and similar mistakes are clearly counterindicated. The individual is charged to find his or her own comfort point or set point, and to deviate from that only with due care. Most South Chinese are in fact careful, and many are continually concerned. They regulate every activity so that it does not take them far from their perceived balance points. This is particularly pronounced in regard to diet, but it affects all aspects of life, notably including physical exercise. These and other benefits seem inadequate to explain the enthusiasm with which the system is accepted.

The need to have some overarching, all-connecting symbol or value is also clearly present. Every system needs something to tie it together at the top—to connect all parts and make them all meaningful in relation to each other. This allows people to store and retrieve information much more easily. Any medical system must have a simple way of organizing its facts, for the convenience of its practitioners. Ordinary laypersons then take over this simple algorithm and simplify it again. Often they then go on to make it more complicated again, but in their own, nonprofessional ways. While international scientific medicine has the idea of rationality and the concept of experimentally verified fact, the Chinese concepts of balance and harmony serve to link medicine to the homologous systems (or subsystems) of thought represented in social management, landscape management, and cosmology.

Yet this leaves the question of why one overarching symbol system is picked over another.

Balance and harmony are picked, in my opinion, because they place the locus of control squarely on the individual, and specifically on the individual in society. If the elite did deliberately sell this belief system to pacify the masses, they captured a Tartar. The overarching message of the valuation of balance, in both social life and personal health, is that the individual exists in relation to the environment and has to take control of how he or she interacts with that environment. Social life is not simply a matter of passive adjustment to a social order; it is a matter of developing wider and deeper personal networks, and working on balancing one's responsibilities. Health, similarly, requires a continual balancing act. One must react to the environment and take control of one's responses to it. This may be related to the concept of "somatization," used by the psychiatrist and anthropologist Arthur Kleinman to describe Chinese medicine's treatment of what Westerners call "psychological" problems.[35] The Chinese use physical therapy, nutrition, and similar methods to deal with what they see as a bodily matter. The idea of a "mind," divorced from the body and subject to its own diseases, is foreign to China.

Life in traditional China is sometimes thought to be constrained. The individual is said to be dominated by gentry, lineage elders, and a rigid code derived from neo-Confucian philosophy. This was true up to a point, but the ordinary people had many ways of maintaining their own integrity and power. Recent studies such as those of Hill Gates, Robert Marks, and Robert Weller have focused on resistance: the ways in which ordinary people managed their lives in spite of elites and rules, and prevailed over these when opportunity afforded.[36] Not only did ordinary people have many means of direct resistance; they had to run their own farms and their own communities. Even the state had to work with them, not against them; the state could not manage every farm, and it depended on the revenue. Therefore, life for the average adult was one of actively negotiating and renegotiating one's place in society and the cosmos.

If one were to write a book on China comparable to Ruth Benedict's *The Chrysanthemum and the Sword*, it would not focus on hierarchic terms but on terms associated with managing cooperation and fine-tuned social relationships. In addition to *he* and *ping*, one would discuss *ho* "cooperation" (as in *lien-ho*—a different word from "harmony"), *kuan-hsi, kan-ch'ing, min* ("face"), and the folk concepts of leadership and friendship.[37] If the Japanese are highly social and Americans highly individualistic, the Chinese may be thought of as combining (balancing!) both: they are individuals-in-society. Certainly the Cantonese word *ian* ("person") conveys this idea. Castle Peak Bay persons put a very high value on individuality, even eccentricity, but an even higher value on being actively participating members of communities and networks. Independence, resistance, and control of one's life grew from such roots. And medical aspects of balance grew as a logical corollary of this view of the world, which in turn developed from the needs of the ordinary person to survive and function in a highly complex social environment. E. P. Thompson has shown how a working class forms as individuals strive to exercise what control they can. Jean Comaroff, among anthropologists, has applied similar concepts to the use of ideology as a means of constructing passive resistance.[38] The Chinese have always used their medical system as a means of asserting individualism. By connecting it directly with the social system, through the concept of balance, they made explicit a concern with internalizing the locus of control over personal life in society and in the environment.

The health consequences of such a belief system are not trivial. Richard Schulz has written a paper describing the human need to feel able to cope with one's life.[39] Psychologists, especially Albert Bandura and Ellen Langer, have stressed the psychological and physical importance of perceived control. Health and even survival under stress depend (in part) on maintaining control.[40]

The traditional Chinese folk system based on humoral medicine, herbal therapy, tonic and strengthening foods and medicines, exercise, and other forms of "nourishment of life"[41] demands that the individual take some control over life, and encourages even more. A person must actively, thoughtfully take over health maintenance for himself or herself, and (to varying degrees) for those for whom he or she is responsible. This is a deeply empowering ideology, and part of the tough, resilient network of grassroots power that allows Chinese to work both alone and together for the common good. It is part of an ideology that grows from practice and, in turn, affects practice. As such, it has been one key part in the survival of the Chinese people over the millennia.

Balancing hot and cold is not the only matter of serious importance in Chinese nutritional medicine. Strengthening, cleansing, and dealing with poisons are also daily concerns. These draw on a very different logic, perhaps more ancient, certainly less social. To understand these systems, we must invoke other theories of how people process knowledge and how they feel about what they know.

Pu p'in ("supplementing things"; *pou pan* in Cantonese) are part of a complex widely known in Asia. My friend Najma Rizvi, who has studied food beliefs and medical practices in the Indian subcontinent, has told me of similar foods used for strengthening, especially for women after childbirth.[42] More research is needed on how far the complex spreads, but there are similar belief systems in Southeast Asia and elsewhere.[43] *Pu p'in* include many medicinal herbs, as well as foods. They supplement energy, tone up the system, and above all strengthen. Some strengthen the whole body; others, a specialized group, strengthen particular organ systems. On the whole, *pu p'in* supplement depleted *ch'i*. They may also repair damaged tissue, or they may act by invigorating *ch'i* and thus empowering the body to repair itself.

The most basic and widespread *pu p'in* is chicken soup, which is as popular with Chinese grandmothers as with proverbial Jewish ones. The Chinese variant should ideally be simmered very slowly for a very long time, with warming and *pu* herbal drugs.

In general, all poultry are *pu,* but wild ones are more so than tame ones. Most meat is *pu,* at least when stewed slowly and delicately in a closed container. As with birds, wild meat is more *pu* (on the whole) than tame. Among herbs, ginseng is the most famous, but there is a vast lore of *pu* herbs. Many fungi are especially important. Especially valuable for preserving the *pu* qualities (while preventing too much heat from getting into the food) is a steaming process known as *tun*. This involves putting the food in a covered dish that is then put in a larger vessel with some water, rather like a bain-marie. A similar cooking process is known by the similar sounding word *dum* or *dam* in India, and there too it serves to retain virtues of the food. I suspect a relationship between the words *tun* and *dam*. After all, the concepts of "strengthening foods" are clearly related.

Almost all *pu p'in* are cooked this way or in a casserole or soup. Almost all *pu p'in* are gently heating; this sort of cooking reduces or tempers their heat still more. The idea is to provide a gentle warming rather than a sudden shock of heat. Prepared this way, *pu p'in* are easy to digest, by both Chinese and Western standards. Such items as chicken are often stewed with enough vinegar to leach calcium and other minerals from the bones.

In explaining *pu* foods, the first and most obvious factor is that they work. The focal situations in which *pu* foods are prescribed are—above all—recovery from childbirth; convalescence from disease or trauma; and the waning of powers that accompanies aging. The *pu p'in* are all either foods that are high in protein and minerals while being low in fat (poultry, game, mushrooms), or else plants with tonic effects that are known (ginseng and its relatives) or likely. The traditional Chinese lived on grain with relatively small amounts of vegetables. Even in the diet of the rich, meat was not heavily represented, vegetables and fruits being choicer than most meats. Protein and mineral nutrition was adequate for ordinary life but marginally adequate for tissue repair. Women got a disproportionately small share of meat and other high-quality protein and mineral sources. As I often observed in the field, pregnancy and childbirth very often pushed them over the edge into out-and-out anemia. At best, they needed all the help they could get. A good diet meant not only their own survival or welfare, but that of their infants. Thus all Chinese women recovered from childbirth by "doing the month":[44] they spent some days, ideally a month, lying still and eating *pu* foods. Many of the foods at this time were explicitly intended to increase milk supply, and these were high in fat or calcium. Others, such as liver, were rich in iron and vitamins. All in all, they worked superbly for their intended purpose. It is impossible to imagine China reaching its current population without the "month."

But the effectiveness does not by any means account for all the facts concerning *pu p'in*. Many highly nutritious items were neglected. More strikingly, many items were considered to have supernaturally spectacular effect, especially on the aged.

One reason to think that a food was a *pu p'in* was a Chinese equivalent of the Doctrine of Signatures. Roots shaped like the human form, for instance, were naturally held to strengthen the actual human body. This is one reason why ginseng was so highly regarded (the other reason is that it actually does contain effective chemicals, apparently tonic to the immune-response system). Also, parts of an animal's body were especially strengthening to corresponding parts of a human's. This was validated by the obvious beneficial effect of animal blood on humans with weak blood; anemia and the effect of pig's and chicken's blood on it were very well known. Red jujube fruits also improve blood, and they too have some iron. By the time we get to port wine, however, we are in the realm of pure magic. Perhaps Westerners, introducing it, convinced the Chinese of its value in order to sell more of it, though many native wines were always believed to have tonic effects, if only because of their alcohol content.

Consuming liver was seen as an ideal way to supplement one's own liver. As in so many other cases, observation had made clear the actual health benefits of liver consumption by anemic patients. This observation was logically extended. Pigs' lungs help the lungs of the eater. Brains improve brain power, and so do walnut meats, which look like brains.

Genitalia, of course, strengthen the genitalia; and it follows, logically (but wrongly), that the best would be from a notoriously randy animal. A male deer can service a whole herd of several dozen does. The same is true of at least some kinds of seal. Their genitalia can be found in all Chinese drug stores, commanding a very high price among men who feel old age creeping upon them. This was even more true in the old days of polygamy. A man was expected to satisfy all his wives. Deer antlers in velvet are also highly valued as a general strengthener with special effect on the male genital system; antlers in velvet do contain hormones and minerals of uncertain effect. *Pu* items such as this are often translated as "aphrodisiacs" by salacious Westerners, but the action is not seen as aphrodisiacal. They improve, strengthen, and repair the system, and—as with ginseng—they act as general tonics. They do not excite the genitals directly, the way Spanish fly does.

Finally, *pu* effects are ascribed to items that appear strange or uncanny. This recalls the work of Lévi-Strauss and of Mary Douglas. The Lele people, whom Douglas studied in Africa, regarded the pangolin as magically powerful, because it seems both mammal and reptile and because it both burrows and runs on the surface or even climbs.[45] The Africans taboo it. The Chinese also see the pangolin as anomalous, but instead of tabooing it, they seek it out as one of the most *pu* of foods. I have seen a recipe from Kweichow for pangolin, which recommends stewing the pangolin for hours with every strong-flavored food item available. Obviously the strong taste of ants and grubs is not one of the animal's selling points; never have I seen the Chinese work so hard to kill a taste.

Other bizarre creatures that are spectacularly *pu* are edible birds' nests, sea cucumbers, sea horses, flying lizards, rhinoceros horns, vultures, and raccoon dogs. It is clear that their bizarreness, their anomalous nature, is the reason they are considered so powerful. Less strange items with comparable nutritional value are less *pu*: white fungus, abalone, and the like. Still less so are wild ducks and pigeons. Finally, ordinary barnyard creatures are *pu*, but only mildly so. My informants were quite realistic about the value of these as food.

In short, the more strange a food, the more power is ascribed to it. Fishermen at Castle Peak Bay ascribed particular potency to a small crustacean parasite of the giant grouper. They held that the *ch'i* of the grouper entered this small creature when the fish died. Thus the strange little crustacean held all the potency of a fish that could run to five hundred pounds of fighting muscle.

This last example gives us a clue to the logic of the system. Weirdness is taken as proof that the animal in question has potent *ch'i*. Strange-looking rock formations such as stalactites (high in calcium!) are also pressed into service. If a creature seems to be two things at once (like the pangolin), or if it simply looks striking, or if it has the appearance of twisted, tortured, knotted energy flow, it is assumed to be a good candidate. In the end it must also exhibit some empirical effect.

A partial opposite of *pu* is *tu*, "poisonous." Often this really means "poison-potentiating." *Tu* foods bring out poisons already present in the system, and thus make disease worse. They are especially dangerous for cancer patients. *Tu* foods include uncastrated male poultry. In a study of cancer epidemiology, M. L. Anderson and I found what our Chinese colleagues already knew: cancer patients rigorously abstained from any poultry that they did not actually see killed and cleaned, and even from chicken broth, for fear that they would get a tiny bit of a male, which would potentiate the cancer. Beef and sheep meats are often considered poisonous, the latter potentiating epilepsy. Several fish are poison-potentiating, especially if they are heating and wetting. Informants and classical herbals differ as to just which foods are *tu* for which conditions. As Carol Laderman points out, allergic reactions such as hives are often at the root of such ascriptions.[46] Rashes are often diagnosed in Chinese folk practice as being due to internal poisons breaking out.

Most *pu* foods are nonpoisonous, but the poison-potentiating foods seem generally *pu* to some degree. Many herbal remedies are poisonous, "using poison to drive out poison," much as the Chinese "used barbarians to control barbarians" in classical political strategy. It seems that such things as uncastrated male poultry combine *pu* and heat in a degree that makes them *pu* to poisons in the human system. They nourish the cancer or the toxin. The tremendous yang energy of a rooster or drake converts it from a gentle nourisher to an uncontrolled, angerous force.

Harder to explain are the many poisonous combinations. Here the belief is not in poison-potentiating; certain foods eaten together react to produce actual, virulent poisons. Gould-Martin gives some examples: "in Taiwan, crab and pumpkin, pork and licuorice, mackerel and plums and, in Hong Kong, garlic and honey, crab and persimmon, dog meat and green beans . . ."[47] Very long lists can be compiled by anyone with access to medical books. The lists differ so much from place to place and person to person that they defy all explanation. A delightful article by Libin Cheng recounts his daring experiments. He and his experimental animals survived unhurt, but his gingerly approach to testing the combinations on himself rings clearly through his medical prose! He suspects the whole complex may be due to experiences with allergy, bacterial contamination, adulteration, and the like.[48] Perhaps so; this would explain the lack of system in the whole matter. Yet we find similar beliefs around the world. Growing up in Nebraska, I was solemnly assured by almost everyone around me that eating ice cream at the same meal with fish or shellfish would "kill you for sure." Some combinations appear to be illogical, wrong, uncanny; people suffering indigestion blame it on a union of foods that, to them, seems basically wrong or unacceptable.

We may pass briefly over such minor problems as foods said to be bloating or flatulence-causing; here people merely describe reality. The one other key concept is the one that underlies *ch'ing,* "cleansing," and *hsiao,* "dispelling, clearing away." Foods in these categories are low in calories, mild in flavor, easy to digest, frequently astringent, and almost always herbal or vegetal. They include "honey, brown sugar, sugarcane juice"[49] in Taiwan; honey and sugarcane (juice included) in Hong Kong. They get rid of waste products, poisons, impurities, excess wetness, excess "wind" (i.e., rheumatism and other conditions thought to be related to internal effects of winds on the body), and other pathogenic forces. Their common denominator is that they are bland. They are either astringent or soothing.

It will be immediately evident that they form a contrast set as opposed to strengthening and poison-potentiating foods: bland versus flavorful, soothing versus exciting, cool versus hot, plant versus usually animal, cool-colored versus hot-colored. The set of cleaning foods heavily overlaps the set of bland and cooling foods. However, it is not quite identical; see, for example, brown sugar in Taiwan. More research is needed on these matters. There seems a good likelihood that the Chinese are aware of some quality in many of these herbal remedies that is new or not very familiar to Western medicine and that would repay further investigation. But, so far, all we know is that they are soothing, mild, low-calorie foods that would seem to act by calming an overwrought digestive system or diluting systemic irritants.

In all these cases, we have a group of foods that actually have some obvious physical effects, that seem experientially to hang together, and that make good sense as a unit. Yet, in no case did the Chinese see the unity as being produced by an obvious organoleptic or analytic quality. They inferred subtle energies or qualities. They inferred, on the whole, according to a very simple and straightforward set of rules:

1. Assume the simplest possible linkage. Like goes with like.
2. Assume the widest possible linkage.
3. Assume the linkage that is most consonant with the theories of *ch'i.*
4. Assume that weirdness marks effective power. Anomaly and "mixed signals" are instances of weirdness.

Chinese nutritional therapy, therefore, is a beautiful case of fitting empirical data into a logically derived theory and then making deductions based on that theory. The theory is dubious (but still respectable) by modern scientific standards. The deductions are almost all wrong. So are some of the empirical observations, notably the poisonous nature of certain food combinations. This seems typical of human thought. People are good, but far from perfect, observers. They tread on more dangerous ground when they abstract—inferring theory or generalization. But when they make deductions from inferred and necessarily imperfect theory, they make their really major mistakes.

People classify things by seeing some shared qualities that they think are, somehow, more basic than other qualities. They then overgeneralize and overextend these classifications to produce overarching high-level systems. They then deduce new "truths." Often the deduction is so confidently made that real-world observations are claimed to support it, even when they actually do not. People misperceive the facts, or they count only the hits and explain away the misses. If a cooling food seems heating to a particular person, that person simply has a unique nature. If a *pu* food fails to tone up a patient, that patient was too far gone.

Generalization, chunking of data, and inference are at work. We need not deal with schemas in any strict sense (as my sometime colleague in these researches, the cognitive psychologist Sheng-ping Fan, points out). We are dealing with lists and taxonomies and with simple information processing.

Something very close to a schema does exist in the form of analogic thinking. This is a classic process in Chinese philosophical thought, having triumphed over syllogistic logic in early centuries.[50] Analogic arguments drew on perceived parallels between events. In proving the certainty of mortality, the Chinese were more apt to say that all animals and plants die, so humans must die too; the Greeks, with their syllogistic logic, gave us the classic "All men are mortal; Socrates is a man; therefore Socrates is mortal." The Greeks argue from the general to the particular; the Chinese from one datum to a parallel datum at the same level of generality.

Chinese thinkers recognized that there were analogies and analogies. The idea was to find cases that were more than mere coincidental resemblances— cases where analogy was due to a real, underlying driving dynamic, a cause or process that produced like effects in like situations. There were qualities that were pure labels imposed by humans (such as value judgments). There were qualities that were real and shared but rather superficial and trivial (whiteness). There were still other qualities that are truly basic (*ch'i*). In the end, analogic incorporated syllogistic logic. One can recast much of the medical system syllogistically: Anomalous appearance is caused by potent *ch'i;* the pangolin looks anomalous; therefore the pangolin has potent *ch'i.* The Chinese focused on existential reality seen as process. The whole Western tradition of idealism (focusing on essential reality and on permanent, unchanging ideal forms) was unacceptable to the Chinese, even though it was often introduced, especially by schools of Buddhism.

So far, we have dealt primarily with "cold" cognition: cognition that does not involve the emotions. But the sense of uncanniness one gets from anomalous animals is emotional in nature: this is "hot" cognition in modern psychological terminology. (How readily we fall into using heat and coolness as natural metaphors! Will future psychologists believe in true heat and cold in the mind?)

However, there is more at work. The most salient feature of Chinese traditional medicine, and especially of herbal therapy, is unquestionably its relentless focus on a holistic, somatizing, naturalistic, individually localized view. The locus of control is in the individual, and in that whole individual. Thinking, knowing, and emotional feeling are viewed as clusters of functions of the body, not as a separate "mind" or even a set of functions localized in the brain. Thinking takes place in the brain, but emotion is of the heart and liver. Kleinman, in his discussion of somatization, has not quite shaken the Western notion of a separate "mind" somewhere in there, and wonders why the Chinese do not pay more attention to it.[51] But for the Chinese, mentality is not a thing, but a class of functions, like digesting.

I was raised, like most Westerners, with the belief that bad things are basically external. I would "catch a bug" or get accidentally hit by something. The Cantonese of Hong Kong were more concerned with "nourishment of life."[52] Illness is primarily a destabilization of the body, not an external insult to it. It is caused, usually, by one's own lifestyle, not by accident. Of course, the distinction is far from total. The humoral system affected my own childhood. I was taught that getting my feet wet would cause me to catch cold—a purely humoral statement. And the Chinese could see that many an accident was just chance. But the difference was real. Their medicine localized control basically within the individual; mine localized it outside the individual.

Moreover, the Chinese of Hong Kong saw most illness as natural. It was not sent by gods, witches, or demons. People I have known elsewhere in China were more afraid of the spirits, but they still saw most illness as naturalistic in causation. This can be contrasted with those many African and Oceanian peoples who ascribe all illness to malevolent or vengeful conscious entities. George Foster and Barbara Anderson make a contrast between "naturalistic" and "personalistic" medicine.[53] They rather overdrive the distinction, but it is nonetheless of interest, especially since Paul Unschuld has shown that Chinese medicine has changed from an ancient personalistic emphasis to its modern naturalistic one.[54] In rural Hong Kong when I did fieldwork there, even the spirits (speaking through spirit mediums) usually diagnosed illness as due to natural causes.

Unschuld points out that the rise of the naturalistic system, with its focus on individual control, tracked the rise of the rational bureaucratic state. Once again, as in the case of the theme of "balance," the connection lies in the desperate need of the Chinese people (both elite and folk) to assert as much control of their lives as they possibly could. Confronted with an impersonal power state and its impersonal, hyperorganized cosmology, they bent that cosmology to their own ends. They deduced a system of medicine that gave them as much control of their lives as possible. This, of course, is what made personalistic medicine succeed so little. When it did succeed, it often succeeded when all other hope had gone, or among marginal populations—in other words, it succeeded among people who had lost even the pretense of maintaining much significant control. Of course, the doctors' view could be very different from the patients', as each side jockeyed to retain or expand their power and control.

Charlotte Furth has given us a brilliant Foucaultian analysis of how this game was played in Ch'ing Dynasty gynecology.[55] Foucault saw that medical discourses are discourses about control—of the body, the mind, and the society—as well as (or, even, instead of) discourses about healing the wounded and the ill. And when an entire people locate control of health firmly in their own individual bodies, we must assume that they are trying to maximize control over their lives. Perhaps they do it to resist the bureaucratic state, using what James Scott calls the "weapons of the weak."[56] Perhaps, in this case, they are not so weak.

Chinese medicine could be bent to the service of doctors, herbalists, and even rulers, but it was superbly used for self-empowerment by the broad people of China. This is what gave it force. They could weave their empirical observations into a pragmatic of power. This is, of course, exactly the same force that is making Chinese medicine popular with some of its Western devotees today. As my student William Bowen has often pointed out to me, the Chinese explicitly attempt to take back control of their health from what they see as an alienated and alienating medical establishment that is trying to take too much control of their lives.

Many ordinary Westerners today concern themselves with "stress" and downplay genes and other aspects of fate, hoping to maximize feelings of control. Recent research shows that cancer and heart disease patients, for instance, focus on the aspects of life they can control, such as diet and stress, and ignore or try to ignore the role of uncontrollable factors such as genetics.[57]

Indeed, the modern world could do worse than see the human body-mind system as a dynamic swirl of energy, which must be kept in balance and vigor by proper "nourishment of health."

To some extent, the Chinese had little choice. They had to control their lives and their health, in the old Imperial days, when government officials comprised only 0.1 to 0.2 percent of the population. (About one in ten workers in the United States today is a government employee.) And the Ch'ing didn't even have telephones. Doctors were also few in number. Druggists and herbalists were numerous and widespread, providing much care and also a cultural pipeline between educated elite and ordinary folk. But individuals had to assert control in the teeth of government, community, and kinship organization.

Psychologist Robert Zajonc argued that humans cannot know or think anything without at least some involvement of emotion, if only a vague sense of "good" or "bad."[58] As Zajonc would lead us to expect, the deeper generating dynamic of the special characteristics of the Chinese medical system is "hot," not "cold." As Bandura would lead us to expect, it is a function of the human need to negotiate self-efficacy.[59]

This, and the cosmology of ch'i and its transformations, gives Chinese medicine a very different language from Western therapy. Translation can be dangerous—a fact only now beginning to be realized.[60] Real explanatory dictionaries are needed; Liu and Liu make a good start.[61]

Chinese society required that every science be applied. The Renaissance concept of "pure" science was a revolutionary development in the West, but had strong roots going back to Classical Greece. Plants were to be studied primarily in relation to other plants, and only secondarily in regard to their value to humans. Physics was to be studied as pure work, or motion, and only secondarily in regard to human work. Mathematics became a wonderful sport. The need to classify newfound plants and model newfound heavenly motions had much to do with this, but it was philosophically congenial. To the Chinese, on the other hand, botany was ever the handmaiden of agriculture and herbal study; mathematics of engineering; anatomy of medical practice. There was a felt need to understand things in themselves, just as there was a pure mathematics. But people were too busy with the practical matters of life to go into either one in very much depth. Chinese applied science went as far as it could without a pure science to back it up, but then it foundered on a maze of reefs: untested inferences, untested mistaken deductions. Even so, it is well to remember that a malnourished person would have been far better advised to trust himself or herself to a Chinese grandmother than to a Western nutritionist, right up into the first part of our own century.

As it confronts the Western world, Chinese medicine is accommodating in methodology and discourse. Medical anthropologist Karin Hilsdale argues that Chinese medicine shows signs of losing its paradigm and becoming a disunited bundle of techniques, as Western concepts of cosmology, biotechnology, and so on are incorporated.[62] Arthur Kleinman's and William Bowen's current research adumbrate on this issue as well.[63] While the demise of the Chinese paradigm is hardly imminent, there is a real chance of losing certain strengths.[64] The irony of adopting an increasingly analytic, if not alienated, approach is evident. *Scientific American* (1985) reports that one recent study concludes that almost a third of deaths in the United States are hastened by abuse of tobacco, alcohol, and other drugs. Add to this the toll of suicide, eating disorders, and other self-destructive behavior, and we probably can say that most deaths in the United States are caused or hastened by processes under the full control (conscious or subconscious, if you will) of the individual.

Chinese medicine has persisted so well because it has a comprehensive, overarching framework that can accommodate everything from spirit mediumship to literally cut-and-dried herbal remedies and because it satisfies its users' need to take control of their lives. I extend Karin Hilsdale's call to preserve the framework in extending Chinese medicine to the West.[65] We not only need to preserve it; we need to transmit it outside the bounds of traditional Chinese practice.

Thus, for confusing and complex reasons relating to human information processing, Chinese nutritional science has moved back and forth from everyday empirical reality to a highly abstract and complex logical scheme that, in turn, influences perception of everyday reality. The net result is better nutrition for billions of people over countless years.

4

Learning from the Land Otter: Religious Representation of Traditional Resource Management

Throughout the forests of the Northwest Coast of North America—those few forests that have not been logged—one finds cedar trees from which long strips of bark have been removed. These strips were taken, at various times in the recent or distant past, by local Native American peoples, to use for a wide variety of reasons. The trees were never cut for their bark; only one long, narrow strip was removed. The process made it necessary for someone to climb high up in the tree to cut the top of the strip.

This difficult and dangerous climb was economically reasonable; cutting a cedar is a long job, and would, in any case, eliminate the chance of future bark. But the climb was required for a more immediate and compelling reason: the cedar is sacred, and its indwelling spirit must be respected. Wanton cutting of a cedar is unthinkable. Before a cut is made, prayers and apologies are made to the tree. The cutter explains that he or she really needs the bark, and often adds that he or she will take as little as possible, in the most careful way.

In spite of two centuries of contact with, and borrowing from, the outside world, this reverence for the cedar continues today. It is part of a wider religious involvement with the landscape—with water, mountains, plants, and animals—that incorporates environmental management rules as part of sacred ethics.

Across the Pacific from China, the Native American peoples of the Northwest Coast maintained, until recently, a way of life based on fishing. While the Chinese changed from foragers to farmers, and slowly built the world's most populous civilization, the Northwest Coast Indians developed more and more sophisticated ways of harvesting the abundant fish and shellfish resources of their cold and rainy coastlines and rivers. Although they built no cities and wrote down no literature, they created a brilliant, complex culture that had an extremely fine-tuned adjustment to its environment. These were no primitive hunters-and-gatherers roaming over the landscape hoping to find a dead deer; they were settled peoples, living in large villages with class systems, spectacular art, elaborate oral literature, and a superb knowledge of ecology and environment.

Here, as in China, we find an unsurpassed knowledge of the fish and mammals of the region coexisting with what seem, to Western biologists, truly incredible errors. The Indians of the northern Northwest Coast believed, for example, that the "land otter" (Northwest Coast English for the river otter, *Lutra canadensis*) could steal their souls. (Herein I will use the local name to distinguish the otter of local belief from the river otter of science.) Frequently, a land otter would drown a man alone in a canoe. Or it might appear to a man alone in the forest, seeming to be his wife or sweetheart, and lead him away never to return. These beliefs are by no means extinct today.

As with *feng-shui,* I will argue that:

1. Such beliefs are logical, following from the best model that the Northwest Coast people could make of their world.

2. This model (counterfactual beliefs and all) serves as a powerful conservation device.

This chapter focuses on religion. I draw heavily on the sociological theories of Emile Durkheim.[1] Following him, I take religion to be the ritual representation of the community, and a device for sanctioning moral codes.

The reason for religious representation of resource management seems clear. By using religion as the carrier wave, a society invokes the religious system's emotional power and intellectual authority. This point has been made for the Native peoples of Canada by Robin Ridington.[2] Religion is used to sanction conservation and to teach environmental knowledge (see chapter 10). In short, ecology and religion are inseparable.

Recent research on Canadian and Alaskan Native cultures makes explicit the workings of traditional resource management and its relationship to ideology. This is especially well covered for the Cree, but also attested for the Beaver, the Koyukon and their neighbors, including the Kaska, the Inland Tlingit and Tutchone, the Tlingit, and several other groups.[3] Almost all sources speak of rules that command a user to take no more of a resource than absolutely necessary. Studies of the Cree and Beaver show actual conservation of animal stocks. However, they also show much variation in this regard, over time and over space. Robert Brightman's studies of the Rock Cree reveal periods of waste and periods of relatively better management.[4] Variation in such matters is to be expected. The argument of the present chapter is not that traditional peoples are natural conservationists, but that they *sometimes* conserve, and that, when they do, it is because of religiously coded moral rules as well as (or instead of) rational planning.

The above mentioned studies, of course, do not describe aboriginal conditions. Richard Nelson, in his study of the Kaska, even allows the possibility of white influence.[5] Brightman postulates the same for the Rock Cree. However, serious Anglo influence on such systems is extremely unlikely. These systems are well described by careful ethnographers working with old informants who remember traditional times. They are phrased in, and thoroughly embedded in, the language of arcane ideological discourse—quite traditional, and very far from Anglo discourse. Historical studies show the conservation-ideology linkage is respectably old.[6]

Moreover, the Anglos with whom the North Woods Indians have had contact have never been 1960s hippies filled with ecological dogma. They were old-time pioneers and woodsmen and modern corporation representatives. Their attitudes toward the environment were, and are, almost purely exploitative. As I can testify from research on the Northwest Coast, Indians continually have to assert their traditions against local whites who are militantly opposed to conservation in any form—and who frequently convince younger Indians to forget old ways.

Finally, at least some of the ethnographers went out explicitly to disprove the "myth" of the conservationist Indian, and stayed to be convinced.[7] We are not dealing with a case like that of the famous speech of Chief Seattle, some of whose conservationist words are now known to be spurious.[8] The very popularity of this speech among Anglos is revealing; its discourse is all too Anglo. Its nature lore is unmistakably that of the 1960s eco-movement, not of a world of giant demon-otters and talking dogs.

Throughout the American subarctic, there is a broad commonality of beliefs about animals. It is very general, but also absolutely critical. In a word, it is the idea that animals and humans are bonded very closely; they are part of one community, and as such are involved with each other in relations of empowerment, emotional interaction, and even sex. Adrian Tanner's book's title, *Bringing Home Animals,* is intended to stress the fact that animals are not simply brought home as dead hunks of meat and hide. They are brought *home.* They are part of the community, part of the wider family. Further than that: they are, in some sense, people. For many groups, they are actual humanlike beings, who can take off their animal skins and appear as thoroughly humanoid. For others, they are not human persons, but they are persons all the same. We must here escape from the Western concept of human versus inhuman, inanimate, soulless.

However, Lévi-Strauss's opposition of "culture" and "nature" is apposite. The point is that the boundary between culture and nature crosscuts the boundary between human and animal. There are humans and humanoid beings who are uncultured: wild men, crazed cannibals, and the various mythic beings ancestral to the "Sasquatch" and "bigfoot" of American folktales.[9] The major animals, on the other hand, live in humanlike societies, or become humans.

Thus on the Pacific Coast the salmon are viewed as humans who put on fish skins to sacrifice themselves to their human relatives. When white men first appeared in ships, the Nuu-Chah-Nulth (Nootka) people of Vancouver Island thought that the salmon had, for some reason, appeared in their human form. The strangers were fish-belly white, and appeared from the ocean in vast houses of the sort the salmon inhabited under the sea. The Nuu-Chah-Nulth still refer to the whites as *mamalni*—"floating-house people." Nowhere in the Northwest were salmon used as a family- or lineage-crest animal. Salmon were not important animals in art. The salmon were very much the "ordinary people" of the nonhuman world; they were not special in the ways that made a creature spiritually and socially powerful. They were the yeomen, not the chiefs—the staff of life but not its head.

Plants, mountains, rocks, and even weather phenomena were all regarded as persons (human or not). The South Wind, bearer of storms on the Pacific Coast, was a blustering old man in the mythology of the Haida of the Queen Charlotte Islands. He is still regarded with a lively sense of personhood by many Haida. Not a few Anglo-Canadians on the Charlottes have acquired some of this viewpoint; the violent, dangerous, sudden storms that blow up from the south seem almost to demand that one postulate an active malevolence behind them.

The Katzie Salish of the lower Fraser River, near what is now Vancouver, believed that their creator/culture hero had had a son who begat the Katzie and a daughter who became a sturgeon. She is still instantiated in the sturgeons that once made Katzie territory their main spawning ground. Thus, when a Katzie caught one of the sturgeons that made up their staple food, he thanked his beloved sister for sacrificing her life for her brotherhood.[10]

As elsewhere in the world, the dog is a revealing creature, being between humans and animals in its home and habits; it was often regarded as very human, but could be rather terrifying—especially when, in myths, it grew human enough to talk or to father children.[11] Human and nonhuman realms should be separate. The dog flouts this separation. It is not human, yet it is part of human society: it lives with humans and eats their food. There was (in myth) always that frightening chance that a dog might suddenly talk, turn humanoid, and carry off a human girl or boy for a spouse.

The Haida, Tlingit, and Tsimshian peoples of the northern Northwest Coast, in northern British Columbia and southern Alaska, believed that certain animals had particular power. The land otter, black oystercatcher, octopus (devilfish), and raven were associated with magic and shamanism. Other animals, such as bears and eagles, had less dangerous but socially important power. Animals were classified not only in biological terms but in terms of the types and intensities of their spirit power. The system grew from the interaction between careful and pragmatic observation and a shamanic worldview. It was mediated through intense emotional involvement with the animals, their capture, and their management as a vital resource.

Some animals are far more important and powerful than others. Specifically, on the northern Northwest Coast, the raven (*Corvus corax*), octopus (*Octopus* spp.), oystercatcher (*Haematopus bachmani*), and river otter (*Lutra canadensis*) are especially associated with the vitally important powers of killing and healing. They are thus powerful magic for halibut fishing and for shamanic curing and bewitching.[12] Halibut fishing is an exceedingly dangerous occupation; it is carried out on the open sea, often far from land, and the halibut are often huge. It is also notoriously chancy. It is also necessary for survival, for halibut are a staple fish along the outer coast. Shamanism is, of course, even more culturally salient and psychologically charged.

The most distinctive and striking belief complex in this cluster is that relating to the land otter, a common and easily observed animal in the area. (The sea otter, *Enhydra lutris*, formerly common in the area, has no special magical associations.)

The land otter is believed to get power over humans—especially drowned persons—and turn them into land otters. The otters lure people to drown, in hopes of capturing them. However, lone individuals far out in the woods or marooned on isolated islands are also at risk.[13] Any human alone in the wilderness and at risk of death is easy prey. To these, the otters appear as friends and loved ones. If the human is seduced by these apparitions, he or she will turn into a land otter. It is particularly dangerous to enter into loving relationships. A man alone in the woods is lost if he has sexual relations with a land otter who has taken the form of his wife. A child is lost if she accepts as true parent a land otter who has taken the form of her mother or father. Quite apart from Freudian implications, these human relationships are highly charged—powerful—and, of course, create close social bonds. It is no wonder that the land otters rely on such methods. The land otters are used to scare children into staying near camp and not straying in the woods.

A few especially powerful individuals can meet the land otters on their own ground and remain safe. This requires many precautions as well as tremendous personal power. A dramatic Haida story tells of a man canoewrecked on a small island, who resisted the land otters though they took the form of his wife and other dear ones. He had to refuse all food and keep his anus stopped up tight. He also had to kill his dog, skin it, cover himself with the blood and skin, and hold its ulna bone; dogs are antipathetic to land otters. With the ulna bone he could test the otters' canoes, since the bone would penetrate them. He put their paddles in the fire and the paddles turned into minks and ran away. Many other precautions had to be taken before he was rescued.[14]

More important culturally is the Tlingit story of KAka'.[15] This individual resisted the land otters and got much power from them, innovating shamanism or at least greatly contributing to its depth and knowledge among the Tlingit. Frederica de Laguna, ethnographer of the Tlingit, discusses in detail their fear of the animals, and the precautions taken in everyday life, such as keeping iron or similar metal about one's person.[16] A person changed into a land otter is called a *kucdaga* in Tlingit, a *gagixit* in Haida. The latter term has actually crept into Queen Charlottes Islands English, and the Anglo-Canadian residents of the islands have picked up some of the belief; many of them are genuinely afraid of the "gogeet," regarding it as a bogeyman or bigfoot of the woods. This reveals the extreme power of the whole belief complex; no other Haida belief has been so generally adopted by the whites.

Tlingit myths and tales include countless stories about the land otters. The otters are regarded as having towns of their own, where captured humans live more or less as they would have at home. Otters are shape-changers and magicians.

A would-be shaman must go out alone and meet the land otters on their own ground. Here they will challenge him. If he is strong enough, an otter will come to him and fall dead, or appear to. The shaman then takes its tongue and prepares it in a ritual way, and the dried tongue becomes a terrifically powerful item, to be kept in his *shluch* ("power bundle," "medicine bundle").[17] Apparently in reality the shaman kills an otter and takes its tongue. It is possible that visions of otters are involved here. Tonguelike objects found after seeing real or imagined otters may sometimes be collected.

The other animals require less comment. The raven is, of course, the trickster, creator and transformer of Northwest Coast myths. He was more important at the beginning of time, when he made the world as it is today. Now he is just a bird—however important as symbol and clan crest. However, among the Tlingit, the raven's first call of the day has the function that the dawn crowing of roosters has elsewhere: at the first raven call, supernatural beings must return to their homes, and humans must stop any particularly magical or supernaturally charged activities.

The octopus is seen as a weird, scary creature and little more. Stories of giant octopi are as common on the Northwest Coast as elsewhere. Heroes conquer gigantic octopi in Tlingit versions of the worldwide story of the hero who must perform magical tasks to win the chief's daughter. The oystercatcher seems completely absent from stories and accounts, but assorted unidentified shorebirds are referred to in myths and tales. Otherwise, the oystercatcher appears only as a bird in art, represented on halibut hooks, shamanic equipment, and especially on the bird-shaped rattles used by chiefs and shamans. These are either ravens or oystercatchers.[18]

Other animals, though important in myths, are not magically dangerous, as the foregoing are. More gentle or more distant beliefs attach to many other animals, including porpoises, killer whales, bears, salmon, kingfishers, cranes, geese, and most of the other salient creatures of the coastal world. Even wrens, sparrows, and chickadees have their roles in stories, and the mouse is a very important character in Haida tales, appearing as a woman who repays many times over any favor done for her. But none of these compares with the land otter in sinister reputation.

Aldona Jonaitis, authority on the art history of the northern Northwest Coast, has revealed and explained an underlying pattern in Tlingit animal lore.[19] I believe, from my own research, that her findings hold for the less well known Haida and possibly for the Tsimshian. The highly charged magical animals—land otter, octopus, oystercatcher, raven, and kingfisher—are shown on halibut hooks, rattles, and a few other kinds of magical equipment and on shamans' charms. The land otter is far and away the most important of these, represented on these items—especially on almost every shaman's charm. Land otter persons (humans changing into otters) are widely depicted in northern Northwest Coast art. In contrast, the art of the chiefs and descent groups rarely shows any of these except the raven. The land otter was, however, a Tlingit crest animal[20] and was occasionally shown in Tsimshian art. There is a totem pole in front of Paris's Musée de l'Homme, for instance, that appears to show a land otter. Thus, the separation is not uniform. However, there was a clear contrast between magical and chiefly art.

Chieftainship and descent are eminently public, social phenomena, whereas shamanism and food-quest magic are private and personal. The animals of the secular/social world are bears, wolves, whales, beavers, mosquitoes, seals, wealth-giving monsters, and so on. Land otters are apparently *never* found on boxes, blankets, robes, chests, and other everyday items. Neither are oyster-catchers, as far as I know. Wolves and bears, conversely, are rare or absent on shamanic and magical gear. (Apparent exceptions seem, often, to be misidentifications.) Dogs, interestingly, seem virtually absent from Northwest Coast art. Only the raven seems to move easily between both worlds, and the raven is truly privileged, as the original shaper of all things.

Jonaitis has pointed out, I believe correctly, that the magical animals are all highly anomalous. The land otter, for instance, is able to move easily in the underworld (its burrow), in water, and on land. It is also humanlike in its playful nature, social behavior, and dependence on fish. I can testify from considerable personal contact that meeting an otter is a unique and striking experience. Otters are often uncannily fearless, being quite prone to come toward humans and look them straight in the eyes. Otters in the water often play around a canoe, or a person on the shore, and try to incorporate the human in their games. They seem to be quite genuinely trying to lure the person into the water to play with them. Having seen this behavior on several occasions, I am convinced that the otters' apparent desire to involve humans in their world has given them their reputation.

What are we to make of these beliefs? At least some of them are far more than mere symbolism. Land otters are not symbols of descent groups or of religious concepts. They are not simply artistic devices. The land otter beliefs are not a trivial or minor part of the culture. Land otters are important animals. They are genuinely and deeply feared—so much so that, as we have seen, fear of land otter–men has spread to many whites. Thousands of hours were once spent in carving land otter representations on shamans' goods, including grave goods and memorial poles.

The following is a letter by Mrs. Mabel Sport, an elder of the Nuu-Chah-Nulth people. Her 1985 letter to the Nuu-Chah-Nulth tribal newspaper, *Ha-Shilth-*

Sa, deals with the need to protect even the smallest and most humble of fish. "Bull head" is Northwest Coast English for any of various small sculpins, often caught today by children, sometimes in informal "derbies." Like most other wild creatures, they were of considerable mythological importance to most of the Northwest Coast peoples. They do not resemble the small catfish called "bullheads" in most of North America. This letter says more about Nuu-chah-nulth belief in the value of all living things than about ichthyology. Especially important is the second paragraph; Nuu-chah-nulth culture does not allow such things to be said lightly.

> Dear Editor:
>
> As one of the natives of the Nuu-Chah-Nulth tribes, I am compelled to write and let people know of the teachings I had as a child concerning the bull head.
>
> I get very hurt feelings inside whenever I hear about the Bull Head Derby.
>
> As a child I was taught about the sacredness of life. The natives believe that every living thing has a spirit.
>
> The bull head is the guardian of the waterfront and rivers. It keeps the water clean by eating things that make the water unclean. That is why he has a lowly Indian name.
>
> It also guards the small coho fry until maturity. The more plentiful the bull heads are in the river, the more plentiful the fish.
>
> As children we were not allowed to catch and kill the bull head, because the elders of our tribe said the bull head screams the loudest when it is killed and this causes the Sea Spirits to get very disturbed and this is why the west wind blows very hard.
>
> These are only some of the stories about the bull head.
>
> Thank you for your attention to my letter.
>
> Mrs. Mabel Sport

Northwest Coast myths and tales routinely teach that people should not take more game or fish or plant materials than they can use, or more than the environment can spare. Frederica de Laguna provides superb examples of Tlingit moral teachings.[21] At the beginning of the twentieth century, John Swanton recorded tales with conservationist morals from Katishan, a Haida of the Queen Charlottes.[22] Practical teaching of conservation is thus made more persuasive by teaching it through powerful religious and social documents. The intense emotional relationship that Northwest Coast peoples have with animals is made powerful by the inclusion of animals in the social, and thus the religious, structure and system. There is no necessary reason to conserve animals simply because one is emotionally involved with them, but conservation as a specific moral teaching is more easily enforced if people feel this involvement.

In any case, the involvement of animals in the human world—or, rather, the extension of the social world to include animals as well as humans—entails some logical corollaries. Most obviously, if the human world includes an opposition of secular/social and shamanic/private, the animal world must have such an opposition as well. It follows that the more ordinary animals would seem to inhabit the social realm, while the apparently uncanny and strangely powerful ones would sort with shamans and loners. In particular, if humans are to receive power from animals, they should expect to receive social and chiefly power from ordinary (if physically strong) creatures like wolves and bears, and to receive shamanic powers from uncanny creatures like land otters. The all-transcending, all-transforming raven participates in both sectors of life, even more as overarching mythic figure than as direct power-giver.

Probably arising among the Tlingit, the land otter belief was a logical corollary of shamanistic thinking, in a society where animals figure as persons and as givers of power. Many other groups saw the otter as a mythic creature, but only among the Tlingit and their neighbors did the otter become so important. The pervasive fear of witchcraft among the Tlingit seems strongly associated with the belief in a power-animal with such frightening properties.

To paraphrase the Northwest Coast way of knowing: we humans live in mutual-aid relationships with most of those other persons, the nonhumans. We eat them or use them; they empower us. We have increase rites for them, remember them in songs and ceremonies, and sometimes can give them goods. This is especially important if we eat them or if they eat us.[23]

Necessary for the consociation of humans and nonhumans was profound mutual respect. Some nonhumans had powers far beyond anything an ordinary human could muster. Others moved with ease in worlds impassable to humans: deep water, air, or the underground. Others sacrificed themselves, regularly, as food. Since they were persons, and universally believed to be endowed with some degree of humanlike cognitive abilities, they must recognize their danger when humans were hunting them. If they were caught, it must have been by their choice. The hunter's ability was critically important, to be sure, but game and fish simply disappeared from an area where they were ill-treated.

Far more serious was the fear that outraged animals would descend on a village and destroy it for its lack of respect, as they had done many times in the mythic past. Chief Kenneth Harris of the Gitksan is one who has recorded the stories. In his book *Visitors Who Never Left* we read of beavers that avenge themselves on a boy who broke their dam, of the revenge of the heavens on others who used a bear's stomach for a football, and of the climactic destruction of the original Gitksan village by mountain goats outraged because of over-hunting: "They had defied the laws of nature, the laws of their god, the laws of their Father-in-Heaven who had instructed them not to torment animals, not to laugh at them, not to waste, and not to use any portion of the animal for amusement."[24] I have seen the site of the old village. It appears to have been buried by a landslide. I assume the landslide, whenever it occurred, was taken to be the revenge of the mountain goats.[25] There are comparable stories, or versions of the same stories, throughout North America. My Maya Indian friends in Quintana Roo phrase their hunting morals in very similar terms to Chief Harris's.

Respect was tinged with gratitude and with awe. Universal in the Northwest, and possibly everywhere, was the custom of apologizing to a tree, plant, or animal for taking it. The taker had to apologize, thank, and explain that he or she genuinely needed the individual for his or her family—not just his or her own welfare. People even apologize to trees for taking strips of bark (as I learned from the Nuu-chah-nulth of Vancouver Island).

The rules of conduct varied from group to group. Among the Beaver and their neighbors, animals appeared to men in dreams, telling the men which way to hunt. Trails came from the skyworld, crossed human trails, and led to the animals' sacrificing themselves if the hunter did not violate proper rules of behavior.[26] Among the northern Northwest Coast tribes, hunting and fishing were more prosaic, but wandering in the wild could involve the risk of encountering spiritually powerful animals, especially the otters.[27]

Among the Salish peoples of the coast, each individual had a spirit guardian. This guardian gave him or her all his or her special powers, inclinations, and abilities. The spirit power thus included what Christians of the recent past knew as "one's vocation." In fact, the spirit gave the recipient a song, and so one's special ability was often referred to as one's "song."

Among other groups, the spirit guardian was called "knowledge," leading to the rather strange English usage of "so-and-so doesn't know anything" meaning "so-and-so has not yet received spirit power." This usage lies behind the title of Robin Ridington's book *Little Bit Know Something*, an account of his research among the Beaver Indians.[28]

Thus, conservation of animals and plants was a burning, emotional, personal issue. A properly socialized individual had a powerful sense that the wild world was feeding him, and he ought to be as grateful and as anxious to act decently as he would to any human who fed him out of sheer kindness.

Naturally, wanton killing was virtually tantamount to murder, and ungrateful murder at that.[29]

Ownership and management of most resources rested with the local descent group. In the northern Coast this was the localized, coherent, chief-led lineage segment (as opposed to the larger lineage, a somewhat vague entity).[30] For the Kwakwaka'wakw ("Kwakiutl") it was the numaym. The Salish had localized patrilineal winter-village groups. The Nuu-chah-nulth (who possess an ineffable fondness for large kinship groups with fuzzy boundaries) had bilineally accreted winter-village groups of frequently shifting membership. The local chief assembled whatever band of people he could hold by right of superior generosity and prowess. In all cases, the chief of the local descent group had power as representative, spokesman, and leader to direct the management of resources. The authority of the chief seems to have been high among the Tsimshian, at least in historic times, but chiefs had less power among some Salish-speaking peoples. The Nuu-chah-nulth, Kwakwaka'wakw, Haida, and others seem to have been somewhere in between, having strong chiefs but frequent shifts of power. A strong chief could even lose a major battle or potlatch competition and see his followers decamp to a rival establishment.

In all cases, someone had to be responsible for management. Ownership could be a complex matter. Individuals owned their own means of production—bows and arrows and the like—and managed these as they saw fit. Smaller or larger groups than the localized descent unit might own property.[31] Chiefly authority could organize production and enforce conservation. Among the Gitksan and their neighbors, salmon fishing was highly organized and directed by chiefs.[32] But individuals had a good deal of power and autonomy, and had to have internalized quite firmly management strategies and rules. Local chiefs and rich people organized potlatches, powerful incentives to amass food and wealth; but chiefs had little direct ability to force independent followers (as opposed to slaves) to produce. Individuals worked hard for popular leaders, and for the greater glory of their descent units, but they had considerable control over how much effort they put into this. Chiefs could and did exert enough control over resource management to affect the levels of resource use by whole descent groups, but they did not have anything close to total power in this regard.

In such a situation, a public ideology of resource management and wise use was maximally valuable and maximally likely. Chiefs could not simply amass wealth for themselves and let their followers suffer. Individuals could not ignore the group. Chiefs and commoners were mutually dependent, and both groups depended on the workings of a system that had to maintain itself through particular strategies. This demanded a validating ideology.

The religion did more than that: it provided direct emotional involvement with natural resources. Individuals got their spirit power, their calling, their very personhood from transactions with the nonhuman world. They also lived in fear of the magic otters, the powerful natural forces, and other nonhuman powers. Nothing could be farther from the vague and fuzzy "oneness with mother nature" of the environmentalist rhetoric that has recently been foisted on the Indians. Such rhetoric is, in fact, a way of distancing oneself from nature; it is the product of urbanites who do not deal with ecological realities. The Northwest Coast Indians confronted nonhuman beings with an intense personal love, a sense of direct personal empowerment, and frequently a healthy respect or even fear. Beings had their own special powers and abilities, natural and supernatural. Fish, bears, wolves, and eagles were part of the kinship system, part of the community, part of the family structure. Modern urbanite ecologists see these as Other, and romanticize them; but for a Northwest Coast Indian, an alien human was apparently more Other than a local octopus or wolf. It was this direct and total involvement, this intense and personal relationship, that allowed reasonable resource management. If these people had had the cold, distant relationship that modern Anglos have with nature, they would not have been able to involve themselves enough in resource management to function in the system.

Specific ecological knowledge was taught by myth. The hero destroys the weir that is taking all the salmon, and decrees that henceforth weirs shall allow salmon to escape.[33] The bad children of a village kill animals wantonly, and the village is destroyed, except for those who warned against such behavior.[34] Salmon capture a boy who was not respectful of them and explain to him the proper way to treat them.[35]

The most important question in all this is, of course, whether conservation was actually maintained by this ideology. This breaks down into two separate questions: First, did the Northwest Coast Indians really conserve? Second, did this ideology drive that behavior?

As to the first, there is no serious doubt that some deliberate managing of populations was practiced. For plants, there is no question: deliberate burning to maximize healthy plant populations, deliberate cultivation, and even planting of resources was general.[36] For animals, the most dramatic case is the Nuu-chah-nulth custom of planting salmon eggs in streams. Gilbert Malcolm Sproat, an excellent nineteenth-century observer, describes this as a "common practice."[37] Since he was the first Anglo in the area of which he writes, the Indians can hardly have learned it from local whites. In fact, whites were not planting salmon eggs in streams anywhere near the Nuu-chah-nulth area at that time. Unfortunately, early ethnographers simply were not interested in resource management. They not only didn't ask about it, they apparently deliberately steered away from it, so as to spend their time finding out about more patterned behavior, such as language and folktales. We must rely on recent ethnography of nearby interior groups who preserved more or less traditional lifeways until more modern days (see above) and on ethnohistoric research; a very important beginning in this regard has been made by Steve Langdon.[38]

But we can see the existence of effective conservation at work. Fish populations survive, for instance, in even the tiniest creeks. It is a simple matter, with thoroughly traditional Indian methods, to "rob" such creeks: set a net or weir across them and take all the salmon, eliminating the run. This is, alas, commonly done today.

The myth of Northwest Coast abundance has long been defunct.[39] True, the groups at the mouth of the Fraser River would have had a hard time wiping out its resources.

However, even on the vast Skeena and Fraser River systems, runs could fail.[40] John Pritchard found that the Haisla, in such a situation on their own rivers (far smaller than the Skeena), took refuge with relatives.[41]

Over eight thousand Haida try to make a living from the Queen Charlotte Islands. These desolate and impoverished islets have no large rivers and only two streams large enough to have respectable salmon runs. The Haida were frequently reduced to real hunger, and relied heavily on deep-sea fishing and on trade for grease with the mainland. Only someone who has been out on Queen Charlotte seas can appreciate the desperateness of such a position. The survival of large populations of salmon and land game on the Charlottes must necessarily be due to careful management; the Haida had the numbers and the technology to wipe out essentially everything. Haida villages moved every generation or so, in part because they had eaten the local seacoasts bare and had to give the resources time to recover.

Other upriver or island peoples were in a similarly vulnerable position. Except for the groups at the mouths of major streams, the Northwest Coast Indians were pressing on their environment; their very large, sedentary populations occupied a land where fish runs did fail, game could be decimated by a bad winter, and food was exceedingly scarce outside of the overwhelming and sometimes unstorable abundance of the major fish runs. One reason for the myth of abundance is the sheer tonnage of food that can be obtained. However, this is misleading because of the exceedingly low caloric value of berries, wild roots, and sea food. There was a large focus throughout the Northwest on grease: from ooligan fish, sockeye salmon, whales, seals, anything. The climate and active lifestyle demanded a high-calorie diet. My own experiments with gathering food reveals that, although one can gather a great deal of food in undisturbed parts of the Northwest Coast, the easily gotten items are so low in calories that they rarely repay the effort expended in gathering them.

Were children taught by myth and ritual to transport salmon eggs or stop fishing when runs were reduced? It seems impossible to believe that people could kill wantonly in good conscience, but what about killing just a bit more than was directly necessary? Obviously, there was some waste of food in the potlatches—though all researchers seem to agree that the excessive waste at potlatches of the late nineteenth century was a postcontact phenomenon.

In short, on the Northwest Coast, conservation was managed by political regulation supported by appeal to individual morality. This involved administrative control over fish and fishing activities. Control was usually vested in the whole group (kin or community) and administered by chiefs. In other areas, there was management through ritual regulation using religious specialists.[42] Individual morality was also involved, at many levels.[43]

Chiefly power, ritual power, and the personal power of individual morality maintained the system. This required a tremendous knowledge of the ecosystem. It also required a political system that allowed specification of the resource base to eliminate tragedies of the commons by vesting control of resources in the local community, and providing actual means for enforcing that control.[44] It also required that everyone, or almost everyone, be aware of the need and committed to preserving the life-support system.

Conscious management of resources for long-term use seems to have been widely characteristic in North America.[45] In the Great Basin, straight-trunked juniper trees suitable for bow staves were exceedingly rare; they were carefully managed. Staves were cut off the living tree, the tree being allowed to heal and recover between cuts. This meant that only one stave could be taken every decade or two, and people for miles around had to know this and respect the trees.[46] Management of oasis farming by the Tohono O'o'dham of northern Mexico led to maintenance of wild plant and bird populations; by contrast, even attempted conservation of oases by modern governments is less successful.[47]

Community management strategies and the individual knowledge of ecology, morality, and cultural rules had to be passed on to rising generations. This leads us to the questions, how do people learn such matters, and how are they taught? To my knowledge, there is only one full-length study of how children in a traditional society learn about ecology: Kenneth Ruddle and Ray Chesterfield's book *Education for Food Production in the Orinoco Delta*.[48] Richard Gould in Australia and Carobeth Laird in California are among those who have touched on this issue.[49] Myths and folktales function as, among other things, devices to teach the young about their environment. Both Gould and Laird describe how children learn myths that include the travels of culture heroes around the water holes in the territory. For these desert peoples, as for others, a list of water holes is a great deal easier to memorize if it is embedded in a racy story with lots of sex, violence, and religion. A boy who tried to memorize the bare list would easily become confused and perish in the sand. Nor is this an isolated instance.

Ralph Maud has reviewed the use of myths as teaching devices in the Northwest Coast cultures.[50] Early ethnographers simply recorded myths without the exhortations and lectures that typically accompanied them. These were an integral part of myth-telling, as Chief Harris has shown (see above). The overarching message is be respectful and reverent to animals and plants, for they and we depend on each other.

In practice, this led to eleven corollaries, which represent the shamanistic religion of the Northwest.[51]

1. Cultural and natural worlds are distinct but interpenetrate constantly. Each depends on the other and must maintain harmony.[52]

2. These worlds are not separate. Human souls are reincarnated in killer whales, wolves, and other animals. Humans and animals can marry, and many groups trace their ancestry to such marriages in mythic time. Humans and animals are, therefore, frequently kin.

3. Supernatural power routinely crosses the gap. People draw power from nature and can use it in the cultural sphere. Just as food and other material goods derived from the environment, so spiritual power can be gained from the nonhuman world. The Northwest Coast Indians were, and still are, profoundly aware of their dependence on the natural world around them. It was reasonable to extend this dependence from material to nonmaterial goods.

4. To obtain this power, individuals must leave the social and cultural world. They must go alone into the wilderness in as bare a state as possible. Here, without human contact and with minimal food and clothing, they must

subject themselves to cold bathing and other ordeals, making themselves not only pitiable but also free of human or cultural taint.

5. Animals are culture-bearing beings too, in their own realms; there (inside mountains or under the sea) they are people with houses, fires, cooking, clothing, valuables, and all the rest of the paraphernalia of culture. They also, often, participate in human kinship and political systems. The opposition between nature and culture does not separate humans from nonhumans. Instead, the contrast is between beings-in-their-communities (people in villages, salmon under the sea) and beings-in-the-outer-world (people on vision quests, salmon in the rivers). The links and separations between humans and nonhumans are complex.

6. Animals that act like humans—animals that are social carnivores or that live on fish—are especially powerful and can transfer especially great powers to humans.

7. Humans who get power from the natural world can use it to control things not normally under human control: sickness, luck, weather, and the like.

8. Powers must be exhibited, like other social distinctions and goods, in public rituals.

9. A reverent, caring, thoughtful, and grateful attitude toward the natural world and its inhabitants is absolutely necessary to survival. Without proper ritual treatment—and all traditions make it explicit that the ritual is an expression of the reverent gratitude—the animals and plants will cease to sacrifice themselves for human welfare. (If the salmon and mountain goats are people, indeed relatives, who put on animal skins to sacrifice themselves for us, it behooves us to treat them as honored relatives and as guests when they are with us. Without that, they will naturally be offended and go away.) Failure to do so, dishonesty in the explanation, or taking unneeded materials will lead to alienation of the animals and plants and of their spirit guardians.

10. In some Northwest Coast societies, there is an opposition between the realm of chiefs and the realm of shamans. The chiefs are exemplary within the social and cultural realm. Chiefs are supposed to exemplify polite and proper behavior. The shamans are in the wilderness so much that they become wild themselves, and act in a way that is opposed to social behavior. Indeed, their behavior is typically the exact opposite of correct, proper etiquette. The Tlingit are perhaps the extreme case; their chiefs are more secular, their shamans more wild and religious, than seems to be the case elsewhere.[53]

11. The natural world, especially animals, provides not only powers but also symbols. These include the kinship-group crests that figure so spectacularly on totem poles and other art, and the shamanistic portrayals of power

animals. These higher-order symbols portray a complex and elaborate order that communicates both the religion and its practical applications.[54] Higher-order symbols in this system routinely link across the culture-nature boundary. In contrast, ordinary language, small-scale art, houses, cooking, and other daily activities maintain the boundary. Most Northwest Coast folk knowledge of animals was conveyed by art, ritual, and myth.

It is natural for humans to distort their view of the world such that it is simpler, more manageable, and more generalized.[55] It is natural for us, as humans and as individuals, to see the rest of the world as more like us than it is. The Northwest Coast peoples see animals as humanlike. We do similar things in modern America: ascribing human virtues to pets, delighting in Mickey Mouse and Donald Duck. The Northwest Coast peoples do more. Their belief system goes far beyond our trivial anthropomorphization of animals. Through the millennia, the Northwest Coast peoples have evolved a religion that integrates the cultural and natural spheres so much that people feel involved with nonhuman lives. Emotions, ethics, and morals all are invoked. Moreover, people are involved with the natural world at the most intense possible level: animals and other beings provide us with our powers, our abilities, our vocations.

In Western psychological terms, this means that these beings of the wild are used to validate a sense of self and of personal self-efficacy. The beings of the wild take on the function of validating what really matters to us—what we "really are"—just as God does for devout Christians, just as Science does for devout academic rationalists, and just as one's family, friends, and psychotherapists do for ordinary Americans. Shamans heal with animal powers just as doctors heal through "science" and evangelists heal through the Holy Spirit.

In the Northwest Coast societies, social and personal construction of self and of self-efficacy is negotiated not only with humans but with the entire cosmos. This I take to be the true key to Northwest Coast philosophy. It is both a necessary part and a driving dynamic in any ongoing sustained-yield management of resources. The Northwest Coast cultures build from that involvement an elaborate system that both validates individuals and maintains the sustained-yield management strategies. This is yet another reason for counterfactual beliefs. Humans appear to be more apt to believe counterfactual, exaggerated claims about those with whom they negotiate selfhood. In modern American society, extreme and clearly counterfactual beliefs are held about other people.

Racism is one case in point. Another is the belief that humans are fundamentally savage and competitive. People who negotiate their selves with animals and plants would humanize the animals and plants, and come to believe strange things about them; by contrast, in an urban and political world, strange beliefs involve other people and their politics.

The relationship of ideology to actual management practices seems to me like the relationship of a driver to a car. Without ideology, regulation by laws and communities would be a dead letter. Without a community that can enforce its needs through an actual system of rules and an actual hierarchy of leaders, ideology is impotent. On the Northwest Coast, ideology validates the ritual management of resources by the chiefs and other leaders.[56] I have also observed, that ideology validates a stunningly effective psychological healing system.[57] Indeed, the effectiveness of shamanic psychological treatment has affected profoundly the actual forms the system takes. The ideology can thus be seen as a higher-order integrative device that validates, encodes, and makes salient a range of personal, social, medical, and ecological wisdom. The system may not be the most accurate way to represent the animal world, but for the Northwest Coast Native peoples it may well be the most useful.

We may expect to find that traditional subsistence-oriented cultures will encode a tremendous amount of intensely emotional and personal material about animals and plants, and that this material is highly structured and organized into a simple, memorable worldview that is dramatically highlighted in myth and ritual.

Thus the land otter does give power to the Tlingit, by serving as their prime symbol of the power of nature and of their own human nature as well. The guardian spirits of the Salish are so transparently symbols of personal, human, social, and individual empowerment that the fiction of nonhuman naturalness wears very thin at times in this modern secular world, but without this fiction people would be just people—alienated from all that is most powerful and most important to them. Even university-educated Native Americans today maintain the ideology of direct spiritual empowerment by the creatures of their universe. For some, the beliefs are weakening. But all of them realize that, in conservation as in other moral matters, *human beings make sacrifices for what they love,* not for what they regard as merely a rational means to a material end.

In order to persuade people to do what is empirically known to be sensible or necessary, a culture must encode a great many plausible and believable explanations and justifications.

I end this chapter with grateful acknowledgment to the otters of Vancouver Island.

5

Managing the Rainforest:
Maya Agriculture in the Town
of the Wild Plums

Noemy Chan, a young Maya woman of Mexico, looked up from her cooking and spied her children switching butterflies out of the air with twigs. She immediately dropped her knife, ran to the yard, picked up the butterflies—and made the children eat them. The lesson was explicit: You kill only for food.

In the traditional Maya world of the interior rainforests of Quintana Roo, animals are killed only from pressing need. If they are not to be eaten, they can be killed only if they are eating the crops on which humans depend. Ideally, they are slain only when both motives operate. Early one morning I met a family carrying a dead coati in a bag; they said, "It was eating our corn, so we are going to eat *it*." In Noemy's home town, Chunhuhub, even the sale of game is confined to local marketing to other subsistence farmers. The unfortunate habit of poaching game for sale to cities has not—so far—spread into the bush.

Noemy and her husband are well off by Mexican standards—he manages heavy equipment for road construction. They saved their money and built an urban-style concrete block house. It stands empty; they live in a traditional Maya pole-and-thatch hut, of a style used continuously for thousands of years in the area. As they correctly point out, the hut is much cooler, cleaner, less damp, and in every way more efficient than the European-style house.

The Maya civilization, one of the greatest of the ancient cultures, is by no means dead. Millions of Maya Indians, speaking two dozen related languages, still live in Central America. They practice traditional corn agriculture and maintain many pre-Columbian rituals. Yet they are no more "survivors" of the "past" than are modern Englishmen who still eat bread and beef and worship in the Church of England. Maya civilization is dynamic, living, changing, and, above all, creative. Tough and independent, its bearers have adapted to the modern world; many are doctors, lawyers, and degree-holding professors. They still speak Maya languages, and usually Spanish as well.[1]

Noemy and her husband are among the half million Mexicans whose native tongue is Yucatec, the language from which our word "Maya" comes. The Yucatec call themselves *maaya* and their land *maayab*. "Yucatec" derives from "Yucatán," a name that immortalizes one of those marvelous mistakes in history. Spanish explorers asked a canoeful of Indians about the name of the mainland. One helpful soul, observing the puzzlement of his canoemates, answered something like "he didn't understand you": *ma' u yu'ca t'aan i*. The Spanish picked up the accented part of this sage remark, and were satisfied. This story would not be worth repeating were it not so revealing. It was not the first time that outsiders have lost important truths by misunderstanding the Maya.[2]

The Maya of central Quintana Roo and nearby parts of the peninsula successfully rebelled against Mexico in the mid-nineteenth century and remained completely independent until well into the twentieth. Chunhuhub was depopulated during this time, being resettled by the rebels after peace was finally achieved (on *their* terms, many say). They retain a fierce independence. Paul Sullivan, in a delightful book called *Unfinished Conversations,* captures the flavor of their discourse: fascinated with the outside world, yet determined to hold their own against it.[3]

Chunhuhub—"Wild Plums" or "Trunk of the Wild Plum Tree"—is a large *ejido* that lies where the dry hills of the interior Yucatán Peninsula meet the lush rainforest of the southeastern coastal plain. An *ejido* is a communally owned tract of usable land. A product of the Mexican Revolution, the *ejido* system was abolished by government decree in 1991. However, individual *ejidos* could maintain their collective system if they wanted to do so, and Chunhuhub opted for this. They were managing well. Seventy-five percent of the *ejido* is forest land. It can only be managed on a large scale, and it provides plentiful income from mahogany and other valuable woods. The rest of the *ejido* is cultivated. Most of the cropland is in the dry but fertile hills. This land can be cropped for only two or three years at a time. After that, it must be rested until nitrogen-fixing, litter-producing trees have grown up, restoring the soil's fertility. This sort of "shifting agriculture" has been described as wasteful and backward, but it is actually an exceedingly sophisticated management system, and it is the only system that is productive and sustainable in most of the Yucatán Peninsula. The shallow, rocky soils of the peninsula degrade rapidly under cultivation, and only long fallowing can restore their fertility. Thousands of years of both accidental and deliberate selection have produced a forest of trees, most of which either fix nitrogen or provide useful products, or both.

Agriculture is based on something structurally reminiscent of the infield-outfield farming of Europe. Around the house are magnificent dooryard gardens, in which up to a hundred species of fruit trees, vegetables, medicinal and cooking herbs, and ornamental plants are grown. Pigs, chickens, and turkeys abound. Cows, horses, ducks, and occasionally a peccary or deer may be seen in big yards. The trees are many-layered: tall coconuts, and giant mameys and sapotes with trunks a meter thick, shade oranges, limes, and many native fruit unknown to temperate lands. Below these are shrubs and annuals. To the untrained eye, the system looks chaotic: trees are planted irregularly, tufts of vegetables seem randomly placed, and herbs hang from the trees in buckets and old boxes. The practiced eye quickly sees that each tree and bush is planted in the best spot for its growth. Wet places are scarce; Yucatán's stony ground does not provide many pockets of deep soil for roots to grow. Each farm family knows exactly what to plant in a shallow wet hollow, a rocky knoll, or a shady flat space.[4]

The outfields—milpas in Mexico, col to the Maya—are irregular patches of cut-and-burned forest, planted to maize and often intercropped with pachpakal (assorted vegetable, fruit, and root crops). Beans climb the cornstalks to the light. Squash spreads its great leaves, shading out weeds and killing pests with its bitter, toxic leaf sap. The maize yields about a ton per acre, which is poor by Iowa standards but excellent for the Yucatán Peninsula. On those thin soils, even the best modern technology can give no more.

Countless medicinal herbs are grown or appear spontaneously. Chunhuhub residents know at least three hundred medically active plant species, many of them tested and proven by modern biomedicine. Much of Maya medicine has been summarized in the recent monumental study by the Maya doctor Gilberto Balam Pereira.[5]

There are several reasons why these fields and gardens are productive and sustainable in the Yucatán Peninsula. First, they are diverse—not only in species composition but also in genetic variety within each species. Second, the land races are tough and well adapted to local conditions. The traditional maize varieties, for instance, are genetically variable and are able to produce well in spite of drought, thin soil, and pests ranging from corn smut to earworms to deer. Third, the structure of the gardens is similar to that of the natural forest, with its varied composition and its many layers. Fourth, the structure of the *milpas* is similar to natural burns that are regrowing. Maize replaces the natural grasses; beans and squash replace wild beans and gourds; other plants also have their equivalents. The original trees regrow from stumps and roots, just as they do after a natural fire. Fifth, each plant is carefully placed in the microhabitat best for it. On rocky, pitted soil, even individual corn kernels have their carefully selected natural crevices and hollows. One often sees a flourishing cornfield on what appears to be absolutely naked rock. Sixth, the main plant and animal pests are often eaten or otherwise used, turning a "cost" into a benefit. Seventh, all wastes are returned to the land, thus closing the cycle. (Alas, the Maya have not quite learned that modern wastes do not compost, and Chunhuhub is fringed by small dumps that include some dangerous items.)

In short, the Maya work with nature rather than against it. This requires an intimate knowledge of the habitat.

Many Maya still live by subsistence agriculture. They live mostly on maize; it provides 75 percent of the calories in the rural Yucatán. This figure has been remarkably constant over time and place,[6] though affluent families in Chunhuhub eat less maize and more wheat products. The rest of the diet is about evenly divided among meat, fruit, and a large range of vegetables. Beans do not grow well, and thus are less important than they are in most of Mexico. Subsistence agriculture does not mean poverty. In Chunhuhub, the goods produced by an average subsistence-farm family would cost $2,000 to $3,000 in U.S. currency if bought on the open market. There is plenty to eat, and always a surplus to sell, providing cash for machetes and clothes. Anyone serious about farming can go into intensive vegetable production,[7] or can get long-term use of a piece of land for an orchard. Oranges are the main crop, but more than a dozen exotic fruit species are produced for sale. Bees provide another option. The Maya have been zealous beekeepers since time immemorial.

The need for communal landholding is clear: if land must be fallowed for anywhere from five to thirty years, and if maize, vegetables, and orchards provide three different time frames for use of a given parcel, the only way to keep much sanity in the allocation process is to keep the land public and share it out every year according to family needs. This is done in a big, noisy assembly, to which all heads of families come—often with spouses (many family heads are women) and children. Others, especially people who have recently moved in and are not actually members of the *ejido* community, are accommodated on land left over from this division. Chunhuhub has a substantial land base, and many family heads are taking up town jobs, thus freeing up land for distribution.

All the ingredients for a classic "tragedy of the commons"[8] are here: collective ownership, lack of supervision, and a slowly recovering resource base that would be easy to mine. Indeed, some resources have been exhausted. For instance, the ideology of killing only for immediate use is adequate to protect prolific, adaptable animals, such as peccaries and deer (both still common), but is not adequate to save the vulnerable species. Wild turkeys, once abundant, are now gone. Gone, too, are the big cats—the jaguar and ocelot—whose predatory habits and valuable skins provided motives that overrode ideology. Rapid population growth is now endangering even the peccaries and deer, and will force the people to make hard choices in the near future.

Similarly, the magnificent forests have flourished and reproduced themselves under careful selective logging. The traditional ideology of conservation and sustainable management is still operative—partly because government foresters, based in the town, keep the *ejido* self-consciously on its best behavior. The Maya do not want government interference; the government wants more management rights (and fees) and waits for signs of waste that would give them an excuse to take over.[9] But here, too, population growth and market demand are putting almost unbearable strains on the traditional management system.

Any lingering doubts about the self-conscious, deliberate invocation of a conservationist ethic are removed by attending an *ejido* assembly devoted to management of the forest. Old men recall the great forests of the past. Young men and women become more and more vocal, shouting down those who want to cut railroad ties, crop the infertile rainforest soil, or sell more trees than can be produced. Antonio Azueta quietly mentions his work in collecting and growing seed of valuable trees; the forests are full of seedlings, some planted, some protected. The *ejido* council balances need for cash against the strong urgings of the protectors.

Many, perhaps most, people believe in the Lords of the Forest (the *yuntziloob*), and Lords of the Animals (*yum il ba'alche'ob*). These beings guard the forest and the animals. They punish people who take more than necessary. Fernando Tesucun, just across the border into Guatemala, told Charles Hofling of men who had been taken away to the cave of the Lord of Animals, there to be reprimanded for careless, unnecessarily destructive hunting.[10] This is a Maya version of a story told by Native peoples all over North and Central America.

Mistakes are made, and the forests have suffered; but one need only drive through the nightmarish deserts of southeastern Quintana Roo or southern Yucatán to see what might have happened. There, thousands of acres of forest were wantonly cut down, mostly to make cattle pasture. Weeds invaded, soil gave out, range deteriorated. Worthless grassland or a few stunted, unsalable cattle remain. Forests that once produced hundreds of thousands of dollars' worth of valuable woods are now a memory. Some of the land has been maintained as good pasture, but the effort and capital necessary to do that are beyond Maya peasant capabilities, and the cost-benefit ratios are sobering. Forest destruction for rangeland is common in Latin America, as in the United States; it rarely pays in either place. It is usually maintained, in the Yucatán and elsewhere, by enormous government subsidization at taxpayer expense.[11] The elite want their beef.

Maya agriculture, like that of the Chinese, is labor-intensive and knowledge-intensive. It depends on intimate knowledge of the resource base. The people of Chunhuhub recognize well over four hundred plant species and probably as many animals. Of birds alone, they recognize more than a hundred kinds, and can identify them by either sight or sound. They know uses for almost every plant and animal except the smallest and the rarest. They grow almost two hundred species of plants in their gardens and fields. Householders exchange plants and plant products and take care that neighbors grow different things, so as to maximize diversity within their immediate social networks.

For every common tree in the forest—and central Quintana Roo has dozens of common species—they know the value of the fruit or seeds, the forage value of the leaves, the medicinal qualities or lack of them, and the usefulness of the wood for construction, sale, and firewood. A trip to collect fuel is a whole botany course: "Don't bother with that one, the wood's too soft to burn long. That stick isn't dried out enough yet. Pick up that piece of *dzidzilche;* it's the best right here."

Sharp images from the forest remain. Felix Medina Tzuc told me how he trained his dog to hunt deer: he had it smell a deer and then got a wasp to sting the dog's nose, ensuring an unforgettable experience. Miguel Casanova and his family, displaced by Hurricane Gilbert from a coastal town, took over a barren rocky knoll at the edge of Chunhuhub and turned it into a flourishing farm; they left wild herbs growing, and planted more, so they had more than sixty medicinal plants growing among the rocks. Andres Sosa, educated in the local technical school, explained to me the ancient Maya traditions of companion planting: squash to suppress weeds in maize, fruit trees planted in mixed-species stands to minimize competition, various weeds left because they repel insects or have medicinal qualities.

Not much capital is invested in a Maya landscape, but the total investment in labor and learning is incredibly high.

Thus the discount rate is set to cover long, slow returns. One spends a lifetime learning the forest and a lifetime using it. To reap any benefit, one must be in that wood for a long life, and leave it in good shape for one's daughters and sons.

Newcomers to the area usually learn Maya strategies. If they do not, they can only fail. In southern Quintana Roo, where many outsiders have settled, one often sees melancholy farmsteads that are either abandoned or reduced to desperate poverty. They cleared the forest, planted what few crops they knew, and then found the soil deteriorating. Many sold out and fled to the city. Some turned to crime to survive.

Only through profound knowledge can this difficult landscape yield food. Modern capital investment can develop rice in some areas and cattle in others, but these are precarious operations, and vast sums have been lost. The Maya have survived the millennia by knowing every use of every significant living and nonliving thing, and by managing these in a sustainable way to safeguard the investment of time and effort embodied in that vast learning pool. Maya men and women take their children with them to the forest. Together they collect wild resources, together they farm, and together they work in the home garden. Children learn by doing, but they also receive continual instruction. Education is no mindless matter of copying the parents. Parents work hard to motivate their children. They are incredibly long-suffering teachers, but, as we have seen, they are quick to sanction appropriately when children do wrong.

Maya civilization sustained itself for more than a thousand years, in a land where soil lies shallow and erodible over the barren bedrock. Yucatán's limestone blots up water like a sponge. Chunhuhub, with eighty inches of rain a year, has no surface water at all. Until very recently, when electric pumps came to hand, the people had to do as the ancients did: catch water in wells and cisterns. Under these circumstances, it is no wonder that the ancients developed many complex, sophisticated methods of farming.[12]

They probably failed more than a few times. The collapse of Maya civilization around 800–900 A.D. seems to have been due to escalating war.[13] I suspect that scorched-earth policies did the real damage. However, exhaustion of the soil and forest by ordinary agriculture may well have been a factor in the Maya collapse. If so, the Maya appear to have learned something. Perhaps their conservationist ideology received a powerful boost from the problems of crowding and intensive cropping in late classical times. Today they face another test: rising population and increasing outside encroachment are driving more and more communities to desperation. There has been much governmental pressure to "modernize" by willy-nilly introduction of machines, new crops, and agricultural chemicals. Even Chunhuhub, one of the most fortunate of Maya towns, has had its problems. A tractor sits irrevocably broken in a thicket of tough nonnative grass. Pesticides languish on shelves after some early, unfortunate incidents. Widespread poverty, disease, and malnutrition remind everyone that there is a long, long way to go. The easy money of Cancún calls the young away, and farms languish for lack of labor power.

Yet, even today, Maya strategies do better than others. Where the Maya are poor, no one else can farm at all. Where others survive, the Maya are more successful and prosperous. Countless schemes have been introduced from the outside. Most have failed. Those that have succeeded are those that fit in with Maya ways. Fruit-growing, that ancient staple activity, is particularly prominent among the successes.[14] Maya can easily move from home-garden fruit-growing to commercial production, as many have done in Chunhuhub. Carefully done, fruit-growing reproduces the forest canopy, slowing the degradation of the soil.

Hilaria Maas Colli spent her girlhood in a small village north of Chunhuhub. Unlike most traditional village Maya, she went to university, and there she discovered anthropology. Her *licenciada* thesis, unfortunately languishing unpublished in the files of the University of Yucatán, casts brilliant light on the ways that the Maya learn their culture.[15]

Maas Colli focuses on the progress from girlhood to womanhood; she underwent it herself, then returned to observe it from an ethnographic point of view. Her thesis moves from ceremony to ceremony. Starting with birth, and then the unique *hetzmek* ceremony, when the baby is first carried on its mother's hip into the great outside world, children are taught sex roles and gendered behavior. Adulthood brings great rites that reaffirm the traditional ways of being man and woman: marriage, curing, death, and burial. Ceremonies mark every transition, dramatically highlight and foreground every important tradition, and bring the whole community together in a powerful emotional catharsis. Rules are taught in the most powerful, intense, compelling possible way.

The success of this method is perhaps all too great when gender is involved; a girl's lot is far from ideal in southeast Mexico. When conservation is the issue, however, the traditional education is satisfactory. Noemy makes her children eat the butterflies they thoughtlessly killed. Felix Medina Tzuc cradles a young pet bird with loving attention or carefully moves an insect off the path; his children and grandchildren watch attentively. Ariel Gongora trains his barnyard *chachalacas* (pheasantlike native birds, often tamed) to fly to his shoulder. These countless small acts construct a reality that reaches its climactic expression in the great rituals that integrate humanity and the cosmos.

No Maya cosmos can stray far from agriculture. Maas Colli's thesis on gender cannot fail to discuss it. The boy and man, from *hetzmek* to grave, is identified with the machete, digging stick, and sack of seed corn. The girl is quickly introduced to the *koben,* the hearth and tortilla-making area in which she will spend so much of her life. His job is to grow maize; hers is to turn it into food. He lives by the fertility of the land and the life-giving rain; she lives by fire and by the captured water of well and cistern. Every ceremony sets up these ancient oppositions, and in every one, the world begins from maize production. In ancient Maya myth, humans were shaped by the gods from maize dough into which the gods mixed their own blood. The handsome young maize god had vast power over life and death. Indeed, with maize (often mixed with animal flesh and blood) providing so much of their food, the Maya are quite literally made from the golden grains.

Thus the great ceremonies are still alive, in spite of the five-hundred-year encounter with Christianity. The *ch'achaac,* "calling the rain gods," comes just before the rainy season. The *hanlicol,* "feeding the field," originally provided food for the guardian spirits of the *milpa,* but modern Christian Maya may interpret it otherwise. The magnificent *hanlicol* held by the Tun Xool household, for instance, was described as a thanksgiving to God; the household had converted to Protestantism after healing experiences that seemed almost miraculous, but were not about to abandon the old sacred ways.

These rites involve ritual sacrifice of many chickens—turkeys, in past times—and production of incredible quantities of tamales and maize pies to be cooked in great pit barbecues.[16] A number of other specifically agricultural rites exist, but are not now practiced in the Chunhuhub area. At one time, the entire farming cycle, from cutting and burning the forest to bringing home the sheaves, was ceremonialized; rituals inaugurated every phase and consecrated every action.[17]

As in the Northwest Coast case, these ceremonies are not simply a matter of "reverence for nature" or "living in a sacred manner." The practical role of shoring up social bonds is well recognized. The necessity of the interplay between reason and religion, between technology and ceremony, is also clear to everyone. Like the Chinese and the Northwest Coast peoples, the Maya do not make an artificial separation between religion and daily life. Religion is a way of representing and facilitating daily life—economically, socially, sacrally. It ties together, in one package, technology and society.

Religion, therefore, serves as the natural vehicle for carrying messages about conservation and wise management. It provides the overarching moral sanctions. It also provides the community structure necessary to enforce these. The "tragedy of the commons" is averted. Most people internalize the norms—they develop a biological conscience—after such experiences as those which Noemy Chan provided for her children. The few cheaters can be controlled, because the community is united.

To the extent that the modern world intrudes, reorienting people toward urban media and urban values, this old order breaks down. It has broken down all too thoroughly in many communities nearer the city. Yet, even in the outskirts of Mérida and Cancún—those foci of the encroaching Spanish-speaking world—Maya gardeners patiently reproduce an ecological vision that was ancient before Spanish evolved from Latin.

As with the process of growing up, these ceremonies have a major teaching function. They involve the Maya emotionally in their agriculture. They mark out stages and processes for all to see. Children learn the world through ritual and are thus taught not only the facts but how to react to them. They learn to be grateful to the forces of nature, to God or gods. They learn that their food is the product of a complex interaction between themselves, the natural world, and whatever powers lie behind all of this. They learn that food production is serious, indeed passionately and intensely serious. They learn, above all, to treat resources with respect, and not to use everything up. Moreover, the social bonds that allow people to work together are affirmed.

The proof of the value of these strategies is there: Chunhuhub and its neighbor villages have lush forests, abundant game, high yields of crops, and a thriving, prosperous, commercial economy. Other well-known villages to the north and south are reduced to poverty by over-driving the system or by invoking simplistic strategies of "modernization" that were ultimately suicidal. These have ranged from monocrop agriculture to commercial sale of game, and from overuse of pesticides to intensive pig-farming that polluted the groundwater.

Maya in areas that have lost the ceremonies, and lost other marks of cultural integrity and pride, have succumbed to such strategies. There is no way they can organize to resist the blandishments of government agents or ill-advised aid workers. The decline of religion may not make people bad, but it does deny them one way of organizing the good. The loss of ceremonies does not destroy the conservationist worldview outright. It works its devastation in two ways: first, through undermining the education of the young, and second, through undermining the community's ability to force its will on cheaters. Without ritual to bring people together and weld them into a community, they are possibly more likely to cheat in the first place, but the real problem is that no one is likely to stop them.

The future, then, depends on several things. The traditional conservation ideology must be maintained and strengthened. Traditional rituals must be encouraged. Modern methods must be introduced, but only when compatible with sustainable, labor-intensive, knowledge-intensive farming styles. Existing methods of mixed farming are being enriched by more productive new ways that yield much greater amounts of highly marketable vegetables, fruit, and livestock.[18] Marketing these, in restaurants and stores of Cancún or farther afield, is a challenge for the future.

Most difficult of all will be coping with population expansion and technological progress. Traditional controls cannot be expected to track a rapidly moving target. Sustainability will have to depend, more and more, on the Maya working with government and private individuals to carry the spirit of Maya agriculture forward into a more crowded, busy world.

If all this can be done, Maya civilization's real worldwide importance may be yet to come. It provides an example of practical, sustainable, intensive, low-capital, high-yield agriculture. The tropical world at large desperately needs such systems and can benefit enormously from the Maya lesson.[19]

The dry season of 1991 was long and severe. Even the rainforest was shedding leaves, and the dry hill forest was nearly leafless. Dos Aguadas, the village east of Chunhuhub, called in an expert.

Fernando Caamal is a slight, dignified, elderly man from a northern village in Yucatán state. He is a *hmen,* "one who knows." He was called in to hold a *ch'achaac,* to call the rains up from the Caribbean.

On May 15, he came to Dos Aguadas, whose "two waterholes" are the reservoirs of an ancient Maya town. The town was abandoned centuries ago and resettled in recent decades by people from the Chunhuhub area. He set up an altar of leaves behind the little Catholic chapel. The leaves are of *ha'abin,* the most common local tree, whose spectacular flowers cover the forest just before the rains. Before the altar he carried out long and complex chants, calling down both Catholic saints and ancient Maya powers. Slowly, thirteen calabash bowls were arranged, in which were honey mead and corn gruel, the sacred foods of the ancients. Meanwhile, a great pit barbecue was made by the men, while the women cooked chickens and prepared corn dough. A feast of tamales was entombed to bake. There was a long, relaxed waiting period, while Don Fernando chanted softly on. A man explained to a group of playful boys that the visiting anthropologist "is going to take you to California, where you will be made into sausage." The boys responded with hilarious amusement, and the men joined in.

After the festive foods had been prepared and everyone partook, the chanting became more serious. Shares of food were offered on the altar. The bowls were set up in complex array, with corn-husk cigarettes and resin incense from the *pom* tree. All were purified by being brushed with the leaves of a medicinal plant. The glory of the flowering forest had reached its climax, as the leaves of the dominant tree reminded us. The foods that made us were here, offered back to the gods who used them to create our life. The incense and the smoke of the narcotic tobacco carried the scent of the burning forest to the sky. Smoke wound and twisted upward, like storm clouds. Life had been sacrificed and the blood consumed. Above all, the holy maize pervaded everything: wrapping the food, thickening the gruel in the bowls, providing the husks for the cigarettes, and yielding great tamales marked with the cross that is sacred in both Christian and pre-Columbian Maya traditions. To the Maya, it represented—and still represents—the sacred ceiba tree, another aquatic symbol because it grows near water and leafs out with the rains.

While all this took place, dark clouds gathered directly above the little chapel. With every chant, they grew darker and thicker. Nothing like this had been seen for four weary months. Yet, at the end of the ceremony, the clouds immediately dispersed; they began to break up as the altar was being dismantled. People returned stoically to their homes.

The next day dawned hot and clear. By noon, a tiny cloud appeared and began to grow. Suddenly, it seemed to explode; a vast dark mountain covered the universe. Winds whipped the trees and the laundry on the village clotheslines. Birds flew up, then dived for shelter. Then, blazing with lightning and roaring continual thunder, the Chaac gods rode in.

6

Needs and Human Nature

The preceding chapters raise complex and deep issues about why people act and believe as they do. Clearly, people are not only acting "irrationally" in many cases, but they are often basing their most "rational" actions on completely false premises or basing utterly "irrational" actions on perfectly accurate (but irrelevant) beliefs.

This forces us to take a whole new look at human action, right from its bases. The following two chapters explore in some detail the ways in which humans understand environments. This will take me rather far afield from ecology into the somewhat arcane realm of cognitive psychology. The relevance will, I hope, become clear in the following chapters.

The first, most basic, question is: Why do we act at all? What are the ends of behavior?

Economists take the structure of "final demand" as a given. Economics is the study of how people choose between *ways of reaching* predetermined ends. Final demand is outside the system: it is what the system works to satisfy. Similarly, environmental damage is "external" to this system.

The difference between economics and cultural ecology is that cultural ecologists do not exempt these matters from our calculus. We work final demand into our system. We also deny the existence of "externalities." Nothing produced or consumed on earth is an externality to us. Even the satellites shot into space have to be counted; they cost the world a tiny bit of metal and fuel.

Moreover, culture often determines "final demand," and we try to explain culture. Everybody has to have protein, but why is it that Americans prefer that protein come from a cow, while high-caste Hindus are horrified at the thought? A traditional economist would have to take this as given; cultural ecologists try to explain it.[1]

Lately, anthropologists have emphasized the highly culture-bound and contingent nature of human wants. However, all humans do have pretty much the same physical survival needs. Since these survival needs are the ultimate determinants of resource use, and since they have been neglected in recent literature, it is necessary to list them here.

Most Americans claim they work "for money," but no one really does that. Scrooge McDuck is a figure of fun precisely because he literally does enjoy money for itself ("I like to dive around in it and throw it up and let it hit me on the head"). For the rest of us, money is strictly a means to obtain what we really want, and is disposed of as fast as (or faster than!) it is acquired. We spend it on food, clothing, and shelter; on prestige and status; on love and caring.

For the serious money-makers I know, money is a counter in a game. The game is played for the prestige of winning or simply for the excitement of play. The rest of us are more interested in food, clothing, and shelter, or functional equivalents, and tend to stop work when we have what we want.

Unlike money, food is a real end in itself. Even food, however, could be seen as a mere means—a way of staying alive but not a reason for living. The same could be said of most of our physical survival needs. Once food and shelter are taken care of, human beings spend their time in the pursuit of other things—especially social goals.

Biologists tell us that all our inborn needs must be related, in the end, to reproduction—to keeping our genes going. We act to leave descendants, or at least to help our close relatives leave more descendants. At some ultimate remove, all our actions are no doubt related some way to "maximizing our inclusive fitness," but this is not the way most of us think. Indeed, the main question of this book is precisely why we are *minimizing* our inclusive fitness in the ways we manage the environment.

The most basic human needs can be classified under seven general headings. I am not suggesting that this is the only way of classifying needs; it is simply one that is convenient in studying human ecology. One could easily rearrange this classification—for instance, by including food and water as part of the need for health and safety, or by separating needs for health from needs for security from violence, or by separating the needs for friendship from those for love. This list owes a great deal to the writings of Abraham Maslow.[2] Such undefinable entities as a "need for self-actualization," postulated but later abandoned by Maslow, are not included here.

1. Food and water. This is not a single need, but it is a fairly natural category, embracing our needs for protein, carbohydrates, fats, vitamins, mineral nutrients, water, fiber, and whatever else may turn out to be valuable in the diet.

2. Temperature regulation. Shelter, clothing, staying cool in extreme heat, and the like are all part of a need to maintain our ambient temperature at a level that we can handle physiologically.

3. Health and physical safety. A vast mass of specific medical needs, including safety from violence, is subsumed under this heading.

4. Sleep and arousal. Sleep is, of course, a physical need. Less obvious is a real physiological need for—and inability to prevent—considerable variety in both type of sleep (deep sleep versus rapid-eye-movement sleep) and type of arousal (drowsiness, excitement, boredom, intense stimulation, ecstasy, etc.). Much activity is dedicated to manipulating arousal level; trillion-dollar drug and entertainment industries depend on this, to say nothing of the world trade in alcohol, caffeine plants, and similar drugs. A large percentage of the tropical and subtropical montane forests of the world has been cleared for coffee and tea production.

5. Sex and reproduction. Sex is not a survival need for anyone. Indeed, for the individual, it is risky, difficult to manage, and generally "costly" in terms of satisfying one's real survival needs. But, obviously, reproduction is necessary to the continuance of the species.

6. Social needs. Humans cannot survive without some social life. A normal life has its share of friendship, social contact, support, and all the various forms of love. A normal person devotes much of his or her economic resources to maintaining social life: wining and dining a date, buying a gas-burning car to show off status, buying engagement and wedding rings, wearing special costumes to mark particular roles, and so on. Gift exchanges are perhaps the most common: gifts of equal value are exchanged; no one is *materially* better off, but a *social* payoff comes from the transaction.

7. Control over one's life. This includes a need to understand one's surroundings and situation and to feel some control over them—a need for "perceived control" and for "self-efficacy."[3] It has been shown that some sense of this is actually necessary for health and even survival among all mammals. Laboratory rats will die of sheer stress if subjected to continued, unpredictable events. When placed in a new cage, laboratory rats and mice, and indeed all mammals tested, will explore before they do anything else; even if very hungry, they will not eat until they have explored the new habitat. The novels of Franz Kafka drive home the emotional effects of being in

unpredictable, uncontrollable situations. The research of psychologists such as Albert Bandura and Ellen Langer has provided sober, factual confirmation of Kafka's perceptions.

Related to this basic need is the need to manage and process information. Information management is sometimes just for fun (as in the game Trivial Pursuit), but more usually it is a necessary part of survival, and it is exquisitely attuned to our survival needs.[4]

All the above needs are satisfied by drawing on the environment. Obviously, we depend on the environment for food, shelter, medicines, and the like. But even the needs for social life and for control influence environment use. The social need, for instance, often expresses itself in status consumption—wasting vast amounts of resources in "position goods" like Cadillacs and huge houses. The control need expresses itself in a range of activities, from scientific investigation to "dominating nature" by off-road vehicle use.

These seven categories of needs are not confined to humans or even to mammals. Even a lizard needs to find a mate, recognize his neighbors, feel secure in his hole, decide whether to fight or flee from a threat, explore his territory, and move around to get warm. His life is much more than sleeping and eating. More complex animals that take care of their young have to have social bonding too, at least within the family.

That choice of fighting or fleeing from threat may be peculiarly important here. How do people cope with environmental problems? They may panic if they don't understand the situation (control need unsatisfied). They may go into self-defeating rage if they feel they are deliberately attacked (social need directly stressed). They will cope rationally only if they feel they can; they have to know how. A lizard, deciding whether to eat, fight, or flee from another animal, need only see whether the other animal is smaller, the same size, or bigger. We have a far more demanding set of dimensions to consider.

Overriding, crosscutting, and integrating all these survival needs is the rich, complex life of the mind. We live a life of feelings and moods, emotions and thoughts. Most social science—especially economics and ecology—conveys the impression that people are always coldly rational. Indeed, economics is often defined as the rational allocation of means among conflicting ends. But everyone is aware that humans are far from rational in the normal usage of the term. (Other usages will be discussed later.) Indeed, we need formal economic analysis (often with the help of linear programming) precisely because we are so frequently less than perfect in our rationality. We are creatures of love and hate, joy and sorrow, loathing and desire. In particular, humans react emotionally when survival needs are at stake. Frustration of a felt need arouses fear and anger. Sudden satisfaction of a deeply felt need produces happiness.

Psychologists such as Robert Zajonc have shown that we must react with some emotion—if only a vague feeling of interest, liking, or aversion—to notice a stimulus at all.[5] Zajonc is talking about raw basic feelings—the primal feelings that are similar in the lizard and the human. In humans, emotions become more complex, and are subject to cognitive construction.[6] We think about our emotions, just as emotions always color our thoughts. Moreover, cultural traditions influence our feelings; we are taught how and when to feel particular emotions.[7] Reason may help us decide among conflicting means to an end, but our ends are set by needs and emotions, and our perceptions are necessarily and inextricably involved with feelings.

Our social needs are particularly, and notoriously, involved with emotions. Love and hate are social matters, negotiated with our companions and rivals. Social needs force us to accommodate, to support, to help, and to worry about rejection. They also permit society to reproduce itself. Reproduction is not an individual need; many people get along happily without sex, let alone children. For humans, the *individual* need that is satisfied by sex—as well as by love and family—is the social need.

Sociability also entails a need for some sort of social system, including a decision-making system and some sort of ethical code. The social system is, of course, put to use to satisfy all the other needs as well. All books on society begin with this awareness—complex human needs entail a social order—so nothing further need be said about it here. However, one related point does deserve special attention: the built-in tension between the need for social life and the need for control of one's life. Everyone wants to be part of a social order, but everyone wants autonomy.

In resource management, as in other domains, the need to have a moral code and the need to have autonomy in behavior often take a collision course. Few have made that point. We all know that maintaining social harmony depends on having a moral code. Murder has to be *wrong,* not just unprofitable. Yet, environmentalists and environmental economists write as if environmental issues can be handled by rational self-interest in the narrow sense. This is false. Morals and the social contract must be involved.

Permit me, then, a brief excursion into the question of moral codes, human nature, and what society can and cannot do.

An ethical code must be more demanding than necessary, and it must be effectively enough "sold" that most people behave better than they need to do to keep society functioning. This is because there are always "cheaters," and the rest of the population has to be "extra good" to take up the slack. If one or two people take more than the legal limit of fish, the fishing laws must be set such that honest people take fewer fish than they could theoretically take without reducing the fish stocks. If one or two people kill—and every society has a few pathological murderers—the rest of the population must be kept from falling into the classic pattern of "an eye for an eye, a tooth for a tooth" and creating a pattern of revenge killing that exterminates the society. If group survival depends on sharing food, there *must* be a strong and *widely observed* ethic of generosity to make up for the inevitable Scrooges that occasionally appear.

We frequently condemn moral codes for being impossibly strict and the people who observe them carefully for being "goody-goodies" or "hypocrites." The fact is that all moral codes are stricter than the actual working rules of society, and the actual working rules are too strict for many people to follow. This is an inevitable fact of life. *All functional societies have very strict and rather strictly enforced ethical codes*—much stricter than they would be if people were always unfailingly honest and cooperative.

All well-socialized humans act better than they "need" to, and most of us know it, too; we realize that we are taking up the slack to make up for a few outrageous sinners. This is never a pleasant thing to realize, and a society must have ways of persuading us to do this and of rewarding us for doing it. A society in which people are "no better than they should be," or in which direct police enforcement is necessary to maintain minimal law and order, usually collapses into chaos; sometimes it reforms itself, usually via a bloody period of struggle, rarely through a peaceful "revitalization movement." Only one society of truly rational individual maximizers has been well described in the anthropological literature: the Ik of Colin Turnbull's *The Mountain People*.[8] The Ik were starving to death due to pressure by more powerful groups. Under this stress, social rules had broken down, and they lived by scrounging, begging, and stealing. It was not a society that could have lasted long.

In conservation and resource management, this whole problem becomes acute. The temptation is almost irresistible to "take just one more," especially since "it can't hurt." In a well-run society, it really can't hurt; there is enough play in the system to allow for a few poachers. Most people have to be honest in spite of this. There are not enough people in the world to provide a trained game warden for every stream and hillside. In California, four-fifths of the deer shot by hunters are poached. There have to be laws to preserve the deer, and they have to be set such that honest hunters get only one-fifth of the deer they could otherwise take—unless the state is willing to put far more effort into enforcement. England's experience shows that even the death penalty does not deter poaching very much; remember Robin Hood.

Civilizations have formal law codes and police. Simpler societies, and also isolated, self-contained communities in modern states, do not. They must enforce their regulations and management schemes by sheer weight of public opinion. Sometimes a local chief has some authority, but never very much; he cannot call out the troops. He can sometimes threaten, but on the whole he must rely on persuasion and on community solidarity.

Thus we conclude that all societies exploit their environments to satisfy not only physical needs, but also social and other "intangible" needs. All societies must have ethical codes, including environmental ethics, and must have some way of persuading the majority to follow those codes even more strictly than long-term economic sense would dictate. All societies must have ways of persuading their members to sacrifice short-term, narrow interests to long-term, wide ones.

Recently, several attempts have been made to understand human behavior from a sociobiological viewpoint.[9] This enterprise is based on the growing awareness that behavior, including complex behavior, can be selected in the evolutionary process. Many sociobiologists postulate a future in which they can totally explain all human behavior as narrowly determined by complex instincts. Behavior toward the environment, for instance, is seen as so instinctive that nothing we do can alter it.

Fortunately, environmental behavior is not tightly determined by instinct, as most sociobiologists would now agree. Sociobiologists have pointed out that complex instincts are inefficient. It is easier to design a brain that learns and reasons. Selection on environmental behavior must be very indirect. It acts on the consequences of behavior, which are, notoriously, not always predictable from the behavior. Moreover, behavior itself is somewhat decoupled from the genes. Evolutionary psychologists maintain that our brains evidently evolved for complex learning situations and for integrating complex social action. We have particular skills, not some sort of generalized single-factor "intelligence."[10]

People may not all be siblings under the epidermis, but they are all closely related genetically. In a stable social group, individuals sometimes need help and at other times can give it. As long as the individuals in the group are related and are often in need of each other's support, evolution should favor a strategy of extending cooperation and returning any favor that results. Evolution should not favor following up on the uncooperative; they should be cut off or worse. People who initially cooperate may survive because they get into networks of mutual aid; nonreciprocators may die off, because sooner or later no one is there to help them.

In an unstable group, however, nonreciprocators—"cheaters"—can prosper at the expense of the cooperative. Over time, mechanisms evolve whereby cooperators can detect cheaters, and cheaters evolve mechanisms to get around these mechanisms, and so the world goes on. Among sexually reproducing organisms, there must be at least enough cooperation to get a pair together to mate, and most of the work on "cheaters" and their detection has centered around mating. But among humans, social life is all-important. Humans are rarely alone. Child-rearing is invariably a social process, and lasts for many years. Siblings, parents, and usually a much wider network of kin and non-kin must get along and be involved in the enterprise. All human groups share food to some extent, and practice some sort of cooperation in the quest for food.

This makes it seem very likely that humans are naturally altruistic to their immediate family groups and prone to extend aid more widely in the hope of reciprocity; but, also, humans should also be quick to detect cheaters and summarily discipline them. There is much evidence for both points. The natural tendency of humans to cooperate is well established.[11] Humans clearly evolved as social beings, foraging together much of the time and sharing food.[12]

There is now evidence that humans do indeed have genetic guidance for prosocial behavior. It appears to be highly heritable—much more so than antisocial behavior. An anonymous report in *Science* reports research indicating that violent, socially unaccepted behavior is associated with poverty and with a violent, abusive background—in other words, is predictable from environment—while prosocial behavior seems pretty much the rule otherwise.[13]

Humans are also intensely emotional creatures. Love, in all its complex forms, is the cement that binds social groups together and gives meaning to individual lives. Hate arises when cheating, or indeed any threat, menaces the integrity of the group. This seems to me to lie behind some of the classic views of humans, as basically "good," or at least growth-oriented, creatures. This might include Carl Rogers's humanistic approach[14] and Viktor Frankl's concern with "meaning."[15]

As philosophers such as David Hume have pointed out, our everyday experience of what we like in people is a pretty good guide to morals.[16] Even a thoroughly amoral person will act sociable and "good" out of sheer self-preservation. Moreover, Hume reminds us that "bad" people often operate by using an inverted moral scale, which shows that they are perfectly aware of "good" social behavior—they are just at war with it because of some deep hurt.[17] Anatomists, in fact, often find physical brain damage in such cases.

This view contrasts with two widespread views of human nature: the *tabula rasa* view and the negativist view. According to the former, humans have few or no innate behavioral tendencies, and all their behavior is the result of training. This view is inherently unlikely, and it is not supported by the evidence.[18] We have clearly evolved physically; it is hard to believe that we do not have any behavioral programming. There are many behaviors that are universal among humans: smiling, crying, complex language, the basic emotions (but not the subtle shadings), the fight-or-flight response, and, of course, a strong tendency to be social and to cooperate.[19]

However, obviously, humans do learn a great deal of their behavior. All humans have a complex language based on a hierarchy of grammatical structures, but the particular language varies enormously. All humans love, but the subtle cultural nuances given to love in different places are a never-failing source of inspiration to writers the world over. An extreme *tabula rasa* view of the emotions, defended most persuasively by Catherine Lutz, holds that there are no basic human feelings—all is cultural.[20] This is hardly defensible in view of the fact that we can not only recognize all the standard emotions and expressions across cultures,[21] but we can even identify fear, rage, happiness, and the like in a dog or cat. But Lutz is pointing to an important, if overstated, truth: the subtleties of emotions, and also the discourse used to talk about them, differ from culture to culture.[22] Indeed, it differs from family to family and from individual to individual. Truly, as a proverb has it, "everyone is like all other people, like some other people, and like no other people."

A negativist view of human nature is often credited to Thomas Hobbes, but it actually goes back long before him. David Hume traced it back to Cicero and even Plato.[23] It maintains that humans are innately aggressive, selfish, and cruel, and that—in Hobbes's oft-quoted phrase—"the life of natural man . . . is solitary, poor, nasty, brutish and short."

Hobbes actually had a less "Hobbesian" view than this is usually taken to imply. He saw people as rational and relatively decent—his "state of warre" was the ancestor of Hardin's "tragedy of the commons," not a claim that people fought all the time.[24] "Warre" meant not permanent conflict, but lack of institutionalized order. Marshall Sahlins has revived the term "warre," as opposed to "war," to cover this situation,[25] so "warre" now has some modern English currency. Hobbes saw rational, potentially decent people as forced into cutthroat competition by lack of a social contract. He expected that they would soon end it by forming a contract and picking a leader—not by continuing a dog-eat-dog existence.

It is, in fact, clear—and was surely clear to Hobbes—that such savage, vicious people as those postulated by neo-"Hobbesian" sociobiologists could not possibly have made a social contract or created any society. They would have eaten each other instead. A society based on self-interest to such a degree cannot provide for anyone's self-interest. Hume argued, very reasonably, that the family was most likely the source or basic model for society—not a rational, voluntary, hard-to-enforce contract.[26] Modern anthropology tends to support this idea.

However incorrectly, Hobbes's name has become associated with the more negativist view, which is, in fact, far more widespread than Hobbes's real viewpoint. A large and increasing percentage of people today hold a view of people as inherently vicious, cruel, and selfish—in spite of conclusive proof to the contrary.[27]

The negativist view is demonstrably false.[28] Available evidence supports the general psychological position of humans as strongly social and disconfirms the Freudian and sociobiological viewpoints. This should not surprise us.

Why does the negativist view sell, then? In part, it has value as a self-serving view. If I think, inside, that I am a bad person, it makes me feel better to think that others are even worse. If I, in fact, am acting pretty badly, it makes me feel even better to think that others are acting worse.

Moreover, the negativist view has always been used to justify absolutism. Hobbes used it (in the milder form that he actually stated) to justify the centralization of the state under an autocratic ruler. So did the early Chinese proponents of the same view. So did Hitler.

The negativist view also animates anti-environmentalists. There is a cynical hopelessness about it that allows it to excuse them from care for the future. Faith in humanity and hope for the future are seen as impossibly romantic, woolly-headed, idealistic, and so forth. This becomes an excuse for selfish waste or equally selfish withdrawal.

However, a great deal of environmental mismanagement is based on narrow self-interest. Less widely realized is the fact that a great deal is also based on destructiveness without even the excuse of the crass selfish greed so often postulated in the environmental literature. People hunt simply to kill—not just for food—and off-road vehicles are used to destroy and "conquer" terrain rather than to get to wild places.

Thus, a theory of antisocial behavior is a necessity for our purposes. Antisocial behavior varies a great deal from society to society. Aggression varies about as far as it possibly can. The Senoi of Malaysia virtually never show it.[29] Among the Yanomamo and Jivaro Indians of South America, on the other hand, murder is one of the leading causes of death. The same is true of inner-city slum dwellers in the modern United States. Even worse situations occur during some civil wars. The province of Szechuan, China, lost perhaps 70 percent of its population when the Ming Dynasty fell. In all cases known to me, obvious economic and political pressure leads to such moral cascades. The South American Indians, for instance, are under intense attack and pressure by whites.[30]

Common experience suggests that bigots vote for politicians who will hurt their (the voters') interests, simply because the politicians promise to hurt the "other guys" even worse. Indeed, wars are often fought for the same dubious ends. Politics everywhere is often conceived as a zero-sum game, in which one group wins only by taking from another. (This led to a not-unreasonable flight by scientists of the early twentieth century from the political arena. They wanted positive-sum games, and found that politics was uncongenial. Unfortunately, they eventually found that there was no escape; politics caught up with them even in the ivory tower.)

When community breaks down, then Hobbesian dynamics do come into play. A moral cascade takes place. With no stable code, people are forced into the "war of each against all," whether they want it or not. Obviously, they do not—rational people prefer peace, as Hobbes pointed out—so they try to found a stable community, to regulate this sort of thing. Communities do this not by "social contract" under a despot, but by giving people a chance to live normal lives.

It is under such circumstances—not in the normal course of social functioning—that Hardin's "tragedy of the commons" takes place.[31]

Ironically, anthropologists have found that the most simple societies are the most tightly regulated by moral codes, and Hobbesian "warre" exists mainly in the autocratic states that Hobbes idealized! In other words, it appears to be the *actual breakdown of a complex society*, not life in a simple state, that causes selfishness and violence to become prevalent. (Hobbes was, of course, thinking of the breakdown of English society in the Civil War—not of tribal peoples.)

Mismanagement of resources is often, perhaps usually, due to psychological pressures that have nothing to do with the resources.

This is most obvious in cases such as that of the United States, where people elect, for quite other reasons, politicians with unpopular environmental policies. These cases are part of a wider problem that stems from one particular type of emotional response: the tendency to deal with stress by panicking rather than by rational coping.

Thus, responsible behavior toward the environment is apt to be a function of people's general overall socialization—*not* just of their knowledge of ecology or their economic self-interest. The need is then to teach people better coping strategies as well as better ecology.

Individuals vary greatly along a number of dimensions. The old concept of one-factor intelligence (IQ) has been replaced by views of the mind that emphasize multiple abilities only weakly tied to each other.[32] Similarly, views of personality that speak of a simple, straightforward "normal" personality from which everything different is "deviance" have been replaced by views that emphasize the enormous differences, along many dimensions, of perfectly normal people.[33] A well-run human society will, as all the above authors point out, make use of many gifts and abilities instead of insisting that only one is valid or worthwhile. People's needs are fairly uniform, but their ways of getting those needs satisfied are many and various. The ideal society is one in which people have a chance to realize their differing potentials and to work together with each other, so that each one complements the other. It will also be based on mutual aid and support.

Two things follow from this diversity: First, it is lucky for us and the environment. Think if we all liked exactly the same two or three foods, or if we all had exactly the same patterns of damaging our immediate environments. Second, *we must design our moral codes and social contracts to accommodate a wide range of people.* This rules out, among other things, the tightly entailed, rigidly defined "New Age religions" and "environmental spirituality" movements as effective solutions. The Inquisition that would be needed to enforce these religions staggers the imagination.

Scapegoating is easiest when a real, immediate problem preempts attention, but isn't easily solved. If the problem is inescapable but the cause unclear, people tend to blame the nearest "different" person.

For the cultural ecologist, such situations are interesting because they lead to a breakdown in conservation and resource management. People become uninterested in protecting things. Moreover, they lose interest in the world and long-term perspective, both of which are necessary to manage any resource. They shift from opposing the very concept of toxic waste dumps to the "not in my backyard" psychology: put that toxic waste dump in someone else's backyard, not mine.

Thus, although people very often do act in their self-interest, they very often act against their material and economic self-interest, because of emotional reasons. Most commonly, these emotional reasons are defensive reactions, especially hate of other human groups or of any outsiders. Sometimes, people attack the environment deliberately, shooting up inedible birds or deliberately driving over rare plants. Far more common, however, is a simple breakdown of control over resource management, because a country has gone off into a negative-sum political game.

In the United States, election figures allow some estimate of how often people vote against their economic self-interest. In the 1988 election, 42 percent of people with incomes under $20,000 a year voted for the Republican candidate. In the 1992 election, in spite of the independent candidacy of Ross Perot, the figure stood at 29 percent. The previous years of rule (since 1980) led to a massive, indeed revolutionary, wealth transfer from poorer to richer people. Few of these less affluent voters could have been seriously expecting better economic times for themselves. They evidently voted out of other motives. Conversely, about the same percentage of individuals with over $40,000 incomes voted Democratic—fully 36 percent of those with over $75,000 a year, in the heavy 1992 Democratic winning totals. At least by conventional wisdom, they could be seen as sacrificing their self-interest for other reasons, among which hatred of Republicans must have figured in more than a few cases, though serious worries about ecology and economic stability were demonstrated to be important among these voters. On the whole, it appears that a considerable majority of voters in 1988 voted with perceived material self-interest, but a good 30 to 35 percent voted from what must have been emotional factors—fear of rival groups, solidarity with reference groups, or blind opposition to "big government" or "big business." No doubt many others voted out of charity and goodwill, but—alas!—we have no measure.

It would appear that people often vote their fear; they vote against the person, or people, whom they fear or hate most. They vote on economic ground when their greatest fear is for their economic future. Otherwise, they vote against blacks, or criminals, or welfare mothers, or whatever other group seems most threatening to their sense of their proper or secure world. This subverts ecological voting. In France in the 1993 elections, the "green" parties got less than half of the vote they were expected to receive; neo-Fascist groups got 20 percent of the vote, far more than the greens. Concern about immigrants and Jews outweighed concern about a rapidly deteriorating environment.

If people were simply creatures of emotion, or simply creatures of "rational self-interest" in the old sense, we would have an easier time explaining behavior. Unfortunately for the social scientist, people persist in creating complex political ideologies that imperfectly and confusingly combine emotional and material interests. These cultural constructions change rapidly. I remember when conservation of natural resources was more a "conservative" than a "liberal" cause, and Republican President Dwight Eisenhower appointed the great environmentalist Stuart Udall as Secretary of the Interior. In those days, following Franklin Roosevelt's public-works tradition, it was the liberals who were the big-dam people.

In a world where the traditional "little community" is no more, and where networks and individuals replace families and societies, what can save us from a general collapse? Can resource management reassert itself in an increasingly Hobbesian world? Sociologists such as Robert Bellah and his collaborators hold that we should develop new community institutions. Otherwise, decline of old institutions makes it easier to rip off those weaker than oneself but harder to go after those stronger.[34]

But, on the other hand, networks, support groups, work groups, and special-interest groups are on the rise. Even voluntary charity and help are on the rise; it is reported that 57 percent of the citizens of the western United States are involved (at least as passive members) in organizations or groups dedicated to help and support in some form. The human spirit endures even in times of breakdown. The rise of fear and the decline of secure social life lead to anger and defensiveness. Resource management by the dog-eat-dog method leads to a lot of eaten dogs. Yet, creative responses appear as well.

This means that we not only *need* not, but *should* not, try to "sell" a whole religion. If we wait for the whole world to convert to goddess-worship or spiritual ecology, we will all be dead. I have my utopian social dreams, but the need now is to set medium-term goals. This does not mean accommodating to the status quo, as advocated by Martin Lewis.[35] Serious debate is needed to establish a minimum of basic points that *must* be shared, and that would be acceptable to all men and women of principle—not just to eco-radicals, but to liberals and conservatives as well.

The rise and decline of civilizations has been ascribed to environmental misuse. Perhaps it is more accurate to say that environmental misuse is due to the decline of civilizations. At least, environmental management is a function of politics. We cannot understand it without understanding why people want what they want and why human groups act in such varied and often self-destructive ways.

7

Information Processing:
Rational and Irrational
Transcended

A large and probably increasing proportion of literature on the environment is based on the assumptions of rational choice theory. People are
held to be almost errorless maximizers of individual utility. They are seen as
being quite clear about their goals, having perfect information about the means
to achieve those goals, and being able to calculate rapidly and precisely the exact
trade-offs and Bayesian optima that allow them to reach their goals by the most
cost-effective method. A further assumption, often unspoken (occasionally
even denied) but in practice almost always accepted, is that people's goals are
narrowly individualistic—short-term and narrow, not long-term and wide.
This assumption is not really entailed by rational choice theory, but rational
choice theorists often make it. Rational choice theory has its uses, but these
assumptions are questionable (at the very least).

Perhaps the commonest counterview in the environmental literature is
based on the assumption that rational individualism is a product of the modern
capitalist world, and that other peoples have based their lives on more communitarian and ecologically sensitive intuitions. Carolyn Merchant, chronicler of
Radical Ecology, provides a particularly powerfully argued summary of the
variants of this view.[1] Unfortunately, anthropological evidence shows fairly
conclusively that many premodern cultures ruined their environments through
shortsighted and wasteful practices (see chapter 8).

This chapter argues for a different way of understanding human successes and mistakes. A number of lines of evidence suggest that humans do indeed practice something like the rational calculus but that they are not perfect at it and that they are greatly influenced by social and emotional factors. The result is that their decision making often closely approximates rational choice but often deviates from rational choice models in dramatic but often predictable ways. This fact goes a long way to explain many of the mistakes we see in environmental management. It also helps explain the question posed earlier in this book: Why do people often use religious and mythic institutions to motivate rational behavior? If rational choice theory were adequate, people would not need the panoply of religion and myth to get them to act sensibly. But they do appear to need religion or myth in many cases, and it is the cultural ecologist's job to understand why.[2]

My career has been devoted to understanding traditional systems of folk science. I am mainly concerned with their practical value. Most of the folk wisdom of the world's farmers, fishermen, hunters, gatherers, and craftsmen is correct, and it is exceedingly important for the modern world. Villagers in tropical forests know literally tens of thousands of useful plants that are imperfectly known—or not known at all—to international science. Peasants know countless farming techniques that would benefit modern agriculture. Folk and non-Western medical traditions have already given us discoveries that have saved millions of lives: quinine, digitalis, ephedrine, and much more. Borrowing from the folk is increasing, not decreasing. Entire books of such useful knowledge have been compiled.[3] Most of the work in studying folk science systems is chronicling their practical, valuable knowledge.

But, as everyone knows, folk beliefs are a mélange of truth and inaccuracy. Much of the world's ancient belief systems seems like preposterous nonsense to the modern scientist. The same can be said of modern views—including (perhaps) more than a little of the environmentalist and anti-environmentalist rhetoric. Error creeps into even the most rigorous science (think of the story of "cold fusion"), to say nothing of the more open world of political and social thought.

Thus, a great deal of modern environmental policy is founded on mistakes and half-truths. Understanding why and how people come to hold false views is essential to cultural ecology, and is one central program of this book.

This chapter is about how people make mistakes. It is not intended to be as depressing as it will probably seem to the reader. I provide what I believe to be a fairly complete list of psychological findings on human error. However, at the beginning, I wish to emphasize that people usually do well enough. If we hadn't had *something* going for us, we would not have survived the last couple of million years. The findings on human nature reviewed in the preceding chapter suggest that people are not so much vicious and cruel as well-meaning and naive.

In spite of recent books that revive all the old myths of the Savage[4]—violent, cruel, trapped in superstition, and so forth—people in most societies manage well enough to survive and multiply. The problem is that they do not necessarily do any better than that. Evolution and adaptation are about satisfying—about just getting by. And sometimes societies fail to do even that; the Sumerians and the Roman Empire are no more.

Thus, since this is a book about why people mismanage the environment, I focus on the difficult questions we often fail to answer adequately. In this chapter, I focus on the more general process that lies behind environmental misperceptions.

How can the same Chinese medical system that gave us ephedra and chaulmoogra oil also hold that the mud from the footprint of an eastbound horse can prevent a sleeping man from getting up if it is rubbed on his navel?[5] A comforting bit of snobbism holds that the elite thought up the correct ideas, the stupid masses the rest. This is not the case for any tradition known to me. If anything, the reverse is true; certainly, in my experience, Chinese peasants have more solid empirical ideas of medicine than more elite consultants. My Chinese fishing friends, like the old fishing masters of Ponape,[6] knew much practical lore that was unknown to Western ichthyology—let alone the Chinese elite.

Conversely, many of the old errors sell as well in the modern United States as they ever did in the prescientific world. Astrology, telekinesis, the neo-Hobbesian view of humanity, fortune-telling, and poltergeists seem to be even more popular than they were before they were conclusively disproved. Here we have to deal with errors whose entire theoretical and empirical basis has been utterly demolished. Why does modern science fail to dislodge them?

One view holds that people, in areas where they lack direct knowledge, invent beautiful and poetic systems of symbol, metaphor, and dream. This view, however, would predict that the counterfactual knowledge encoded in traditional science systems is essentially arbitrary or poetic. This is not the case. These mistaken views are logical and patterned; they are often predictable; and, most astonishing, the same beliefs crop up over and over again, around the world.

Thus, I must regretfully reject the "postmodern" and "cultural constructionist" views, in this regard. In some realms, people do construct arbitrary systems of meaning, and "interpretive anthropology" is valuable. But in this book I am confining my attention to directly instrumental behavior toward the environment. Studies of "meaning" and "cultural construction" are simply not adequate to tell us anything we want to know about the feedback between the external environment and our instrumental ideas of it. The case would be quite different if I were discussing differences in the philosophies of various deep ecologists or environmental ethicists. Then, arbitrary individual differences would make all the difference, and I would invoke the appropriate interpretive and postmodern theories.

For widespread and relatively straightforward theories, we must seek more universal processes.

The belief that certain foods are "heating" to the system while others are "cooling," for instance, has spread worldwide, and almost certainly was independently invented in vaguely similar forms in several regions, for example, Greece and the Near East Malaysia, and Native America.[7] The belief in a sacred tree that serves as the world-pole is also widespread.[8] Astrology, too, has been independently invented in several areas. The only theory that addresses these widespread errors is that of Carl Jung, who held that we have certain inherited "archetypal ideas" in our heads.[9] This theory, in its original form, cannot be taken seriously in the light of modern genetics. Moreover, the widespread ideas are never quite completely universal, as they would be if they were genuinely archetypal. But Jung was on the right track: the universal workings of the human mind do predispose us to reason in a certain way, and thus people in similar situations come to similar conclusions.

Another widespread and plausible mistake is the belief *post hoc, ergo propter hoc*. Indeed, many of us do assume that if *x* precedes *y*, *x* has caused *y*. However, usually, *x* is followed by lots of different events. Why do people pick out *y* rather than *w* or *z*?

With what we now know of human information processing, some problems seem solvable. Claude Lévi-Strauss first realized this, basing his theories of dyadic opposition on the gestalt and phenomenological psychology of his day.[10] Since the work of Daniel Kahnemann, Amos Tversky, and their followers and associates, more seems explicable.[11] New subsequent advances have brought a great deal more to light, and enabled those of us who are not psychologists to incorporate the new findings into theories of human action.[12]

As I now see it, traditional and modern systems of supposedly factual knowledge can be analyzed as follows:

1. Look for the practical information.
2. Anything that does not look obviously practical and empirical should first be analyzed to see if it is merely a perfectly ordinary, accurate observation

described in a culturally unique way. For instance, many cultures use demons as explicitly imaginary constructs when they talk about diseases. Not all references to demons should be interpreted to mean literal belief; the term "Demon Rum" does not necessarily imply literal belief in an alcohol devil. Even more trivially: many European medicinal references to "dragons" refer not to imaginary monsters but to the very real—and pharmacologically active—plant *Dracunculus vulgaris,* known as "dragons" in herbalists' English.

3. Much more is actually empirical observation, *confirmed* by experience but *explained* by recourse to imaginary constructs. The phlogiston theory in seventeenth-century European science is an example: European savants knew about heat and burning; they inferred a peculiar material, phlogiston, in an attempt to explain what they saw.

4. Most outright errors can be explained as logical deductions from known principles—but with the logic (and often the observations too) distorted by the habitual biases in human information processing. Francis Bacon pointed out something like this long ago, in his "idols." Even earlier, much of Greek and Roman rhetorical study was devoted to avoiding errors. Modern psychology sheds increasing light on this key aspect of thought. Such counterfactual statements can range from the trivial errors we make every day to the wondrous and high-flown poetry of traditional creation myths.

5. Finally, some counterfactual knowledge creeps into belief systems as the result of teaching devices. Since time immemorial, people have known that myths and fables are great ways to teach morals to the young. It naturally happens that the young may get some unintended messages. The story of the fox and the grapes is *not* about fox biology, or even about the souring of grapes.[13] But generations of children have learned from it that foxes talk. Medieval European bestiaries began as treasuries of moral tales but became accepted as serious treatises on zoology, leaving us a residue of wonderful nonsense that still surfaces in folk beliefs. In traditional societies, the boundary between myth and reality can be very fuzzy indeed, and a cluster of ideas may spread simply because the ideas reinforce each other in learning. Indeed, as any good politician knows, the same is true today.

What interests me most are the systems that combine good empirical observation with creative (and therefore often inaccurate) inference and explanation. Folk medicine, general agricultural strategies and decision making, site planning, geography, beliefs about the powers or behaviors of plants and animals, and similar knowledge systems are invariably mixtures of truth and assumption (even in modern university departments).

Perhaps the most difficult and demanding, and the most inevitable, subject of questioning is: What is a person? What does it mean to be human? The very question is part of the answer. What other animal wonders about such things?

Thus, modern psychology makes it clear that human action is based on a calculus that must take into account a range of needs. All of them must be satisfied for survival. No one, not even a computer, can calculate how to satisfy *optimally* all those needs at once.

This has caused the brain to evolve as a mechanism for brilliant approximating. It is impossible to find the one perfect solution to the problem of maximizing satisfaction in food, shelter, excitement, rest, sociability, and efficacy all in one day. However, most human beings find a bearable solution on most days. Most of the rest could do so if they were not overwhelmed by poverty or oppression.

Culture is an enormous aid in the process of finding some kind of bearable solution. Culture is preeminently a storehouse of ways to kill two, three, or many birds with one stone. In all societies, food is not just nutrition: it is a symbol of family and sociability, a mark of security, and often a medicine. A house not only provides shelter, it provides a "home," symbol of security and social warmth. Less pleasant are the widespread tendencies to mix up food or sex with control. Particular social institutions, such as the family, serve to satisfy many needs. Religion, as we have seen, becomes a carrier wave for ecological knowledge, and thus joins that knowledge to the more classically "religious" issues of reassurance, social sanctioning, and cosmology.

All this raises important questions about "rationality" and the rational calculus that underlies modern economic and political theories.[14] Rationality has been variously defined in modern writings. Often the same person will use it in two senses in the same book.

The narrowest definition opposes reason to emotion, impulse, and whim. Philosophers of the Enlightenment sought to make people more reasonable, or rational, in this sense, so that they could make better decisions. We have seen that such unemotionality is simply not humanly possible. An enlightenment scholar might answer, Surely, but the nearer we approach it, the better off we are. In other words, rationality (tightly defined) is a *normative* thing.

There is a second meaning of "rational," covering acts that are generally seen to be sensible. Under this definition, voting appears rational, because we all know that voting is a good thing to do, even if one's chances of casting the deciding vote are less than one's chances of being run over on the way to the polls. Similarly, carpooling and public transportation is seen as more rational, because it ultimately benefits society, even though each individual loses (or thinks so, anyway) by giving up the independence and flexibility of driving alone.

Rationality in modern economic literature has yet a third meaning, quite different from the other two. For the neoclassical economist, rationality consists in calculating the best way to use available means to get desired ends. This implies knowledge of alternative means and of which ones are best in which situations. It also implies some kind of ranking of the ends. For instance, food is more important than sociability to the starving. (*Erst das Fressen, dann die Moral*—first feeding, then morality—as Bertolt Brecht said.) Once well fed, most people reprioritize their ends, and sociability outweighs food.

Unfortunately, this definition is so loose and begs so many questions that no one can really use it.

This third meaning of "rational" lies behind the "maximization of utility" beloved of neoclassical economists. Anything anyone wants is taken to be a "utility." This has the very real advantage of allowing economists to model any and all behavior—to work it into their equations. This is no mean feat; Gary Becker won the Nobel Prize for it. But, under this definition, all behavior is thus rational, since it is all directed toward some sort of end-state. "Joe loves Susie" is redefined as "Joe puts a high level of utility on Susie and on being with her." This has the advantage of cutting the Gordian knot of deciding what is rational and what is not. It also has the advantage of allowing one to calculate the trade-offs. (Does Joe love Susie enough to spend on her the money he had saved for a new car?) It allows one to analyze, by normal decision-making research techniques, such "irrational" behavior as buying a brand of beer or cosmetics because a football hero or female politician endorses them, or buying more of a perfume when its price goes up. (It's rational to wear a perfume that seems more snobbish, surely . . .)

Unfortunately, it also makes the word "rational" almost totally meaningless. It does not help us predict when people will trade off short-term for long-term benefits, or material for emotional ones. They will do so "when it maximizes overall utility," but that description, by definition, fits *any* end-state.

Other problems of this approach appear in practice. Economic calculus depends on our having a very firm sense of our means and ends. In reality, we rarely have that kind of knowledge of our means and ends. This is where brilliant approximation comes in.[15]

We also have limited ability to calculate optima. As Richard Thaler says, "An economist who spends a year finding a new solution to a nagging problem, such as the optimal way to search for a job when unemployed, is content to assume that the unemployed have already solved this problem and search accordingly. The assumption that everyone else can intuitively solve problems that an economist has to struggle to solve analytically reflects admirable modesty, but it does seem a bit puzzling."[16] Any economics journal contains papers on conceptually very simple problems that require several pages of advanced calculus to solve optimally. If humans—especially in premodern societies without calculus or economics journals—manage to cope with such problems in the real world, it must be because of more or less inspired approximation, tested over many trials, and summed up and transmitted culturally.[17]

There are deeper logical problems with the whole agenda, especially if whole societies are considered. One person's means are another's ends. In regard to the environment, for instance, a forest is loved for itself by some, while others regard it only as a source of lumber for profit, and still others as merely junk to get out of the way so that the land can be used for some other purpose. Saving bird species is an end for bird lovers, a means for people interested in genetic diversity, and neither end nor means for many other people. Moreover, for the same person, on the same day, food can be an end in itself at dinnertime and a mere means—an excuse to get away from the office and socialize—at lunchtime.

As the philosopher Alexander Rosenberg puts it, "The relationship between beliefs, desires, and behavior just does not permit us to isolate one of these variables from the others and to sharpen up our measurements of it in ways that will lead to identification of the point at which the whole story goes wrong. So, it is not just that compared with other theories, rational choice theory cuts nature farther from the bone. It is rather that we have no idea how far from the bone it cuts, and no way to find out."[18]

Cultural institutions have to balance out means and ends, and they have to do it through individual negotiation. Rational choice theory provides a beginning, but it cannot be adequate in itself.

A good deal of economic hand-waving has been expended in trying to prove that this or that act was "rational." Economists like to argue that the act of suicide is rational. They mean, of course, that it is goal-directed, and that the suicide thinks he or she is maximizing utility. Death appears preferable to life. Economists often imply that they have thus shown that suicide is a carefully considered, unemotional choice—"rational" in the Enlightenment sense. This is, of course, mere deliberate confusion of the issue by mixing up two or three different definitions of the word. Most suicides occur in fits of depression.

Many people kill themselves because of incurable illness or long-continued psychic agony, but many suicides are by people who would—and did—choose life for many years. For a moment, they may have been optimizing satisfaction by ending their lives—but the moment was brief, and foreclosed forever on countless other moments. Is it "rational" for them to foreclose on their futures?

Obviously not. But—and here is the stinger—*economists use the same logic to claim that modern resource use is rational.* Humanity is clearly acting suicidally, on the basis of a self-destructive whim, in its current behavior toward forests, farms, fish, and wildlife. The economists argue "rationality" because some people are indeed maximizing profits. However, the satisfaction for billions of people over countless decades or centuries is foreclosed forever. This and other questions begged by the application of rational choice theory to ecology have been thoroughly addressed by Dryzek in his book *Rational Ecology* and need not be considered here.[19]

Modern economists and sociobiologists are also fond of pointing out that all behavior is "self-interested" in the sense that our most socially "altruistic" acts are done because we want to. David Hume pointed out long ago that this is obviously true, but obviously not a very serious point. The real question is: When do we get enjoyment—or "utility," in modern jargon—from helping others, and when do we get it from hurting others? By definition, people cannot want to do what they do not want to do. It is far more important to figure out why some people want to be altruistic and others do not.[20]

This suggests that people need moral systems, not so much to force them toward altruism as to *encourage long-term, wide-flung self-interest at the expense of short-term, narrow self-interest.* The ordinary human tendency is to go with the latter, *even when the former would clearly bring more ultimate benefits.* Today's tiny pleasure is very persuasive compared to tomorrow's much greater one. Ask any dieter.

The persistence of belief systems that have been repeatedly disproved, such as astrology, proves that people are not rational in the everyday sense of the term (as opposed to the economic usage). So does the continuation of flagrantly self-destructive behavior, be it drug addiction, compulsive gambling, or environmental overuse. But even the more general, less falsifiable sense of the term leads to paradoxes and produces wrong expectations.[21]

Thus, it seems to me that the most important task of the modern social scientist is to explain why people make mistakes and hold counterevidential beliefs. Once we understand that, we can understand why people act in ways that seem self-destructive or irresponsible.

No wonder students of rational choice are known as "rat choice people" in academic slang. Yet, I depend on their models in this book. If people's choices are "rat choices" only in a very special sense, at least people *do* make choices and those choices are usually comprehensible. My complaints about rational choice theory deal with its limitations to some extent, but mostly with its abuses. In particular, I protest mixing up rationality in sense 3 (rationality as unemotionality) with rationality in sense 1 (rationality as optimization). Motivated choice is *not* unemotional or objective choice. All I want is acknowledgment that the rat is an impassioned rat.

As of this writing, the major published collection of anti-environmental and anti-conservation writings is titled *Rational Readings on Environmental Concerns*.[22] Most of the book is political advocacy, but there are essays that actually try to live by the "rational" implications of the title. In these, the major issue and the source of the word "rational" is the need for perfect information. Most, if not all, the authors agree that we should not stop pollution, ban chemicals, or save wildlands unless we have essentially *perfect* information on the effects. This would, of course, foreclose on all action taken to avoid risks. Indeed, this is a rational point: the rational thinker will not act unless sure. "If it ain't broke, don't fix it" is a valid enough point. Unfortunately, it is not so valid when we are dealing with nuclear power plants, or even with one's family car. Preventive maintenance and preventive precautions may be irrational in some economic models, but they are practical in the real world.

Of course, one can always point out that the contributors to Lehr's book are putting their "rational" calculus to the service of emotional ends. One suspects that, in daily life, the authors look before crossing streets, and change the oil in their cars.

However, the question is not trivial. How do we calculate risk and uncertainty? What is "acceptable risk"? If we genuinely have no idea what a drug will do, should we allow it to be sold in the hope that it is safe? Should we assume that it is as safe as the "average" drug and not test further? If we do test it, how much should we test? There are some technical questions here, such as the validity of rodent models, but the main questions are ethical and social, and cannot be decided by narrowly rational calculus. Indeed, even the definition of the word "rational" cannot be decided by rational calculus. Is Lehr right? Or is the rational person the one who ensures against future disaster?

K. S. Shrader-Frechette, in *Risk and Rationality*, has argued for the latter view.[23] Evidently, the very definition of rationality is subject to irrational distortions. Lehr is an advocate of uncontrolled capitalist development;

Shrader-Frechette's book is subtitled "Philosophical Foundations for Populist Reforms." Clearly, emotional commitment has, for these authors, determined their very use of the word!

Some rational economists—it is not only Lehr who uses the word this way—would put a nuclear power plant in a heavily populated area and then never maintain or inspect it. The rational Soviet planners did exactly that at Chernobyl. Rational planners in the tropics wiped out the rainforests for trivial or insignificant per-acre returns, in spite of the virtual certainty that drug plants potentially worth billions of dollars were being exterminated. The difference between virtual certainty and absolute certainty made all the difference here.

No one, except a compulsive gambler or a cocaine addict, would run his or her personal life this way. What seems preposterous for the individual case should seem even more preposterous for the general polity. This is not the case, however, because of the extreme problems of calculating long-term, wide-flung costs and benefits.

And how much satisfaction are we to forgo, today, for the benefit of our futures? Our future selves, or the unborn future generations, might very well wish that we use no resources at all and leave them the lot. This seems to us impractical and unnecessary. At the very least, though, we and they will certainly wish that we had managed the world sustainably.

Both dispassionate analysis and careful weighing of means and ends are absolutely necessary in dealing with the environment. It is precisely the difficulty of doing them that makes them so important. As so many philosophers remind us, *the extreme problems that humans have in thinking rationally make the attempt to do so even more important.* We are easily fooled by emotional appeals and over-optimism.

The philosophers of the Enlightenment knew that reason—in the sense of careful calculation of how to reach thoughtfully chosen goals—is a rare thing in this world. It was left to twentieth-century economists to claim that everyone is fully rational all the time. Their rationality has given us pollution, deforestation, extinctions, mass starvation, and urban sprawl. It is time we recognized that the philosophers (and not the economists) were right. Calculation of one's best interest is difficult, demanding, and absolutely imperative.

Thus, many anthropologists, myself included, have come to believe that much human behavior toward the environment can only be understood by looking at how people process information. Up to a point, this is obvious; humans can't see ultraviolet light, and thus (without special equipment) can't act on the basis of seeing ultraviolet patterns on flowers, as bees can and do. Less obvious but far more serious distortions in our perception result from other biases.

Roy Rappaport has argued that religion serves to code ecological knowledge.[24] This begs the question: Why religion? Why not just common sense? The answer, simply put, is that religion involves emotions, involves the community, and reaches people in ways that logical, rational argument cannot do. Nor is it the only emotion-laden belief system that codes knowledge, for good or ill. Sometimes our information-processing idiosyncracies lead us to error. However, traditional cultures have often found ways of using them, so to speak, to "sell" economic messages. One can extend Rappaport's argument (which, itself, has roots in the work of Lewis Henry Morgan, Karl Marx, Franz Boas, and other social science classics) by adding new knowledge of information processing to the theory, thereby increasing its explanatory power.

The economists' models of rational behavior usually assume perfect information. Obviously, in this imperfect world, we never have that. Herbert Simon first began serious modeling of economic decision making under imperfect information.[25] His work not only won him the Nobel Prize; it also set off considerable research, not only in the rather arid realms of economic modeling, but also in the empirical world of experimental and social psychology. For an anthropologist interested in resource management, the most interesting reading imaginable is the body of literature that has accumulated since Simon's work on decision making cross-fertilized with social psychology, especially the individualistic and skeptical tradition that runs from George Herbert Mead through George Kelly to the modern students of decision making and the construction of reality. These people—psychologists such as Richard Nisbett, Lee Ross, and Paul Slovic, and economists such as Jon Elster—have provided major advances in the understanding of human irrationality. "Irrationality," in this case, refers to the inability to evaluate alternative means well enough to see which is optimal. Both logical paradoxes and failure to predict behavior ensue from rigid application of rational choice theory.[26] Often, the behavior that mystifies a rational choice theorist is perfectly comprehensible if one assumes that people are trying their best but just can't get perfect information or process it optimally.[27]

It even appears that people are not always able to rank their goals or their preferences in any stable manner.[28] The economists' assumption of stable preferences is not always justified. People often change their minds or cannot decide between alternatives.

Even when our preferences are stable, we frequently misunderstand the world because of our prejudices and preconceptions. This returns us to Khayyám's quatrain. In our minds, we literally shatter the world to bits, and reassemble it to accord with our wishes and biases.

However, the extreme phenomenologists are wrong; we cannot simply construct any reality we choose. We are forced to deal with a world that is out there, that has its own structure, and that will not let us forget it. We, in turn, impose our own structure on it—and, especially, on our perceptions of it.[29] There is a constant feedback between self and environment.

Given imperfect information, horribly complicated goals, rationally insoluble dilemmas, and the ultimate indeterminacy of the "means-ends" distinction, it is no wonder that our brains function according to quite a different calculus from the "rational" one of microeconomics.

Real-world cognition and decision making rest on a number of cognitive processes that allow humans to simplify the world enough to operate in it. Many of these run counter to rational decision making to optimize utility.

Emotion is, of course, the most obvious. Think how different the "objectively" same touch of the hand feels when the touch is given in love, in physical therapy, or in an aggressive encounter with an enemy. Some amount of emotion enters into all information processing, and some amount of cognitive construction seems to enter into all human emotional experience. Cognition and affect are not, in practice, separate (and perhaps should not be analytically separated).

Cognitive psychologists often differentiate between "cool cognition" and "hot cognition." The first is logical, "rational," unemotional thought. Mistakes of cool cognition involve miscalculation and plain foolishness. Hot cognition is emotion-driven. Mistakes of hot cognition are mistakes of passion, of desire, of love and hate. For a while there was hope that many of our mistakes were of the "cool" type,[30] but of late psychologists have generally agreed that emotion and mood (however defined) profoundly influence all our thought. We do not even react consciously to any stimulus without evaluating it.[31]

This being so, the goal of dispassionate, cold, calculating rationality is unattainable for humans, and is to be written off. The planners, engineers, and developers of this world have usually banked on getting to purely "rational" solutions for their problems. Indeed, we can and should be as accurate and reasonable as possible; but we have to recognize that the goal of a perfectly unemotional, dispassionate plan is absolutely beyond us. In particular, no political question (and, therefore, no real-world question) can be addressed without some sort of emotional involvement. The best we can do is be as conscious of emotionality as possible, so that we can actively minimize its distorting effect—while, perhaps, making use of its intense drive.[32] In regard to environmental concerns, David Orr has pointed out that biologists who love their subjects of study do a disservice by pretending to be coldly rational; they are not only dishonest, they are failing to motivate others.[33] Politicians, of course, have long been aware of this truth. If they are statesmen rather than just politicians, they will operate by balancing opposing emotional views, and coming to their conclusions by considering all sides. If they are mere "politicians" in the popular, derogatory sense of the word, they will try to inflame the less worthy emotions, and get power by manipulating the mob. This distinction, of course, was well recognized by the time of Aristotle.

Intelligence is situational and interactive.[34] We learn, understand, and influence others through interaction with them and with the environment. This wide interaction is usually a complicated, unstructured, and only partially conscious process. Learning runs ahead of conscious systematization, and action often runs ahead of reflection.

Once an individual makes the move from action or experience to concept, the next step is to generalize and simplify the concept further. This is another point at which trouble enters. Inevitably, some overgeneralizing goes on.[35] There are those who believe that "once you've seen one tree, you've seen 'em all," with the one tree being, I would suppose, their original focal tree. This assumption that the world is much less diverse than it is, and much more like us, lies behind a huge percentage of the mistakes human beings make.

The application of this point to the environment becomes obvious. The remark about trees was made, of course, to excuse clear-cutting and destruction of the western forests. But there is a broader problem that underlies it: the problem of overgeneralization. Of this, we are all guilty. We all are too prone to ignore diversity in environments, plants, and people.

For the Northwest Coast Indians, hills, fish, trees, and other non-human beings are persons, and most of them talk and have villages with something like human culture. This operates to keep people attending to the specific creature and its particular value. It thus provides a spiritual alternative to overgeneralizing.

Humans also are bad at calculating probabilities. They will choose a ten-in–one hundred chance, and even an eight-in–one hundred chance, over a one-in-ten chance.[36] They will assume that, when a coin has come up heads five times in a row, it "must" come up tails next time.[37] They will attend to a single salient bit of information over an overwhelming mass of data; thus, if my highly respected brother-in-law tells me a make of car is a lemon, I will be all too prone to disregard *Consumer Reports* and all the car magazines.[38] Also, people expect too much consistency of the world; this is so universal that it has been called the Fundamental Attribution Error. For example, they expect people to have highly consistent personalities, in spite of much evidence of human changeability.[39]

Humans can deal with probabilities better than the Kahnemann-Slovic-Tversky and Nisbett-Ross teams originally believed. A number of authors have pointed out that these groups used artificial and inadequate experimental designs and probability reckonings.[40] Gert Gigerenzer, in particular, has shown that more reasonable situations and more comprehensive calculations of probability clear up some of the probability errors. Unfortunately, not even he can prove that humans do not make mistakes. Nor are his optimistic arguments always convincing. We all do make mistakes due to sloppy calculation, and we know it.

Teaching, fortunately, has been shown to be effective in improving performance in these matters.[41] It follows that such teaching should receive a very high priority in any curriculum.

Humans also weigh an improvement in life less than an objectively equivalent decline. I am less cheered by a salary raise of 5 percent than I am depressed by a salary cut of 5 percent. This makes sense in terms of the human security need and in terms of the fact that I have arranged my life on the basis of a certain income. A raise would not be a great improvement, but a cut means serious and unpleasant restructuring. The implications of this belief for environmental economics are regarded as serious.[42] The human tendency to discount the future inordinately is an even more serious problem.[43]

All these and many other home truths can be deduced from the need to simplify the world. Moreover, they make some sense in daily practice; it is usually reasonable to assume that events are non-random, and certainly more sensible to try for prediction than to give up all hope and expect a fluctuating, random universe.[44] It has also been argued by psychologists such as Leda Cosmides and Gert Gigerenzer, as well as by anthropologists such as David Kronenfeld, that people do much better with probabilities in "natural" settings, or when approximating, than in the laboratory; some cultural ecologists have taken heart from this.[45]

I have not found much consolation in this view, though it undeniably is correct in some cases. The fact remains that we are not perfect information processors. We make mistakes. We are better at rapid, rough calculations than at detailed figuring. All this is consistent with the imperative human need for a comprehensible, meaningful world. We have to approximate. Many of the simplifying assumptions uncovered by Nisbett and Ross are necessary if we are to operate in a complex world. Unfortunately, they also lead us to oversimplify and overgeneralize in dealing with the environment.

In practice, all cognition involves at least some emotional reaction, if only a vague sense of "good" or "unpleasant."[46] Love, hate, and fear distort our perceptions in obvious ways. Moreover, we make a tremendous number of trade-offs in which we damage ourselves, in the long run, to protect our precious self-images. Roy Baumeister and Steven Scher have documented the dismal roll of self-destructive things people do just to feel good.[47] I am reminded of the U.S. Forest Service's sober prediction, some thirty years ago, that Humboldt County's lumber industry would collapse in twenty-five years at then-prevailing rates of cut. The figures were unimpeachable, but the loggers went right on. When twenty-five years rolled around and the industry collapsed, both corporations and loggers professed surprise and wonder. They had, all along, been hoping that somehow . . . So they blamed the environmentalists.

It is depressing to remember, too, that people are more accurate in self-perception when in fits of depression than when in their usual more cheerful mood. (I have learned to delay making key decisions until I'm miserable about something.) Now and then people react the opposite way, making the world worse than it is, or deliberately destroying themselves, but such cases are rare. (Still, flagrantly self-destructive behavior, and depression so black that it leads to unwarranted pessimism, are both common enough to need cultural recognition and cultural coping mechanisms.)

George Ainslie has recently argued at great length that humans are hopelessly prone to value the immediate over the distant.[48] In a particularly dismal and pessimistic review of all human error, he argues that great future happiness is sacrificed for even the most trivial or self-destructive present pleasure. He cites alcohol and drug abuse as his model system.

Fortunately, the world is not always so bleak. Most people escape alcoholism, and many or most alcoholics become securely sober at last. Nor are humans trapped in the present time. Most groups find ways of deferring gratification. The problem lies in finding the means to escape it—to use religion, morality, law, or other institutions to offset whatever bias toward the present is actually "wired into" our brains. This problem is, of course, exacerbated when rapid population growth renders traditional controls less and less adequate.

A popular and reasonably successful set of psychotherapies has stemmed from the "cognitive therapy" of Aaron Beck.[49] These methods make us aware of cognitive problems, and provide ways of asserting control over our cognitive processes. This being so, it is logical to suppose that a great deal of cultural wisdom must have the function of saving people from themselves. Indeed, my experience with shamans, spirit mediums, and other folk healers confirms that they are often extremely effective cognitive therapists. They may credit the gods with the cures they effect, but the visiting outsider sees a process that shares much with a cognitive therapy session.

Culture *must* provide institutions that force people to act rationally *in spite of* their tendencies to distort everything in pleasant or unpleasant directions. There are some particular distorters that are extremely unfortunate for society and are also extremely predictable. In addition to the obvious—lack of information, prejudice, and so on—there is the whole complex of distortions that go with hierarchic social systems. The more we feel that power is unequally distributed in society, the more we become prey to certain habits of thought. Immortalized in song and story is status emulation: the desire to keep up with the Joneses, to achieve Bourdieu's "distinction" (which, he usefully reminds us, has a huge and direct financial payoff in many cases).

Insofar as people are defined as isolated individuals whose only relationship is with the all-powerful Center, they cannot form communities or even act responsibly. A problematic mentality develops from this, often hostile to community action.[50]

Insofar as decisions are taken out of people's hands, they become victims of "learned helplessness." If an animal or person has tried long enough to control his or her world, and has been actively frustrated in that enterprise, he or she eventually gives up trying. People in this situation cease to learn, and ultimately cease to hope, or even to think, beyond a minimal level.

Another great distorter, not unrelated to power hierarchies, has been discussed at length by Jon Elster in *Sour Grapes*.[51] People "make the best of things," "trim their sails to suit their cloth," and dismiss the grapes out of reach. Elster points out that this habit leads to suboptimizing. People learn to be content with what they can get. If the parameters change and they could in fact get much more, they are slow to change. People also learn to go for what they can get easily rather than for what might be more desirable but would take very much more work to get. In environmental politics, this very human tendency has had an absolutely devastating effect. Southern Californians, in my lifetime, have learned to live with levels of smog, traffic congestion, and environmental ugliness that would once have been unacceptable.

Of all attacks on the belief that humans act in anything like their economic self-interest, the most radical is *Positive Illusions* by Shelley Taylor.[52] Modest in its apparent message, this book is profound in its implications. Taylor, a psychologist at UCLA, summarizes the many studies that show how people can distort their perceptions in a positive direction. Lionel Tiger, in a book called *Optimism,* had earlier argued that this habit of thought is actually instinctive.[53] Our ancient ancestors who had unrealistically rosy expectations about children and about foraging would go forth, breed, hunt, and gather with more enthusiasm and abandon than their more realistic neighbors. Since wild gambles do pay off occasionally, the optimists would leave more descendants. Indeed, people start families everywhere. A modern parallel of hunting may be afforded by an attempt to open a small restaurant in a spot where many have failed before it. As Nisbett and Ross point out, and as many of us have plenty of occasion to observe, the same bad location attracts hopeful entrepreneurs year after year.[54]

Logically, leaders and heroes should be more unrealistic than the rest of us. "Pride goeth before a fall," and leaders continually blunder into wars and other disasters because of overconfidence.[55] The more powerful a society's leaders are, the more unrealistic they can afford to be. Conversely, the rest of us, insofar as we are cautious realists, don't act—and leave the more deluded in charge of all the entrepreneurship. This makes for a growth economy, but is not way to manage the environment.

Positive illusions account for much resource overuse. They are the beliefs behind the familiar lines: "It can't hurt to take just one . . . There's always plenty more . . . Natural populations are very resilient . . . We'll just try it this once . . . Surely, they wouldn't be allowing this if they didn't know it was safe . . . There's as much game as ever, it's just hiding . . ."

A leader may be old and wise enough to have lost the rosy visions of youth. Unfortunately, the opposite is also true: a leader, buoyed by success, may get more and more unrealistic with age. Morris Rossabi has brilliantly documented how this undid Coleridge's idol Kublai Khan.[56] It also helps explain Lord Acton's law: "All power tends to corrupt, and absolute power tends to corrupt absolutely"—which historian Page Smith has recently called the only law of history.[57]

Still, the studies all seem to confirm Taylor's position. Neil Weinstein, for example, shows how unrealistic we are about personal risks.[58] Like the writers in Lehr's collection, individuals often trust in the future: their car will always perform well, their neighborhood is safe.

This is one of the principal reasons why conservationists must expand their appeal beyond economic logic. If people routinely overestimate their chances, they cannot coolly and rationally assess their situation, experience or no. Our only protection is to have a population with very high goals and quick responses to threat. They must be willing to work hard for small returns.

Positive illusion theory predicts the "hits" of rational choice theory at least as well as rational choice does. It predicts the "misses" far better. Thus it explains human action better than rational choice theory.[59]

Taylor does not spell out rules, but one can abstract them from her account:

1. The more a person has invested in a belief, the more illusion sets in. The more deeply desired the goal, the greater the illusion.

2. A corollary, remembering how important sociability is, emerges from experiments as well as logic: one key domain of self-delusion, in all people, concerns how well liked they are.

3. The more one can avoid hard facts and other real-world feedback, the more one can self-delude. Reality checks teach rationality.[60]

Taylor follows Albert Bandura in seeing humans as in need of a sense of effectiveness in the world.[61] A major area for positive illusions is self-efficacy. Most people think they can do much more than they really can. When reality catches up, it often throws them into a depression. Thus, people act to prevent such reality checks—which explains the findings of Baumeister and Scher, mentioned above.

As Taylor points out, positive illusion theory also predicts much about racism and prejudice. She cites Melvin Lerner's famous book, *Belief in a Just World: A Fundamental Delusion*.[62] Lerner showed that people tend to believe that the world is a more fair and just place than it is, and thus tend to believe that people who are down and out deserve their fate. Such people thus think that African Americans deserve to be slaves or street people, alcoholics deserve no help, sick people are being punished by God for something, and the environment is not going to be hurt by ozone depletion or global warming.

Positive illusion theory does have some problems as a theory. It predicts opposite things in this case; some people see criminals as deserving the worst, others as good people in bad company. Both these views are positive illusions of a type. Moreover, Taylor uses positive illusions to explain both high achievement (wild hopes led them to it) and underachievement to protect one's self-image ("I failed because I didn't try"). Yet the theory is clearly true in the main and needs only minor tinkering to handle these discrepancies.

Taylor raises an important question. The goal of psychotherapy is usually to make the client more realistic. But is this desirable? Should we strive to make people more positively self-deluding?

I think not. The goal should be to get people to focus on the real good in the world, but not to ignore the bad. Reasonable strategies for maximizing one's use of one's abilities depend on having some understanding of what one's abilities really are. Above all, though, environmental management of any kind relies wholly on combatting the human tendency toward positive illusions.

It is evident that positive illusions are one of the most important causes of the human failure to trade off short-term against long-term payoffs, to plan adequately, and to deal realistically with the environment.

In summary: Contrary to the views of the economic determinists, people live for many non-material ends, and can't calculate their material self-interest very well anyway. Contrary to the teachings of many social scientists of phenomenological persuasions, people do not usually fill their minds with flights of arbitrary but beautiful speculative fantasy. They construct their realities, but they test these constructions against their ongoing experience. They routinely distort these constructions according to their hopes and dreams. This leads them to have beliefs that are close to the realities of the external world, but that "remold it closer to the heart's desire."

The brain has evolved, and is the product of a very special sort of evolution. Barkow, Cosmides and Tooby, arguing for this view, see human intelligence as made up of various faculties that adapt us to our lifestyle—specifically our original niche as social foragers and omnivorous, opportunistic feeders.[63] Early humans found it necessary to size up complex situations very fast, move in quickly to take advantage of them, and organize complex and fine-tuned group action for the purpose. The same needs are still with us today. It is at least possible that there is a worldwide "common sense" about the environment, underlying cross-cultural similarities in the perception of nature—a point defended by some cognitive anthropologists, such as Scott Atran and Brent Berlin, but still very much under investigation.[64]

Social needs may be thought to be only indirectly involved with the environment. The same cannot be said of our need to feel in control of our world. Our most basic drive, in relation to the environment, is the need to understand it, predict what will happen to us in it, and control it enough to get some sense of empowerment or efficacy. Elderly people in nursing homes given plants to care for lived longer and healthier lives than those given plants that the staff cared for. This study is discussed in detail, with much other relevant material, in Ellen Langer's book *The Psychology of Control*.[65]

Fear is based in great measure on a sense of helplessness—not just in the face of immediate threat but as a result of our perception of our ability to cope with that threat.[66] Learned helplessness can ensue when an individual's attempts to cope are constantly thwarted. Depression typically follows; the differences between it and learned helplessness are slight indeed.[67] The application of all this to political apathy are obvious enough; from the ancient Greeks to modern times, philosophers and writers have held that despotic regimes make passive and alienated publics.[68] Conversely, it has also been noted that the control needs of the power-hungry can be insatiable.

This would seem to be taking us a long way from resource management. It is not. It becomes directly relevant to resource management when one considers the coping strategies that hurt people invoke.

Neither hate nor withdrawal necessarily affects the man cutting down a tree for firewood or shooting ducks for food. What they do affect is politics—in the broad sense—and politics determines the resource management rules and strategies of a society.

A society that has degenerated into an ethnic or ideological rat fight will not waste time or effort on conservation. Indeed, it will probably end up in a state of war, or at least of Hobbesian "warre," and resources will suffer accordingly—especially the "ultimate resource,"[69] the human beings caught in the vortex. The United States is only one of many societies riding the ragged edge of this very situation today. Yugoslavia and the ex-Soviet Union went, tragically, beyond the edge. (The Soviet Union was doing nothing for its ecology before, but Yugoslavia is a particularly tragic case; it was just beginning to move toward being a real ecological success story when ethnic hatred tore it apart.)

Even without open war, withdrawal of the alienated and dispirited leads to resource mismanagement. They become the helpless victims of toxic-waste dumping and the like—all the things that more vocal or affluent people can keep out of "their backyards." They become the helpless victims of resource depletion, national or international in origin. Anything that divides such people and keeps them from combining into a political force contributes to such processes.[70]

Also, hurt and anger animate some of the more extreme players in the environmental discourse. In fact, across the board, the extremes of current political debate have become so clearly divorced from reality that they can only be explained as anger and hurt gone out of control. This is not new; the philosophers made the same complaint about politics in ancient Greece.

It is necessary to separate emotional rhetoric from the rational grounds for a political stance. All political rhetoric goes beyond the narrowly rational, almost by definition. The forces pulling it beyond rationality are many and various, but all lie in the dark realms of the psyche. This is true even if the rhetoric is culturally and socially standardized and constructed, as, of course, it invariably is. Socially shaped though it be, it is invoked only because it gets an emotional response in the individual voter. Recall that the voter must overcome a possibly rational desire to stay home—one vote won't make a difference. The rhetoric has to be emotional enough to get the voter out. An empty social form won't do it; any lingering doubt on that score is dispelled by the fact that, indeed, most people do *not* turn out.

Naturally, extremism feeds off extremism. "Wise Use" advocates can correctly point to the excesses of the animal rights extremists, and vice versa. Extremists of all stripes stick together and often share beliefs. Racism, sexism, and the like are widely and broadly linked to environmental and especially to anti-environmental extremism.[71] Once again, it appears that the beliefs are due to deep-seated emotional factors, rather than to any encounters with evidence or logic.

Yet extremist scapegoating is not instinctive. Observation of children shows that bias is learned, and that it is driven by a kind of logic. Positive illusions make people think the best of their own reference group. Oversharpening of differences makes them think the worst of its main or most obvious rival. Displacement makes people project their own failings: we hate most in others what we secretly hate most in ourselves. Thus, one's most salient opponent group tends to be regarded as the repository of all vileness, and is blamed for every bad thing.

Environmentalists are, increasingly, occupying this position, in the minds of polluters, large logging companies, and other users of the environment. In the nature of things, people typically blame their scapegoat group even for the consequences of their own folly. Thus, loggers blame environmentalists for the loss of logging jobs in the Pacific Northwest, when in fact the loss of jobs is due to overcutting. The forest is gone except for a few tiny protected scraps. The loggers blame the environmentalists for protecting the last few acres, rather than the lumber companies for cutting the other 99 percent. This is a logic familiar to those who have followed the sordid history of racism and anti-Semitism.

The enemy is denigrated and ultimately satanized. All too typically, the scapegoat is a weaker group. This is the playground-bully syndrome: if abused or scared, find someone weaker to beat up. The alternative—going after one's abusers, going after the more powerful—is unthinkable for those who are themselves weak, abused, and isolated.

Only solidarity and new courage can get them out of this trap. Solidarity and courage, however, depend on directly dealing with reality. In the modern (postmodern?) world of images, fragmented lives, and sound bites, people become more passive and weak. The old cultural institutions—religion, kinship, local politics—dealt with such issues, often successfully. What can we use now?

Thus, conservation, like every consideration of the long term, depends not only on people's felt needs, but also on their ability to work together. Cooperation and solidarity are necessary not just for political reasons, but for inspiriting or "empowering" the individuals. This is one of the reasons that institutions and political movements succeed where individual choices fail to improve a situation.

Culture usually operates to keep people in line—to keep them from making egregious mistakes. ("Culture" here is shorthand for institutionalized knowledge in a society.) Often, it harnesses mistakes in the service of wisdom, as we have seen with Chinese nutritional beliefs. But culture can also institutionalize mistakes. In simple societies, feedback teaches people rapidly that their behavior isn't working. In the modern world, feedback is slow and confusing. Large polities and diverse cultures cannot incorporate learning fast enough.

Cultures can show astonishing consistency across time and space; one can predict some modern Latin American behavior fairly well by studying sixteenth-century Spain.[72] On the other hand, cultures can change fast; consider the rise and decline of cigarettes in the Western world.

One of the key issues is reproduction. Passing on culture is part of raising children. The children always rebel, at least a little bit. Thus they change culture—often slowly and subtly, sometimes rapidly and dramatically. Indeed, "reproduction" is a bad word. Sexual organisms do not *re*produce. They produce genuinely new organisms—unique creatures, like nothing ever seen before, like nothing that will be seen again. Only asexual cloning is literal *re*production. All this makes education a difficult and distinctive game. Its most difficult task is teaching people to make informed and thoughtful decisions.

And this brings up the whole question of how cultures encode information and rules.

8

Culture: Ecology in a Wider Context

Culture can be seen as a way out of the limits set by information processing. Culture, at its best, institutionalizes sensible, corrective views—usually through the negotiation of various individuals and groups within society. Unfortunately, at its worst, culture institutionalizes the mistakes, and makes them that much harder to correct.

The key question is how particular beliefs about resources become accepted as canonical in particular cultures. In other words, the question is, Why do *societies*—groups of people with specific social organizations—accept particular beliefs as part of their *cultures,* their accepted repertoires of learned, shared behaviors and texts? Societies and cultures exist only as emergent phenomena, without the flesh-and-blood reality of individual people, but they have their independent structures and dynamics. However, they cannot act or think—only individuals can do that.

Conservation is basically *about people,* not about resources. It is a problem in resource use, but the real problem is not managing the resources but managing the people. We know, more or less, how to manage the resources—at least how to conserve them. The problem is how to motivate people to do it. Motivation is an emotional matter. Knowledge is necessary, but knowledge without emotional drive does not produce action. It produces the detached sage, whose knowledge may be potentially useful but whose actions are confined to arcane trivia.

World Bank expert Michael Cernea has recently observed that "social variables are not just an 'aspect,' another side of a basically technical issue, but rather lie at the structural core of environmental problems."[1] Cernea opposes both psychological and economic reductionism in explaining environment use. He points out that social institutions actually direct the managing; we must look at actors, social contracts, cultural and social authority systems, and rules— more or less what Marx called the "relations of production" and the "social superstructure." This being the case, environmental economists have recently become acutely conscious of social systems and institutions.[2]

Case studies show that belief systems become accepted and propagated if they seem to fit empirical reality, and if they fit well enough with the rest of the culture to seem consistent or coherent with it—in other words, if they are useful. Overgeneralization, oversharpening of distinction, and positive illusions account for most of the distortions and mistakes that get encoded. The closer a belief is to empirically observed fact and daily practice, the more accurate it is. Beliefs based on long chains of inference are apt to be highly distorted. Beliefs about everyday but unimportant matters can also be far from truth.

Conversely, highly important but quite abstract and inferential beliefs are subject to a great deal of feedback from the real world, and often move toward accuracy over time. This applies, inter alia, to conservation. The Maori of New Zealand seem to have exterminated the moas and perhaps other species and to have introduced much negative environmental change in their pioneer days.[3] Yet, modern Maori culture presents a classic case of conservation religiously represented.[4] Evidently, the Maori learned from experience.[5] Other Polynesian pioneers overused the Easter Island forests and exterminated many bird species on a wide variety of islands.[6] However, later Polynesian cultures were excellent managers.[7]

Change can also be for the worse. Often this is due to modernization, but J. R. McNeill, in a superb and unique study, *The Mountains of the Mediterranean World,* shows that deterioration began early and worsened during various times in history.[8] The worst damage to the montane environments did indeed take place under modern capitalism, but damage was apparent in the days of the Roman Empire.[9]

In spite of all that is said today about the reality and rapidity of change in "traditional" cultures, we often assume they never learned anything. This, clearly, is not the case.

However, it is also true that, due to the human propensity for positive illusions, the more important a realm of knowledge may be, the more subject it is to distortion by wishful thinking. It seems that most knowledge is either so arcane as to be easily distorted by ignorance, or so important as to be easily distorted by "remolding it closer to the heart's desire."

The major corrective is one that has attracted the attention of too few philosophers: simple interaction with reality. Marx and, especially, Engels stressed this. Unfortunately, they dressed it up in gratuitous jargon about "dialectics," and so it has been ignored. Latter-day philosophers, especially phenomenologists and postmodernists, appear to talk as if they know only of the viewer's first conception of an object. Indeed, a first impression is typically incomplete or wrong. Experience, however, can be corrective. Reality fights back against mistaken impressions. As Marx said, the nonswimmer who *believes* he will not drown is in for a rude shock if he falls into the water.

One major problem for modern environmental management is that urban life decouples most of us from direct experience with ecological reality, and overspecialization decouples even the rural workers from a broad ecological view.

In the specific case of biotic resource management, daily experience with sustainable and unsustainable resource use strategies acts to keep people realistic. Wishful thinking—"it won't hurt to take just one . . ."—plays against this. The more important the resource, the more pressures exist in both directions.

Culture is a great feedback system—either negative or positive. Typically, for everyone distorting the truth in one direction, there is someone else distorting it in another. Thus a rough balance results. In the United States, farmers overconfident about the quality and safety of our food are offset by highly reactive consumers who dread even the slightest contamination, and a semi-rational balance results. It does not follow from careful attention to fact so much as from negotiation. The apple scare of the 1980s stands as a case in point: farmers were not at all concerned about the pesticide Alar; consumers over-reacted to insignificant doses of it; a more or less reasonable compromise eventually emerged after a great deal of unnecessary rhetoric. Initially careful and rational responses would have been preferable, but we can expect only so much in the real world.

Culture can also promulgate positive feedbacks. Through interaction, people in cultural groups develop sanctions for good behavior. Artists stimulate each other to do better work. Scientists discuss their findings, and thus get both ideas and inspiration for further work.

Unfortunately, not all "positive" feedback is positive in its effects. People can whip each other into mass hysteria, often in racist or chauvinist causes. As we have seen, this is often associated with fear and insecurity in the body politic.

Bad results can stem from even less evil impulses. Indeed, in resource management, simple mistakes and hopeful dreams may do much more damage. Environmentalists have been quick to blame resource depletion on "selfish greed," but sometimes it is done for the best of motives. Subsidizing the family home and the family farm have been standbys of American democracy; these subsidies have sometimes produced pernicious effects on the environment, such as urban sprawl and overuse of chemicals on economically nonviable farms.

Social mechanisms sometimes produce an insensate desire for some one item because of its high prestige, with consequent unbearable pressure on that resource. Nothing could save the sea otter and the beaver from overexploitation in the nineteenth century. Prices were so high that the animals were hunted to extinction in many areas. (A valuable but inessential item is the least likely to be saved; people are more careful with subsistence matters and have no incentive to destroy trivially valued ones.) Even worse is the modern destruction of tropical forests to make cattle pasture. In our beef-obsessed society, the thousands of benefits of the tropical forests are economically outweighed by cheap (and unhealthy) steak and hamburger. A wholly irrational and inaccurate East Asian belief in the healing virtue of bears' gall is now causing the extermination of most of the bear species of the world.

Cultural beliefs, then, cannot be taken as necessarily right, wrong, or indifferent. In recent years there has developed a truly ridiculous controversy between people who idealize "the primitives" as happy children of nature who are "natural" ecologists[10] and those who see them as foolish squanderers incapable of learning from experience. In fact, as we have seen, traditional people are like modern people: they try to make the best of the situations they are in; they make mistakes; they usually (but not always) learn from the mistakes. They are careful when they have to be and often careless when they can get away with it.[11]

We have examined certain Northwest Coast Native American management strategies that were effective. Other northern peoples also had good conservation strategies,[12] and these appear to have been very ancient, though there is a minority opinion that they developed after the whites came.[13] (This latter opinion is unlikely, because of the extremely widespread nature of the institutions in question, their grounding in Native religion, and their lack of resemblance to white codes.) The California Indians also managed their lands intensively and successfully.[14] They reduced a few vulnerable species to rarity—the abalone is one example[15]—but preserved and even tended most of their subsistence stocks.

Good environmental management is, in fact, reported for most Native American peoples[16] and for many other groups around the world.[17] On the other hand, many South American groups that had small populations in vast tracts of forest did not practice conservation or have the concept; they had no need of it—until recently.[18] Near Eastern peoples overgrazed their lands even before cities arose.[19]

The immediate need is to document actual systems of management, with the entire ideological apparatus included as part of the picture.[20] We must learn from societies with long experience in managing resources, but we cannot expect any societies—ours or others'—to have all the solutions. We need all the help we can get, so it is extremely shortsighted and foolish to dismiss traditional peoples out of hand. On the other hand, we can move forward only by pooling existing knowledge. No group, traditional or transformed, has a perfect relationship with its environment.

The optimal way to deal with local knowledge, then, is not usually to accept it as gospel—but certainly not to dismiss it. Billie DeWalt has recently provided long-needed guidelines on how to combine, creatively, local knowledge with outside ideas. He advocates consultation at all levels and stages, and use of modern scientific advances to supplement or complement local techniques, always assessing the resulting package for ecological effects.[21] The emphasis here is on actually working with local producers. They are treated as the experts they are, but neither they nor outside experts are regarded as omniscient.

Another red herring that is typically raised in such arguments is "cultural relativism." Cultural relativism is a standard anthropological working principle. It has been attacked, in some quarters, under the false assumption that cultural relativity is a claim that we should make no value judgments about particular cultural institutions. No one actually believes any such thing. No anthropologist has championed human sacrifice, slavery, or genocide.

Cultural relativism, in reality, is the principle of looking at cultural beliefs and practices in their own terms, in relation to their cultures.[22] Anthropologists as individuals retain the right to judge the general benefit of a particular cultural practice.

Thus, I am trying to analyze Chinese medicine in its own terms, as a cultural system. I try to see how the beliefs in the medical value of bears' gall and *Platycodon* plants fit into the system, and why they are logical and reasonable in terms of that system. I am *also*—as a quite different enterprise—seeing what effect Chinese medical beliefs have on biotic resources. I am *also*—in yet a third mode—interested in their actual, demonstrable value in treating disease. To some extent, I judge them accordingly. A wholly erroneous belief that endangers a species, such as the beliefs in the medical value of bears' gall, pangolin scales, and rhinoceros horn, has to be seen as pure cost in the modern world. On the other hand, more or less accurate perceptions of the medical values of some herbs, such as the *Platycodon,* have led to their preservation, cultivation, and propagation. Culturally, all these are interesting beliefs. Medically, they are all under study by those more qualified than I. Ecologically, they have different values.

Some of the conflict about the conservationist nature of traditional people has come about when biologists, who typically want perfect protection of all species, argue with agronomists and anthropologists, who are usually more interested in sustainable management as it relates to people. Balancing these two divergent goals can be very difficult. Conrad Kottak and Alberto Costa have provided the best insight to date, arguing that only enlightened cooperation between international agencies and local peoples can provide any hope.[23] They point out that expertise at all levels is necessary. Local peoples may not have the knowledge or capability to stop an ecological decline they recognize. Outside experts may not have any idea of the social and economic pressures operating in the area, and thus will have little sense of why local people make the decisions they do. Constant dialogue and mutual accommodation is often necessary.

The record of the Maya provides a case of both successes and failures. For five thousand years, the Maya have managed to make a reasonably good living from a very difficult environment. For a thousand years, they supported one of the greatest and most unique and creative civilizations of the premodern world. This civilization collapsed in the ninth century A.D., with ecological damage showing clearly in the archaeological record. The fall of the Classic Maya civilization seems to have been due in large part to escalating wars,[24] but environmental deterioration, no doubt caused in large measure by the wars, occurred in tandem. Wars probably destroyed the orchards, carefully built-up fields, and complex water catchment systems on which ancient Maya cities were based. In any event, the population crashed, wars became more trivial, forest refuges protected isolated villages, and Maya culture stabilized at a lower level of complexity. Evidently, ancient Maya society was able to manage its environment well enough to keep a civilization alive for a very long time. Where it failed was in controlling war. Uncontrolled aggression seems to have gradually led to scorched-earth policies that ruined the great cities. Perhaps vitally important orchards were cut, waterworks disrupted, or high-yield but delicate crop varieties lost.

Similarly, the civilizations of the ancient Near East, from the Sumerians to the Roman Empire, are no longer with us, and the biggest reason may well be ecological.[25] Deforestation, erosion, and deterioration of pastureland and farmland are sadly obvious in the archaeological and historical record. Long ago, agronomist Sheldon Judson found that up to a meter of soil had eroded away since classical times in the core areas of the Roman Empire.[26] If these factors did not bring down these states, they certainly created economic stresses that exacerbated a broad economic decline.

Culture, thus, is not a straitjacket or an unchanging body of tradition. It is the result of countless human decisions. Culturally coded knowledge systems are "emergent phenomena": they are not totally predictable from those countless decisions. But these systems do not decide, nor do they act. Only individuals (alone or in organizations and groups) can do that. Actions, and the results of actions, lead to changes. Unexpected outcomes, in particular, make people conscious of their plans, and may make them invoke new plans. A broken traffic light makes us aware of our rules and options. Similarly, the breakdown of a resource utilization system forces people to take notice, and they sometimes develop institutions to motivate better management.

Basic to accounting for ecological belief systems is the perception that they are not determined by strictly materialist concerns. I agree with Marvin Harris and Eric Alden Smith that one should start with the direct material costs and benefits of a system.[27] However, I do not find that one can ever stop there. Harris has accounted for India's non-slaughter of cows by appeal to the usefulness of the cow—a theory already adumbrated by Al-Biruni in the 1100s.[28] Granted the cow is useful; Americans use almost as many cows as Indians, and take much better care of them, but do not worship them. The difference is explained not by material interest, but by India's general pattern of religious nonviolence, as Martin Orans has found through careful historical study.[29] I would also hazard a guess that the Indians felt a need to involve people emotionally in communal care of cattle. Ordinary economic interest suffices for Americans. In India, however, cattle were sacred long before they were protected. Cattle protection arose as population increased and the dangers of theft, raiding, and bad care escalated. Emotional involvement with cattle rose apace.

Eric Alden Smith applies the materialist calculus to Inuit hunters in northern Canada.[30] He shows that they hunt efficiently—they go after the resource that provides the most meat. However, close reading of his book reveals that most of the hunters make their real money by wage work and carving tourist souvenirs, and could get more calories by buying bread than by hunting. They hunt because they like the meat—their culture has long encoded a fondness for wild game and fish. Even the hunters who live by their quest must piece out the odds by trading or selling meat to others who work for pay but want the meat for cultural reasons. In a world of guns and snowmobiles, hunting costs a lot of money, and cannot be justified by materialistic economics. However, Smith is certainly right in his claim that we should start with the material side, both because it is highly important and because it is, after all, the natural thing to look at first when one looks at a hunting society. If you don't understand the game animals and the chase, you certainly will not understand anything else about such a group.

However, as we have seen, no resource management system is comprehensible without looking at the institutions of a society—rules, ideology, scientific knowledge, and all.[31] Historical accident and incident, and the logic of the social order, both affect the system.

The beaver example cited earlier makes a case that is extreme enough to be particularly revealing. In the 1830s, a craze for beaver hats swept Europe. The result was the virtual destruction of the world's beavers. This led to massive erosion, gullying, and lowering of water tables in many areas. The results are still with us. In the American Southwest, for instance, a vast cycle of gully-cutting, with consequent ruin of rangelands, desertification, and economic decline, began in the late nineteenth century. Quite often, this has been alleviated by building concrete floodways, which have their own environmental costs—so the vicious circle expands. While overgrazing and possibly climate change were involved in this, trapping out the beaver was certainly a cause and may actually have been the main cause. I have observed, in areas where the beaver has been recently reintroduced, the reversal of this deadly cycle. In the San Bernardino Mountains near my home, the upper Santa Ana River has been controlled, turned into a permanent stream bordered by lush meadows, reforested, and otherwise greatly improved by the beavers, *in spite of* extreme drought and massive human damage by logging, roads, recreation, and off-road vehicles. The brief fad for beaver hats caused incalculable damage that has only rarely and locally been reversed.

The other side of the coin is more relevant to our concerns, of course: an "irrational" taste that is ecologically beneficial. Such a taste is found in American bird-watching. Thousands of acres of habitat that would otherwise have been "developed" into wasteland were saved as bird sanctuaries. These acres have now turned out to be invaluable for other reasons: they saved important genetic resources, medicinal plants, new industrial crops, and pollution-absorbing wetlands. An uneconomic, emotional motive led unexpectedly to real economic benefits.

Another example is the Chinese ginkgo tree, saved from extinction as a temple ornamental and minor nut tree. It is now widely valued as a shade tree, nut producer, scientific research resource, and medicinal plant with considerable potential.

Thus it occurs that some resources are saved because people take them as *ends in themselves*. Birds are saved because people want them around. Spectacular scenery, wilderness areas, salmon, and game animals have been saved because people enjoy them or at least enjoy eating them. They are loved; they are cherished ends in themselves. By contrast, saving obscure plants because of potential scientific and medical value, or recycling garbage because it would otherwise pile up and endanger health, are cases of conservation for purely instrumental, "rational" motives.

However, economics and culture usually interact in more complex ways. Let us return to a case considered in several contexts in this book. Americans used to prefer pork to beef and eat little of the latter. After the Civil War, beef became cheap due to expansion on—and from—the Texas range. The rise of the cowboy as the Great American Hero added romance. With both economics and emotion going for it, beef displaced pork, and became the preferred meat of the twentieth century. The vast majority of American households ate it almost every day, and many ate it twice a day. During all this period, cheaper and equally good-quality protein was available from beans and grains. From the 1960s, health concerns became prominent. Beef remained the leading meat, but consumption per capita has declined by about a third. Chicken and fish, seen as more healthful, increased in sales.

Throughout the entire period, it would have been more efficient to use a wider variety of animals and to eat less meat overall. Economics would have dictated far more use of vegetable proteins and cheap fish. But tastes conditioned by late nineteenth century economic and social factors led the vast majority of Americans to act against economic and medical self-interest. The result was a cattle-dominated economy that has done incalculable ecological harm. Unlike many environmentalists, I would not phase out the cow. The problem is not cattle, but overstocking of cattle. I would simply propose instead that people act in their economic and medical self-interest. If they did, the cow would be too rare to do much damage.

A countercase is seen in South Chinese rice agriculture. For similarly complex and not wholly rational historic reasons, the South Chinese became devoted to rice. Traditional rice agriculture, based on water management in paddy fields, builds up the soil, extends farmland seaward, recycles nutrients, requires a varied and species-rich agro-ecosystem, benefits many wild organisms, and in general is both ecologically sane and capable of feeding dense populations.[32] Most of China's worst famines were in the north—outside the rice zone—though the rice zone had a much higher population density. Rice agriculture had its costs—deforestation was and is the worst—but it succeeded in feeding billions of people for thousands of years.

In these cases, ecological effects are, to varying degrees, the unintended consequences of strategies based on cultural tastes.

Culture serves to emphasize certain things and reduce others to the background. It also serves to create wants. The fad for beaver hats and the American taste for beef were culturally created wants that had devastating ecological impact. On the other hand, the world "subculture" of bird-watchers has bonded together those who love birds into a powerful force for saving environments. Obviously, saving the environment depends on making love of the environment a "foregrounded" concern in all cultures.

In anthropology, there has been a long-standing debate over how tightly structured human thought may be. Recently, Pierre Bourdieu has emerged in something of a middle ground.[33] His ideas are not new, though he has coined some new terms. His success and popularity in anthropology are due to his providing a sane alternative to cultural irrationalism, narrow material or individual rational choice, and extreme structuralism. He sees people as learning a great deal from their social surroundings; much of what they learn is half-understood, or overlearned to the point of being unconsciously invoked, like grammatical rules. This mess of cultural stuff is blended into, and reinterpreted in terms of, their personal dispositions. The result is the *habitus:* a persistent collection of ideas and preferences. It is not a neatly structured display shelf, but rather a typical garage, with all kinds of useful items mixed in with old junk and unread newspapers. Like Lévi-Strauss's *bricoleur,* people then make their independent decisions on the basis of this mass of loosely structured mental material. They do a lot of improvising, and a lot more reacting to other people's improvisations.

Social pressures lead people to seek new knowledge or to stick with the tried and true. Social pressures guide us to be curious about nature or to study machines instead. Social pressures lead us to be curious about processes or about mere facts alone, curious about ultimate causes or quite indifferent to them. Conforming to a subculture can make us seem to move away from conformity to the dominant society while we are actually serving its interests. Paul Willis's classic study of English working-class youth reminds us that society can manipulate rebellion to make it serve the very social order that the rebels attack.[34] The general case has been argued by Bourdieu and Passeron:[35] Education reproduces society, complete with any evils therein. They argue, for instance, that the lecture system teaches passivity rather than knowledge. Certainly, we all know that the appreticeship system is better.[36] Robert Orr argues—surely with reason—that if we injected emotion into the cold textbooks, we would arouse more interest.[37]

With these ideas in mind, the key question of this chapter may be rephrased: How do culture and society construct or embed institutions that can permit management as a social choice?

In *The Cement of Society* Elster discusses the value of social norms for facilitating action.[38] Elster defines social norms as those codes that have no obvious function, except to show belonging—and the purest social norms do not even do that, but are quite unconscious and arbitrary, such as wearing coat sleeve buttons or using the grammatical rules of one's subculture or dialect. There is a sort of continuum from these through useful but somewhat arbitrary codes (everyday politeness) to clearly desirable but highly conventionalized acts (moral codes, bargaining rules). Elster shows how rules and conventions are necessary to bargaining, especially collective bargaining; the process would be total chaos if it were simply people arguing for their individual self-interests. He thus proves that society cannot run on individual rationality alone. It is, in the end, cemented together by a great deal of arbitrary convention. (Elster doesn't say it, but the extreme of this is language: How could a language possibly exist without arbitrary convention? Everyone has to agree that "dog" is "dog" and "cat" is "cat," and that questions end with a rising inflection, and that "dog" shall be pronounced "dawg" and not "diplodocus." If everybody decided to create a personal phonemic and grammatical system according to what felt most rational in terms of narrow self-interest, no one could agree enough to talk. On the other hand, if everyone agreed on everything, there would be nothing to talk about.)

The applications of all this to resource management are straightforward. Whoever sets the rules, by whatever standard, the real problem comes when people decide whether to accept or reject the rules. In much of the world, hunting regulations and park protection are dead letters. Indeed, in Costa Rica, there are professional squatters—people who make their living by invading protected land, destroying its natural cover, and selling the resulting *de facto* opened land to actual farmers when the government has given up on it. Costa Rica has the highest percentage of protected land of any Latin

American country, but much of that land has gone to these professional wreckers.

There has been a strong tendency in recent years to move increasingly toward command-and-control strategies for "saving" the environment. Governments pass laws and set up armed enforcement agencies.

The large and increasing body of anthropological evidence suggests that this strategy is dangerously wrongheaded. Successful environmental practices around the world depend on *grassroots-level management and moral suasion*. Typically, the people actually dealing with the resource are the ones who set immediate management goals and practices. They plan rationally, but in terms of the wider moral and ethical systems of their societies.

The very strong implication, for modern resource management, is that *higher levels of management should set general goals and back them up by moral suasion* but should *leave actual management to the people on the ground*. This is not wholly adequate. It will not work for pollution that blows over a whole continent or for species that migrate from Canada to Argentina. Here international laws and policies are obviously necessary.

But, even in these cases, *local communities must be considered*. Whooping cranes, which migrate from Canada to Texas and Mexico, have been saved by a combination of international treaty and local suasion. Communities all along the route of the cranes not only have to know that the big white birds need special protection—they also have to want to protect them. By contrast, game in South Mexico is theoretically protected by the government, but local enforcement agents share a values system in which immediate needs of local people are ranked well above survival of game species. There is charity and even nobility in this view, though in the long run it hurts the people (who are often deprived of their only meat source) as well as the animals. Here, the laws are adequate; but they clash with local cultural norms, and no one—until recently—has tried to deal with the resulting tragic problems.

Getting rules actually institutionalized in a society—actually passed and actually accepted—is thus very much an emotional process. It involves deep feelings, which may be socialized as moral responsibility, or religion, or politics. To these we now turn.

9

In and Out of Institutions

Institutions, including a society's structure from kinship to kingship, exist for a purpose. That purpose, as Douglass North points out, is often to lower transaction costs.[1] In other words, they make it easier for people to get together to act. (At least, that is what they are supposed to do; sometimes they make it harder.) Usually they are created to make it easier to do something that people were doing already, but often they are created to satisfy a whole new want. By "institutions," writers like North understand the rules of society, written or unwritten. The actual organizations are specific instances of institutions informing people and situations; the general principles and laws behind the organizations are the institutions. Other writers, of course, use the word "institutions" to include actual organizations, such as prisons and colleges.

The discussion that follows is general enough to avoid conflicts over definitions. It is not intended to provide an adequate account of institutions or of environmental economics. It is intended solely to extend my comments on human information processing, and thereby raise some questions about our current economic interpretations. These questions follow from this book's central premise that humans are emotional, and that emotion often displaces rational calculation. This is, of course, the point classically made by Max Weber; it keeps being rediscovered by institutional economists like Douglas North.[2]

The success of a given society at building institutions thus is related to its success at ecological management. This is obvious when the institutions in question are related to conservation. It is not so obvious, but actually more important, when the institutions are more general in scope and purpose, serving the society at large.

The most extreme and spectacular case is that of highly centralized, authoritarian polities. It is safe to say that such polities are always a catastrophe for the environment. The farther control gets from the local people who actually benefit or lose by resource management, and the more control is vested in people remote from the scene, the worse the management. These people are decoupled from the results of their actions.[3] They do not pay the costs of their mistakes; therefore, they do not change their behavior. This is reasonable enough, and it has been observed in countless cases.[4] The tragedy of the USSR is an extreme case. Soviet writers (and their Western sympathizers) had argued for decades that centralized planning saved the environment from self-interest, ignorant misuse, capitalist tragedies of the commons, and so on. We now know differently. China, less centralized and overplanned, has suffered less, but has still done roughly as much damage to its environment in fifty years of Communism as it did in five thousand years of feudalism.[5]

The countercase is, of course, that of societies so weakly organized that even local communities have little control over resource use. Cheaters and misusers proliferate. This is most typical of frontier situations, as in the settlement by Europeans of America and of Polynesia, and of at least some native Polynesian settlers too.[6] It is also found when societies break down or simply fail to develop effective social regulation. This is a much rarer case than many writers believe. Close inspection of most cases of resource abuse discloses not a failure of institutions, but quite the opposite: effective institutions dedicated to shortsighted overuse.

Ultimately, the institutional problem boils down to one of specifying the costs of production on those who benefit. Resource mismanagement cases can be described, in general, as cases in which someone (or some group) benefits but can pass on the costs of those benefits to other people. This is the point first made by Ronald Coase,[7] and subsequently developed in detail by Earl Murphy.[8] Thus, person or group A gets a disproportionately good benefit/cost ratio, while B has a disproportionately bad one. The textbook case of this is river pollution. The upstream users get pure water and pollute it. The downstream users face pollution through no fault of their own.

Such things as overfishing can also be described in these terms. A tragedy of the commons occurs when early, nonconserving fishers take too much, leaving later or conservationist fishers with nothing. The latter are paying the costs of the sins of the former; the former are getting all the benefits. The beaver trappers of the 1830s captured the benefits of overdrawing the beaver resource—and very small benefits they were, too. The modern ranches and cities pay the costs—literally thousands of times the benefits, producing what may be the worst benefit/cost ratio in the history of resource misuse. On Long Valley Creek in northeastern California and on the upper Santa Ana River in the southern part of that state, one sees eroded sandy banks, and the stream often dries up—except where beavers have been reintroduced. Over the years I have watched the renewal, as the beavers produce permanent ponds, lush vegetation, and a restoration of stable banks. Wildlife, grazing, and water conservation have all benefited where the beavers have reestablished themselves. The beavers cause concern by eating a few young trees, but without the big rodents, floods soon take out *all* the trees.

Lack of specification of costs also lies behind the insane discount rates that characterize much of the modern world. Enormous future benefits—not even very distant future benefits—are routinely sacrificed for the tiniest and most insignificant of current returns. Tropical rainforests are cut in order to run a few scrub cattle for a year or two—until the soil is gone and a desert is created. Endangered species with enormous potential are exterminated for very small local profits. The problem in these cases is that the people doing the cutting or exterminating are not in a position to capture the future benefits of good management *or* to pay the costs of bad management. At this point, society has to intervene and provide some means of compensation. So far, the transaction costs of doing so have often been unbearably high. Moreover, the voluntary conservation organizations that try to stop the damage are forced to pay all these transaction costs. We therefore conclude that new institutions are needed. Bargaining and sanctioning are both in need of better institutionalization.

Naturally, *A* fights tooth and nail to prevent specification of costs. *B* has to be in a position to fight harder. This is possible only under certain circumstances:

1. *B* has to have legal recourse: standing to sue, ability to vote, or recourse to regulatory institutions.
2. *B* has to be suffering enough to make the recourse worth invoking. (If lawsuits cost a lot, *B* will endure substantial costs in silence.)
3. *B* has to be able to enforce the legal recourse on *A*. (It's too late to sue the beaver hat industry. In an election, if *A* has more votes than *B*, *B* is in trouble.)
4. *B* has to be safe in doing so. (In many countries, *A* is usually the government or someone in league with it, and *B* is often jailed, tortured, or killed for protesting.)

5. There has to be an impartial judge. (The U.S. Supreme Court has occasionally been deliberately "packed" to favor extractive business, as in the early 1900s and again in the 1980s.)

This list provides one obvious explanation for the bad record of authoritarian regimes: they do not provide any of the institutions mentioned here.

The same is true of any unjust situation. Racism and prejudice set up the stigmatized groups to be dumping grounds. Robert Bullard has thoroughly investigated and treated this point in his definitive research on toxic waste disposal in the United States.[9] John Bodley has done the same for those who pay the costs of resource overuse.[10] This is known in high places; Vice President Al Gore has traced out its implications.[11] Social inequality and injustice create the situations that permit some people to be victimized and deny them recourse.[12] Indeed, such economic motives often keep victimization going. If the powerful have rights and the weak do not, then the weak will be abused environmentally as well as in other ways.

Thus, an unjust or ethnically polarized society is inevitably worse at environmental management than a fair one. In a fair society, everyone has enough recourse to prevent excesses of toxic waste dumping, forest overuse, pollution, and so on. This provides incentives (strong ones) for polluters and destroyers to cease and desist or to improve their behavior. The more unfair the society, the more pollution and waste can be treated as "externalities"—in effect, passed on to the politically powerless.[13] Similarly, more and more resources have to be redirected toward maintaining "law and order" and keeping the social infrastructure functioning. The society can collapse if these costs become insupportable.[14] Thus, matters such as education and ecologically sound behavior require a more or less equable society with a moral base that recognizes the importance of long-term and wide-flung considerations.

In the now-vanished frontier societies of old, some system costs were true externalities. They could be simply ignored. Nature would take care of the mess. Today, in a crowded world, no such situations remain. Pollution, waste, destruction, and erosion cannot be escaped. Even trivial sources of pollution can be health risks now—Los Angeles has had to regulate backyard barbecues because of the smog danger. "Externalities" exist only insofar as some humans are disenfranchised, and can be made to suffer.

Outside of authoritarian and racist states, the most common problem is one of dispersed cost. If A is a small group getting lots of benefits, and B a very large group each member of which is paying quite small costs, then it often happens that no one in B protests. This is true even if the total costs to B are many times the total benefits to *A*. This is notoriously common in pollution situations. It also occurs in such cases as the exhaustion of one among many fisheries; consumers switch to other fish unless the fish in question is culturally preferred. The United States saved salmon and trout but has not done much for gar and paddlefish.

This is only one of the problems with cost/benefit accounting.[15] Cost/benefit accounting is subject to all the information-processing biases and mistakes chronicled throughout this book.[16]

Government has usually been the institution of recourse in environmental matters. Laws restricting fish catch, hunting, deforestation, and pollution are universal (if frequently ineffective). Direct governmental management of reserves, refuges, and parks is also very old, and has increased in the twentieth century. There are problems with this approach. Governments cannot solve all the problems. Big governments tend to get out of touch with local conditions and with the people on the ground. Governments are also apt to be too soft-hearted, or under too much political pressure, to phase out ecologically destructive but politically popular programs. Big dams and subsidized agribusiness[17] provide some cases in point. Dams and farms tend to become uneconomic when they are unecological, for obvious reasons, but governments keep them going at a loss.

Thus, there has recently been increasing interest in returning power to the grassroots. Local management has been revived as a serious option.[18] Under this philosophy, communities that actually depend on the resources in question have a major (but not exclusive) share in managing them. Of this more below.

Free-market approaches are also receiving much more serious attention than in the past.[19] In this sense, the "free market" is not the unrestrained rape, looting, and pillage that American environmentalists and anti-environmentalists agree in calling "free enterprise." (The former execrate it, the latter idealize it.) The "free market" of people like Terry Anderson and Donald Leal is a very different thing. It is a special institution that requires full government support. It is an economic arrangement in which individuals have rights to resources (property rights, in a broad sense) and have equal standing before the law. They thus have opportunities to use resources profitably, but also have the right to sue others who damage their resource holdings. This, theoretically, effects a balance, via the familiar "Invisible Hand." The landholder profits by using resources in the most efficient, sustainable manner. Anyone hurt by externalities (pollution, overfishing) can sue.

Anderson and Leal point out that the diffuse, small-scale, bottom-up, resource user–managed world that results from "free-market environmentalism" is like a natural ecosystem, while government is not: "Both the scientific management approach and the societal adaptation approach to sustainable development violate basic principles of ecology. It is impossible to concentrate knowledge about all of the possible variations in an ecosystem, especially if the ecosystem is taken to mean the global environment . . . [or] seek static solutions to dynamic problems. . . . Information about the environment is so diffuse that a small group of experts cannot manage the planet as an ecosystem. Individuals must be relied upon to process time- and place-specific information."[20] This, of course, applies also to local communities that depend on local resources.[21] They have more opportunity to gather information and manage wisely than individuals do.

In practice, of course, this is a difficult condition to create. The Invisible Hand is a mystical, even religious, concept—more so, perhaps, than the dragons in the hills or the magic of the land otter. In real-market situations, inequalities in power quickly lead to unfairness. Moreover, there is no guarantee that long-term interests will prevail over short-term ones, though the cited authors all maintain that long-term interests are better served than under other plans. Most important of all, the government must maintain, regulate, and umpire the free market—by enforcing and encoding property rights, judging suits, guaranteeing political freedom and equality, and preventing total takeover of resources by the most politically powerful. Thus, the extreme free-market position seems self-destroying.

Such arguments are currently hotly debated. International free trade (or approximations thereto) has been particularly contentious, possibly because the extreme libertarian position is still viable, as it is not within the nations themselves. Free trade has sparked major clashes in several journals recently.[22] No one seems to have won these debates conclusively, but there seems a rough consensus that markets by themselves cannot be adequate regulators, for reasons both pragmatic and theoretical.[23] "Free-market environmentalism" can serve a function by informing the debate, but other options need to be considered, as even the most narrowly economistic writers are admitting.[24]

This brings government back in, but perhaps in a more effective way. For government to set taxes on pollution, or standards for pollution, the government must be very responsive. Not only must it pass effective laws, but it must change them very rapidly, when new pollutants or new industries appear. This problem is alleviated if government merely sets the ground rules for individual action. If this fails, variable taxes at least provide some measure of economic incentive.

However, strict rules rather than economic incentives are necessary if the costs of pollution are inordinately high—as, for example, in the case of lead, which causes massive brain damage to humans. In such cases the free-market argument breaks down. The social costs of supporting millions of brain-damaged children are bad enough; the morality of permitting such a situation to arise is more serious still.

It is often forgotten that Adam Smith inveighed against mercantilism, the ancestor of monopoly capitalism and giant multinational conglomerates. He saw the Invisible Hand operating only in situations where many firms competed more or less as equals. His name is now invoked to excuse predatory rip-offs by giant monopolistic firms with preferential government backing; he is probably turning in his grave.

So far, no government has been forbearing enough to allow a real free market to exist. (Hong Kong under the British may have come closest, but it wasn't very close. British preferential treatment of whites and of rich Chinese as opposed to poor saw to that. Even so, Hong Kong's economic growth amazed the world. Unfortunately, so did its levels of pollution.)

It is in such cases that cultural institutions such as religion come into their own. Religion can provide an emotionally compelling moral argument and an institution that carries that argument. Religion can also act in the opposite direction, by creating despised and therefore victimized pariah groups (Jews in medieval Europe, burakumin in Japan, etc.). Much depends on the teachings of the religion and the integrity of its practitioners. However, there is a key point here: many other things—racism, ethnic hate, and so on—can define pariah groups, but *only* an emotionally compelling, culturally accepted moral institution can help the weak, justify a new institution, or motivate behavior. Laws cannot, for laws can be bent or ignored. Governments can, up to a point, but not when the government is itself the offender. (Rarely, *B* can effectively appeal to one government agency against another, but usually through the claim of wider moral standards.)

The weak have many resistance strategies, including a sort of social jiujitsu in which they use the strong against themselves, but these flourish only in a moral ground.[25] Religion often provides the strong with an excuse for abuse of power, but it also provides the poor with an ideology of resistance. Other political codes do not. Democracy at least gives them a voice, but gives power to the majority, thus making difficult the case of an out-voted minority. Here we must carefully separate literal democracy—majority rule—from American-style democracy, whose concept of minority rights is firmly rooted in religion and civil morality rather than political tradition. (The Founding Fathers denied the vote to slaves, non-whites, women, and the poor; the changes since their time owe much to religious activists, from the abolitionists to Martin Luther King.)

With fair recourse and with institutions that mobilize people against abuses, the less powerful can look out for their own interests. If this happens, costs of production will be specified on the producers (and ultimately the consumers). Sustainable or reasonable use will become economically necessary, or at least economically attractive.

In short, fairness, equality and recourse for the weak are more important to resource management than any directly conservationist actions. This is a point that has been made rather often in the relevant literature.[26] It needs to be made even more strongly.

All this, however, is premised on the assumption that people know the value of a resource and are willing to fight for it or spend money on it. (If they can't buy it, they can contribute to campaigns to save it through legal action.) If a resource has been chronically undervalued, *and* poorly specified in terms of capturing what value is recognized, a whole array of institutions need to be invoked to protect it. This is the case with wetlands.[27] It is more serious with endangered species, which can be exterminated before anyone has found out what values they have. It is probable that we have exterminated plants with potential value in treating cancer, AIDS, and other problematic conditions.

It is possible to develop a number of plans and schemes for environmental management that are based on principles very different from those above. One of the best examples is the work of John Dryzek.[28] Dryzek classified and evaluated various types of institutional arrangements according to their success in dealing with ecological issues. He defines an "ecological rationality" in which people focus on maximizing ecological benefits (by analogy with terms like "market rationality" in the sense of being as rational as possible about the workings of the market). He sees a need for ecologically rational institutions to further homeostasis (negative feedback), coordination, flexibility, robustness, and resilience. Certainly the common-property management groups show these traits. He then evaluates standard types of institutions— markets, command-and-control bureaucracies, law, moral suasion, grassroots organizations, and others—in regard to those five traits, and finds all of them wanting. He proposes (rather tentatively) an "open society" in which people get together to formulate institutions at all levels of management—from grassroots to worldwide. He stresses the need for people to keep reviewing and revising these institutions.

Dryzek is strongly skeptical of moral suasion because of its tendency to dogmatism. On the whole, one can only agree, but one is also tempted to ask how the open and self-reflexive society is to keep from turning to mush. Some sort of general pattern of guidelines, values, or overall system rules will have to guide the whole process of reviewing and revising, or the society could redefine itself out of the whole ecology game. This brings us back to the need for traditions and for an overarching code defining moral responsibility.

There is another institution not considered by Dryzek: the institutionalized business of collecting knowledge. The ways of waging science are relevant. The search for knowledge is inevitably a part of all human life. All societies have science. All have generalization procedures that routinely turn individual knowledge into culturally constructed knowledge; all culture is generalization. All have large knowledge bases and specialized experts. Even the simplest hunting-gathering groups have their expert hunters and their herbalists. The differences between their scientific traditions are due in large part to the ways that science is institutionalized.

In the Western world, science developed a unique form during the Renaissance. Science today has become a vast enterprise, with its own culture and secrets. This has created obvious problems. The dispassionate quest for truth is alive and well, but a great deal of modern science has little to do with it. The environmental cause, like other causes, has suffered from bad science. In particular, there has been a lack of scientific attention to organisms and ecosystems. Biology has tended recently to specialize in the molecular and chemical level, and social science has neglected human–environment interaction. There were good reasons for this in the past, but the time has come to focus primarily on ecology and human ecology.

Among the emergent phenomena of societies are certain simple classes of games. For purposes of resource management, the prisoner's dilemma is particularly famous, but there are some other broad classes of games that need attention.

First, an important distinction can be drawn between zero-sum, positive-sum, and negative-sum games. Most "real games" are zero-sum: if you win, I lose. If we bet a dollar, one of us winds up with two dollars, the other with none. There is zero overall change—merely a redistribution from one person to the other.

In positive-sum games, the game increases the total amount of stuff. A beach competition in sand castle building is a passable example. We begin with nothing but random beach sand, and wind up with several impressive sand castles.

A negative-sum game makes everyone worse off. The fight between the cats of Kilkenny (who ate each other up) was an extreme case.

To some extent, of course, the difference is in the eye of the beholder. A real-world boxing match is, on the face of it, zero-sum; one person wins and one loses. But there are positive-sum aspects—both contestants get some glory—and some negative-sum aspects—both contestants get mashed up.

It is possible to understand whole social policies in this light. The United States was a positive-sum society in the good old days (if those ever existed). Firms competed to develop resources, and everyone got richer, though the resource base was depleted. By the 1980s, we were, as Lester Thurow pointed out, a zero-sum society.[29] By the 1990s, we were a negative-sum society. Real wealth was shrinking, and the rich got richer by making the rest of us very much poorer. Corporate mergers and real estate speculation, rather than productive investment, swallowed up money. Forests were cut and the money lost in paper games; the trees were gone, but there was nothing to show for it.

It has been argued that positive-sum games are typical of the private sector, zero-sum games of politics—politics being all too much like a football game, with a winner, a loser, and no net gain.[30] This is not necessarily true. Private individuals in a poor society without opportunities are the classic zero-sum players.[31] In the United States, the predatory takeovers of the 1980s illustrate negative-sum playing, on a mammoth scale, in the private sector.

The perceived nature of a game has major effects on the psyches of the players. In a positive-sum situation, people naturally tend to be hopeful. A zero-sum society leads to a dog-eat-dog attitude. A negative-sum situation leads to real desperation. People are afraid to cooperate, and tend to become defensive. George Foster developed a model of the "image of limited good": in societies where the total economic pie is constant or shrinking in size, people become more and more defensive, suspicious, envious, and secretive.[32] Foster developed this model from work in Mexico, where a non-growing economy has to accommodate an exploding population, leaving each successive generation with less real wealth per capita. This model has received considerable empirical support—it certainly fits my own observations. Of course, positive illusions guarantee that a chancy, hard-to-predict situation will generally be seen as positive-sum, even when it is not. Only a quite serious negative-sum situation will be perceived as such.

Cutting across this spectrum is the question of cooperation. When should we cooperate and when should we compete? It has been shown, by computer simulation in the "Tit for Tat" program, that when the choice is a simple one of "cooperate or don't cooperate" a player should begin by cooperating, then cooperate when the other player cooperates, and default when the other defaults. This is, indeed, how people usually live their social lives: presume trust and friendliness until these are not reciprocated, then cut the person in question until he or she apologizes and does better. This game gives us a simple model of how to live in the world. The problem with it is that it does not offer much guidance if the other player is apt to kill rather than just default. Thus it has provided little help to international politics or gang warfare. (Hobbesian footnote: it is certainly significant that statecraft and inner-city dope-dealing share an identical game plan.)

Real-world situations tend to favor cooperation or competition. Where it takes the whole village working together to plant the fields and then get in the harvest, cooperation will be favored. Hunting-based societies also tend toward cooperation, because, though people may hunt as individuals, they have to share the meat. One hunter will be lucky one day, another hunter the next; they have to exchange. The United States exemplifies the opposite extreme: a society based on a great deal of competition (as well as a lot of cooperation).

Culture, of course, institutionalizes such matters. Working with children too young to have much to do with economic activity, psychologists such as Spencer Kagan constructed games in which the children can play either "positive-sum" or "negative-sum," depending on how they choose to operate. Village Mexican children, in spite of the Limited Good image, play cooperatively to get a higher total. Anglo-American children play to defeat each other. If given a choice of cooperating so that each child gets a big reward or competing such that the "winner" gets a small reward and the rest get nothing, they will invariably opt for the latter. Urban Mexican children, and Mexican-American children, are intermediate. The Mexican villagers are used to cooperating in agricultural work; Americans are schooled in playing to beat the others.[33] The sad effects of this attitude on American social and economic life in the last twenty years are certainly all too obvious. The recession of the 1990s was caused by many factors, but probably the most important single factor was the behavior of high-flying financiers in the 1980s. Legal changes connected with Reaganomics allowed men like Michael Milken and Charles Keating to enrich themselves at the expense of the system. The losses to the system were far greater than the profits of the financiers.

Now, obviously, a particularly vicious circle can easily be imagined. A fiercely competitive negative-sum game, played by a whole country, can cause people to become more and more angry and defensive. This, of course, makes them more competitive and merciless.

This brings us to Ibn Khaldun's cycles of dynastic rise and fall. Part of his model can be stated in the above terms. A new, rising empire is rather low in population, has lots of resources, and has a spirit of conquest and hope. People cooperate or compete, but in either case they expect to get ahead, and act accordingly. A mature empire moves toward zero-sum: population is expanding, the economy is expanding at something like the same rate, and people are rich but not getting richer. Finally, population keeps growing, resources are overstrained, and the government needs more money to operate. There are more and more poor to support, more and more children to educate, and more and more bureaucrats to pay. People get poorer, and thus more and more angry and defensive—especially about the increasing taxes. The empire breaks down.[34] A Hobbesian war of each against all follows. With luck, a strong leader emerges and puts the country back together (as happened in the American Civil War). All too often the war goes on until the population of the country is so reduced that the survivors have lots of resources, and the cycle starts over again. China's dynastic cycles provide cases in point.

These games are not mere neutral, rational pastimes. They absorb people's lives. They are thus intensely emotionally experienced.

The theories of Foster and Ibn Khaldun bridge from abstract games to real human emotions. The course of empire can be predicted only if we take into account human emotional responses to economic trends. An economist could easily show that a Khaldunian empire need not break down. When the economy begins to stagnate, people should work harder to find new and more efficient ways of doing things, develop new resources, and the like. The problem is that any downturn is apt to bring out defensiveness and destructive competition, not redoubled efforts toward improvement. In a declining economy, it is, apparently, easier (psychologically if not economically) to rip off one's neighbor than to work with him or her. This simple observation goes some way to explaining the rise of fascism in the 1930s depression. The exceptions require special explanation. The United States, for instance, still had a huge and relatively less developed resource base in the 1930s and a good deal of hope and solidarity that was lacking in war-scarred Europe. Even so, polls in the late 1930s showed one-third of Americans supporting Hitler and his policies.

There are several implications of these observations for resource management.

1. Waiting until things are really bad is disastrous. Planning must start when people are hopeful and cooperative—especially when the economy is seen as expanding. Otherwise, the "jobs" argument for resource overuse is overwhelmingly persuasive, and people have little desire to forgo benefits.

2. Resource management being essentially cooperative in nature, conservationists need to further cooperative behavior and ideology in every way possible. The rise of extreme, destructive competitiveness in the United States

is a matter of concern.[35] The solution proposed by sociologist Robert Bellah is to return to a more "communitarian" universe, with communities and firm traditional rules.[36] Bellah's position has been criticized, rather unfairly, by those who fear that "community" automatically implies a hierarchic social order with women and minorities at the bottom. Bellah, however, explicitly seeks an egalitarian communal order. However, it would also be possible to argue for a world no less individualistic (or even more so) but based on responsibility and long-term considerations rather than short-term emotional politics.

3. The austere, ascetic, puritanical attitudes of conservationists of the 1960s and 1970s were a mistake. Fortunately, most of us know better now. "Affluence" and "consumption" have their problems, but no good is accomplished by constantly jawboning people to make themselves poorer. Conservationists should have pointed out that forests, animals, and even beautiful scenery are riches, and that destroying them impoverishes everyone.

4. Especially in the impoverished Third World, the very opposite is true: the only hope for conservation lies in making it a part of economic growth.[37] Even if conservationists succeed in convincing Americans to lower their standard of living to save the environment, they will not be able to succeed with this message among starving inhabitants of the Sahel or of rural Mexico or Brazil. Nor would it be very moral for them to try. For the desperate rural poor of the Third World, self-denial does not provide a viable option.

Too often, rural modernization, in both rich and poor countries, has meant ecological and social devastation.[38] Most readers of this book know the litany: Monocrop culture, agricultural chemicals, unrestricted hunting, massive clearing of land in ill-advised schemes, social disruption, takeover by giant firms or government plans, and the rest. The net result of such "development" is not usually economic benefit, even by the distorted measures criticized by Repetto.[39]

Fortunately, ecologically and economically successful development is not totally unknown in the world. As we have seen, local ways of life are often ecologically reasonable, or can be made so with some changes. Rural China and India would be vastly benefited, for instance, by a massive return to protecting and increasing sacred groves. The modern Maya can intensify their traditional mixed-use plot cultivation, and can systematize and make rigorous their control of game exploitation. A large literature now suggests that this is the best path, and sometimes the only path, for local development.[40]

Planning for this would, among other things, require major changes in current economic accounting methods.[41] Today, subsistence farming and other vitally important local goods are not counted in world economic balance sheets. Damage to the poor is undervalued. If pollution ruins their lives, no one notices. The costs of wasting human potential, through disease, poverty, and oppression, are systematically undercounted—if they are counted at all.[42] Economic benefits of conservation are also valued at a very low rate in too many economic assessments. It is common to ignore even the health benefits of pollution control—let alone the benefits of aesthetics and mental health. Potentially more serious is underestimation of the value of genetic diversity. Destruction of genetic diversity, whether by cutting tropical forests or losing ancient crop varieties in Turkey or Peru, is probably the most serious problem for the future—far more dangerous than even the population explosion or global warming. Yet, when Turkish farmers convert to modern high-yield varieties and we lose thousands of strains of disease-resistant wheat, no one counts the damages. The farmer gets more wheat—that is the only thing counted.

This situation is chronically made worse by subsidies. The United States is not the only country that subsidizes destructive logging. Subsidies for uneconomic, unsustainable logging is common in the tropical rainforests.[43]

Recently, the people of Chiloe Island realized they were sitting on something worth more than all the gold mines in the world. Chiloe Island has more potato varieties than any place of its size on earth. Araucanian Indians—expert farmers and plant breeders—long ago hybridized potatoes with local wild relatives, producing tougher, more adaptable, more resistant strains. Today, plant breeders from around the world flock to Chiloe. After years of graciously handing out free potatoes to seed companies that made millions from them, the good farmers of Chiloe have taken to charging hefty fees for their potatoes. This gives them an incentive to preserve their strains. This simple device may save the world from a repetition of the Potato Famine of 1846–48, which was caused by a blight that affected the one strain of potato that was then widespread in Ireland and Europe. Millions of people died then because of lack of genetic diversity.

Much of the interest in institutional studies of resource management has recently centered on management of common property.[44]

Common property management is often called "common pool resource" management, since totally open-access common goods are not "property." However, "property" in reference to open-access goods calls our attention to the fact that *somebody* has real control over them, and is *abnegating* management— deliberately deciding not to specify.[45] Arthur McEvoy in *The Fisherman's Problem* compares Native American and modern Anglo-American fisheries management in California. The Native population took huge numbers of fish, but rarely overexploited the resource base. Since the nineteenth century, the fisheries have been destroyed or decimated. Similarly, Carl Safina recounts the destruction of the bluefin tuna resource, in spite of full knowledge by all participants of the costs of their behavior; short-term thinking supervened.[46] Even the deep ocean is under the international Law of the Sea and related treaties. We do not live in a pre–Social Contract world of Hobbesian "warre." If a commons is being depleted, someone is at fault. Decision making at too high and remote a level is usually the problem. Heads of state are busy with other matters, and often indifferent to local concerns. Poor valuation of the resource follows from this. If it is the subsistence resource of local or indigenous people, they may starve to death, but the heads of state are not touched, so they react with indifference. This is the situation I have most often observed in my work in Third World countries and in rural parts of North America.

Rapid population growth destroys all regulation systems. If the quota is ten fish, doubling the fishing population means that the quota has to be cut to five fish. It also means that there are more fishermen to argue and vote against being cheated of their forebears' rights. If the population doubles again, pollution probably wipes out the fishery. Modern plans for integrating conservation of wildlife with traditional local resource-use patterns can founder on this rock if planning is poorly done.[47]

The classic remedy for common-pool problems is to privatize them. This does not always work. Many resources can only be managed at a high level, and privatizing only makes the tragedy of the commons worse. The classic example is soil erosion in a large watershed. Before the United States formed the Soil Conservation Service, each small farmer found it to his advantage to cultivate intensively, but not to check erosion. A given small farmer could not make a difference. Erosion control can be managed only at the watershed level. Private ownership of land led to people wanting to protect the land, but without an overarching, stable institutional structure they could not do it. They could theoretically have created their own institutions, as irrigators do.[48] However, erosion control, unlike irrigation, does not yield an immediate high payoff. Small farmers couldn't afford it, or at least did not think they could. The Soil Conservation Service provided an institution that alleviated the problems, but it worked effectively only when it served to bring farmers together and persuade them, rather than "shoving ideas down their throat" in bureaucratic style.

Private ownership has also failed to stop overgrazing in the West. America's literal "common pastures," the Bureau of Land Management's vast holdings, are devastated,[49] but so are many private ranches. Some ranchers take good care of their lands. Others do not. I often observe a model ranch, with lush grass and abundant cattle and wildlife, next to another ranch that has become an eroded waste. The problems are revealing, in terms of general theory. First, many ranchers are gentlemen farmers who raise cattle only as a tax write-off; they do not care about good management, and they make their money somewhere else. Second, the full-time ranchers are often small-scale ranchers who lack information on sustainable grazing levels. If they have the information, they may be forced to overgraze the range to stay in business—the classic tragedy of the commons, played out here because each rancher's bit of private land is so small.[50]

By contrast, grazing in Switzerland has long been regulated as common property by local communities, and there are landmark studies of these systems.[51] Here, too, government influence is important—but this time the government acts to support and back up commons management, not to erode it.

It can be shown by a simple model that problems with opportunity costs and information are endemic to all situations in which small operators compete for a resource that can be depleted.[52] In such cases, privatization fails—unless the small operators can form grassroots regulatory institutions. This they routinely do.[53] However, social factors can prevent this. Civil unrest, government interference, or an extreme ideology of competitive individualism can make organization impossible.[54]

An advocate of privatization could maintain that the Invisible Hand would weed out the inefficient ranchers if they were not heavily subsidized by the government, but irrevocable damage would be done to the grasslands before the Invisible Hand accomplished this goal. This is the real problem with environmental management: even an ideal Adam Smith scenario may not be good enough. If a Smithian shoemaker fails, no one but his family loses. If a modern chemical company or nuclear power reactor fails, hundreds of thousands of people could be killed. Privatization does not cure this.

If open access is controlled by specification, and if the small operators can group together to regulate a resource, there is still the problem of demand structure. A perverse or subsidy-distorted demand structure can lead to mismanagement of a resource. The ranches, again, provide an example: as we have seen, subsidization of cattle has made it uneconomic to consider the benefits of scenery, food plants, game animals, and the like on ranch land.

Even if this problem is eliminated, and "multiple use" becomes an economic fact rather than a pious hope, the discount rate must be made realistic. In a relatively open-access situation, this is, of course, an obvious problem.

Clearly, managing common property resources is a difficult art—not an easy, cut-and-dried matter of accounting. Yet traditional peoples have worked out the problems, often slowly and painfully through trial and error, and their solutions deserve our attention.[55]

Minimally, there must be an actual community—a group of people who interact—which depends on, or feels deeply involved with the use of, a resource; and this community must see that the resource is under pressure.[56] The community is the critical variable. Only it—that is, its members, negotiating and agreeing—can define the resource for management purposes, or perceive the pressure, or organize to deal with the issue. In all studied cases, one finds a general ethic of mutual responsibility within the community, as well as the specific laws and enforcement structure involved in resource regulation. One also finds that multiple pressures from different points tend to overwhelm a community. In general, community solidarity has a lot to do with success. All the standard measures of community solidarity—shared values, frequent interaction, working together for common causes, and so on—may thus be directly relevant to conservation.

In many but far from all traditional societies, the general and specific rules are religiously maintained. If they are not maintained through religion, they are at least emotionally salient and are maintained through strong public opinion. One must admire especially the fishermen who succeed, usually without special religious missions and without help from the state, in preserving fish stocks.[57] Fish are notoriously hard to manage.

Common-property management is one subspecies of management. General management rules apply. Among these are the rule to leave lower-level decisions to the lower-level managers, and local management has indeed proved effective in common-pool resource situations.[58] Managers and bureaucratic systems tend to try to maximize their power, however, and the results can become nightmarish.

Elinor Ostrom, in *Governing the Commons,* points out that poor regulation leads to worse cheating. She also notes that public regulation may lead to bureaucratization, but private regulation may lead to expensive risk-spreading schemes (I assume this includes high insurance costs and runaway lawsuits). She points out the needs of decent resource management, common or other:[59]

clear boundaries and memberships

congruent rules (rules that fit local conditions)

collective-choice arenas

monitoring

graduated sanctions (minor punishments for minor crimes, and so on)

conflict-resolution mechanisms

recognized rights to organize

nested units (high levels make broad decisions, low make narrow)

Ostrom provides studies of cases where these needs were met, and closely matched cases where management failed for lack of one or another of these requisites.

The total number of decision makers, including the number minimally necessary, is also important; the discount rate in use and the leadership competence of the managers are, of course, relevant.[60] Costs of learning and of getting information must be factored in. Simple, direct rules are easier to learn, accept, and monitor—a point notoriously forgotten by government agencies. Rule enforcement is easier if the group is small, stable, and more or less mutually trusting. This is another point in favor of local-level management.

Ostrom has a healthy skepticism of perfect rationality: "Models that use assumptions such as complete information, independent action, perfect symmetry, no human errors, no norms of acceptable behavior, zero monitoring and enforcement costs, and no capacity to change the structure of the situation itself help the analyst derive precise predictions" but are totally worthless; the precise predictions will all be wrong in any real-world situation.[61]

Ostrom has been criticized by Sara Singleton and Michael Taylor for paying too little attention to the importance of strong communities in all this.[62] Reanalyzing her data, they show that success occurred in strong communities, not in others. Of course, there are also cases where active disagreement ruins a management scheme. Ostrom and Singleton and Taylor both discuss the failure of water management along the Mohave River, and ascribe it to failure of people to get together. What really happened was that certain giant corporations, mostly upstream users, got together quite effectively to resist overall watershed planning, to protect their own water rights, and stop excessive downstream development that could challenge their position.[63] The moral is that the community must be reasonably unanimous in wanting to manage in the first place.

Any common-property management group, then, must have institutions that create and maintain solidarity and further responsible action, as well as enforcement and distribution rules.[64] The question of enforcement brings up another advantage of communities: they can rely on community pressure—moral suasion, social reinforcement, jawboning—to enforce formal and informal rules. This reduces enforcement costs to a very low level. By contrast, top-down command-and-control systems run quickly into skyrocketing enforcement costs. Both monitoring and sanctioning are difficult and expensive for a national government.[65] Again, the advantage of working with the people on the ground is obvious.

Moreover, a community can be expected to socialize its members. Self-interest of adults guarantees that children are socialized into local responsibility codes early on.

A household, after all, faces its own ecological problems in its small world.[66] Even for capitalist firms, management is, in the end, very much a question of institutionalizing loyalty and emotional support for the enterprise.[67] The more long-term the planning horizon, the more true this tends to be. A community, with its accumulated store of memories, its concern for children and grandchildren, and its attachment to place and site, has both more need for solidarity and more emotional and cultural resources to meet this need.

Common-property management works best if it is vested in the hands of small user groups. Once a group gets large—larger than about 150 participating members—decision making and management become very difficult.[68] The Hutterite colonies, for instance, tend to break up when they have more than 150 adults.[69] This may be more than a little related to the fact that humans seem to have evolved in groups of 50 to 150. In most mammals, brain weight correlates very well to body weight. However, social mammals have relatively larger brains. The larger the group, the more the animal's brain/body ratio exceeds the norm. Humans' huge brains fit perfectly with a group size of 150.[70] Thus, we probably evolved in groups of 150, and that is the group size we should therefore be expected to find effective. Thus, imposing levels of management may be necessary. Each level should have fewer than 150 people interacting and should make no decisions that are better left to people at lower levels.

If people were rational in the narrow sense, it would be easy to construct institutions that would manage common property well. The problem is that when people confront a threat or stressful event, their ancient mammalian heritage is apt to take over, and the fight-or-flight response swamps reason. They confront the problem with blind rage or with frantic attempts to escape. Rage leads to damaging oneself, and one's surroundings, just to hurt the enemy—something evident in much voting behavior and in much oppressive governing. Escape, in the modern world, is usually not through running but through alcohol, television, or shopping; but it is escape from stress all the same. It takes not only effort, but also emotional strength and support, to take the harder choice of rational coping. An overly stressed, disunited community becomes a most unpleasant place.

Likewise, if people were really interested only in consuming to satisfy physical needs, we could easily invoke Ostrom's and Pinkerton's plans. But people also consume to show off status, to fill psychic emptiness, and to give themselves a feeling of power and control. The rich are, arguably, more prone to this than the poor. They have more chances to satisfy their consumption needs, and, also, the less affluent imitate them (status emulation). Thus, the tastes of the rich often prevail over the efficient resource use of the poor. The prime example is the deforestation of Latin America for cattle-raising. The Maya Indians of Mexico use at least two thousand species of plants and several hundred animals. This incredibly intensive, diverse, sustainable, knowledge-rich pattern of forest management is giving way to cattle-pasturing. The cattle produce far less utility per acre, but they pay better because the rich will pay for beef. The Maya, kept poor by an oppressive social system, cannot pay much for forest maintenance.

In all these cases, we must invoke institutions that provide motivation and emotional support for those faced with hard decisions. This is particularly true in times of rapid and progressive change, such as the present, when traditional management strategies must be steadily transformed in the face of growing population and consumption. This can be seen in cases such as that of slash-and-burn agriculture, in which shorter fallow cycles lead to soil erosion and failure of forests to regenerate. The rapid growth of the world economy—internationalization—also puts increasing pressure on local systems. It is in such cases that mutual responsibility breaks down, self-interest takes over, and narrow short-term considerations dominate long-term ones. The individual sees less benefit in following old codes, and more in ripping off the system. Thus, monitoring change and getting information out become critical. Most important of all, though, is the invocation of a moral system that pays enormous attention to real ultimate goals and is less committed to particular strategies for reaching those goals.

On top of this, there are such strange attitudes toward the resource base, as that of an early-day California judge quoted by Arthur McEvoy that it is "better to exterminate the game at once than to preserve it for the special benefit of a favored few."[71] This judge seems to have failed to see the possibility of a middle ground between the tragedy of the commons and the aristocratic game parks of old England. Such views prevailed; McEvoy's monumental study shows how they conditioned the devastation of the California fisheries.

With all these problems, it is both surprising and hopeful that so many peoples around the world have successfully managed to avoid the tragedy of the commons. As we have seen, the success stories are those in which strong social and cultural management rules are sanctioned by moral, ethical, and usually religious institutions. If humans find it naturally difficult to calculate their rational self-interest, they find it strikingly easy to organize moral communities. The human need for social life, and the moral codes that emerge from social interaction, make this possible.

Privatization, common-property management, governmental institutions and all other foci of study must be reinterpreted to deal with the realities of human political choice: how information and emotion are negotiated in society. This can involve anything from theological debates in a world religion down to an escalating argument between preservationists and developers over a local meadow. General principles of common-property resource management can be stated more easily than they can be enforced. To enforce them, one normally needs some ideology that will mobilize people to oppose cheaters and stop them from cheating.

Understanding this will require some rethinking of social issues. Most social science theories tend to deal with highly intellectualized and passionless actors, and are thus incomplete. Examples include structuralist and structural-functionalist theories, as well as most of economic theory. This is why economists have proved successful at predicting specific market or firm behavior but poor at predicting social change. Other theories (such as culture-and-personality) analyze feeling without thinking.

Such theories do not allow prediction of changes in ecological morality. Americans have accepted protection of songbirds (a major food source in the nineteenth century), changed their attitudes on cruelty to domestic animals, and learned to live with game limits (though poaching is still not uncommon). These changes came about through moral suasion, not because of economics. Today, vegetarianism for moral reasons is on the increase, and wearing fur is unacceptable in many circles. Of course, far more important changes, such as the abolition of slavery and the rise of civil rights and women's rights, have also come about from almost purely moral motives. (The economists always seemed to figure out, *after* the fact, that these things were economically rational! This, for instance, is often argued *now* for slavery—but try to find any such thinking in the early nineteenth century.)

By themselves, such changes in morality are not enough to save the world's forests or stop soil erosion. The point is that economic rationality, in the narrow sense, is not adequate either. Action follows from moral and practical factors acting in concert.

For a case study, consider the modern United States—the antithesis of the traditional, religiously coded worlds of old China or the Northwest Coast Native peoples.

At the end of the millennium, the United States is still the richest and most powerful country in the world, though Japan and Germany are closing fast. The United States is also the home of the sharpest and most important environmental fights in the world. It is the home of the largest and most politically active environmental movement, and also of the largest and most active backlash from industry and extractive producers.

The United States has been, up till now, surprisingly successful at protecting its environment and its citizens. The mistakes are obvious, but consider what might have happened. At the logging rates typical of the nineteenth century, America would have cut its last tree around 1920. The last extinction of a major, economically important species took place when the last passenger pigeon died in a zoo in 1914. Pollution control has cleaned up Lake Erie and stabilized the air quality over Los Angeles, in spite of massive economic growth in those regions.

The reason for the successes is simple: a large number of people were, and are, outraged at being made to pay the costs of other people's profits. These people formed groups. The groups have recourse to the ballot box and the lawsuit. By contrast, the USSR followed the course that the American anti-environmentalists wish for: production at all costs, with no account taken of the environment or of environmentalists. The result has been not only environmentally devastating, but also economically so. The daughter countries of the USSR now average about a third or less the per capita GNP of the United States, and the gap is widening fast. The environmental damage is notably worse than America's. Life expectancy is falling steadily, and currently stands about ten years behind the United States'. The infant mortality rate is several times as high as America's, even though the American rate is the highest in the developed Western world.[72]

The Third World is worse off still, partly because of the activities of the developed countries, partly because of population growth. On the whole, local people are worse fed than they were a century ago.[73]

Clearly, the United States could do a lot worse. At least, American per capita income has grown. And the United States has so far avoided catastrophes on the level of Chernobyl or the Union Carbide plant in Bhopal. It is significant that the latter involved an American firm. Operating in the United States under publically negotiated laws, Union Carbide has caused no serious problems. Operating in India under India's less accountable government, Union Carbide's supervision failed.

However, the United States has its own catastrophes, not least in the matter of agriculture. A general idealization of technology and progress has led to capital overinvestment and to energy waste and chemical pollution. Government policies and incentives for row-to-row, monocrop cultivation are a problem. Farm subsidies are among the important causes of overcultivation that has led to the destruction of wetlands, prairies, and forests, and to pollution through excessive use of chemicals. Even tobacco production is still very heavily subsidized, though smoking is responsible for approximately one-fourth of all deaths in the United States. Farm subsidies were theoretically intended to preserve the small farm, but they have failed to do this. The United States has probably the highest concentration of land and wealth in private hands of any agricultural economy in the world. Most American small farms are part-time, recreational, or retirement farms that do not contribute much to the economy. Much of the subsidy system was developed not to help the economy, but to preserve the small farm, seen as virtuous and freedom-building since the days of Thomas Jefferson. There still exists a tiny but healthy and important small farm sector that deserves all the support it can get, but the current system is not an effective way to do that.[74]

In the forests, there are similar incentives to damage the environment for other than market-economic reasons. The National Forests heavily subsidize logging. On any good aerial photograph of the Pacific Northwest, one can tell the private from the public forest land by the better condition of most of the former. Private land is often cut and sometimes overcut, but it rarely shows the moonscapes covering thousands of acres that are the legacy of uneconomic, taxpayer-subsidized logging on the public lands. It is, of course, ironic that the very institutions that were set up to protect the forests are now doing the worst job of it. In fairness, it should be said that the Northwest situation is extreme, and many National Forests are well managed and in good shape. However, once again, policies designed to help local industries—loggers and sawmills—have protected a "way of life" at considerable expense to the total economy as well as to the ecosystem.

Similarly, overgrazing on public land depends on very low fees, heavy subsidization by government construction of roads and restoration of pastures, and government tax breaks to ranchers. This has led many people, most notably Lynn Jacobs, to advocate banning of grazing on public land.[75] One does not have to agree with this extreme view to see that subsidization of grazing, on or off public land, must result in uneconomic behavior. Cattle are so artificially favored that watershed, scenery, wild plants, nuts, game, and all the other benefits of rangeland are squeezed out of the picture. Attempts to compensate by passing countless regulations have given the livestock industry an understandable lack of enthusiasm for the Bureau of Land Management, which thus finds itself attacked by both stockmen and anti-livestock activists. Eliminating the subsidies would allow eliminating this bureaucratic load. Again, the subsidies were originally passed to preserve a way of life that is not only an American myth and dream but also politically powerful because of its voting power in the Western states.[76]

Authors such as Martin Lewis argue for retaining the existing system of government-guided economics, but redirecting it from favoring production at all costs to favoring conservation.[77] This Lewis calls "guided democracy." The Mexican[78] and Communist experiences suggest that this will not work. *Any* government-favored sector of the economy will become a problem in time. The National Forests, after all, were created to guide forest use in the paths of good management. They are now, all too often, managed worse than private forest lands. Logging firms have incentives to lobby for unrestricted use of National Forest lands, but no incentives to protect or restock them. Private forests, in contrast, can be economically managed for the long term. Any subsidy, of any kind, is simply an invitation to wasteful use of resources.

All of the above have been used to justify free enterprise as the best thing for the environment.[79] Certainly, both government control of the economy (compare Mexico and the USSR) and governmental special favors for particular economic sectors are, almost invariably, disastrous for the environment. However, unregulated private enterprise simply leads to tragedies of the commons and to competition to see who can pass on the most costs to the general public, as "externalities." Competition can lead to the best winning out (Smithian competition), but it can also lead to the worst winning, by resorting to dirty tricks (Reaganian competition), or to the slickest and most dishonest winning (Barnumian competition). Government policies determine which will prevail.

American experience has certainly not been consoling to those who believe in the value of unfettered freedom of anyone to do anything. The extreme case of the beaver during the Fur Trade era was far from the only case of outrageous waste on the frontier. The passenger pigeon was exterminated and the buffalo nearly so, all for no clear benefit to anyone. Sustained cropping—such as we now do with ducks—would have obviously been preferable, by any standards. We now know the buffalo is far more efficient and economical as a grazing animal on the high plains than are domestic cattle. Even more efficient is a mixed stocking system with buffalo, antelope, and elk. But we have foreclosed that option; we are stuck with the cows.

In short, we cannot eliminate this problem by diving indiscriminately into "free enterprise" or "government regulation." Both the market and the government share the guilt for the mess we are in. Both the market and the government share the credit for the fact that things are no worse.

Many Americans are becoming more and more anti-conservation because of genuine doubts and worries about the near-term, expressed through voting "against" everything: big government, other ethnic groups, and the environment.

This appears to lead to a general principle that illustrates the main point of this book, and that should be disturbing to environmentalists: when things go wrong, the human tendency is to look for other people to blame, rather than to look to proper resource management. Scapegoats in the form of structural opponent groups are more emotionally salient. Worst-case results of such thinking can be seen today in the former Soviet Union, in the former Yugoslavia, in Malaysia, in Guatemala, and elsewhere.

Thus in America, as in China and the Northwest Coast, conservation cannot be looked at in isolation. It is part of the whole strategy of social responsibility, of sacrificing immediate self-interest for long-term benefits. Conservation is not an isolated issue. It is inseparable from other issues that involve such trade-offs, notably education and tolerance.

Either way, the general point raised by Bellah and his collaborators is valid:[80] moral and ethical changes are at hand, and should be discussed in a more serious way than the average political campaign manages to do.

10

The Disenchanted: Religion as Ecological Control, and Its Modern Fate

Conservation must be rationally planned, but inevitably it becomes a political issue. Policies and plans must be debated in the political arena and decided there. Politics is the art of managing passions and conflicts—either to control or resolve them, or to whip them up for selfish reasons. It is necessary for environmental management to minimize conflict and achieve specific social contracts. This involves playing the highly impassioned game of politics, as well as appealing to truth and reason. Neither of those two things can be separated from the other. Politics without rationality soon degenerates into mindless conflict. Reason without passion carries no political appeal.

Politics thus comes to rely on wider and more personally compelling belief systems. Religion is notable among these. It has been shown that traditional societies use religion to sanction their resource management strategies, and that this appears to be a successful strategy. This point has long been argued.[1] More recently, it has become a cornerstone of one branch of cultural ecology theory. Roy Rappaport has expanded his argument that religion can encode wise management strategies to include a more general theory of religion, encoding information and involving human emotions.[2] Lansing has provided a classic test case.[3] Victor Toledo has incorporated Rappaport's observations in a wider theory of what he calls "ethnoecology."[4] The following discussion takes off from their insights, and draws some further conclusions.

The advantage of religion in traditional societies where religion is still a major force is that it involves emotion in moral codes. A moral code based only on emotion or only on practical reason will not sell. To succeed, a moral code must have something to do with reality, but it must be strongly *believed*—people have to have a lot of emotion invested in it. Belief, in this sense, does not mean dogmatism. One can be open and reasonable about a belief. The difference between a belief—in this sense—and an ordinary bit of knowledge is the emotional investment.

The question posed herein is: How do religions sell moral codes?

Perhaps the best insight into the reasons for religion is provided by a quick review of modern books on ethics. Technical philosophy, such as is found in the works of John Rawls, Jurgen Habermas, or Derek Parfit, is so abstruse that no ordinary mortal could use it for guidelines.[5] The public remains unmoved by debates about "deontological" and "assertoric" ethics. Also, the schemes of these modern ethicists do not command agreement even among scholars.[6] Among other things, these scholars tell us rather little about motivation. Parfit finds little consistency except in the Present-Aim Theory—the ethic, if such it can be called, of believing I should get what I want, right now. Given the slipperiness of the concepts "self" and "want," and our problems with rational ordering of preferences, even this minimalist ethic cannot stand really searching challenges.

Habermas resorts to appeals to ordinary social morality. I am not the first to point out that a German should know that ordinary social morality may not always be a perfect guide. The ordinary social morality of Germany in the 1930s and early 1940s left something to be desired. So does that of the modern United States. The fact is that ordinary social morality is an even worse guide than the experts. In any event, ordinary social morality is derived to some extent from earlier religious and philosophical teachings. Little originality, inspiration, or authority are provided in popular codes. It is true—as noted above—that all societies must, and do, place high values on generosity, self-sacrifice, and mutual aid. However, they do not all value conservation, to say nothing of tolerance, nonviolence, fairness, and liberty. At best, conventional social morality arises from everyday interactions. It thus works well in these face-to-face interactions but is not adequate for long-term, wide-flung calculations.

It is fairly likely that Jesus, Buddha, Muhammad, and St. Francis will be remembered long after Parfit and Habermas are forgotten. Persuasive and comprehensible rhetoric, and a firm grounding in broad ethical codes that actually assert something, ensure this. More to the point, religion directly deals with human emotion and suffering. Relatively few people read Parfit or Habermas for refuge, meditation, solace, or excitement. Much of the considerable

literature on environmental ethics is little better—with the significant exception of works by poets and writers such as Gary Snyder or Edward Abbey.

The obvious objection is that religion has often been bent to serve the
most murderous and destructive ends. This stems from a less severe, but actually
more damaging, critique: religion has been bent to serve all possible ends.
Religion is not a code or a system but a general term that has become established
in the Western world for a whole class of social codes and rituals.

Religion is, in fact, a cultural system that "sells" a moral code by embed-
ding it in an emotionally compelling communal system of symbols, beliefs, and
ceremonies. Thus, the content of the moral code is negotiable, and is not in
itself a part of the religion. We can have a moral code without a religion.
"Secular humanism" has liberated the standard Judeo-Christian moral code
from its ritual embeddedness, thereby gaining some credibility with atheists,
but losing much emotional appeal. Conversely, the pseudo-fundamentalist
doctrines that have vocally opposed themselves to secular humanism have kept
many of the rituals but have lost the moral code of standard Christianity,
substituting quite different ones.

Religion also "sells" economic behavior patterns, as Marx and, later, Max
Weber pointed out.[7] Even if one accepts the revisionist point that the economic
behavior came first and the religious representation of it came later,[8] the main
point stands: capitalism flourished only when, and insofar as, religion could be
bent to motivate people to save, invest, and work hard.

It follows, then, that environmental management depends on the following:

1. A strong, simple ethical code. As noted in chapter 6, this must be a
stricter code than seems "necessary," rather than a logical, "adequate" code.

2. Some form of religion or other system that involves people emotionally
in their ethical and moral world.

It is possible, and indeed common, for such cultural systems to flourish
without being "religions." Soviet Communism became a religion by some
definitions, since it created symbols, elevated Marx to the status of holy writ, had
its own embalmed saints, and so forth. The French Revolutionaries tried to create
a state cult that was something of an atheistic religion. It has even been argued that
American patriotism was a kind of secular religion, creating community by
shared symbols.[9] One might argue that the same could be said about modern
mass-media worldviews. The communities are loose and the meanings hardly
shared, however, so this seems to be stretching the definition too far.

Still, it raises an important point. A religion need not, and usually does
not, "represent the community" in the very tight sense that Emile Durkheim

made famous.[10] World religions like Christianity and Islam are held together by allegiance to a few symbols. They create a community only in a very loose sense—a minimalist community. Many Christians and Muslims reject as heretical most of their co-communicants. Therefore, we do not expect a perfect equation of one religion with one moral code, even in a small community. In fact, a religion must have some ambiguity if it is to spread widely. It must also have few enough rules that it can succeed in a variety of communities.[11]

At the margin, then, religion blurs into generalized philosophy and cosmology. Belief in supernaturals need not co-occur with moral codes, rituals, or cosmological ideas.

The points that are important, in the work at hand, are not doctrinal but functional. Religions, and similar cultural systems, serve primarily to bind emotional appeals to codes for living. This is done by appealing to as many channels of appeal as possible. Normally, a religion is based on a sacred book—written or unwritten—and a set of symbolic rituals.

The sacred book is not only "canonical" but also poetical. The close correlation between a religion's success and the appeal of its main texts has been noted for millennia.

The ceremonies and rituals—more generally, all the activities connected with the faith—usually have something for everyone. There are ascetic periods for those who delight in self-denial as well as feasts for the rest of us. There are opportunities for ecstatic trance as well as for quiet meditation and for ordinary cheerful interaction. Ideally, the whole span of human activity and emotion is covered. A good Chinese temple fair or Maya saint's-day fair maximizes sensory experience. Smells, tastes, colors, noises, human activities, and ritual moods are as intense as they can be made. No one can ignore or forget such occasions.

In short: religious activity must involve *some* sharing of moral and emotional foundations of society. It should go on and call up, structure, and manage *the full spectrum* of emotions and ideas. Thus, everyone is involved, both as sharers and as different individuals. As St. Paul said, we share the basic creed, but "having then gifts differing," we live and teach it in our different ways—and this is a strength, not a weakness.

The effectiveness of traditional ethical and religious teachings in conservation has been very abundantly documented.[12] The need for moral ecology has also been argued in both the abstract and the concrete.[13] This is not, of course, to argue that religion is ever a perfect regulator. Particularly important is the argument of Stephen Lansing that religion does not so much create an ethical standard as supply the cultural and emotional involvement that motivate people to keep following an eminently pragmatic management system.[14] Lansing's model study of Balinese use of temple organization to manage irrigation water remains one of the best demonstrations of the role of religion in traditional common property management.

Religion is especially necessary as a counterbalance to positive illusions. As we have seen, people tend to think the world is the way they want it to be. The active, enterprising people who are apt to be doing the most to the environment are often the most optimistic people. Thus, they are even more apt to say "a little pollution won't hurt," "environmentalists are Chicken Littles," and "it won't hurt to kill just one more whale" than are the rest of humanity. Against this enterprising spirit—laudable in most contexts—religion must pose firm rules against shortsightedness. Most religious morality turns out, in fact, to be the familiar trade-off between short-term narrow interests and long-term wide ones.

In a modern society, the "disenchantments" of which Max Weber spoke happened long ago. The first Weberian disenchantment came when we gave up seeing all nature as spiritual; the second, when we relegated religion to its present-day rather minor status in society. (The Islamic world and some other areas have yet to reach this second disenchantment. This is nothing against them; Weber was anything but enthusiastic about this bit of "progress," as the word "disenchantment" implies.) We must, therefore, not hope for religion to save us. Fortunately, other emotional codes suffice.

Education provides an example. As long as education was a good in itself, people supported it—and it paid off. So educators began to sell education as job training and economic investment. The support dried up. Once education was merely instrumental, it was just one more investment to balance against more immediate needs.

The most important feature of religion (or any belief system) is its role in involving the children. Children first delight in Christmas gifts and foods, or in the feast at the end of Ramadan, or in the awe-inspiring Passover ritual, and are won over to the moral code by its association with those events. Anyone who has attended a Passover seder and seen the youngest child ask the traditional questions about the ritual has a strong sense of this.

Adults do convert, but only rarely, and only when they are dissatisfied seekers who finally find a congenial congregation. The overwhelming majority of recruits to any religion are the children of its communicants. Obviously, they are not brought to the faith by its abstract theology or its flights of logical brilliance! They are brought in by the emotional warmth and the sensory intensity of the rituals and symbols. They remain because of the emotional ties with the whole community and its most deeply felt representations.

This banal observation should end, forever, the hope of a "rational ethics," environmental or otherwise. Even if you could explain Rawls or Parfit to a three-year-old, you couldn't make her care. By the time she is far enough along in school to worry about communicative ethics or consequentialism, she has already made her key moral choices. Conventional social morality can be—and is—taught by ordinary rewards and punishments, and arises from the interactions of daily practice and inborn predisposition, but we have already seen how far conventional social morality can get us. The very point at issue lies here. Conventional morality arises from daily experience. It follows that anything beyond daily experience requires something more.

Religion also involves the community in sanctions. Since religion is a huge part of the constitution of community, or at least of some network of social support, people will actively work to maintain it and to sanction violators. "Cheating" in the formal sense is correctly seen as a direct challenge to the whole society. Without some such representation of community, there is no way to mobilize people to exert sanctions, negative or positive.

In short, the problem of communal morality resolves itself into two necessarily linked problems:

1. The nature and content of the moral code.
2. Its linkage with a compelling, emotionally satisfying, rich network of symbols, texts, and activities.

The various systems of thought described in this book are appealing for three reasons: They fit the empirical data (they work); they are logical and coherent within the terms of their cultures; and they are directly, personally involving. Dragons in the hills and *feng-shui* rites fit the Chinese worldview and appeal to its symbolic repertoire. Animal conservation is persuasive in a shamanistic society because of the emotional salience of animals, their spiritual involvement in the community, and the authority of the shamans with their animal-inspired texts and rituals.

This is not to say that traditional cultural systems are all good. Obviously, they are not. Religious cannibalism, ritual warfare, and human sacrifice do occur. Other, less damaging, systems of thought seem highly plausible in terms of cultural cosmologies, yet have few real-world benefits; one thinks of Puritanism, eremitic mysticism, and ritualism. Every religion, and every non-religious moral code, has clauses that allow for withdrawal from human action. These clauses may allow meditation on the value of nature; they also, however, may cause brilliant, good-hearted people to withdraw from doing any tangible good in the world (whatever the ultimate spiritual benefit).

And there are, of course, inquisitions. Inquisitions go on in spite of, rather than because of, religious codes. All world religions explicitly condemn violence and cruelty, and all inquisitions and fundamentalist massacres are flatly illegal under the rules of their own faiths. Close investigation of such sordid episodes usually discloses motives far more mercenary that religious. The Albigensian Crusade had more to do with looting than with anything else, and the Spanish who denounced purported Jews and Muslims to the Inquisition received all the property of the victims as their reward. The Chinese court made a regular practice of tolerating Buddhism until the monasteries got rich, and then launched religious "reforms" that consisted of appropriating the wealth. It is also well to remember that Nazism and Soviet Communism went farther than any world religion in purifying their ranks, thus shattering Voltaire's dream of ending intolerance by ending religiosity.

Nevertheless, this problem should convince the New Age spiritualists who hope for an ecological religion that they may be buying some very unpleasant merchandise.

Another tendency of religion is toward puritanism: denial of the flesh and an attack on enjoyment. As we have just seen, this attitude has influenced the conservation movement. However, it is an intensely anti-conservation tenet, since enjoyment of nature and wildlife is the essence and foundation of the emotional involvement that is necessary to save those goods. What is less obvious is the relationship between puritanism and "rationality" in the narrow sense. The unemotional and calculated thinking that was called "rational" in many quarters over the last two hundred years is a direct descendant of Puritanism.

All of this proves that moral codes must be constructed carefully, and that even if constructed carefully, they will be subverted in time. The moral codes of a society, community, cultural group, or worldwide network have to be worked out by negotiation. Making them acceptable to the people involved, and especially to new generations who were not part of the initial negotiation process, involves use of emotionally compelling materials. These new generations must have the power to renegotiate the codes, on mutually acceptable terms, to prevent the drift toward intolerance and inquisition.

I am not advocating—or condemning—use of religion to sell conservation. I am neither interested in starting a new Green Religion nor in forcing religious beliefs on anyone. The point is a factual one:

All traditional societies that have succeeded in managing resources well, over time, have done it in part through religious or ritual representation of resource management.

The key point is not religion per se, but the use of emotionally powerful cultural symbols to sell particular moral codes and management systems.

The conclusion is not that ecology must be religious, but that anyone interested in convincing people to manage the environment in any particular way would be well advised to embed it in a rich texture of emotion and experience. Nature walks do better than classroom lectures. Weekend workshops and week-long eco-tours do better than nature walks. Even these only begin to tap the surface. Above all, think of the children. Environmental education has made great strides in the last few decades. Print and TV are increasingly supplemented by hands-on involvement. This must increase. Ideally, the hands-on activities would be the core, and print and TV the supplements.

In traditional societies, religion, worldview, and resource management strategies are often inseparable. This occurs in two ways. First, religious sanctions are invoked directly to support conservation. Second, people are emotionally involved with their natural surroundings. This emotional involvement—as we have seen—reaches the level of actually incorporating plants and animals in society. They are not human persons, but they are persons.

This brings us back to Lansing's study of water regulation in Bali.[15] Lansing found that management of irrigation water is in the hands of the water temples and their priests—administrators of a religion that involves sacred waters and sacred mountains. When international engineers and bureaucrats tried to take over, they botched the job so badly that the priests had to resume control.[16]

Cases of ideological regulation without real religious sanctions have also been documented. In Japan, Tokugawa forest and fisheries management was exemplary. The Tokugawas set general policy but left responsibility for implementing it to local communities. This and other systems, some more religiously represented, are considered by Kenneth Ruddle and Tomoya Akimichi.[17] Of course, the United States and other developed countries provide the major cases. Duck and deer management is wholly secularized but is very effective, except where duck habitat has been destroyed by farming operations (mostly uneconomic but heavily subsidized). A few fisheries have also been adequately managed in the modern world, in spite of pressures. Religious construction of sanctions is not necessary, at least in developed societies with separate law enforcement agencies and a general respect for the law. There are many ways to manage such broad ideological representations, running the gamut from strict "secular religions" to untrammeled free enterprise within a responsible universe.[18]

Conversely, it should not be thought that traditional societies all have conservation ideologies. Several, living in areas without pressure on resources, have no concept of conservation or sustained yield. For example, the Amazon rainforests were, until recently, thinly populated, and many local peoples had no conservation traditions.[19] Other Amazon areas, of course, had denser populations—and conservation traditions.

However, religion is also used to sanction environmental destruction. We are now too sophisticated to blame anything as vague and undefined as the "Judeo-Christian tradition" for the rape of the Western world, but some Christian societies have regarded destruction of nature as a divine mission. Other traditions, also, can justify waste, especially when pioneer communities confront a new landscape.

The Judeo-Christian tradition (if there is one) is too broadly and vaguely defined to provide many guidelines. The Old Testament provides many model ecological teachings while also providing examples of environmental damage through scorched-earth warfare (sowing salt on the ashes) and overcultivation. When prophets such as Isaiah want to give us portraits of ravaged landscapes, they often provide graphic images of the salt marshes that form in the Near East when overirrigation leads to buildup of groundwater and salt. Here "the cormorant and the bittern" find lodging.

Modern American Christianity accommodates widely differing views on the matter of environmental management. Some Christians are fighting a literal holy war against conservation and environment.[20] At the same time, others are developing a radically conservationist Christianity.[21] All possible shades of opinion between these extremes can be found.[22]

Max Weber saw modern society as having become progressively "disenchanted" with the world.[23] The pun is perhaps more forceful in English than in Weber's German. We have lost the enchantment of life in a spiritual cosmos; we have cut ourselves off, by a narrow rationality, from the great unity of things. Yet religion continues to flourish (against all Weberian predictions) and is being revived in many circles as a source of ecological sensitivity.[24] Indeed, the modern and Western world is not so much a secular world cut off from "Nature" as a deeply ambiguous, divided, and contested world. Community and its religious representation declines. The result is not so much an ideological assault on "Nature" as a failure to unite on any management strategy at all.

Thus, religion is not just an ethical code. It is a way of linking ethical codes to deep emotional and cosmological forces in society. A vast, all-embracing, widely followed religion like Christianity is not in itself a bearer of a particular ethical code. It is a carrier wave, facilitator, or authoritative justification for whatever ethical code a community or group wants to empower. Even the far more tightly defined and entailed religions of traditional "primitives" allow for a good deal of play.

The need, then, is for a given group to develop an ethical code and find an emotionally compelling, authoritative belief system in which to embed it and with which to validate it. The ethical code, in turn, should be developed on the basis of actual experience in the world: what works best. Going the other way—from emotional belief to practical application—is the sure formula for disaster. The whole record of religion proves that.

The place to seek such codes and such emotional constructions is in the realm of societies that have successfully managed resources. In these, we find that a direct, emotional, religiously "socialized" tie to the resources in question is the most salient factor. In the modern world, it is neither necessary nor possible to missionize for animism and shamanism. What we can do is work toward involving people in a genuine love of their environments, discussing openly and freely the moral issues and choices involved in conservation. The opposite approach—leaving ecology to "scientists" and "experts"— is not viable. The experts preach objectivity, rationality, and dispassionate examination of the facts. Yet, being human, they are necessarily impassioned and biased.

In ethnobiology and cultural ecology, worldview is even more important than food, medicine, or industrial crops. Cancer cures are certainly desirable, but the human race will survive even if cancer is not eliminated. The human race will not survive without stronger conservation ideologies. We need all the help we can get from all the traditions that have embodied good management in any form.

Melvin Gilmore, the father of academic ethnobiology, wrote in 1929: "Among Indians generally, as I have known them in a number of different tribes or nations, there is a comon feeling of reverence for life in all its forms, whether that life be manifest in human form, in the various species of animals, or in plants. . . . They teach their children to have respect for all living things, however lowly."[25] Gilmore goes on to decry the lack of interest that Americans of European origin show toward the prairies. Raised in the wilds of frontier Nebraska, Gilmore first trained for the ministry but fell under the influence of Charles Bessey and studied under him—along with Frederick Clements. (Thus ethnobiology and ecology were linked from his early days.) Gilmore transferred his missionary fervor to the ethnobiological realm. His book *Prairie Smoke* was an attempt to capture the Siouan and Pawnee attachment to the prairie country of the Midwest, to inspire other Americans to love it as well.

"Outsider" and "insider" views of traditional resource management provide a case in point. Typically, the outsider makes the people seem coolly calculating and narrowly rational. The insider describes them as warm, emotional, and intensely involved with religious ritual.

This should be very sharply and carefully distinguished from the romantic, Rousseauian view of "the primitive" that is championed by some extreme outsiders.[26] These simple, happy children of nature exist—fortunately—only in the imagination of such uninformed reporters. Nor am I under the illusion that all traditional peoples always manage resources well. They are human and make mistakes. What insider accounts present is something very different: *extremely detailed, pragmatic, empirical knowledge, religiously represented, and bound up with an emotional tie to the land.* The Nahuatl of Mexico, for instance, had a complex cosmology in which humans had animal companions, could become mountains after death, and were equated with clouds or flowers. Richard Haly, who has carefully studied this complex worldview, finds it less a matter of belief in a sacred Mother Earth than a complex deduction from respectful interaction: They "relate to the landscape in a manner that does not question its authority."[27] Within such a framework, conservation can be invoked if necessary.

The "outsider" literature of ethnobiology and cultural ecology ranges from materialist to idealist. Smith provides a good example of "practical reason" at its most practical.[28] Much of the agricultural decision-making literature is also narrowly devoted to microeconomic visions.[29] Other writers are more attuned to ideology, religion, and emotion.[30]

The classic ethnographies of the Malinowskian tradition were particularly good at integrating "biological functionalism," or at least biological observations, with social and religious lore.[31] Malinowski's most famous student, Jomo Kenyatta, produced the most famous of all insider ethnographies, *Facing Mount Kenya*.[32] Malinowski, of course, achieved notoriety by tying "magic, science and religion" closely together, and defining them contrastively, according to a matrix that is still hotly debated.[33] He regarded magic as an attempt to control the unknown or uncertain by instrumental means, and thus closer to failed science than to religion—the latter being considered as an overarching social ideology rather than a practical, manipulative system.

By contrast, "insider" accounts that deal heavily with ethnobiological and cultural-ecological matters do not separate religion from practical reason. They also often describe highly emotional relationships with the landscape and biota. The most striking recent example is the stunning ethnographic work by Jesus Salinas Pedraza, recorded by Russell Bernard in *Native Ethnography*.[34] Salinas is a Nyahnyu (Otomi) Indian from the Mezquital Valley of Mexico. His account of local plants and animals is brilliantly detailed and thorough, with uses exhaustively recorded. He lists enjoyment of the flowers, delight in the antics of the animals, and pleasures of the hunt along with the more prosaic uses—no separation is made. He finds the greatest value of hunting pack rats is in providing men with an excuse to get away from their wives and tell dirty jokes. This was the real reason for much of the hunting and fishing in the Midwest of my childhood, too. One wonders what Smith would make of this. Is obscene repartee a part of our genetically coded strategy for optimal foraging?[35]

All these accounts deal in detail with religious and ideological matters. In some cases this may reflect an ethnographer's interest, but many of these accounts were done either without benefit of ethnographic midwife[36] or with minimal control by the ethnographer,[37] to say nothing of the cases in which the "native" *was* the ethnographer (Kenyatta, for example). Surely, it should give pause to Eric Smith and other cultural materialists that no "insider" has ever seen fit to produce an unemotional, materialistic account. Neither have outsiders who, like Gilmore or Firth, have spent really long periods in the field.

On the whole, most ethnobiological "outsider" accounts confine their attention to "practical reason" in Sahlins's sense. In matters relating to inner emotion and personal experience, this is necessary, or at least desirable. Claims of deep empathy with insiders are highly suspect, especially if the ethnographer spent only a few months with the people in question.

These considerations, however, pale into insignificance beside the one raised by Gilmore and by so many since: religion is the standard way that biological knowledge, including conservation and management, is taught and sanctioned among traditional local-level societies. Often it also provides the organization that is put to use in managing the resource, as in the Balinese case.

This links the "outsider" and the "insider" literature. It also brings us back to the seminal work of Roy Rappaport, Robert Netting, and other cultural ecologists who have long taken an institutional view.[38] Rappaport, in particular, has argued for a generation that religion served as a carrier wave for ecological knowledge.[39]

This is a key point. Religion in modern Western societies is usually relegated to a small part of life. It is usually confined to metaphysics and higher-level ethics. Not only everyday practical knowledge but also everyday morality is left strictly to the secular arm. The few exceptions involve cases where religion makes outrageously counterevidential claims (faith healing, creationism, etc.). Western scientists often go into the field with the unexamined assumption that the same is true of religion and ideology everywhere. This, is, of course, a completely false assumption for the Balinese, and also for the Chinese, the Dogon, the Hindus, and countless other groups. Among these peoples, higher-level ecological and environmental knowledge is typically represented religiously. It is thus discussed in a manner that seems otherworldly to the skeptical Western outsider. As even Paul Radin—an anti-religious cynic if there ever was one—[40] wrote of the Winnebago: "The Indian does not interpret life in terms of religion, but religion in terms of life. In other words, he exalts the world around him and the multifarious desires and necessities of the day, so that they appear to him bathed in a religious thrill."[41]

Key, also, is the role of religion in providing a basic social and emotional ground in educating the young.[42]

As we move into resource management questions, we move into higher-level representations of the environment. These higher-level representations, in particular the management strategies, are almost invariably coded as religious systems in traditional societies. The naive Western assumption that all religion must be nonsense is simply not defensible in such cases. Strategies that are "objectively" (a word that often means "in Western terms") perfectly scientific and empirically valid are religiously represented in many cases. Moreover, the people are often quite conscious of this, even if they do not or cannot discuss it in Western scientific terms.[43]

Most important of all, however, is the role of emotion, ideology, and perhaps religion in modern resource management. Biotic management today has become the province of engineers, bureaucrats, and others who share the narrowest of "rational" views. This point has been amply discussed by sensitive conservation biologists such as David Ehrenfeld and David Orr, who point out the need for scientists to acknowledge that people—and often the scientists themselves—may often love the plants and animals they observe and live with. Orr notes that many (most?) field biologists love their subjects, and study them because they love them, yet seem afraid to admit this in public or to talk of emotions in their writings. As he points out, this is no way to organize conservation action.[44]

Yet, broader policies involving the environment are created politically, and politics is a field noted for emotionality and bias. The greatest need in conservation and resource management today is for some sort of meaningful dialogue between scientists, politicians, and the public. By this I do not mean that they should merely talk to each other; I mean that the politicians should learn some science and the scientists should learn that people, especially in groups, are motivated by powerful emotions and by social constructions of these emotions.

This does *not* mean that we have to revive (or, worse, fake) some sort of ancient spirituality. Attempts to adapt shamanism, Goddess-worship and the like to the modern world have found little credibility and are often based on sad misunderstanding not only of the religions in question but of their role in society. Like it or not, we are separated by vast Weberian disenchantment from a world in which such cults can persuade.

However, this does not stop us from invoking an aesthetic and moral system that allows us to care. Like the Nahuatl, we can deal with the landscape in a way that respects it, though we may not personalize it as they did. Such a relationship is not necessarily religious. It goes deeper than religion, into the respectful and concerned emotionality that provides the common ground for religion and ethics.

For this reason, I will avoid discussing the enormous and rather indeterminate literature on environmental ethics. My sense is that much of this literature is too general, and much of the rest is too specific.[45]

The solution, for us, must involve creation of an ethic that is specific about the basics but dispenses with sectarian dogmas (be they the Virgin Birth or the Great Coyote in the Sky). A bare minimum, or at least a beginning, would include the following:

1. Mobilizing active love for plants and animals and the environment.

2. Representing this love by a morality of caring for and cherishing living things, and acting with social responsibility toward them.

3. Wanting to learn more about living things and keep informed about their situation.

We do not need religion to do this. We simply need to expand our ordinary everyday morality of family, neighbors, and reference group. We need to define the natural environment as part of our personal community.

This will not be easy. We have not succeeded brilliantly in making communities of our multiethnic cities. Nature may be easier to deal with— plants are less scary than ethnically alien human neighbors. But no one should think that this will be an easy task.

The way to do it is to keep it simple, concentrating on the three points made here and not insisting that everyone become a shaman or a sectarian. The way to do it, above all, is to focus on bringing people into the natural environment in such a way that they love it. Then practical reason can take over, and people can be trusted to act to preserve what they love.

A Summary, and Some Suggestions

The world's traditional societies have come to some kind of terms with their environments, or they would not have lasted long enough to become "traditional." Most of them encode in their moral teachings practical wisdom about the environment and the individual's duty to treat it with respect. These injunctions are lived; they enter daily practice, as when Noemy Chan makes her children eat the butterflies they thoughtlessly kill. They structure whole landscapes, as South China was structured by *feng-shui*. They stimulate deep personal involvement with actual plant and animal species, as on the Northwest Coast.

The common theme of all these traditional resource management ethics is not spiritual harmony with some disembodied and abstracted Nature, but actual personal and emotional involvement with the actual landscape and its nonhuman inhabitants. People interact with their surroundings. In all cultures, these surroundings become meaningful—not just as sources of food and shelter, but as sources of beauty, power, excitement, and other human values. In those cultures that endure and do not collapse, the meanings of nature are bound up in systems of respect and protection. Often, mutual obligations exist between people and the beings or forces they believe to exist in the wild.

From the lived experiences of people in cultures around the world, we can extract a number of general principles for environmental management. We can also, mercifully, learn that we need not go to the extreme lengths of ideological reform proposed by some modern environmentalists. Many societies have lived in balance with their environments without devoting their lives to ecology and without invoking elaborate laws. It is not only easier, but apparently more productive, to persuade people to live by a few simple principles of caring for, and enjoying, the world.

No group has yet come up with a perfect plan for managing the environment. However, all societies have something to teach. The great benefit of anthropology is that it can bring together the combined wisdom of people from all times and places. Today, we need all the wisdom we can get, and only by pooling a wide range of human experiences can we survive.

People are emotional; society, including resource management, must be structured to take account of that.

This is not to say that humans are solely creatures of emotion. In practice, knowledge, emotion, and social institutions are inseparable, and all are involved in all significant action in the environment. Trying to separate one from the other as "the most important" is like trying to decide whether carbon, hydrogen, or oxygen is "the most important" ingredient in sugar or alcohol. In fact, what matters to us about sugar is an *emergent* property of the combination of the three. Sugar differs from alcohol—and particular sugars and alcohols differ from others—because the three ingredients are combined in different ways. Perhaps it would be better to analogize the carbon chain to the basic rational calculus, the hydrogen and the oxygen to the various emotions, and the overall structure to the institutions. The point is not to make a perfect analogy but to stress the indispensability of the factors.

Economists have tended to look only at individual rational decision making. Some economists add institutions, but few economists discuss the role of emotion. Conversely, "deep ecologists" and "spiritual" ecologists deal only with emotion, and sometimes institutions, forgetting or downplaying the rational calculus. No wonder ecological planning has been fragmented and contested.

Humans are imperfect planners. They value very small but immediate returns over much greater, but more distant or chancy, returns. Indeed, they often go with the most short-term, narrow plans and strategies possible.

Scholars and environmentalists have erred by assuming that people act in their rational self-interest. They do not. Positive illusions, including discounting the future and overvaluing one's own considerations, interfere. People are "rational" only in the tautological sense that allows economists to say that schizophrenics are as rational as business accountants.

Only experience or a strong social code will make people sacrifice immediate self-interest to long-term, wide-ranging interests. Without long experience and accumulated wisdom, people do not know what their interests are, and assume the best or simply don't think. Thus modern urbanites, cut off from the world of plants and animals, become more and more alienated from the issues at hand. Even farmers have changed; traditional cultivators are still forced to come to terms with their environments, but agribusiness and absentee landlords can avoid any such awareness.

Humans are also prone to react emotionally rather than sensibly. Often, this means that they solve a problem by attacking or repressing other people rather than by working for more creative and constructive solutions. Underdevelopment in the modern world is not caused by ignorance so much as by oppression. Everywhere, the powerful suppress those below instead of building, investing, and creating. In the long run, this is foolish; it makes everyone poorer. In the short run, it appears more economically "rational"—often because fear makes cruelty seem to be the height of rationality. The person on top fears those below, thus hates them, and thus prefers to rip them off than to develop human or natural resources wisely. The anti-environmental movement in the United States is based on hate more than greed; it is funded by the extractive industries, to be sure, but its troops on the ground are the racists, the religious bigots, the "sick and tired." The environmentalist view that these people are ignorant and misled is untrue. They are not a random selection of the gullible, but a "total sample" of the defensive.

There is no reason to think that the United States is unique. France, as we have seen, shows similar voting patterns. Other countries with ecological problems have suppressed debate for related reasons. To the degree that this holds true, the world environmental problem is not an environmental problem. It is a problem with human emotions. On the one hand, stressed, frightened people often react by attacking scapegoats rather than by working soberly to deal with the actual problem. On the other hand, good environmental management depends on harnessing the more prosocial emotions for the common good. Institutions such as Northwest Coast religion and Chinese *feng-shui* accomplish this.

Human society—specifically, as a resource-managing institution or set of institutions—depends on the ability of people to provide ways to *maximize correct empirical knowledge, emotionally involve people therein, and educate children in the tradition.* To the degree that this is accomplished, the society succeeds. To the degree it fails, the society fails.

We have seen that some systems of thought that seem strange to modern scientists—*feng-shui*, spiritual kinship with animals, and similar beliefs—have worked effectively in preserving the environment, while modern "rational" political economy has not. Emotional involvement, on a community level as well as among individuals, is necessary.

Conservation and resource management require a moral code and social institutions to maintain them. Without that, people will value short-term, narrow considerations over long-term, wide ones. In "tragedies of the commons," they are *forced* to do so.

Humans make mistakes, have positive illusions, and cheat. Therefore, the code and the institutions that enforce conservation and resource management must have many fail-safe mechanisms, *including, above all, democratic rights of recourse.* There must be free debate about errors and full rights to sue over mistakes. Above all, *the code and the institutions must be better than they appear to "need" to be.* We must err on the side of caution.

The coercive role of government is limited. Neither is coercive government desirable. Thus, the current environmentalist tendency to rely on big government, and heavy regulation, is *dangerously misguided.* We cannot and should not put a soldier behind every tree and bird. Even if we did, it wouldn't work; if society reached the point at which such a course was necessary, nothing could save the environment.

Thus, solutions *must be found in motivating individuals, especially those individuals who actually use the resources, to conserve.* This point seems almost universally agreed on by modern environmental economists and anthropologists. This is true whether they are classic conservatives (actually nineteenth-century liberals) like Terry Anderson and Donald Leal, classic liberals like Elinor Ostrom, or radicals like Evelyn Pinkerton.[1] Blue-ribbon panels such as the National Commission on the Environment argue for tax restructuring and ending subsidies to achieve such goals.[2] Unfortunately, even such rational motives, let alone emotional ones, are not often enough considered by environmentalists and policy-makers.

Failure often comes from reacting with self-defensive anger rather than cool reason. Evolution did right in giving us a quick, emotional response to lions and sabertooth cats. The problem is domesticating it in a world where the threats demand the coolest of cool thinking.

Failures follow from people getting caught up emotionally in scapegoating or withdrawal. These in turn are predictable from social coherence, and specifically from perceived "fairness."

The normal course of failure is predictable. In a society that fails to manage its resources well, a few get richer, but most get poorer. As rich and poor grow farther apart and the whole society gets more diverse, rules become more and more distorted to favor the powerful. This leads to more and more hurt and anger among all (even the powerful). This, in turn, inevitably leads to pathological coping mechanisms: hatred, scapegoating, withdrawal. These increase at the expense of rational coping. The crisis comes when people's emotions are caught up in the fear and rage, rather than in the preservation of knowledge and good management. By this time, the society has reached a stage where few people see it as worth preserving. A period of collapse sets in, ending when new institutions offer some hope.[3]

Successes occur when people get caught up emotionally in the task of learning more useful facts. Often, successes at using resources wisely can follow from deeply inaccurate (or at least "enchanted") views of reality, as in the Chinese and Northwest Coast cases. Failures can follow from more scientific views—misapplied—as in many examples from the technologically sophisticated United States. America is the homeland of conservation science and a center of nutritional research, yet traditional Chinese were better nourished (when they could afford it!) and traditional Northwest Coast Indians still conserve animals better.

Ultimately, people most often work to maximize security, not "happiness." They are also more concerned, ultimately, with society and control issues than with food, clothing, or shelter. Society and control are partially contradictory. It is notoriously hard to find the optimal trading off of sociability and autonomy. Many marriages founder on that rock.

People are, however, brilliant approximators—evolution has made sure of that. We are not so good at achieving perfection as at acting quickly to produce tolerable though imperfect solutions, and then improving those imperfect solutions by trial and error.

There is no free lunch, but some lunches are cheaper than others. In modern America, we are paying an appalling price for very unnutritious and tasteless fare—literally and figuratively.

Conservation cannot be separated from economic equity—benefits for all—because as long as there is gross inequity, the rich will be predatory and indulge in conspicuous consumption, and the poor will do everything possible to get a chance to consume more. Situations will be created such as we see with transportation: "everyone" needs a car.

It is obvious, also, that conservation is hardly going to flourish unless there is justice in the sense of fairness, and security from random violence.

The most direct approach is the best. Providing a wonderful social life does not guarantee conservation. Only direct consciousness of the need for conservation can do that. Economic development doesn't automatically do it. Love alone doesn't do it; many off-road vehicle users genuinely like the outdoors, but thoughtlessly damage fragile environments.

Human survival depends on educating everyone, especially the rising generations, in ecological morality. We must use the world for long-term, wide-flung benefits. We must emotionally involve everyone in the project of working toward such use.

The first and most obvious requirement is to get as much information out as possible, to minimize the danger of *solely* emotional action. Education, specifically environmental education, is necessary. This must involve people in their environments directly. It must also present choices and teach people to make decisions. Current educational strategies, which make people into mindless, passive sponges for information, are counterproductive. As Thomas Jefferson said: "I know of no safe depositor of the ultimate powers of the society but the people themselves; and if we think them not enlightened enough to exercise their control with a wholesome discretion, the remedy is not to take it from them, but to inform their discretion."[4]

The present book is about information processing and the making of mistakes, not about moral prescriptions. Others, more qualified, have examined the moral issues of modern environmentalism from many points of view, and have suggested moral codes.[5] However, it is not out of place to provide, here, some working notes toward the construction of a rough-and-ready moral code, specifically for environmental action. These notes do not comprise a moral code; they are some psychological and anthropological considerations that must be taken into account in creating one.

First and more important, the conservation movement must stick together and stop the current tendency to break down into rival agendas. Second, the movement needs to set priorities and hold to them. Saving the rainforests, for instance, should be a particularly high priority, because of the many benefits to people that are involved—to say nothing of the fact that the rainforests are the most species-rich habitats. This should take precedence over saving a pretty but ecologically altered neighborhood park. "Think globally, act locally" is a good proverb, but it has its limits; we can save the rainforests only by global *and* local action. Similarly, finding ways to make technology more efficient, and thus get more economic benefits from less resource use, is likely to benefit the environment far more than any quixotic crusades against technology could do.[6]

I do not believe that environmentalism needs a religion or needs to be a religion. Quite the reverse: I believe, very deeply and for many very good reasons, that narrow commitment to one or another sect is absolutely deadly to the environmental cause. It is not accident that the fiercest opposition to environmental causes comes from entrenched "fundamentalist" and hierarchic religious establishments, whether Protestant, Catholic, Muslim, or other. Thus, I find myself unable to sympathize with the hopeful but deeply misguided eco-radicals who attempt to tie the movement to "alternative" spiritual traditions. If they succeeded, they would create a new orthodoxy—and it would grow as anti-environmental as the rest. For the same reasons, I view with extreme suspicion the philosophizing about "unity (or harmony) with nature," "back to the land," "bioregionalism," and so forth. Such plans become straitjackets. What the movement needs is openness to *all* spiritual traditions, *all* visions and *all* philosophies, *insofar as they embody the simple morals stated here.* Indeed, one hopes for diversity; societies and cultures, like ecosystems, are normally dynamic and diverse. The problems with monocropping are as characteristic of its spiritual and moral forms as of its agricultural manifestations.

All morality is about helping one's friends and hurting one's foes. It takes very little thinking to realize that one is best off maximizing friendship and minimizing enmity. Ultimately, it would be best if all beings were in our "friend" group. This being impossible (I refuse to befriend the malaria parasites), we can at least approach such a state. It follows that wisdom lies in maximizing help and minimizing hurt. (Even so, I will keep taking malaria pills when I work in the tropics.)

All management, maybe all wisdom, lies in taking full account of the long-term and wide-flung costs and benefits of actions, discounting them accurately against the short-term and narrow interests.

It follows that the general solution to all human problems, not just ecological ones, lies in the widest possible extension of helping behavior.

It also lies in the widest possible extension of opportunity for each person to help. We need to make the most use we can of all human creativity; everyone has something to offer. It is thus ecologically imperative that we provide education, freedom of opportunity, and a chance to own a piece of the action to everyone. This last must mean at least some private property, but we have done far too little in the past with community resources and common-property resources. Managing these, and giving local people a real stake in planning that management, is the most serious immediate challenge.

It also lies in limiting as much as possible each person's ability to hurt. "My rights stop where my neighbor's start." Extreme inequalities of power are pernicious. The ability to pass on real costs of production, as "externalities," are worse. *The absolutely basic necessity, and the highest priority, for conservationists today, is to eliminate "externalities."* Consumers and producers who benefit from a production process *must pay the costs.* They *must not* pass them on to the poor, the weak, or the unborn. There are countless plans for doing this.[7] This simple rule would perhaps stop all ecological mismanagement.

The final nexus is caring respect, for humans especially, but ultimately for all beings. It must grow from trust, and produce responsibility.

The moral code has to be simple and even somewhat arbitrary, because a perfectly, rigorously logical moral code is either impossible or at least too complex for the real world.[8] A functioning moral code has to be pragmatic and easily understood.

It has to have, as its fundamental tenets, the following:

dedication to erring on the side of caution in resource use

dedication to truth and learning

dedication to freedom and civil liberties

dedication to social responsibility in the sense of doing more than one's share

absolute intolerance of cruelty and oppression

Morality in society is a *process.* The cure to the criticisms of Parfit and others is to realize that no moral code is ever final. It has to respond to improvements in knowledge and institutions. Thus, above all, we must make a commitment to improve: to be ever more watchful of the world and caring toward it, to be ever more successful at reducing harm, and to come to know and love the environment more and more widely and deeply.

Only such a code can have any effect against the common distorting forces. This general conclusion, specifically as it applies to resource management, has been reached by a wide variety of people, ranging from John Bodley to Martin Lewis and Evelyn Pinkerton.[9] No less than Vice President Al Gore has argued for a version of it.[10] It seems, then, fact-driven enough to prevail over many personal agendas.

More specifically, I think that we must face the fact that it is genuinely immoral to destroy a species or an ecosystem (in the sense of a bounded, self-maintaining habitat). We can crop individual animals and plants from a population, we can develop the ecosystem nondestructively, but we have no right to destroy something that we cannot recycle or re-create. This is exactly the same logic that makes it immoral to destroy a human life, a human cultural group, or a great work of art.

In war, human lives and creations are routinely sacrificed, and I can envision desperate cases in which we would sacrifice a species or an ecosystem. This is reasonable and probably inevitable. The point is that *species and ecosystems must not be sacrificed to the economic system any more than human individuals are.* They should not be bought and sold and should not be destroyed as part of routine economic action any more than humans should be—and for the same reasons: they are unique, irreplaceable, and intrinsically valuable. A religious person (I am one) would add that they are God-given, and we are allowed to use God's creations but not to destroy them utterly. The question of whether we can give animals or plants "rights" in the human sense remains open, but it is a different question.

In the end, though, moral codes are not enough. We must love the world and treat its beauty and diversity as goals to preserve and cherish.[11] All economic arguments have a limit, for economics is about means, not ends. We must thus present people with the best and most wonderful of natural and human creativity. This is, of course, what the big and established conservation organizations do—because they know it to be effective. We can only continue their work. Television, which too often allows people to escape the real world, also can bring the real world to the viewer. It has thus proved a powerful tool for conservation, because it can show, directly, tragedies and successes from around the planet.

Such truisms are valuable as a start, but are notoriously difficult to apply. We know that cooperation is good, but competition is sometimes good too. We know that competition is good for athletes and businesses, yet bad for street gangs and arming nations. We know that hurting, or at least restraining, one criminal is necessary to help or save many innocents. Where do the lines get drawn? At least such problems can be resolved, in theory, by study of cases. Conservation dilemmas, turning as they do on risk and uncertainty, are not so soluble. We cannot wait for certainty, because certainty would be gained only through our deaths. It is this that makes me invoke "erring on the side of caution" as a fundamental part of the code.

Truisms have their use. They provide a touchstone against which to test new plans. Such conservation plans as the idea of depopulating the Great Plains and turning them back to the buffalo may be tested: the certain costs would be enormous, the benefits uncertain and few. It may sound good to the romantic, but it fails any imaginable economic test.

The truisms also remind us that we are not dealing with bounded systems. Even the earth is not a closed system.

The beginning and end of our study is people—*The Ultimate Resource*, in the words of Julian Simon's thought-provoking critique of environmentalist received wisdom.[12] Human abilities, developed as best we can develop them, are both our real raw material and our ultimate goal. People work on an emotional economy of love and hate, acceptance and rejection, help and hurt. That is not discussed in the ecology texts, but it is actually the wellspring of all our actions.

Time is also a resource we often forget: "An inch of time is worth more than a foot of jade," the Chinese say. We do not have much of it left.

Love, including aesthetic delight, is necessary for any broad strategy for environmental management. It is the only early-warning system that works. Love for the peregrine falcons led to the quick discovery of the dangers of DDT. Love for people, ironically, was less evident; "virus X," which turned out to be acute DDT poisoning, was known before the peregrines started to go out, but no one sought to phase out DDT because it was dangerous to humans. We have made progress since.

The "pursuit of happiness" gets new meaning and a new lease on life from this cause. If we had taken literally that wonderful promise, we would never have consented to see a continent trashed for nothing.

In fact, we would be in a utopian situation if people would not so readily confuse happiness with vengeance or with escapism. Unfortunately, they do. Organized hate replaces political thought. Mindless escapism replaces pleasure. People satisfied with a media world will not act to save the real one. People deluded into thinking that their welfare depends on reducing someone else's will not act to save anything at all.

In a world of sober realities, conservationists must appeal to fear as well as love. But we have too many people whose lives are ruled by fear, leaving them little else. We of the environmental movement will have to give them more: the pleasures of living in a world where there is more than desperate need, fear, and hate. Love and enjoyment grow out of hardship as well as simple pleasure. We will have our share of hardship before ecological sanity prevails.

The United States in the 1930s and 1940s faced runaway soil erosion, and combated it by working with farmers, showing them it was in their self-interest to terrace land, install farm ponds and checkdams, plant trees, and keep some vegetation cover. This worked, usually, and transformed the landscape. I well remember these campaigns from my Nebraska youth, and I saw them work. Today, erosion of genetic resources is being fought by government fiat— bureaucracy ordering ranchers and developers to forgo economic benefits to save species, without much explanation as to why. The reaction is predictable. All our lessons from the 1940s have apparently been forgotten.

General economic development does not lead to conservation, though without it there can be no ecological improvement. Strong communities do not guarantee sane resource use. Neither does justice guarantee good resource management, though it comes the closest and is the most basic, absolute necessity for the world ecosystem. Conservation has to be taught directly. This means that we must be more directly involved in spreading the word.

Conservation is basically about cooperation and about fair play in both cooperation and competition. It is about people and about the social contract, not about resources. The cause of conservation is the cause of freedom, justice, and economic progress. The opponents of sound resource management oppose the other three as well. It is not only that all four causes depend on each other. The deeper truth is that the pursuit of happiness is, as the Founding Fathers knew, dependent on all four. It unites them into one stream.

In the end, education of the public, and especially of the young, is the only hope. They must be made aware of these issues and of these moral codes. They must have at least the option of adopting them. They must have the best possible access to the glory of the natural and human world, so that they can make choices *in the full knowledge of what we can lose.*

The solution is simple but comprehensive. Conservation is simply a form of mutual caring respect. Focally, it is respect for our fellow humans. More broadly, it is respect for the world. Conservation, in the sense of sustainable and efficient use of resources, is an absolute necessity for the survival of humanity.

Notes

Preface

1. Carolyn Merchant, *Radical Ecology* (London: Routledge, 1992).

2. Barry C. Field, *Environmental Economics: An Introduction* (New York: McGraw-Hill, 1994).

3. Gregory Bateson, *Steps toward an Ecology of Mind* (San Francisco: Chandler, 1972).

Chapter 1.   Landscape with Figures

1. Shelley Taylor, *Positive Illusions* (New York: Basic Books, 1989).

2. *Earth Island,* Summer 1992, passim.

3. Joel T. Heinen and Roberta C. ("Bobbi") S. Low, "Human Behavioral Ecology and Environmental Conservation," *Environmental Conservation* 19 (1993): 105–115.

4. George Ainslie, *Picoeconomics: The Strategic Interaction of Successive Motivational States with the Person* (Cambridge: Cambridge University Press, 1993); and Barry C. Field, *Environmental Economics: An Introduction* (New York: McGraw-Hill, 1994).

5. Derek Parfit, *Reasons and Persons* (1984; reprint, Oxford: Oxford University Press, 1989).

6. Murray Feshbach and Alfred Friendly, Jr., *Ecocide in the USSR* (New York: Basic Books, 1991).

7. David W. Orr, "For the Love of Life," *Conservation Biology* 6 (1992): 486–487.

8. Arthur McEvoy, *The Fisherman's Problem* (Cambridge: Cambridge University Press, 1986); and Donald Ludwig, Ray Hilborn, and Carl Walters, "Uncertainty, Resource Exploitation, and Conservation: Lessons from History," *Science* 26 (1993): 17–18.

9. Earl Murphy, *Governing Nature* (Chicago: Quadrangle Books, 1967).

10. Garrett Hardin, "The Tragedy of the Commons," *Science* 162 (1968): 1243–1248; cf. Elinor Ostrom, *Governing the Commons* (Cambridge: Cambridge University Press, 1990).

11. Parfit, *Reasons.*

12. Peter Drucker, *The Ecological Vision* (New Brunswick, N.J.: Transaction, 1992).

13. Jon Elster, *Ulysses and the Sirens,* 2d ed. (Cambridge: Cambridge University Press, 1984).

14. Marshall Sahlins, *Culture and Practical Reason* (Chicago: University of Chicago Press, 1976).

15. E. g., Robert Edgerton, *Sick Societies: Challenging the Myth of Primitive Harmony* (New York: Free Press, 1992); and Thomas Lewis, "Cloaked in a Wise Disguise," *National Wildlife* (Oct.–Nov. 1992): 4–8.

16. David Hume, *Enquiries Concerning Human Understanding and Concerning the Principles of Morals,* 1777 ed. of 1772 work (Oxford: Oxford University Press, 1975).

17. E. N. Anderson, *The Food of China.* (New Haven: Yale University Press 1988).

18. See Eric Hobsbawm and Terence Ranger, eds., *The Invention of Tradition* (Cambridge: Cambridge University Press, 1982) for a cynical look at "immemorial traditions" such as the tartans.

19. Robert Netting, *Balancing on an Alp* (Cambridge: Cambridge University Press, 1981).

20. Raymond Firth, *We the Tikopia* (London: G. Allen and Unwin, 1936), *Social Change in Tikopia* (London: G. Allen and Unwin, 1959), and *Economics of the New Zealand Maori* (London: Routledge, Kegan Paul, 1965).

21. Paul Cox and Sandra Banack, eds., *Islands, Plants, and Polynesians* (Portland, Oreg.: Timber Press, 1991); and Denise Yim, "Maori Ideology and Religion: 2000 Years of Ecological Success," *Ms.* (1992).

22. Janis Alcorn, *Huastec Mayan Ethnobotany* (Austin: University of Texas Press, 1984); and Marvin Mikesell, *Northern Morocco: A Cultural Geography* (Berkeley: University of California Press, 1961).

23. Darrell Posey, "Reply to Parker," *American Anthropologist* 92 (1992): 441–443.

24. Conrad Totman, *The Green Archipelago: Forestry in Preindustrial Japan* (Berkeley: University of California Press, 1989).

25. L. Katherine Baril, "Private Property and the Public Trust Doctrine: Developing New Paradigms for Government to Balance Individual Property Rights and Public Resource Protection" (paper presented at the annual meeting of the International Association for the Study of Common Property, 1992); and William Poole, "Neither Wise nor Well," *Sierra* (Nov.–Dec. 1992): 59–61, 88–93.

26. Martin Lewis, *Green Delusions: An Environmentalist Critique of Radical Environmentalism* (Durham: Duke University Press, 1992).

27. E.g., Rifkin, *Journey Beyond Beef* (New York: Dutton, 1992).

28. *Los Angeles Times,* 25 October 1992.

29. Baril, "Private Property."

Chapter 2.   Feng-shui: *Ideology and Ecology*

1. Gary Seaman, "The Material Soul" (paper presented at the annual meeting of the Association for Asian Studies, 1987).

2. Ernest J. Eitel, *Feng-shuii: Or, the Rudiments of Natural Science in China* (Hong Kong: Lane, Crawford, and Co., 1873).

3. E. N. Anderson, "Ecology and Ideology in Chinese Folk Nutritional Therapy" (paper presented at the annual meeting of the American Anthropological Asso-

ciation, 1982, and "Why are Some Rocks and Trees Worshipped?" (paper presented at the University of Southern California China Colloquium, 1982); E. N. Anderson and M. L. Anderson, *Mountains and Water* (Taipei: Orient Cultural Service, 1973); Evelyn Lip, *Feng-Shui: A Layman's Guide to Chinese Feng-Shui* (Singapore: Heian, 1979); and Derek Walters, *The Feng Shui Handbook* (London: HarperCollins, 1991).

4. Cf. Hugh Baker, *Chinese Family and Kinship* (New York: Columbia University Press, 1979); and Steven Feuchtwang, *An Anthropological Analysis of Chinese Geomancy* (Vientiane, Laos: Vithagna, 1974).

5. J. J. M. de Groot, *The Religious System of China* (Leiden: Brill, 1892–1910), 937–938.

6. Eitel, *Feng-shuii;* and Henri Dore, *Researches into Chinese Superstitions* (Shanghai: Tusewei, 1914).

7. Richard Davisson, Jr., "The Dragon in San Francisco," *Landscape* 17 (1967–68): 169–193; Sarah Rossbach, *Feng Shui: The Chinese Art of Placement* (New York: E. P. Dutton, 1983); Rolf Stein, *The World in Miniature* (Stanford: Stanford University Press, 1990); and Derek Walters, *Feng-Shui: The Chinese Art of Designing a Harmonious Environment* (New York: Simon and Schuster, 1988), and *Handbook.*

8. Lip, *Feng-Shui;* Hong-Key Yoon, *Geomantic Relationships between Culture and Nature in Korea* (Taipei: Orient Cultural Service, 1976); and Zozayong, *Diamond Mountain,* 2 vols. (Seoul: Emille Museum, 1975).

9. Edward Hall, *The Silent Language* (Garden City: Doubleday, 1959), and *The Hidden Dimension* (Garden City: Doubleday, 1966).

10. Douglas Fraser, *Village Planning in the Primitive World* (New York: Brasiller, 1968); Amos Rapoport, *House Form and Culture* (Englewood Cliffs, N.J.: Prentice-Hall, 1969); and Bernard Rudofsky, *Architecture without Architects* (New York: Museum of Modern Art 1965).

11. Kevin Lynch, *The Image of the City* (Cambridge, Mass.: M.I.T. Press, 1960).

12. Andrew Boyd, *Chinese Architecture* (London: Alec Tirani, 1962).

13. Cf. Robert Jaulin, *La Géomancie: Analyse formelle* (Paris: Mouton, 1969).

14. Feuchtwang, *Analysis;* Lip, *Feng-Shui;* and Seaman, "Material Soul."

15. Laszlo Legeza, *Tao Magic* (New York: Random House, 1975); and Yoon, *Geomantic Relationships.*

16. Seaman, "Material Soul."

17. W. Hu, personal communication.

18. Lip, *Feng-Shui.*

19. Ibid., 45.

20. Anderson, "Why are Some Rocks and Trees Worshipped?"

21. Lip, *Feng-Shui.*

22. Walters, *Handbook.*

23. Ibid.

24. Ibid.

25. For good popular accounts in English, see Rossbach, *Feng Shui.* and Walters, *Handbook.*

26. Mary Elizabeth Crary, "Chinese Feng Shui in the Context of an American Suburb" (master's thesis, California State University, 1992).

27. For a full discussion see Maurice Freedman, *Chinese Lineage and Society: Fukien and Kwnagtung* (London: London School of Economics, 1966).

28. Baker, *Family.*

29. Anderson and Anderson, *Mountains;* Baker, *Family;* Feuchtwang, *Analysis;* and Freedman, *Lineage.*

30. See the account in Anderson and Anderson, *Mountains,* 134–135.

31. Freedman, *Lineage;* and Feuchtwang, *Analysis.*

32. Vaclav Smil, *The Bad Earth* (Armonk, N.Y.: M. E. Sharpe, 1984).

33. See Boyd, *Architecture;* and Ronald Knapp, *China's Traditional Rural Architecture* (Honolulu: University of Hawaii, 1986).

34. Ian MacHarg, *Design with Nature* (Garden City: Natural History Press, 1969).

35. Cf. Walter H. Mallory, *China, Land of Famine* (New York: American Geographical Society, special publication no. 6, 1926).

36. Smil, *Bad Earth.*

37. Roy Rappaport, "The Sacred in Human Evolution," *Annual Review of Ecology and Systematics* 2 (1971): 23–44, and *Pigs for the Ancestors,* 2d ed. (New Haven: Yale University Press, 1984).

Chapter 3.   Chinese Nutritional Therapy

1. E. N. Anderson, *The Food of China* (New Haven: Yale University Press, 1988).

2. Ibid.

3. Production affects consumption, too, but in China consumption has often been the clear driving force; see Anderson, *Food of China.*

4. Ulric Neisser, *Cognition and Reality* (San Francisco: Freeman, 1976).

5. Anderson, *Food of China;* Henry Lu, *Chinese System of Food Cures* (New York: Sterling Publishing Co., 1986); and Rance Lee, "Perceptions and Uses of Chinese Medicine among the Chinese of Hong Kong," *Culture, Medicine and Psychiatry* 4 (1980): 345–375.

6. E. N. Anderson, "Why Is Humoral Medicine So Popular?" *Social Science and Medicine* 25 (1987): 331–337; and George Foster, "On the Origin of Humoral Medicine in Latin America," *Medical Anthropology Quarterly* 1 (1987): 355–393.

7. Manfred Pokert, *Theoretical Foundations of Chinese Medicine* (Cambridge, Mass.: M.I.T. Press, 1974.

8. For the history, see Anderson, *Food of China.*

9. Walter H. Mallory, *China, Land of Famine* (New York: American Geographical Society, special publication no. 6, 1926).

10. Paul Unschuld, *Medicine in China: A History of Ideas* (Berkeley: University of California Press, 1985).

11. Pokert, *Theoretical Foundations.*

12. For discussions and definitions of Chinese medical concepts, see Paul Buell, "Theory and Practice of Traditional Chinese Medicine" (paper no. 21 presented at the East Asian Colloquium, Center for East Asian Studies, Bellingham, Wash., 1984); Frank Liu and Yan Mau Liu, *Chinese Medical Terminology* (Hong Kong: Commercial Press, 1980); Pokert, *Theoretical Foundations;* Kristofer Schipper, "The Taoist Body," *History of Religion* 17 (1978): 3–4, 355–386; Unschuld, *Ideas, Medicine in China: A History of Pharmaceutics* (Berkeley: University of California Press, 1986), and *Medicine in China: Nan-Ching: The Classic of Difficult Issues* (Berkeley: University of California Press, 1986).

13. See Unschuld, *Ideas.*

14. Ibid.

15. Ibid.

16. Joseph Needham, review of *Ideas* and *Pharmaceutics,* by Paul Unschuld, *American Ethnologist,* 15 (1 [1988]): 182–183.

17. E.g., Taiwan. See Katherine Gould-Martin, "Hot Cold Clean Poison and Dirt: Chinese Folk Medical Categories," *Social Science and Medicine* 12 (1978): 39–46.

18. Linda Koo, *Nourishment of Life* (Hong Kong: Commercial Press, 1982); and M. Topley, "Chinese Traditional Ideas and the Treatment of Disease: Two Examples from Hong Kong," *Man* 5 (1970): 421–437.

19. Paul Unschuld, Illness and Health in Chinese Medicine (paper presented at the annual conference of the Association for Asian Studies, Boston, MA, 1987).

20. Lee, *Perceptions.*

21. Richard Currier, "The Hot-Cold Syndrome and Symbolic Balance in Mexican and Spanish-American Folk Medicine," *Ethnology* 5 (1966): 251–263. See also George Foster, "Peasant Society and the Image of Limited Good," *American Anthropologist* 67 (1965): 293–315; and George Foster and Barbara Anderson, *Medical Anthropology* (New York: Wiley, 1978).

22. Gould-Martin, *Hot Cold Clean.*

23. H. Creel, *Shen Pu-Hai* (Chicago: University of Chicago Press, 1973); and Anderson, *Food of China.*

24. See Anderson, (1982ᵃ), "Ecologies of the Heart," in *Proceedings of the International Chinese Medicine Conference,* ed. Michael Gandy et al. (Oakland, 1984), 205–230, "Heating and Cooling Foods Re-Examined," *Social Science and Medicine* 25 (1984): 331–337, and, especially, "Humoral."

25. Anderson, E. N. "Heating and Cooling Foods in Hong Kong and Taiwan," *Social Science Information* 19 (2 [1980]): 237–268, and "Humoral."

26. Carol Laderman, "Symbolic and Empirical Reality: A New Approach to the Analysis of Food Avoidances," *American Ethnologist* 3 (1981): 468–493.

27. Anderson, "Humoral."

28. Anderson, E. N. "Ecology and Ideology in Chinese Folk Nutritional Therapy" (paper presented at the annual meeting of the American Anthropological Association, Washington, D.C., 1982); and Gould-Martin, *Hot Cold Clean.*

29. Unschuld, *Ideas* and *Illness.*

30. E. N. Anderson, *The Floating World of Castle Peak Bay* (Washington, D.C.: American Anthropological Association, 1970).

31. John Young, *Business and Sentiment in a Chinese Market Town* (Taipei: Orient Cultural Service, 1974).

32. Cf. Foster and Anderson, *Medical Anthropology.*

33. Cf. Diamond Jenness, *The Faith of a Coast Salish Indian* (Victoria, B.C.: British Columbia Provincial Museum, Anthropological Papers no. 3, 1955).

34. Robert Bellah et al., *Habits of the Heart* (Berkeley: University of California Press, 1985).

35. Arthur Kleinman, *Patients and Healers in the Context of Culture* (Berkeley: University of California Press, 1980), and *Social Origins of Distress and Disease* (New Haven: Yale University Press, 1986).

36. Hill Gates, "Dependency and the Part-Time Proletariat in Taiwan," *Modern China* 5 (1979): 381–407; Robert Marks, *Rural Revolution in South China* (Madison: University of Wisconsin Press, 1984); Robert Weller, *Unities and Diversities in Chinese Religion* (Seattle: University of Washington Press, 1987).

37. Anderson, *Floating World.*

38. E. P. Thompson, *The Making of the English Working Class* (1963; reprint, New York: Vintage, 1966); and Jean Comaroff, *Body of Power, Spirit of Resistance* (Chicago: University of Chicago Press, 1985).

39. Richard Schulz, "Some Life and Death Consequences of Perceived Control," *Cognition and Social Behavior,* ed. John S. Carroll and John W. Payne (New York: Academic Press, 1976), 135–153.

40. Albert Bandura, "Self-Efficacy Mechanism in Human Agency," *American Psychologist* 37 (2 [1982]): 122–147; and Ellen Langer, *The Psychology of Control* (Beverly Hills: Sage, 1983).

41. Koo, *Nourishment.*

42. Najma Rizvi, personal communication.

43. See Carol Laderman, "Symbolic and Empirical Reality: A New Approach to the Analysis of Food Avoidances," *American Ethnologist* 3 (1981): 468–493, for Malaysia.

44. Barbara Pillsbury, "Doing the Month" (paper presented at the annual meeting of the American Anthropological Association 1976).

45. Mary Douglas, *Natural Symbols* (London: Barrie and Rockliff, 1966), and *Implicit Meanings* (London: Routledge, Kegan Paul, 1975). The latter book was published with a cover picture of a pangolin printed upside down, anomalous to the end.

46. Laderman, *Symbolic.*

47. Gould-Martin, *Hot Cold Clean,* 41.

48. Libin Cheng, "Are the So-Called Poisonous Food-Combinations Really Poisonous?" Contributions, Biological Laboratory, Science Society of China, *Zoological Series* 2 (9 [1936]): 307–316.

49. Gould-Martin, *Hot Cold Clean,* 40.

50. See, e.g., A. C. Graham, *Later Mohist Logic* (Hong Kong and London: Chinese University of Hong Kong and University of London School of Oriental and African Studies, 1978); and D. Lau, *Mencius* (Harmondsworth, Sussex: Pelican, 1970).

51. Kleinman, *Patients,* and *Social Origins.*

52. Koo, *Nourishment.*

53. Foster and Anderson, *Medical Anthropology.*

54. Unschuld, *Ideas.*

55. Charlotte Furth, "Concepts of Pregnancy, Childbirth, and Infancy in Ch'ing Dynasty China," *Journal of Asian Studies* 46 (1 [1987]): 7–35.

56. James Scott, *Weapons of the Weak* (New Haven: Yale University Press, 1985).

57. Susan Fiske and Shelley Taylor, *Social Cognition* (Reading, Mass.: Addison-Wesley, 1984); and David Morgan, unpublished research.

58. Robert Zajonc, "Feeling and Thinking: Preferences Need No Inferences," *American Psychologist* 35 (1980): 151–175.

59. Bandura, "Self-Efficacy."

60. See important discussions in Pokert, *Foundations,* and Unschuld, *Ideas.*

61. Liu and Liu, *Terminology.*

62. Karin Hilsdale, "The 'Psychiatry' of Traditional Oriental Medicine: An Exploratory Study in Comparative Diagnosis of Depressed Women" (Ph.D. diss., International College, 1985).

63. See Kleinman, *Social Origins.*

64. Michael Gandy et al. (eds.), *Proceedings of the International Chinese Medicine Conference* (Oakland, 1984).

65. Hilsdale, " 'Psychiatry.' "

Chapter 4.   *Learning from the Land Otter:*
Religious Representation of Traditional Resource Management

1. Emile Durkheim, *The Elementary Forms of the Religious Life* (Glencoe, Ill.: Free Press, 1961).

2. Robin Ridington, "Technology, World View, and Adaptive Strategy in a Northern Hunting Society," *Canadian Review of Sociology and Anthropology* 19 (4 [1982]): 469–481. For other areas of the world, see Roy A. Rappaport, "The Sacred in Human Evolution," *Annual Review of Ecology and Systematics* 2 (1971): 23–44, and *Pigs for the Ancestors,* 2d ed. (New Haven: Yale University Press, 1984); and Gerardo Reichel-Dolmatoff, "Cosmology as Ecological Analysis: A View from the Rain Forest," *Man* 11 (1976): 307–316.

3. H. A. Feit, personal communication; Richard F. Salisbury, *A Homeland for the Cree.* (Kingston and Montreal McGill-Queen's University Press, 1986); Tanner, *Bringing Home Animals* (London: C. Hurst and Co., 1979); Hugh Brody, *Maps and Dreams* (Harmondsworth: Pelican, 1983); Ridington, "Technology"; Richard K. Nelson,

Hunters of the Northern Forest (Chicago: University of Chicago Press, 1973), "A Conservation Ethic and Environment: The Koyukon of Alaska," in *Resource Managers,* ed. Nancy Williams and Eugene Hunn (Boulder, Colo.: Westview Press, 1982), 211–228, and *Make Prayers to the Raven* (Chicago: University of Chicago Press, 1983); Catherine McClellan, *My Old People Say* (Ottawa: National Museums of Canada, 1975); George T. Emmons, *The Tlingit Indians,* ed. Frederica de Laguna (Seattle: University of Washington Press and American Museum of Natural History, 1991), 102; and Frederica de Laguna, *Under Mount Saint Elias: The History and Culture of the Yakutat Tlingit* (Washington: Smithsonian Institution, 1972).

4. Robert Brightman, *Conservation and Resource Depletion: The Case of the Boreal Forest Algonquians* (McCay and Acheson), 121–141. Cites to book edited by McCay and Acheson.

5. Nelson, *Hunters,* 155.

6. Calvin Martin, *Keepers of the Game* (Berkeley: University of California Press, 1978).

7. Feit, personal communication; and Tanner, *Bringing Home Animals.*

8. Rudolf Kaiser, "Chief Seattle's Speech(es): American Origins and European Reception," in *Recovering the Word: Essays on Native American Literature,* ed. Brian Swann and Arnold Krupat (Berkeley: University of California Press, 1987), 497–536.

9. For a good explanation of the complex rationale for such beings, see the account of Chipewyan monster in Henry S. Sharp, "Giant Fish, Giant Otters, and Dinosaurs: 'Apparently Irrational Beliefs' in a Chipewyan Community," *American Ethnologist* 14 (1987): 226–235.

10. Diamond Jenness, *The Faith of a Coast Salish Indian* (Victoria, B.C.: British Columbia Provincial Museum, anthropological papers no. 3, 1955).

11. Pamela Amoss, "A Little More Than Kin, and Less Than Kind: The Ambiguous Northwest Coast Dog," in *The Tsimshian and Their Neighbors of the North Pacific Coast,* ed. Jay Miller and Carol Eastman (Seattle: University of Washington Press, 1984), 292–305.

12. Aldona Jonaitis, *Tlingit Halibut Hooks: An Analysis of the Visual Symbolism of a Rite of Passage* (New York: American Museum of Natural History, anthropological papers no. 57 [1], 1981), and *Art of the Northern Tlingit* (Seattle: University of Washington Press, 1986).

13. Jonaitis, *Tlingit Halibut Hooks,* and *Art;* de Laguna, *Under Mount Saint Elias;* and; John Swanton, *Haida Myths and Texts: Skidegate Dialect* (Washington: Bureau of American Ethnology, bulletin no. 29, 1905), *Social Conditions, Beliefs, and Linguistic Relationships of the Tlingit Indians* (Washington: Bureau of American Ethnology, annual report no. 26, 1908), 391–486, and *Tlingit Myths and Texts* (Washington: Bureau of American Ethnology, bulletin no. 39, 1909).

14. Swanton, *Haida Myths,* 358–361. Swanton thinks this story is originally Tlingit, and I agree.

15. de Laguna, *Under Mount Saint Elias,* 749–750; and Swanton, *Social Conditions,* 28.

16. de Laguna, *Under Mount Saint Elias,* 678, 744 ff., 897.

17. For the full story, see especially Emmons, *Tlingit;* de Laguna, *Under Mount Saint Elias,* 678 ff., 702 ff., etc.; A. Krause, *The Tlingit Indians* (Seattle: University of Washington, Press, 1956); and Swanton, *Social Conditions.*

18. Jonaitis, *Art.*

19. Jonaitis, *Tlingit Halibut Hooks,* and *Art.*

20. Emmons, *Tlingit,* 441.

21. de Laguna, *Under Mount Saint Elias,* 814.

22. Swanton, *Tlingit Myths.*

23. For particularly good accounts of the human-nonhuman interface, see Philip Drucker, *The Northern and Central Nootka Tribes* (Washington: Bureau of American Ethnology, 1955), for the Nuu-chah-nulth; de Laguna, *Under Mount Saint Elias,* and Swanton, *Social Conditions,* for Tlingit; and Irving Goldman, *The Mouth of Heaven: An Introduction to Kwakiutl Religious Thought* (New York: Wiley, 1975), and Stanley Walens, *Feasting with Cannibals* (Princeton, N.J.: Princeton University Press, 1981), for the "Kwakiutl."

24. Chief Kenneth Harris, *Visitors Who Never Left* (Vancouver: University of British Columbia Press, 1974), 25.

25. See Leslie Gottesfeld, "Gitksan and Wet'suwet'en Conservation Ethics, Concepts and Practices" (Ms.); and Kitanmax School of Northwest Coast Indian Art, *Wegyet Wanders On* (Hazelton, B.C.: Kitanmax School of Northwest Coast Indian Art, 1977).

26. Brody, *Maps;* and Ridington, "Technology."

27. See Stephen A. McNeary, "Image and Illusion in Tsimshian Mythology," in *The Tsimshian and Their Neighbors of the North Pacific Coast,* ed. Jay Miller and Carol Eastman (Seattle: University of Washington Press, 1984), 3–15.

28. Ridington, *Little Bit Know Something* (Iowa City, IA: University of Iowa Press, 1990)

29. For further information, see Allan Richardson, "Control of Productive Resources on the Northwest Coast of North America," in Williams and Hunn, *Resource Managers,* 93–112, Philip Drucker, *The Northern and Central Nootka Tribes* (Washington: Bureau of American Ethnology, 1955), and Ruth Kirk, *Wisdom of the Elders* (Victoria: British Columbia Provincial Museum, 1986), for the Nuu-chah-nulth and their neighbors; W. W. Elmendorf, *The Structure of Twana Culture* (Pullman, Wash.: Washington State University Press, 1960), Jenness, *Faith,* June McCormick Collins, *Valley of the Spirits* (Seattle: University of Washington Press, 1974), and Wayne Suttles, "The Economic Life of the Coast Salish of Haro and Rosario Straits" (Ph.D. diss., University of Washington, 1951) and *Coast Salish Essays* (Vancouver: Talonbooks and Seattle: University of Washington Press, 1987), for Salish groups; de Laguna, *Under Mount Saint Elias,* for Tlingit; and Harris, *Visitors,* Kitanmax School, *Wegyet,* and Mike Morrell, *The Gitksan and Wet'suwet'en Fishery in the Skeena River System* (Hazelton, B.C.: Gitksan-Wet'suwet'en Tribal Council, 1985), for Gitksan; and Gottesfeld, "Gitksan and Wet'suwet'en," for the Wet'suwet'en.

30. See Kalervo Oberg, *The Social Economy of the Tlingit Indians* (Seattle: University of Washington Press, 1973), for Tlingit, and George Murdock, *Our Primitive Contemporaries* (New York: Dutton, 1934), for the Haida.

31. For the full complexity of the best-known situation, see Suttles, "Economic Life," and "Essays."

32. See Morrell, *Fishery,* for the best-documented case.

33. Ralph Maud, *A Guide to B. C. Indian Myth and Legend* (Vancouver: Talonbooks, 1982).

34. Harris, *Visitors;* and de Laguna, *Under Mount Saint Elias,* 814.

35. Jenness, *Faith.*

36. See, for example, Kirk, Wisdom; Collins, *Valley;* Williams and Hunn, *Resource Managers;* and especially the superb work of Harriet Kuhnlein, Nancy Turner, and their associates, in Dana Lepofsky, Nancy J. Turner, and Harriet V. Kuhnlein, "Determining the Availability of Traditional Wild Plant Foods: An Example of Nuxalk Foods, Bella Coola, British Columbia," *Ecology of Food Nutrition* 16 (1985): 223–241.

37. Gilbert Malcolm Sproat, *The Nootka: Scenes and Studies of Savage Life,* ed. Charles Lillard (Victoria, B.C.: Sono Nis Press, 1987).

38. Steven Langdon, "Technology, Ecology and Economy: Fishing Systems in Southeast Alaska" (Ph.D. diss. Stanford University, 1977), "Comparative Tlingit and Haida Adaptation to the West Coast of the Prince of Wales Archipelago," *Ethnology* 18 (1979): 102–109, and "Alaskan Native Self-regulation of Subsistence Resources: Traditional Practices and Emerging Institutions," (paper presented at the annual meeting of the American Anthropological Association, 1985).

39. Langdon, "Technology"; Suttles, *Essays;* J. Pritchard, personal communication; and my own fieldwork—though see Philip Drucker and Robert Heizer, *To Make My Name Good* (Berkeley: University of California Press, 1967), for a useful reminder that there could be a great deal of food and that populations were kept down to within the subsistence base in normal times.

40. Morrell, *Fishery.*

41. J. Pritchard, personal communication.

42. See the classic paper by Sean Swezey and Robert F. Heizer, "Ritual Management of Salmonid Fish Resources in California," *Journal of California Anthropology* 4 (1977): 6–29; for general surveys in relation to modern needs, see Evelyn Pinkerton, ed., *Cooperative Management of Local Fisheries: New Directions for Improved Management and Community Development* (Vancouver: University of British Columbia Press, 1989).

43. See Jenness, *Faith,* and, for game animals, McClellan, *My Old People Say;* I also refer to unpublished data collected by Evelyn Pinkerton and me.

44. Earl Murphy, *Governing Nature* (Chicago: Quadrangle Books, 1967).

45. E.g., Martin, *Keepers.*

46. Philip Wilke, personal communication.

47. Gary P. Nabhan et al., "Papago Influences on Habitat and Biotic Diversity: Quitovac Oasis Ethnoecology," *Journal of Ethnobiology* 2 (1982): 1224–1243.

48. Kenneth Ruddle and Ray Chesterfield, *Education for Food Production in the Orinoco Delta* (Berkeley: University of California Press, 1977).

49. Richard Gould, *Yiwara: Foragers of the Australian Desert* (New York: Scribners, 1969); and Carobeth Laird, *The Chemehuevis* (Banning, Calif.: Malki Museum Press, 1976).

50. Maud, *Guide.*

51. See Eugene Hunn, *Nch'i Wana, the Big River* (Seattle: University of Washington Press, 1991).

52. Claude Lévi-Strauss, *La Pensée sauvage* (Paris: Plon, 1962), and *The Way of Masks* (Seattle: University of Washington Press, 1982).

53. Jonaitis, similar beliefs among the Huastec and Yaqui, see Janis Alcorn, *Huastec Mayan Ethnobotany* (Austin: University of Texas Press, 1984); and Muriel Painter, *With Good Heart* (Tuscon: University of Arizona Press, 1985). The Huastec even have a belief that a weasel will catch and tickle the prospective curer, giving him power; weasels and their relatives the otters seem naturally evocative creatures (Alcorn, personal communication).

54. Wilson Duff, "The World Is as Sharp as a Knife: Meaning in Northern Northwest Coast Art," in *Indian Art Traditions of the Northwest Coast,* ed. Roy Carlson (Burnaby, B.C.: Archaeology Press, Simon Fraser University, 1983), 47–66, and ms.; and Stanley Walens, *Feasting with Cannibals* (Princeton: Princeton University Press, 1981).

55. Richard Nisbett and Lee Ross, *Human Inference* (Englewood Cliffs, N.J.: Prentice-Hall, 1980).

56. Cf., e.g., Harris, *Visitors;* and Morrell, *Fishery.*

57. Wolfgang Jilek, *Indian Healing* (Vancouver: Hancock House, 1982); and my personal observation.

Chapter 5. Managing the Rainforest: Maya Agriculture in the Town of the Wild Plums

1. The information in this chapter is primarily from my own fieldwork, but much of it emerged from comparing notes with a number of people, especially Betty Faust, Salvador Flores, Arturo Gomez-Pompa, Francisco Rosado-May, and Kathleen Truman. (Francisco Rosado-May is the first Quintana Roo Maya to hold a Ph.D. from an American university; he is now professor at the new University of Quintana Roo.) Otherwise unattributed statements derive from these discussions. Of course, my greatest debt is to the people of Chunhuhub and its neighboring villages.

2. See Inga Clendinnen, *Ambivalent Conquests* (Cambridge: Cambridge University Press, 1987).

3. Paul Sullivan, *Unfinished Conversations* (Berkeley: University of California Press, 1989).

4. Much study has been devoted to Yucatán's dooryard gardens; see Ellen Kintz, *Life under the Tropical Canopy* (New York: Holt, Rinehart and Winston, 1990); and Victor Rico-Gray et al., "Species Composition, Similarity, and Structure of Mayan

196 | NOTES

Homegardens in Tixpeual and Tixcacaltuyub, Yucatán, Mexico," *Economic Botany* 44 (1992): 470–487.

5. Bavera Vasquez, A. et al. (1976).

6. F. Benedict and Morris Steggerda, *The Food of the Present-Day Maya Indians of Yucatán* (Washington, D.C.: Carnegie Foundation, 1936); Maria Elena Peraza Lopez, "Patrones alimenticios en Ichmul, Yucatán" (diss., Universidad Autónima de Yucatán, 1986); and James Stuart, "Maize Use by Rural Mesoamerican Households," *Human Organization* 49 (1990): 135–139.

7. E. N. Anderson, "The Sosa Farm" (paper presented at the annual meeting of the Southwestern Anthropological Association, San Diego, 1993).

8. Garrett Hardin, "The Tragedy of the Commons," *Science* 162 (1968): 1243–1248.

9. E. N. Anderson, "Folk Forestry in a Maya Town," Ms. (1992).

10. Charles Andrew Hofling, *Itza Maya Texts* (Salt Lake City: University of Utah Press, 1991).

11. See Theodore Downing et al., eds., *Development or Destruction? The Conversion of Tropical Forests to Pasture in Latin America* (Boulder, Colo.: Westview Press, 1992); and Arturo Gomez-Pompa and Andrea Kaus, "Traditional Management of Tropical Forests in Mexico," in *Alternatives to Deforestation: Steps toward Sustainable Use of the Amazon Rain Forest*, ed. A. B. Anderson (New York: Columbia University Press, 1990), 45–64; and Lynn Jacobs *Waste of the West* (Tuscon: Lynn Jacobs, 1991).

12. Kent Flannery, ed., *Maya Subsistence* (New York: Academic Press, 1981); and P. Harrison and B. L. Turner, *Pre-Hispanic Maya Agriculture* (Albuquerque: University of New Mexico Press, 1978).

13. Linda Schiele and David Freidel, *A Forest of Kings* (New York: William Morrow, 1990).

14. After a slow start; see Carmen Morales Valderrama, *Ocupación y subrevivencia campesina en la zona citrica de Yucatán* (Mexico City: INAH, 1987); and Margarita Rosales Gonzales, *Oxcutzcab, Yucatán, 1900–1960* (Mexico City: INAH, 1988); I also refer to personal communication from E. Lopez.

15. Hilaria Maas Colli, "Transmición cultural: Chemax, Yucatán" (diss., Universidad Autónima de Yucatán, 1983).

16. We still await a good description of contemporary Maya ceremonialism; for general background on the Maya of the Chunhuhub area, see Alfonso Villa Rojas, *The Maya of East Central Quintana Roo* (Washington, D.C.: Carnegie Foundation, 1945).

17. The classic account of traditional *milpa* agriculture by Augusto Perez Toro, "La agricultura milpera de los Mayas de Yucatán," in *Enciclopedia Yucatanese* (Mérida: Gobierno de Yucatán, 1977), will probably never be superseded. Few authors have been as sensitive to the complex interdependence of biological and ritual technology in traditional agriculture.

18. E. N. Anderson, "Folk Forestry."

19. Gomez-Pompa and Kaus, "Traditional Management."

Chapter 6. Needs and Human Nature

1. Marvin Harris, "The Cultural Ecology of India's Sacred Cattle," *Current Anthropology* 7 (1966): 51–66.

2. Abraham Maslow, *Motivation and Personality,* 2d ed. (New York: Harper and Row, 1970).

3. Ellen Langer, *The Psychology of Control* (Beverly Hills: Sage, 1983); Richard Schulz, "Some Life and Death Consequences of Perceived Control," in *Cognition and Social Behavior,* ed. John S. Carroll and John W. Payne (New York: Academic Press, 1976), 135–153; and Albert Bandura, "Self-Efficacy Mechanism in Human Agency," *American Psychologist* 37 (2 [1982]): 122–147.

4. Susan Fiske and Shelley Taylor, *Social Cognition* (Reading, Mass.: Addison-Wesley, 1984), and *Social Cognition* 2d ed. (New York: McGraw-Hill, 1991); and Ulric Neisser, *Cognition and Reality* (San Francisco: Freeman, 1976).

5. Robert Zajonc, "Feeling and Thinking: Preferences Need No Inferences," *American Psychologist* 35 (1980): 151–175.

6. Richard Lazarus, *Emotion and Adaptation* (New York: Oxford University Press, 1991); and Andrew Ortony et al., *The Cognitive Structure of Emotions* (Cambridge: Cambridge University Press, 1988).

7. Catherine Lutz, *Unnatural Emotions* (Chicago: University of Chicago Press, 1988).

8. Colin Turnbull, *The Mountain People* (New York: Simon and Schuster, 1972).

9. E.g., Melvin Konner, *The Tangled Wing* (New York: Holt, Rinehart, Winston, 1982); and E. H. Wilson, *On Human Nature* (Cambridge, Mass.: Harvard University Press, 1978).

10. Jerome H. Barkow et al., *The Adapted Mind: Evolutionary Psychology and the Generation of Culture* (Oxford: Oxford University Press, 1992).

11. See Daniel Batson, "How Social an Animal? The Human Capacity for Caring," *American Psychologist* 45 (3 [1990]): 336–346; Nancy Eisenberg, *Altruistic Emotion, Cognition and Behavior* (Hillsdale, N.J.: Lawrence Erlbaum Associates, 1986); Martin Hoffman, "Is Altruism Part of Human Nature?" in *Social Cognitive Development,* ed. L. Ross (Cambridge: Cambridge University Press, 1981); Alfie Kohn, *The Brighter Side of Human Nature* (New York: Basic Books, 1990); and D. Lau, *Mencius* (Hardmondsworth, Sussex: Pelican, 1970).

12. Glynn Isaac, "Food Sharing and Human Evolution: Archaeological Evidence from the Plio-Pleistocene of East Africa," *Journal of Anthropological Research* 34 (3 [1978]): 311–325, and "The Food-Sharing Behavior of Protohuman Hominids," *Scientific American* 238 (4 [1978]): 90–108; Richard Leakey and Roger Lewin, *Origins Reconsidered* (New York: Doubleday, 1992); and Owen Lovejoy, "The Origin of Man," *Science* 211 (4480 [1981]): 341–350.

13. *Science* 259 (1993): 33; see also Barkow et al., *Adapted Mind.*

14. Carl Rogers, *On Becoming a Person* (Boston: Houghton Mifflin, 1961).

15. I.e., intense personal involvement with others, or with something beyond oneself; Viktor Frankl, *The Unheard Cry for Meaning* (New York: Simon and Schuster, 1978).

16. David Hume, *Enquiries Concerning Human Understanding and Concerning the Principles of Morals* 1777 ed. of 1772 work (Oxford: Oxford University Press, 1975).

17. Ibid., 226.

18. Barkow et al. *Adapted Mind;* and Michael Gazzaniga, *The Social Brain* (New York: Basic Books, 1985).

19. Donald Brown, *Human Universals* (Philadelphia: Temple University Press, 1991).

20. Lutz, *Unnatural Emotions;* see also Theodore Schwartz, Geoffrey M. White, and Catherine A. Lutz, eds., *New Directions in Psychological Anthropology* (Cambridge: Cambridge University Press, 1992).

21. Paul Ekman, "Are There Basic Emotions?" *Psychological Review* 99 (1992): 550–553.

22. Batja Mesquita and Nico H. Frijda, "Cultural Variations in Emotions: A Review," *Psychological Bulletin* 112 (1992): 179–204.

23. Hume, *Enquiries.*

24. Marshall Sahlins, *Tribesmen* (Englewood Cliffs, N.J.: Prentice-Hall, 1968).

25. Ibid.

26. Hume, *Enquiries,* 190.

27. Kohn, *The Brighter Side.*

28. Ibid.

29. Robert Dentan, *The Semai, a Nonviolent People of Malaysia* (New York: Holt, Rinehart, Winston, 1968); and Clayton Robarchek, "Primitive Warfare and the Ratomorphic Image of Mankind," *American Anthropologist,* 91 (1989): 903–920.

30. This has been denied for the Yanomamo, but see Ettore Biocca, *Yanomamo* (told by Helena Valero) (New York: Dutton, 1970).

31. Garrett Hardin, "The Tragedy of the Commons," *Science* 162 (1968): 1243–1248.

32. Howard Gardner, *Frames of Mind* (Cambridge, Mass.: Harvard University Press, 1983); and Gazzaniga, *Social Brain.*

33. D. Keirsey and M. Bates, *Please Understand Me* (Del Mar, Calif.: Prometheus Nemesis, 1978); and Isabel Briggs Myers, *Gifts Differing* (Palo Alto: Consulting Psychologists Press, 1980).

34. Robert Bellah et al., *Habits of the Heart* (Berkeley: University of California Press, 1985), and *The Good Society* (New York: Random House, 1991).

35. Martin Lewis, *Green Delusions: An Environmentalist Critique of Radical Environmentalism* (Durham: Duke University Press, 1992).

Chapter 7. Information Processing: Rational and Irrational Transcended

1. Carolyn Merchant, *Radical Ecology* (London: Routledge Kegan Paul, 1992).

2. Roy A. Rappaport, "The Sacred in Human Evolution," *Annual Review of Ecology and Systematics* 2 (1971): 23–44.

3. E.g., R. E. Johannes, *Words of the Lagoon* (Berkeley: University of California Press, 1983), and *Traditional Ecological Knowledge* (Gland, Switzerland: IUCN, 1989); and Gene Wilken, *Good Farmers* (Berkeley: University of California Press, 1987).

4. Robert Edgerton, *Sick Societies: Challenging the Myth of Primitive Harmony* (New York: Free Press, 1992).

5. Bernard Read, "Chinese Materia Medica: Animal Drugs," *Peking Natural History Bulletin* 5 (4 [1931]): 37–80, and 6 (1 [1931]): 1–102.

6. Johannes, *Words*.

7. For Greece and the Near East, see George Foster, "On the Origin of Humoral Medicine in Latin America," *Medical Anthropology Quarterly* 1, (4 [1987]): 355–393, and references therein; for Malaysia, see Carol Laderman, "Destructive Heat and Cooling Prayer: Malay Humoralism in Pregnancy, Childbirth and the Postpartum Period," *Social Science and Medicine* 25 (4 [1987]): 357–366; for Native America, see Bernard Ortiz de Montellano, "Empirical Aztec Medicine," *Science* 188 (1975): 215–220.

8. Roger Cook, *The Tree of Life* (New York: Avon, 1974).

9. Carl Jung, *Symbols of Transformation* (New York: Pantheon, 1956).

10. Especially Claude Lévi-Strauss, *La Pensée sauvage* (Paris: Plon, 1962); see also Mary Douglas, *Natural Symbols* (London: Barrie and Rockliff, 1966).

11. D. Kahnemann et al., *Judgement under Uncertainty: Heuristics and Biases* (Cambridge: Cambridge University Press, 1982).

12. Especially Jon Elster's work in economics; see Jon Elster, *Sour Grapes* (Cambridge: Cambridge University Press, 1983), (1983), and *Ulysses and the Sirens, 2d ed.* (Cambridge: Cambridge University Press, 1984).

13. Elster, (1983).

14. Ibid., and *The Cement of Society* (Cambridge: Cambridge University Press, 1989); and Marshall Sahlins, *Culture and Practical Reason* (Chicago: University of Chicago Press, 1976).

15. Kahnemann et al., *Judgement*.

16. Richard H. Thaler, *The Winner's Curse* (Princeton: Princeton University Press, 1992), 2.

17. See also Eric Alden Smith, "Risk and Uncertainty in the 'Original Affluent Society': Evolutionary Ecology of Resource-sharing and Land Tenure," in: *Hunters and Gatherers: History, Evolution and Social Change,* ed. T. Ingold et al. (New York: Berg, 1988), 222–251, especially 224.

18. Alexander Rosenberg, *Economics—Mathematical Politics or Science of Diminishing Returns?* (Chicago: University of Chicago Press, 1992), 239.

19. John Dryzek, *Rational Ecology: Environment and Political Economy* (Oxford: Basil Blackwell, 1987).

20. David Hume, *Enquiries Concerning Human Understanding and Concerning the Principles of Morals,* 1777 ed. of 1772 work (Oxford: Oxford University Press, 1975), 295.

21. Thaler, *Winner's Curse*.

22. Jay Lehr, ed., *Rational Readings on Environmental Issues* (New York: Van Nostrand Reinhold, 1992).

23. K. S. Shrader-Frechette, *Risk and Rationality* (Berkeley: University of California Press, 1991); see also Carl Cranor, *Regulating Toxic Substances: A Philosophy of Science and the Law* (New York: Oxford University Press, 1993).

24. Rappaport, "Sacred," and *Pigs for the Ancestors,* 2d ed. (New Haven: Yale University Press, 1984).

25. Herbert Simon, *Models of Man* (New York: Wiley, 1957).

26. Thaler, *Winner's Curse.*

27. Gert Gigerenzer, "How to Make Cognitive Illusions Disappear: Beyond 'Heuristics and Biases,' " *European Review of Social Psychology* 2 (1991): 83–115; and Thaler, *Winner's Curse.*

28. Kahneman et al., *Judgement.*

29. M. Merleau-Ponty, *La Structure du Comportement* (Paris: Presses Universitaires de France, 1960), *The Phenomenology of Perception* trans. Colin Smith (New York: Humanities Press, 1962), and *Signs* trans. John McCleary (Chicago: Northwestern University Press, 1964).

30. See, e.g., Richard Nisbett and Lee Ross, *Human Inference* (Englewood Cliffs, N.J.: Prentice-Hall, 1980).

31. Robert Zajonc, "Feeling and Thinking: Preferences Need No Inferences," *American Psychologist* 35 (1980): 151–175.

32. C. Wright Mills, *The Sociological Imagination* (New York: Oxford University Press, 1959).

33. David W. Orr, "For the Love of Life," *Conservation Biology* 6 (1992): 486–487.

34. Michael Cole and Susan Scribner, *Culture and Thought* (New York: Wiley, 1974); Jean Lave, *Cognition in Practice* (Cambridge: Cambridge University Press, 1988); Barbara Rogoff and Jean Lave, *Everyday Cognition* (Cambridge, Mass.: Harvard University Press, 1984); and Lev S. Vygotsky, *Mind and Society* (Cambridge, Mass.: Harvard University Press, 1978).

35. See also E. N. Anderson, "Sacred Fish," *Man* n.s. 4 (3 [1969]): 443–449; Scott Atran, *Cognitive Foundations of Natural History* (Cambridge: Cambridge University Press, 1991); David Kronenfeld, *Plastic Glasses and Church Fathers: Semantic Extension from the Ethnoscience Tradition.* Forthcoming, Cambridge University Press. (1987); George Lakoff, *Women, Fire and Dangerous Things* (Chicago: University of Chicago Press, 1987); Lévi-Strauss, *La Pensée,* and *Mythologiques* (Paris: Plon, 1964–1971); and E. Smith and D. L. Medin, *Categories and Concepts* (Cambridge, Mass.: Harvard University Press, 1981).

36. Kahneman et al., *Judgement.*

37. Susan Fiske and Shelley Taylor, *Social Cognition* (Reading, Mass.: Addison-Wesley, 1984); Kahneman et al., *Judgement;* and Nisbett and Ross, *Human Inference.*

38. Nisbett and Ross, *Human Inference.*

39. Walter Mischel, "On the Predictability of Behavior and the Structure of Personality," in *Personality and the Prediction of Behavior*, ed. Robert A. Zucker et al. (New York: Academic Press, 1984), 269–305.

40. Fiske and Taylor, *Social Cognition*, 394–399; Gigerenzer, "Cognitive Illusions"; David Kronenfeld, personal communication; and Peter Richerson, personal communication.

41. Fiske and Taylor, *Social Cognition*, 402–404.

42. David Pearce and R. Kerry Turner, *Economics of Natural Resources and the Environment* (Baltimore: Johns Hopkins University Press, 1990), 129, 158.

43. Ibid., 211 ff.

44. Kronenfeld, personal communication.

45. Richerson, personal communication.

46. Zajonc, "Feeling and Thinking"; and Fiske and Taylor, *Social Cognition*, and *Social Cognition*, 2d ed. (New York: McGraw-Hill, 1991).

47. Roy F. Baumeister and Steven J. Scher, "Self-Defeating Behavior Patterns among Normal Individuals: Review and Analysis of Common Self-Destructive Tendencies," *Psychological Bulletin* 104 (1 [1988]): 3–22.

48. George Ainslie, *Picoeconomics: The Strategic Interaction of Successive Motivational States with the Person* (Cambridge: Cambridge University Press, 1993).

49. Aaron Beck, *Cognitive Therapy and the Emotional Disorders* (New York: International Universities Press, 1976).

50. George Foster, "Peasant Society and the Image of Limited Good," *American Anthropologist* 67 (1965): 293–315.

51. Elster, *Sour Grapes*.

52. Shelley Taylor, *Positive Illusions* (New York: Basic Books, 1989).

53. Lionel Tiger, *Optimism* (New York: Simon and Schuster, 1979).

54. Nisbett and Ross, *Human Inference*.

55. Barbara Tuchman, *The March of Folly* (New York: Knopf, 1984).

56. Morris Rossabi, *Khubilai Khan* (Berkeley: University of California Press, 1989).

57. *Los Angeles Times*, 24 December 1989.

58. Neil Weinstein, "Optimistic Biases about Personal Risks," *Science* 246 (1989): 1232–1233.

59. Elster, *Cement of Society*.

60. Peggy Bartlett, ed., *Agricultural Decision Making* (New York: Academic Press, 1980).

61. Albert Bandura, "Self-Efficacy Mechanism in Human Agency," *American Psychologist* 37 (2 [1982]): 122–147.

62. Melvin Lerner, *Belief in a Just World: A Fundamental Delusion* (New York: Plenum, 1980).

63. Jerome H. Barkow, Leda Cosmides, and John Tooby, *The Adapted Mind: Evolutionary Psychology and the Generation of Culture* (Oxford: Oxford University Press, 1992).

64. Atran, *Cognitive Foundations,* and Brent Berlin, *Ethnobiological Classification* (Princeton: Princeton University Press, 1992).

65. Ellen Langer, *The Psychology of Control* (Beverly Hills: Sage, 1983); see also Bandura, "Self-Efficacy."

66. John H. Riskind and James E. Maddux, "Loomingness, Helplessness, and Fearfulness: An Integration of Harm-Looming and Self-Efficacy Models of Fear," *Journal of Social and Clinical Psychology* 12 (1993): 73–89, provide the latest word in a long literature on this.

67. Michael Gazzaniga, *Nature's Mind* (New York: Basic Books, 1992).

68. Robert D. Putnam, *Making Democracy Work: Civic Traditions in Modern Italy* (Princeton: Princeton University Press, 1992).

69. Julian Simon, *The Ultimate Resource* (Princeton: Princeton University Press, 1981).

70. John Bodley, *Victims of Progress* (Menlo Park, Calif.: Cummings, 1975), and *Anthropology and Contemporary Human Problems* (Menlo Park, Calif.: Cummings, 1976).

71. See, e.g., Rush Limbaugh, *The Way Things Ought to Be* (New York: Pocket Books, 1992).

72. Luis Weckmann, *The Medieval Heritage of Mexico,* trans. Frances M. Lopez-Morillas (New York: Fordham University Press, 1992).

Chapter 8.   Culture: Ecology in a Wider Context

1. Michael Cernea, "Anthropological Variables of Environmental Problems" (paper presented at the annual convention of the American Anthropological Association, San Francisco, 1992), 2.

2. Proceedings of the Conference on Common Property Resource Management (Washington, D.C., 1986); Jon Elster, *Sour Grapes* (Cambridge: Cambridge University Press, 1983); Yujiro Hayami and Vernon Ruttan, *Agricultural Development,* 2d ed. (Baltimore: Johns Hopkins Press, 1985); Gary Libecap, *Contracting for Property Rights* (Cambridge: Cambridge University Press, 1989); Douglass North, *Institutions, Institutional Change and Economic Performance* (Cambridge: Cambridge University Press, 1990), and; and Elinor Ostrom, *Governing the Commons* (Cambridge: Cambridge University Press, 1990).

3. Jared Diamond, *The Third Chimpanzee* (New York: HarperCollins, 1992); Brien Meilleur, "Forest and the Polynesian Adaptation," in *Tropical Deforestation: The Human Dimension,* ed. L. Sponsel et al. (Cambridge: Cambridge University Press, 1992).

4. Denise Yim, *Maori Ideology and Religion: 2000 Years of Ecological Success,* Ms. (1992).

5. See Paul Cox, and Sandra Banack, eds., *Islands, Plants, and Polynesians* (Portland, Oreg.: Timber Press, 1991).

6. Meilleur, "Forest."

7. Cox and Banack, *Islands;* and Raymond Firth, *We the Tikopia* (London: G. Allen and Unwin, 1936).

8. J. R. McNeill, *The Mountains of the Mediterranean World* (Cambridge: Cambridge University Press, 1992).

9. Clive Ponting, *A Green History of the World* (New York: Penguin, 1991); see also, for China, E. N. Anderson, *The Food of China* (New Haven: Yale University Press, 1988).

10. J. Donald Hughes, *American Indian Ecology* (El Paso, TX: Texas Western University Press, 1983); Diamond, *Third Chimpanzee;* and Martin Lewis, *Green Delusions: An Environmentalist Critique of Radical Environmentalism* (Durham: Duke University Press, 1992).

11. The debate between romanticizers of the Primitive and attackers of the Savage provides an excellent example of Kant's aggregation and specification acting to prevent the search for truth.

Those who romanticize the Primitives for alleged closeness to the land and careful cherishing of it usually confuse two things: a religion that represents the environment, and a pragmatic code of conduct that actually preserves that environment. Most traditional peoples have religions that are, indeed, closely bound up with the land. This does not prevent then from overhunting, setting destructive fires, clearing forests, and otherwise altering the land, though it probably does reduce such damage below what might occur.

Those who revive the myth of the Savage paint a picture of traditional peoples everywhere that makes them ignorant, backward, superstitious, careless, and wasteful. Much of the evidence adduced by the critics of traditional societies is wrong or debatable. Martin Lewis, *Green Delusions,* for instance, brings in a number of examples of traditional peoples who have depleted their game animals after receiving guns in trade. As Calvin Martin, *Keepers of the Game* (Berkeley: University of California Press, 1978), and Adrian Tanner, *Bringing Home Animals* (London: C. Hurst and Co., 1979), have pointed out, not only are guns nontraditional, but they invariably enter along with a great deal else, typically including white man's diseases, competition with newcomers for game, new trade relationships, motorized equipment, new status relationships, and new status goods. Obviously, profound changes in the society inevitably occur, and any traditional rules for wise use of the environment are almost certain to become irrelevant. This, of course, should give pause to the romanticizers who want to turn management of resources back to "indigenous" peoples.

Another irrelevant charge made by many critics (mostly by word of mouth; I have heard it from many biologists) involves the Plains Indians and their purportedly wasteful buffalo stampedes. The Plains Indians hunted by driving herds of buffalo over cliffs. This was, however, not wasteful. In the first place, it happened only rarely in pre-horse days. The relatively important Head-Smashed-In Cliff in Alberta, Canada, for instance, was used only about once per generation. Usually only a few buffalo were killed, and all parts of all of them could be used. Very rarely would a whole, unstoppable stampede go over a jump site. (This information is well communicated by the displays at the rather bizarrely named Head-Smashed-In Buffalo Jump World Heritage Site, in Alberta, Canada.)

Lewis, *Green Delusions,* and others have also brought up the "Pleistocene overkill." According to this theory, developed by Paul S. Martin in "Pleistocene Overkill: The Global Model," in *Quarternary Extinctions,* ed. Paul Martin and R. Klein (Tuscon: University of Arizona Press, 1984), 354–403, Native Americans exterminated the megafauna of Pleistocene America by overhunting. This hypothesis is almost certainly wrong. There is absolutely no evidence for it. There is much evidence against it: many small birds and mammals became extinct at the same time; vegetation changed drastically; and many large animals survived and spread (see, for example, Arthur H. Harris, *Late Pleistocene Vertebrate Paleoecology of the West* [Austin: University of Texas Press, (1985)], and E. C. Pielou, *After the Ice Age* [Chicago: University of Chicago Press, (1991)]). Humans came very late to the New World—almost certainly too late to have accounted for much of the die-off. The hot, dry Hypsithermal Period, some four to eight thousand years ago, must be considered. Humans may well have killed off the last few members of particularly vulnerable species, such as mammoths and ground sloths, but certainly were not the major factor in all the extinctions.

12. See Richard K. Nelson, *Make Prayers to the Raven* (Chicago: University of Chicago Press, 1983).

13. Robert Brightman, *Grateful Prey: Rock Cree Human-Animal Relationships* (Berkeley: University of California Press, 1992).

14. Lowell Bean and Thomas Blackburn, eds., *Native Californians: A Theoretical Retrospective* (Socorro, New Mex.: Ballena Press, 1976); Henry Lewis, *Patterns of Indian Burning in California* (Socorro, New Mex.: Ballena Press, 1973); and Florence Shipek, *Pushed into the Rocks* (Lincoln: University of Nebraska Press, 1987).

15. Judy Berryman, unpublished research.

16. Christopher Vecsey and R. Venables, *American Indian Environments* (Syracuse, N.Y.: Syracuse University Press, 1980).

17. See, e.g., Conference on Common Property, Mahdev Gadgil and Fikret Berkes, "Traditional Resource Management Systems," *Resource Management and Optimization* 8 (1991): 127–141; Bonnie McCay and James Acheson, eds., *The Question of the Commons* (Tucson: University of Arizona Press, 1987); Proceedings of the Conference on Common Property; and Kenneth Ruddle and Tomoya Akimichi, eds., *Maritime Institutions in the Western Pacific*, Senri Ethnological Studies no. 17 (Osaka: National Museum of Ethnology, 1984).

18. Janis Alcorn, personal communication; Michael Alvard, "Are Indigenous People Necessarily Conservationists? A Case Study from the Peruvian Tropics" (paper presented at the annual convention of the American Anthropological Association San Francisco, 1992); and Allen Johnson, personal communication.

19. Gary Rollefson, personal communication.

20. Milton Freeman and Ludwig Carbyn, eds., *Traditional Knowledge and Renewable Resource Management in Northern Regions* (Edmonton: Canadian Circumpolar Institute, 1992); Milton Freeman et al., eds., *Adaptive Marine Resource Systems in the Pacific* (New York: Harwood, 1991); R. E. Johannes, ed., *Traditional Ecological Knowledge* (Gland, Switzerland: IUCN, 1989); and Th. W. Overholt and J. Baird Callicott, eds., *Clothed-in Fur and Other Tales: An Introduction to an Ojibwa Worldview* (Washington, D.C.: University Press of America, 1982).

21. Billie DeWalt, "Using Indigenous Knowledge to Improve Agriculture and Natural Resource Management," *Human Organization* 53 (1994): 123–131.

22. See the detailed discussion in Clifford Geertz, "Anti-Anti-Relativism," *American Anthropologist* 86 (1984): 263–278.

23. Conrad Kottak and Alberto C. G. Costa, "Ecological Awareness, Environmentalist Action, and International Conservation Strategy," *Human Organization* 52 (1993): 335–343.

24. Linda Schiele and David Freidel, *A Forest of Kings* (New York: William Morrow, 1990).

25. Ponting, *Green History.*

26. Sheldon Judson, "Erosion Rates Near Rome, Italy," *Science* 160 (1968): 1444–1445.

27. Marvin Harris, *The Rise of Anthropological Theory* (New York: Crowell, 1968); and Eric Alden Smith, "Risk and Uncertainty in the 'Original Affluent Society': Evolutionary Ecology of Resource-sharing and Land Tenure," in *Hunters and Gatherers: History, Evolution and Social Change,* ed. Tim Ingold et al. (New York: Berg, 1988), 222–251, and *Inujjvamivt Foraging Strategies* (Seattle: University of Washington Press, 1991).

28. Marvin Harris, "The Cultural Ecology of India's Sacred Cattle," *Current Anthropology* 7 (1966): 51–66; and E. N. Anderson, "Comment on Marvin Harris' 'Cultural Ecology of India's Sacred Cattle,' " *Current Anthropology* 18 (3 [1977]): 552.

29. Martin Orans, personal communication.

30. Smith, *Inujjuamint Foraging Strategies.*

31. John Bennett, *The Ecological Transition* (New York: Pergamon, 1976); (1976). *Human Ecology as Human Behavior* (New Brunswick, N.J.: Transaction, 1993); Robert Netting, *Cultural Ecology,* 2d ed. (Prospect Heights, Ill.: Waveland Press, 1986); North, *Institutions;* and Marshall Sahlins *Culture and Practical Reason* (Chicago: University of Chicago Press, 1976).

32. Anderson, *Food of China;* and Kenneth Ruddle and Zhong Gongfu, *Integrated Agriculture-Aquaculture in South China* (Cambridge: Cambridge University Press, 1988).

33. Pierre Bourdieu, *Outline of a Theory of Practice* (Cambridge: Cambridge University Press, 1976), and *The Logic of Practice* (Stanford: Stanford University Press, 1992).

34. Paul Willis, *Learning to Labor* (New York: Columbia University Press, 1981).

35. Pierre Bourdieu and J. Passeron, *Reproduction in Education, Society and Culture* (Newbury Park: Sage, 1990).

36. Jean Lave, *Cognition in Practice* (Cambridge: Cambridge University Press, 1988).

37. David W. Orr, "For the Love of Life," *Conservation Biology* 6 (1992): 486–487.

38. Jon Elster, *The Cement of Society* (Cambridge: Cambridge University Press, 1989).

Chapter 9. In and Out of Institutions

1. Douglass North, Institutions, Institutional Change and Economic Performance (Cambridge: Cambridge University Press, 1990).

2. Ibid.

3. Ibid.

4. See Murray Feshbach and Alfred Friendly, Jr., *Ecocide in the USSR* (New York: Basic Books, 1991); Bonnie McCay and James Acheson, eds., *The Question of the*

Commons (Tucson: University of Arizona Press, 1987); and Evelyn Pinkerton, ed., *Cooperative Management of Local Fisheries: New Directions for Improved Management and Community Development* (Vancouver: University of British Columbia Press, 1989).

5. Vaclav Smil, *The Bad Earth* (Armonk, N.Y.: M. E. Sharpe, 1984).

6. On Easter Island and elsewhere; see Jared Diamond, *The Third Chimpanzee* (New York: HarperCollins, 1992); and Brien Meilleur, "Forest and the Polynesian Adaptation," forthcoming in *Tropical Deforestation: The Human Dimension,* ed. L. Somsel et al. (Cambridge: Cambridge University Press).

7. Ronald Coase, "The Problem of Social Cost," *Journal of Law and Economics* 3 (1960): 1–44.

8. See *Ambio,* 20 (2 [1991]) special issue: "Environmental Economics"; Terry Anderson and Donald Leal, *Free-Market Environmentalism* (San Francisco: Pacific Research Institute for Public Policy, 1991); Earl Murphy, *Governing Nature* (Chicago: Quadrangle Books, 1967); and David Pearce and R. Kerry Turner, *Economics of Natural Resources and the Environment* (Baltimore: Johns Hopkins University Press, 1990).

9. Robert Bullard, "Solid Waste Sites and the Black Community," *Sociological Inquiry* 53 (1983): 273–288, "Endangered Environs: The Price of Unplanned Growth in Boomtown Houston," *California Sociologist* (summer 1984): 85–101, and *Dumping in Dixie: Race, Class, and Environmental Quality* (Boulder, Colo.: Westview, 1990); and Robert Bullard and Beverly Hendrix Wright, "Environmentalism and the Politics of Equity: Emergent Trends in the Black Community," *Mid-American Review of Sociology* 12 (1990): 21–38.

10. John Bodley, *Victims of Progress* (Menlo Park, Calif.: Cummings, 1975), and *Anthropology and Contemporary Human Problems* (Menlo Park, Calif.: Cummings, 1976).

11. Albert Gore, Jr., *Earth in the Balance* (New York: Houghton Mifflin, 1992), 149.

12. This is a point that I made more than twenty years ago (E. N. Anderson, "The Life and Culture of Ecotopia," in *Reinventing Anthropology,* ed. Dell Hymes [New York: Pantheon Press, 1972], 264–273), and I am glad to see it vindicated.

13. See Pearce and Turner, *Economics;* and Clem Tisdell, *Environmental Economics: Policies for Environmental Management and Sustainable Development* (Brookfield, Vt: Edward Elgar, 1992).

14. Ibn Khaldun, 1958 *The Muqaddimah,* trans. Franz Rosenthal (New York: Pantheon [Bollingen Books], 1958).

15. Robert Repetto, "Accounting for Environmental Assets," *Scientific American* (June 1992): 94–100.

16. See Peter Drucker, *The Ecological Vision* (New Brunswick, N.J.: Transaction, 1992), 237–239, for some classic errors; and, from a very different point of view, Amartya Sen, "The Economics of Life and Death," *Scientific American* (May 1993): 40–47, for ways to improve the situation.

17. Such as the American sugar industry (see James Bovard, *The Farm Fiasco* [San Francisco: Institute of Contemporary Studies, 1991]) and the Mexican henequen industry.

18. McCay & Acheson, *Question of the Commons;* and Pinkerton, *Cooperative Management.*

19. Anderson and Leal, *Free Market Environmentalism;* John A. Baden, "Business, Science and Environmental Politics: Toward a Political Economy of Hope," *Columbia Journal of World Business,* reprint 273426; and Charles Perrings, *Economy and Environment* (Cambridge: Cambridge University Press, 1987).

20. Anderson & Leal, *Free Market Environmentalism,* 170.

21. Pinkerton, *Cooperative Management.*

22. See *Science* 260 (25 June 1993): 1883–1909; *Scientific American* (Nov. 1993): 41–57; and *The Amicus Journal* (fall 1993): 31–37.

23. For pragmatic reasons, see John Dryzek, *Rational Ecology: Environment and Political Economy* (Oxford: Basil Blackwell, 1987); for theoretical reasons, see Alexander Rosenberg, *Economics—Mathematical Politics or Science of Diminishing Returns?* (Chicago: University of Chicago Press, 1992).

24. Matt Ridley and Boi S. Low, "Can Selfishness Save the Environment?" *Atlantic Monthly* (Sept. 1993): 76–86.

25. James Scott, *Weapons of the Weak* (New Haven: Yale University Press, 1985).

26. Bodley, *Victims,* and *Anthropology.*

27. See the extended discussion in Pearce and Turner, *Economics,* 320–341.

28. Dryzek, *Rational Ecology.*

29. Lester Thurow, *The Zero-Sum Society* (New York: Basic Books, 1980).

30. See, e.g., Anderson and Leal, *Free Market Environmentalism;* and Drucker, *Ecological Visions.*

31. George Foster, "Peasant Society and the Image of Limited Good," *American Anthropologist* 67 (1965): 293–315.

32. Ibid.

33. Spencer Kagan, personal communication.

34. Ibn, *The Muqaddimah.*

35. Bellah et al., *Habits of the Heart* (Berkeley: University of California Press, 1985).

36. Bellah et al. *The Good Society* (New York: Random House, 1991).

37. This is one of the few places where I can wholly agree with Anderson and Leal, *Free Market Environmentalism,* and with Martin Lewis, *Green Delusions: An Environmentalist Critique of Radical Environmentalism* (Durham: Duke University Press, 1992).

38. Angus Wright, *The Death of Ramon Gonzalez* (Austin: University of Texas Press, 1991).

39. Repetto, "Accounting."

40. E.g., E. N. Anderson, *The Food of China* (New Haven: Yale University Press, 1988); and Mahdev Gadgil and Ramachandra Guha, *This Fissured Land: An Ecological History of India* (Oxford: Oxford University Press, 1992).

41. See Herman Daly & John Cobb: *For the Common Good* (Boston: Beacon, 1990); Perrings, *Economy and Environment;* and Repetto, "Accounting."

42. See Repetto, "Accounting."

43. Anderson, personal research; and Repetto, "Accounting."

44. Elinor Ostrom, *Governing the Commons* (Cambridge: Cambridge University Press, 1990), and Pinkerton, *Cooperative Management.*

45. Classic case studies can be found in McCay and Acheson, *Question of the Commons;* and Arthur McEvoy, *The Fisherman's Problem* (Cambridge: Cambridge University Press, 1986).

46. Carl Safina, "Bluefin Tuna in the West Atlantic: Negligent Management and the Making of an Endangered Species," *Environmental Conservation* 7 (1993): 229–238; see also Tisdell, *Environmental Economics.*

47. J. Terrence McCabe, "Turkana Pastoralism: A Case Against the Tragedy of the Commons," *Human Ecology* 8 (1990): 81–104.

48. E.g., J. Stephen Lansing, *Priests and Programmers* (Princeton: Princeton University Press, 1991).

49. Lynn Jacobs, *Waste of the West* (Tuscon: Lynn Jacobs).

50. In regard to ranching, I have profited from personal communication from and the work of Priscilla Weeks, "The State vs. the People: Strategies of Two Texas Communities" (paper, presented at the annual convention of the American Anthropological Association San Francisco 1992), who also reminds us that ranchers frequently have to bear all the costs of protecting an endangered species, even though others who do not pay are gathering all the benefits.

51. Robert Netting, *Balancing on an Alp* (Cambridge: Cambridge University Press, 1981); and Glenn G. Stevenson, *Common Property Economics: A General Theory and Land Use Applications* (Cambridge: Cambridge University Press, 1991), who provides very important general models.

52. Steven Maas, Ms.; Pearce and Turner, *Economics;* and Stevenson, *Common Property Economics.*

53. McCay and Acheson, *Question of the Commons;* Pinkerton, *Cooperative Management;* etc.

54. McCay and Acheson, *Question of the Commons,* and Ostrom, *Governing the Commons,* provide comparisons of "success stories" and "failure stories" in this regard.

55. Fikret Berkes, ed., *Common Property Resources* (London: Belhaven Press, 1991); Fikret Berkes et al., "The Benefits of the Commons," *Nature;* 340 (1989): 91–93; Fikret Berkes and David Feeny, "Paradigms Lost: Changing Views on the Use of Common Property Resources," *Alternatives* 17 (1990): 48–55; Feeny et al., "The Tragedy of the Commons: Twenty-Two Years Later," *Human Ecology* 18 (1 [1990]): 1–20; McCabe, "Turkana Pastoralism"; McCay and Acheson, *Question of the Commons;* Margaret McKean, "Success on the Commons," *Journal of Theoretical Politics* 4 (1992): 247–281; and Patricia Marchak, "What Happens When Common Property Becomes Uncommon?" *BC Studies* 80 (1989): 3–23.

56. Sharon Burton, "Managing the Commons of Tourist Dollars." ms. (1992); and Sara Singleton and Michael Taylor, "Common Property, Collective Action and Community," *Journal of Theoretical Politics* 4 (1992): 309–324.

57. McCay & Acheson, *Question of the Commons;* and Pinkerton, *Cooperative Management.*

58. Pinkerton, *Cooperative Management.*

59. Ostrom, *Governing the Commons,* 90–108.

60. Ibid., 188.

61. Ibid., 191.

62. Singleton and Taylor, "Common Property."

63. I am grateful to William T. Howard for discussion and information in this case, which is fairly well known to me, since I live in the next watershed to it.

64. McKean, "Success."

65. Barry C. Field, *Environmental Economics: An Introduction* (New York: McGraw-Hill, 1994), provides a particularly good introductory discussion of environmental enforcement problems.

66. See, e.g., Richard Wilk, *Household Ecology* (Tuscon: University of Arizona Press, 1991).

67. Drucker, *Ecological Vision.*

68. Sharon Burton, (1992). "Managing the Commons of Tourist Dollars" ms.

69. John Bennett, *The Ecological Transition* (New York: Pergamon, 1976).

70. William Durham, talk of 3 December 1992 in San Francisco.

71. McEvoy, *Fisherman's Problem.*

72. Feshbach and Friendly, *Ecocide.*

73. See, e.g., the significantly titled book by Mort Rosenblum and Doug Williamson, *Squandering Eden* (New York: Harcourt Brace Jovanovich, 1987).

74. Bovard, *Farm Fiasco.*

75. Jacobs, *Waste.*

76. See, e.g., Ted Williams, "Taking Back the Range," *Audubon* (Jan.–Feb. 1993): 28–33—admittedly a biased view—or, for a more balanced view, Weeks, "State vs. People."

77. Lewis, *Green Delusions.*

78. See, e.g., Marilyn Gates, *In Default: Peasants, the Debt Crisis, and the Agrarian Challenge in Mexico* (Boulder, Colo.: Westview, 1992).

79. E.g., Anderson and Leal, *Free Market Environmentalism.*

80. Robert Bellah, et al., *Habits of the Heart* (Berkeley: University of California Press, 1985); The Good Society (New York: Random House, 1991).

Chapter 10. The Disenchanted: Religion as Ecological Control, and Its Modern Fate

1. Raymond Firth, *We the Tikopia* (London: G. Allen and Unwin, 1936); and Melvin Gilmore, *Prairie Smoke* (St. Paul, Minn.: Minnesota Historical Society, 1929, reprint 1987).

2. Roy A. Rappaport, *Ecology, Meaning and Religion* Richmond Calif.: North Atlantic Books, 1979), and *Pigs for the Ancestors,* 2d ed. (New Haven: Yale University Press, 1984).

3. J. Stephen Lansing, *Priests and Programmers* (Princeton: Princeton University Press, 1991).

4. Victor Toledo, "What is Ethnoecology?" *Ethnoecologia* 1 (1992): 5–21.

5. Pierre Bourdieu, *The Logic of Practice* (Stanford: Stanford University Press, 1992), 48.

6. Seyla Benhabib and Fred Dallmayr, eds., *The Communicative Ethics Controversy* (Cambridge, Mass.: M.I.T. Press, 1990); Derek Parfit, *Reasons and Persons* (Oxford: Oxford University Press, 1984, corrected reprint 1989); and K. S. Shrader-Frechette, *Risk and Rationality* (Berkeley: University of California Press, 1991).

7. Max Weber, *The Protestant Ethic and the Spirit of Capitalism,* trans. Talcott Parsons (New York: Scribners, 1905 [German edition], 1958).

8. Kurt Samuelsson, *Religion and Economic Action,* trans. Geoffrey French (New York: Harper and Row, 1957 [Swedish edition], 1961).

9. Lloyd Warner, *American Life: Dream and Reality,* 2d ed. (Chicago: University of Chicago Press, 1962).

10. Emile Durkheim, *The Elementary Forms of the Religious Life* (Glencoe, Ill.: Free Press, 1961).

11. Bronislaw Malinowski, *Myth in Primitive Psychology* (New York: W. W. Norton, 1926); and Rappaport, *Ecology.*

12. For a small sampling of more recent sources in a vast literature, see Fikret Berkes, ed., *Common Property Resources* (London: Belhaven Press, 1991); J. Baird Callicott, "American Indian Land Wisdom? Sorting Out the Issues," *Journal of Forest History* 33 (1989): 35–42; Milton Freeman and Ludwig Carbyn, eds., *Traditional Knowledge and Renewable Resource Management in Northern Regions* (Edmonton: Canadian Circumpolar Institute, 1992); Milton Freeman et al., eds., *Adaptive Marine Resource Systems in the Pacific* (New York: Harwood, 1991); Gilmore, *Prairie Smoke;* and Kevin Lee Lopez, "Returning to Fields," *American Indian Culture and Research Journal* 16 (1992): 165–174. The last, in particular, effectively refutes the countercase.

13. Robyn Dawes, "Social Dilemmas," *Annual Review of Psychology* 31 (1980): 169–193; and Michael Dove, "Perceptions of Property and Equality of Access: Trees in Swidden Systems" (paper, presented at the annual conference of the International Association for the Study of Common Property, Washington, D.C., 1992).

14. J. Stephen Lansing, "Balinese 'Water Temples' and the Management of Irrigation," *American Anthropologist* 89 (1987): 326–341, and *Priests and Programmers;* and J. Stephen Lansing and James N. Kramer, "Emergent Properties of Balinese Water Temple Networks: Coadaptation on a Rugged Fitness Landscape," *American Anthropologist* 95 (1993): 97–114.

15. Lansing, *Priests and Programmers.*

16. For other studies of ritual regulation of ecology, see Janis Alcorn, *Huastec Mayan Ethnobotany* (Austin: University of Texas Press, 1984); Firth, *We the Tikopia, Social*

Change in Tikopia (London: G. Allen and Unwin, 1959), and *Economics of the New Zealand Maori* (London: Routledge, Kegan Paul, 1965); R. E. Johannes, *Words of the Lagoon* (Berkeley: University of California Press, 1983); and Gene Weltfish, *The Lost Universe* (New York: Basic Books, 1965).

17. Kenneth Ruddle and Tomoya Akimichi, eds., *Maritime Institutions in the Western Pacific* (Osaka: National Museum of Ethnology, Senri Ethnological Studies no. 17., 1984).

18. For a selection of very different viewpoints on these issues, see Daniel Batson, "How Social an Animal? The Human Capacity for Caring," *American Psychologist* 45 (3 [1990]): 336–346; Dawes, "Social Dilemmas"; Feeny et al., "The Tragedy of the Commons: Twenty-Two Years Later," *Human Ecology* 18 (1 [1990]): 1–20; Karl Hess, *Visions upon the Land: Man and Nature on the Western Range* (Washington, D.C., and Covelo, Calif.: Island Press, 1992); Rappaport, *Ecology;* and Toledo, "What is Ethnoecology?"

19. Janis Alcorn, personal communication, specifically on the Bora; Michael Alvard, "Are Indigenous People Necessarily Conservationists? A Case Study from the Peruvian Tropics" (paper, presented at the annual convention of the American Anthropological Association, San Francisco, 1992), on their neighbors the Piro; and Allen Johnson, personal communication, on the Machiguenga.

20. L. Katherine Baril, "Private Property and the Public Trust Doctrine: Developing New Paradigms for Government to Balance Individual Property Rights and Public Resource Protection" (paper, presented at the annual meeting of the International Association for the Study of Common Property, 1992).

21. Jay B. McDaniel, *Of Gods and Pelicans: A Theology of Reverence for Life* (Louisville: Westminster/John Knox Press (1989), and *Earth, Sky, Gods and Mortals: Developing an Ecological Spirituality* (Mystic, Conn.: Twenty-Third Publications, 1990).

22. Callicott, "American Indian"; and Shrader-Frechette, *Risk and Rationality.*

23. Max Weber, *The Sociology of Religion,* trans. Ephraim Fischoff (Boston: Beacon Press, 1922 [German edition], 1963).

24. Carolyn Merchant, *Radical Ecology* (London: Routledge, Kegan Paul, 1992).

25. Gilmore, *Prairie Smoke,* 31.

26. See, e.g., J. Donald Hughes, *American Indian Ecology* (El Paso, Te: Texas Western University Press, 1983).

27. Richard Haly, *"On Becoming a Mountain, Or Why Native Americans Have Animals for Souls"* (paper, presented at the annual conference of the Anthropological Association, San Francisco, 1992).

28. Eric Alden Smith, *Inujjuamint Foraging Strategies* (Seattle: University of Washington Press, 1991); and Marshall Sahlins, *Cultural and Practical Reason* (Chicago: University of Chicago Press, 1976).

29. Peggy Bartlett, ed., *Agricultural Decision Making* (New York: Academic Press, 1980), and Agricultural *Choice and Change* (New Brunswick, N.J.: Rutgers University Press, 1982).

30. Alcorn, *Huastec Mayan Ethnobotany;* H. A. Feit, "James Bay Cree Indian Management and Moral Considerations of Fur-Bearers," in *Alberta Society of Professional Biologists: Native People and Renewable Resource Management* (Edmonton: H. A. Feit, 49–65; Lansing, *Priests and Programmers;* and Richard K. Nelson, *Make Prayers to the Raven* (Chicago: University of Chicago Press, 1983).

31. Bronislaw Malinowski, *Argonauts of the Western Pacific* (New York: Dutton, 1922), *Myth, Coral Gardens and Their Magic* (New York: American Book Co., 1935), *A Scientific Theory of Culture* (Raleigh: University of North Carolina Press, 1944), and *Magic, Science and Religion* (Garden City: Doubleday, 1948); Firth, *We the Tikopia, Social Change,* and *Maori;* and Rappaport, *Ecology,* and *Pigs.*

32. Jomo Kenyatta, *Facing Mount Kenya* (London: Secker and Warburg, 1938).

33. Malinowski, *Magic.*

34. H. Russell Bernard and Jesus Salinas Pedraza, *Native Ethnography* (Newbury Park: Sage, 1989).

35. Other classic "insider" accounts include Marcel Griaule, *Conversations with Ogotemmeli* (Chicago: University of Chicago Press, 1965); Gerardo Reichel-Dolmatoff, *Amazonian Cosmos* (Chicago: University of Chicago Press, 1971); and Lucy Thompson, *To the American Indian* (Eureka, Calif.: Lucy Thompson, 1916). There are countless studies and reports from the early days of Native American research. For instance, Gilmore's work is part of a whole literature on Siouan groups, ranging from the early writings of Francis La Flesche (Omaha, with Alice Fletcher), Ella Deloria, Bird Woman (a Hidatsa woman; Gilbert Wilson, *Agriculture of the Hidatsa Indians: An Indian Interpretation* (Minneapolis: University of Minnesota, Studies in the Social Sciences, no. 9, 1917), and Charles Eastman (Siouanname, Ohiyesa; Charles Eastman, *Indian Boyhood* (New York: Dover, 1902, reprint 1971), to the now-classic writings of Black Elk (see R. De Maillie, *The Sixth Grandfather* (Lincoln: University of Nebraska Press, 1984), which is preferable to John Neihardt, *Black Elk Speaks* (New York: William Morrow, 1932) and the Lame Deer (Lame Deer, John Fire, with Richard Erdoes, *Lame Deer, Seeker of Visions* (New York: Simon and Schuster, 1972), not to speak of the countless Crow and Dakota autobiographies recorded in the early twentieth century by writers such as Frank Linderman. This list could be extended indefinitely. We are fortunately quite well supplied with inside accounts that deal in more or less detail with cosmology and ethnoscience.

36. E.g., Eastman, *Indian Boyhood.*

37. E.g., Bernard and Pedraza, *Native Ethnography.*

38. Rappaport, *Pigs;* and Robert Netting, *Balancing on an Alp* (Cambridge: Cambridge University Press, 1981), and *Cultural Ecology,* 2d ed. (Prospect Heights, Ill.: Waveland Press, 1986).

39. See also E. N. Anderson, "Why Is Humoral Medicine So Popular?" *Social Science and Medicine* 25 (1987): 331–337, and "Folk Forestry in a Maya Town," Ms. (1992); and Robin Ridington, "Technology, World View, and Adaptive Strategy in a Northern Hunting Society," *Canadian Review of Sociology and Anthropology* 19 (4 [1982]): 469–481.

40. Paul Radin, *Primitive Religion* (New York: Dover, 1937, reprint 1957).

41. Paul Radin, *The Winnebago Tribe* (Washington, D.C.: Bureau of American Ethnology, annual report for 1915–1916, 1923), 278.

42. Gilmore, *Prairie Smoke;* Carobeth Laird, *The Chemehuevis.* (Banning, Calif.: Malki Museum Press, 1976); Hilaria Maas Colli, "Transmición cultural: Chemax, Yucatán," thesis, licenciada, antropologia social, Universidad Autónomia de Yucatán, 1983); and George Pettitt *Primitive Education in North America* (Berkeley: University of California Press, 1946).

43. E. N. Anderson, and M. L. Anderson, *Mountains and Water* (Taipei: Orient Cultural Service, 1973); and Lansing, *Priests and Programmers.*

44. David Ehrenfeld, *Beginning Again* (New York: Oxford University Press, 1993); and David W. Orr, "For the Love of Life," *Conservation Biology* 6 (1992): 486–487.

45. For introductions or viewpoints, see Robin Attfield, *The Ethics of Environmental Concern* (Athens, Ga.: University of Georgia Press, 1991); Robyn Eckersley, *Environmentalism and Political Theory: An Ecocentric Approach* (Albany: State University of New York Press, 1992); R. Edward Grumbine, *Ghost Bears: Exploring the Biodiversity Crisis* (Washington, D.C., and Covelo, Calif.: Island Press, 1992); Carolyn Merchant, *Ecological Revolutions* (Chapel Hill: University of North Carolina Press, 1989), and *Radical Ecology;* and Holmes Ralston III, *Environmental Ethics* (Philadelphia: Temple University Press, 1988).

Chapter 11. A Summary, and Some Suggestions

1. Terry Anderson and Donald Leal, *Free Market Environmentalism* (San Francisco: Pacific Research Institute for Public Policy, 1991); Elinor Ostrom, *Governing the Commons* (Cambridge: Cambridge University Press, 1990); and Evelyn Pinkerton, ed., *Cooperative Management of Local Fisheries: New Directions for Improved Management and Community Development* (Vancouver: University of British Columbia Press, 1989).

2. *Los Angeles Times,* 12 December 1992.

3. Ibn Khaldun, *The Muqaddimah,* trans. Franz Rosenthal (New York: Pantheon [Bollingen Books], 1958).

4. Thomas Jefferson, quoted by K. S. Shrader-Frechette, *Risk and Rationality* (Berkeley: University of California Press, 1991), 99.

5. E.g., F. H. Bormann, and S. R. Kellert, eds., *Ecology, Economics, Ethics: The Broken Circle* (New Haven: Yale University Press, 1991); J. Baird Callicott, *In Defense of the Land Ethic: Essays in Environmental Philosophy* (Albany: State University of New York Press, 1989); and Shrader-Frechette, *Risk and Rationality.*

6. See the extended discussion in Martin Lewis, *Green Delusions: An Environmentalist Critique of Radical Environmentalism* (Durham: Duke University Press, 1992).

7. Earl Murphy, *Governing Nature* (Chicago: Quadrangle Books, 1967); Ostrom, *Governing the Commons;* Charles Perrings, *Economy and Environment* (Cambridge: Cambridge University Press, 1987); and many other sources.

8. Derek Parfit, *Reasons and Persons* (Oxford: Oxford University Press, 1984, corrected reprint 1989).

9. John Bodley, *Victims of Progress* (Menlo Park, Calif.: Cummings, 1975), and *Anthropology and Contemporary Human Problems* (Menlo Park, Calif.: Cummings, 1976); Lewis, *Green Delusions;* and Pinkerton, *Cooperative Management.*

10. Albert Gore, Jr., *Earth in the Balance* (New York: Houghton Mifflin, 1992).

11. David W. Orr, "For the Love of Life," *Conservation Biology* 6 (1992): 486–487.

12. Julian Simon, *The Ultimate Resource* (Princeton: Princeton University Press, 1981).

References

Ainslie, George, *Picoeconomics: The Strategic Interaction of Successive Motivational States with the Person*. Cambridge: Cambridge University Press, 1993.

Alcorn, Janis. *Huastec Mayan Ethnobotany*. Austin: University of Texas Press, 1984.

Alvard, Michael. "Are Indigenous People Necessarily Conservationists? A Case Study from the Peruvian Tropics." Paper presented at the annual convention of the American Anthropological Association, 1992.

Ambio 20 (2 [1991]). Special Issue: Environmental Economics

Amicus Journal. "Free Trade and the Environment: A Symposium of Views." *Amicus Journal* (fall 1993):31–37.

Amoss, Pamela. "A Little More Than Kin, and Less Than Kind: The Ambiguous Northwest Coast Dog." In *The Tsimshian and Their Neighbors of the North Pacific Coast*, ed. Jay Miller and Carol Eastman, 292–305. Seattle: University of Washington Press, 1984.

Anderson, Beverly, and Leslie M. Johnson Gottesfeld. *Gitksan-Wet'suwet'en Traditional Medicine Program*. Hazelton, B.C.: Gitksan–Wet'suwet'en Education Society, 1986.

Anderson, E. N. "Sacred Fish." *Man* n.s. 4 (3 [1969]):443–449.

———. *The Floating World of Castle Peak Bay*. Washington, D.C.: American Anthropological Association, 1969.

———. "The Life and Culture of Ecotopia." In *Reinventing Anthropology*, ed. Dell Hymes, 264–273. New York: Pantheon Press, 1972.

———. "Comment on Marvin Harris' 'Cultural Ecology of India's Sacred Cattle.'" *Current Anthropology* 18 (3 [1977]):552.

———. "Heating and Cooling Foods in Hong Kong and Taiwan." *Social Science Information* 19 (2 [1980]):237–268.

———. "Ecology and Ideology in Chinese Folk Nutritional Therapy." Paper presented at the annual meeting of the American Anthropological Association, 1982. Washington, DC

———. "Why Are Some Rocks and Trees Worshipped?" Paper presented at the University of Southern California China Colloquium, 1982.

———. "Ecologies of the Heart." In *Proceedings of the International Chinese Medicine Conference*, ed. Michael Gandy et al., 205–230. Oakland: Michael Gandy, 1984.

———. "Heating and Cooling Foods Re-Examined." *Social Science Information* 23 (⅘ [1984]):755–773.

———. "Why Is Humoral Medicine So Popular?" *Social Science and Medicine* 25 (1987):331–337.

———. *The Food of China*. New Haven: Yale University Press, 1988.

———. "Up against Famine." *Crossroads* 1 (1990):11–24.

———. "Folk Forestry in a Maya Town." Ms. 1992.

———. "The Sosa Farm." Paper presented at the annual meeting of the Southwestern Anthropological Association, San Diego, 1993.

Anderson, E. N., and M. L. Anderson. *Mountains and Water*. Taipei: Orient Cultural Service, 1973.

Anderson, Terry, and Donald Leal. *Free Market Environmentalism*. San Francisco: Pacific Research Institute for Public Policy, 1991.

Atran, Scott. *Cognitive Foundations of Natural History*. Cambridge: Cambridge University Press, 1991.

Attfield, Robin. *The Ethics of Environmental Concern*. Athens, Ga: University of Georgia Press, 1991.

Baden, John A. "Business, Science and Environmental Politics: Toward a Political Economy of Hope." *Columbia Journal of World Business* (Reprint 273426 [1992]).

Baker, Hugh. *Chinese Family and Kinship*. New York: Columbia University Press, 1979.

Balam Pereira, Gilberto. *Cosmogonia y uso actual de las plantas medicinales de Yucatán*. Mérida: Universidad Autónima de Yucatán, 1992.

Bandura, Albert. "Self-Efficacy Mechanism in Human Agency." *American Psychologist* 37 (2 [1982]):122–147.

Baril, L. Katherine. "Private Property and the Public Trust Doctrine: Developing New Paradigms for Government to Balance Individual Property Rights and Public Resource Protection." Paper presented at the annual meeting of the International Association for the Study of Common Property, 1992.

Barkow, Jerome H, Leda Cosmides, and John Tooby. *The Adapted Mind: Evolutionary Psychology and the Generation of Culture*. Oxford: Oxford University Press, 1992.

Barlett, Peggy. *Agricultural Choice and Change*. New Brunswick, N.J.: Rutgers University Press, 1982.

———, ed. *Agricultural Decision Making*. New York: Academic Press, 1980.

Barrera Marin, Alfredo, Alfredo Barrera Vasquez, and Rosa Maria Lopez Franco. *Nomenclatura Etnobotanica Maya*. Centro Regional del Sureste, INAH, 1976.

Bateson, Gregory. *Steps toward an Ecology of Mind*. San Francisco: Chandler, 1972.

Batson, Daniel. "How Social an Animal? The Human Capacity for Caring." *American Psychologist* 45 (3 [1990]):336–346.

Baumeister, Roy F., and Steven J. Scher. "Self-Defeating Behavior Patterns among Normal Individuals: Review and Analysis of Common Self-Destructive Tendencies." *Psychological Bulletin* 104 (1 [1988]):3–22.

Bean, Lowell, and Thomas Blackburn, eds. 1976. *Native Californians: A Theoretical Retrospective*. Socorro, New Mex.: Ballena Press, 1976.

Beck, Aaron. *Cognitive Therapy and the Emotional Disorders.* New York: International Universities Press, 1976.

Bellah, Robert, et al. *Habits of the Heart.* Berkeley: University of California Press, 1985.

———. *The Good Society.* New York: Random House, 1991.

Bellant, R. *The Coors Connection: How Coors Family Philanthropy Undermines Democratic Pluralism.* Boston: South End Press, 1991.

Benedict, F., and Morris Steggerda. *The Food of the Present-Day Maya Indians of Yucatán.* Washington, D.C.: Carnegie Foundation, 1936.

Benhabib, Seyla, and Fred Dallmayr, eds. *The Communicative Ethics Controversy.* Cambridge, Mass.: M.I.T. Press, 1990.

Bennett, John. *The Ecological Transition.* New York: Pergamon, 1976.

———. *Human Ecology as Human Behavior.* New Brunswick, NJ: Transaction, 1995.

Berkes, Fikret, ed. *Common Property Resources.* London: Belhaven Press, 1991.

Berkes, Fikret, et al. "The Benefits of the Commons." *Nature* 340 (1989):91–93.

Berkes, Fikret, and David Feeny. "Paradigms Lost: Changing Views on the Use of Common Property Resources." *Alternatives* 17 (1990):48–55.

Berlin, Brent. 1992. *Ethnobiological Classification.* Princeton: Princeton University Press, 1992.

Bernard, H. Russell, and Jesus Salinas Pedraza. *Native Ethnography.* Newbury Park: Sage, 1989.

Biocca, Ettore. *Yanoama.* Told by Helena Valero. New York: Dutton, 1970.

Bodley, John. *Victims of Progress.* Menlo Park, Calif.: Cummings, 1975.

———. *Anthropology and Contemporary Human Problems.* Menlo Park, Calif.: Cummings, 1976.

Bormann, F. H., and S. R. Kellert, eds. *Ecology, Economics, Ethics: The Broken Circle.* New Haven: Yale University Press, 1991.

Bourdieu, Pierre. *Outline of a Theory of Practice.* Cambridge: Cambridge University Press, 1976.

———. *The Logic of Practice.* Stanford: Stanford University Press, 1992.

Bourdieu, Pierre, and J. Passeron. *Reproduction in Education, Society and Culture.* Newbury Park: Sage, 1990.

Bovard, James. *The Farm Fiasco.* San Francisco: Institute of Contemporary Studies, 1991.

Boyd, Andrew. *Chinese Architecture.* London: Alec Tirani, 1962.

Brightman, Robert. "Conservation and Resource Depletion: The Case of the Boreal Forest Algonquians." *McCay and Acheson* (1987):121–141.

———. *Grateful Prey: Rock Cree Human-Animal Relationships.* Berkeley: University of California Press, 1992.

Brody, Hugh. *Maps and Dreams.* Harmondsworth: Pelican, 1983.

Brown, Donald. *Human Universals.* Philadelphia: Temple University Press, 1991.

Buell, Paul. 1984. "Theory and Practice of Traditional Chinese Medicine." Paper no. 21 presented at the East Asian Colloquium, Center for East Asian Studies, Bellingham, Wash., 1984.

Bullard, Robert. "Solid Waste Sites and the Black Community." *Sociological Inquiry* 53 (1983):273–288.

——. "Endangered Environs: The Price of Unplanned Growth in Boomtown Houston." *California Sociologist* (summer 1984):85–101.

——. *Dumping in Dixie: Race, Class, and Environmental Quality.* Boulder, Colo.: Westview, 1990.

Bullard, Robert, and Beverly Hendrix Wright. "Environmentalism and the Politics of Equity: Emergent Trends in the Black Community." *Mid-American Review of Sociology* 12 (1987):21–38.

Burton, Sharon. "Managing the Commons of Tourist Dollars." MS, 1992.

Callicott, J. Baird. "American Indian Land Wisdom? Sorting Out the Issues." *Journal of Forest History* 33 (1989):35–42.

——. *In Defense of the Land Ethic: Essays in Environmental Philosophy.* Albany: State University of New York Press, 1989.

Cernea, Michael. "Anthropological Variables of Environmental Problems." Paper, presented at the annual convention of the American Anthropological Association, 1992. San Francisco.

Cheng, Libin. "Are the So-Called Poisonous Food-Combinations Really Poisonous?" *Contributions, Biological Laboratory, Science Society of China, Zoological Series* 2 (9 [1936]):307–316.

Clendinnen, Inga. *Ambivalent Conquests.* Cambridge: Cambridge University Press, 1987.

Coase, Ronald. "The Problem of Social Cost." *Journal of Law and Economics* 3 (1960):1–44.

Cole, Michael, and Susan Scribner. *Culture and Thought.* New York: Wiley, 1974.

Collins, June McCormick. *Valley of the Spirits.* Seattle: University of Washington Press, 1974.

Comaroff, Jean. *Body of Power, Spirit of Resistance.* Chicago: University of Chicago Press, 1985.

Conference on Common Property Resource Management. Proceedings. Washington, D.C.: National Academy Press, 1986.

Cook, Roger. *The Tree of Life.* New York: Avon, 1974.

Cox, Paul, and Sandra Banack, eds. *Islands, Plants, and Polynesians.* Portland, Oreg.: Timber Press, 1991.

Cranor, Carl. *Regulating Toxic Substances: A Philosophy of Science and the Law.* New York: Oxford University Press, 1993.

Crary, Mary Elizabeth. "Chinese Feng Shui in the Context of an American Suburb." Master's thesis, California State University, 1992.

Creel, H. *Shen Pu-Hai.* Chicago: University of Chicago Press, 1973.

Currier, Richard. "The Hot-Cold Syndrome and Symbolic Balance in Mexican and Spanish-American Folk Medicine." *Ethnology* 5 (1966):251–263.

Daly, Herman, and John Cobb. *For the Common Good.* Boston: Beacon, 1990.

Davisson, Richard, Jr. "The Dragon in San Francisco." *Landscape* 17 (1967–68):12–15.

Dawes, Robyn. "Social Dilemmas." *Annual Review of Psychology* 31 (1980):169–193.

de Laguna, Frederica. *Under Mount Saint Elias: The History and Culture of the Yakutat Tlingit.* Washington, D.C.: Smithsonian Institution, 1972.

de Maillie, R. *The Sixth Grandfather.* Lincoln: University of Nebraska Press, 1984.

Dentan, Robert. *The Semai, a Nonviolent People of Malaysia.* New York: Holt, Rinehart, Winston, 1968.

DeWalt, Billie. "Using Indigenous Knowledge to Improve Agricultuure and Natural Resource Management." *Human Organization* 53 (1994):123–131.

Diamond, Jared. *The Third Chimpanzee.* New York: HarperCollins, 1992.

Dore, Henri. *Researches into Chinese Superstitions.* Shanghai: Tusewei, 1914.

Dove, Michael. "Perceptions of Property and Equality of Access: Trees in Swidden Systems." Paper presented at the annual conference of the International Association for the Study of Common Property, 1992. Washington, DC

Douglas, Mary. *Natural Symbols.* London: Barrie and Rockliff, 1966.

———. *Implicit Meanings.* London: Routledge, Kegan Paul, 1975.

Downing, Theodore, et al., eds. *Development or Destruction? The Conversion of Tropical Forests to Pasture in Latin America.* Boulder, Colo.: Westview Press, 1992.

Drucker, Peter. *The Ecological Vision.* New Brunswick, N.J.: Transaction, 1992.

Drucker, Philip. *The Northern and Central Nootka Tribes.* Washington, D.C.: Bureau of American Ethnology, 1955.

Drucker, Philip, and Robert Heizer. *To Make My Name Good.* Berkeley: University of California Press, 1967.

Dryzek, John. *Rational Ecology: Environment and Political Economy.* Oxford: Basil Blackwell, 1987.

Duff, Wilson. "The World Is as Sharp as a Knife: Meaning in Northern Northwest Coast Art." In *Indian Art Traditions of the Northwest Coast,* ed. Roy Carlson, 47–66. Burnaby, B.C.: Archaeology Press, Simon Fraser University, 1983.

Durkheim, Emile. *The Elementary Forms of the Religious Life.* Glencoe, Ill.: Free Press, 1961.

Earth Island, special issue on Rio de Janeiro Summit, Summer 1992.

Eastman, Charles (Ohiyesa). *Indian Boyhood.* 1902. Reprint, New York: Dover, 1971.

Eckersley, Robyn. *Environmentalism and Political Theory: An Ecocentric Approach.* Albany: State University of New York Press, 1992.

Edgerton, Robert. *Sick Societies: Challenging the Myth of Primitive Harmony.* New York: Free Press, 1992.

Ehrenfeld, David. *Beginning Again.* New York: Oxford University Press, 1993.

Eisenberg, Nancy. *Altruistic Emotion, Cognition and Behavior.* Hillsdale, N.J.: Lawrence Erlbaum Associates, 1986.

Eitel, Ernest J. *Feng-shui: Or, the Rudiments of Natural Science in China.* Hong Kong: Lane, Crawford and Co., 1873.

Ekman, Paul. "Are There Basic Emotions?" *Psychological Review* 99 (1992):550–553.

Ellen, Roy. "Ethnobiology, Cognition and the Structure of Prehension: Some General Theoretical Notes." *Journal of Ethnobiology* 6 (1986):83–98.

Elmendorf, W. W. *The Structure of Twana Culture.* Pullman, Wash.: Washington State University Press, 1960.

Elster, Jon. *Sour Grapes.* Cambridge: Cambridge University Press, 1983.

———. *Ulysses and the Sirens.* 2d ed. Cambridge: Cambridge University Press, 1984.

———. *The Cement of Society.* Cambridge: Cambridge University Press, 1989.

Emmons, George T. *The Tlingit Indians,* ed. Frederica de Laguna. Seattle: University of Washington Press and American Museum of Natural History, 1991.

Feeny, David, et al. "The Tragedy of the Commons: Twenty-Two Years Later." *Human Ecology* 18 (1 [1990]):1–20.

Feit, H. A. "James Bay Cree Indian Management and Moral Considerations of Fur-Bearers." In *Native People and Renewable Resource Management,* Alberta Society of Professional Biologists, 49–65. Edmonton: H. A. Feit.

Feshbach, Murray, and Alfred Friendly, Jr. *Ecocide in the USSR.* New York: Basic Books, 1991.

Feuchtwang, Steven. *An Anthropological Analysis of Chinese Geomancy.* Vientiane, Laos: Vithagna, 1974.

Field, Barry C. *Environmental Economics: An Introduction.* New York: McGraw-Hill, 1994.

Firth, Raymond. *We the Tikopia.* London: G. Allen and Unwin, 1936.

———. *Social Change in Tikopia.* London: G. Allen and Unwin, 1959.

———. *Economics of the New Zealand Maori.* London: Routledge, Kegan Paul, 1965.

Fiske, Susan, and Shelley Taylor. *Social Cognition.* Reading, Mass.: Addison-Wesley, 1984.

———. *Social Cognition.* 2d ed. New York: McGraw-Hill, 1991.

Flannery, Kent, ed. *Maya Subsistence.* New York: Academic Press, 1981.

Foster, George. "Peasant Society and the Image of Limited Good." *American Anthropologist* 67 (1965):293–315.

———. "On the Origin of Humoral Medicine in Latin America." *Medical Anthropology Quarterly* 1 (4 [1987]):355–393.

Foster, George, and Barbara Anderson. *Medical Anthropology.* New York: Wiley, 1978.

Frankl, Viktor. *The Unheard Cry for Meaning.* New York: Simon and Schuster, 1978.

Fraser, Douglas. *Village Planning in the Primitive World.* New York: Brasiller, 1968.

Freedman, Maurice. *Chinese Lineage and Society: Fukien and Kwnagtung.* London: London School of Economics, 1966.

Freeman, Milton, and Ludwig Carbyn, eds. *Traditional Knowledge and Renewable Resource Management in Northern Regions.* Edmonton: Canadian Circumpolar Institute, 1992.

Freeman, Milton, Y. Matsuda, and K. Ruddle, eds. *Adaptive Marine Resource Systems in the Pacific.* New York: Harwood, 1991.

Furth, Charlotte. "Concepts of Pregnancy, Childbirth, and Infancy in Ch'ing Dynasty China." *Journal of Asian Studies* 46 (1 [1987]):7–35.

Gadgil, Mahdev, and Fikret Berkes. "Traditional Resource Management Systems." *Resource Management and Optimization* 8 (1991):127–141.

Gadgil, Mahdev, and Ramachandra Guha. *This Fissured Land: An Ecological History of India*. Oxford: Oxford University Press, 1992.

Gandy, Michael, Mason Shen, and Effram Korngold, eds. Proceedings of the International Chinese Medicine Conference. Oakland: Michael Gandy, 1984.

Gardner, Howard. *Frames of Mind*. Cambridge, Mass.: Harvard University Press, 1983.

Gates, Hill. "Dependency and the Part-Time Proletariat in Taiwan." *Modern China* 5 (1979):381–407.

Gates, Marilyn. *In Default: Peasants, the Debt Crisis, and the Agrarian Challenge in Mexico*. Boulder, Colo.: Westview, 1992.

Gazzaniga, Michael. *The Social Brain*. New York: Basic Books, 1985.

———. *Nature's Mind*. New York: Basic Books, 1992.

Geertz, Clifford. "Anti-Anti-Relativism." *American Anthropologist* 86 (1984):263–278.

Gigerenzer, Gert. "How to Make Cognitive Illusions Disappear: Beyond 'Heuristics and Biases.' " *European Review of Social Psychology* 2 (1991):83–115.

Gilmore, Melvin. *Prairie Smoke*. 1929. Reprint St. Paul, Minn.: Minnesota Historical Society, 1987.

———. *Uses of Plants by the Indians of the Missouri River Region*. Enlarged ed. 1919. Reprint Lincoln: University of Nebraska Press, 1991.

Goldman, Irving. *The Mouth of Heaven: An Introduction to Kwakiutl Religious Thought*. New York: Wiley, 1975.

Gomez-Pompa, Arturo, and Andrea Kaus. "Traditional Management of Tropical Forests in Mexico." In *Alternatives to Deforestation: Steps toward Sustainable Use of the Amazon Rain Forest,* ed. Anthony B. Anderson, 45–64. New York: Columbia University Press.

Gomez-Pompa, Arturo, et al. "Mexico." In *Sustainable Agriculture and the Environment in the Humid Tropics*. Committee on Sustainable Agriculture and the Environment in the Humid Tropics, National Research Council, 483–548, Washington, DC: 1993.

Gore, Albert, Jr. *Earth in the Balance*. New York: Houghton Mifflin, 1992.

Gottesfeld, Leslie. "Gitksan and Wet'suwet'en Conservation Ethics, Concepts and Practices." Ms. 1992.

Gould, Richard. *Yiwara: Foragers of the Australian Desert*. New York: Scribners, 1969.

Gould-Martin, Katherine. "Hot Cold Clean Poison and Dirt: Chinese Folk Medical Categories." *Social Science and Medicine* 12 (1978):39–46.

Graham, A. C. *Later Mohist Logic*. Hong Kong and London: Chinese University of Hong Kong and University of London School of Oriental and African Studies, 1978.

Griaule, Marcel. *Conversations with Ogotemmeli*. Chicago: University of Chicago Press, 1965.

Groot, J. J. M. de. *The Religious System of China*. Leiden: Brill, 1982-1910.

Grumbine, R. Edward. *Ghost Bears: Exploring the Biodiversity Crisis.* Washington, D.C., and Covelo, Calif.: Island Press, 1992.

Hall, Edward. *The Silent Language.* Garden City: Doubleday, 1959.

———. *The Hidden Dimension.* Garden City: Doubleday, 1966.

Haly, Richard. "On Becoming a Mountain, Or, Why Native Americans Have Animals for Souls." Paper presented at the annual conference of the American Anthropological Association, 1992.

Hardin, Garrett. "The Tragedy of the Commons." *Science* 162 (1968):1243–1248.

Harris, Arthur H. *Late Pleistocene Vertebrate Paleoecology of the West.* Austin: University of Texas Press, 1985.

Harris, Chief Kenneth. *Visitors Who Never Left.* Vancouver: University of British Columbia Press, 1974.

Harris, Marvin. "The Cultural Ecology of India's Sacred Cattle." *Current Anthropology* 7 (1966):51–66.

———. *The Rise of Anthropological Theory.* New York: Crowell, 1968.

Harrison, P., and B. L. Turner. *Pre-Hispanic Maya Agriculture.* Albuquerque: University of New Mexico Press, 1978.

Hayami, Yujiro, and Vernon Ruttan. *Agricultural Development.* 2d ed. Baltimore: Johns Hopkins Press, 1985.

Heinen, Joel T., and Roberta C. ("Bobbi") S. Low. "Human Behavioral Ecology and Environmental Conservation." *Environmental Conservation* 19 (1993):105–115.

Hess, Karl. *Visions upon the Land: Man and Nature on the Western Range.* Washington, D.C., and Covelo, Calif.: Island Press, 1992.

Hilsdale, Karin. "The 'Psychiatry' of Traditional Oriental Medicine: An Exploratory Study in Comparative Diagnosis of Depressed Women." Ph.D. diss., International College, 1985.

Hobsbawm, Eric, and Terence Ranger, eds. *The Invention of Tradition.* Cambridge: Cambridge University Press, 1982.

Hoffman, Martin. "Is Altruism Part of Human Nature?" In *Social Cognitive Development,* ed. Ross Lee, 121–137. Cambridge: Cambridge University Press, 1981.

Hofling, Charles Andrew. *Itza Maya Texts.* Salt Lake City: University of Utah Press, 1991.

Hughes, J. Donald. *American Indian Ecology.* El Paso, Tex.: Texas Western University Press, 1983.

Hume, David. *Enquiries Concerning Human Understanding and Concerning the Principles of Morals.* 1777 ed. of 1772 work. Oxford: Oxford University Press, 1975.

Hunn, Eugene. *Nch'i Wana, the Big River.* Seattle: University of Washington Press, 1991.

Ibn Khaldun. *The Muqaddimah.* Trans. Franz Rosenthal. New York: Pantheon (Bollingen Books), 1958.

Isaac, Glynn. "Food Sharing and Human Evolution: Archaeological Evidence from the Plio-Pleistocene of East Africa." *Journal of Anthropological Research* 34 (3 [1978]):311–325.

———. "The Food-Sharing Behavior of Protohuman Hominids." *Scientific American* 238 (4 [1978]):90–108.

Jacobs, Lynn. *Waste of the West.* Tucson: Lynn Jacobs, 1991.

Jaulin, Robert. *La Géomancie: Analyse formelle.* Paris: Mouton, 1969.

Jenness, Diamond. *The Faith of a Coast Salish Indian.* Victoria: British Columbia Provincial Museum. Anthropological Papers no. 3, 1955.

Jilek, Wolfgang. *Indian Healing.* Vancouver: Hancock House, 1982.

Johannes, R. E. *Words of the Lagoon.* Berkeley: University of California Press, 1983.

———, ed. *Traditional Ecological Knowledge.* Gland, Switzerland: IUCN, 1989.

Jonaitis, Aldona. *Tlingit Halibut Hooks: An Analysis of the Visual Symbolism of a Rite of Passage.* New York: American Museum of Natural History. Anthropological Papers no. 57 (1.), 1981.

———. *Art of the Northern Tlingit.* Seattle: University of Washington Press, 1986

Judson, Sheldon. "Erosion Rates near Rome, Italy." *Science* 160 (1968):1444–1445.

Jung, Carl. *Symbols of Transformation.* New York: Pantheon, 1956.

Kahnemann, D., Paul Slovic, and Amos Tversky. *Judgement under Uncertainty: Heuristics and Biases.* Cambridge: Cambridge University Press, 1982.

Kaiser, Rudolf. "Chief Seattle's Speech(es): American Origins and European Reception." In *Recovering the Word: Essays on Native American Literature,* ed. Brian Swann and Arnold Krupat, 497–536. Berkeley: University of California Press, 1987.

Kamenskii, Anatolii. *The Tlingit Indians of Alaska.* Trans. Sergei Kan. Fairbanks: University of Alaska Press. Rasmussen Library, Historical Translations Series, no. 2, 1985.

Keirsey, D., and M. Bates *Please Understand Me.* Del Mar, Calif.: Prometheus Nemesis, 1978.

Kenyatta, Jomo. *Facing Mount Kenya.* London: Secker and Warburg, 1938.

Kintz, Ellen. *Life under the Tropical Canopy.* New York: Holt, Rinehart and Winston, 1990.

Kirk, Ruth. *Wisdom of the Elders.* Victoria: British Columbia Provincial Museum, 1986.

Kitanmax School of Northwest Coast Indian Art. *Wegyet Wanders On.* Hazelton, B.C.: Kitanmax School of Northwest Coast Indian Art, 1977.

Klee, Gary, ed. *World Systems of Traditional Resource Management.* New York: V. H. Winston and Sons, 1980.

Kleinman, Arthur. *Patients and Healers in the Context of Culture.* Berkeley: University of California Press, 1980.

———. *Social Origins of Distress and Disease.* New Haven: Yale University Press, 1986.

Knapp, Ronald. *China's Traditional Rural Architecture.* Honolulu: University of Hawaii Press, 1986.

Kohn, Alfie. *The Brighter Side of Human Nature.* New York: Basic Books, 1990.

Konner, Melvin. *The Tangled Wing.* New York: Holt, Rinehart, Winston, 1982.

Koo, Linda. *Nourishment of Life.* Hong Kong: Commercial Press, 1982.

Kottak, Conrad, and Alberto C. G. Costa. "Ecological Awareness, Environmentalist Action, and International Conservation Strategy." *Human Organization* 52 (1993):335–343.

Krause, A. *The Tlingit Indians.* Seattle: University of Washington Press, 1956.

Kronenfeld, David. *Plastic Glasses and Church Fathers: Semantic Extension from the Ethnoscience Tradition.* Cambridge: Cambridge University Press. Forthcoming.

Kuhn, Thomas. *The Structure of Scientific Revolutions.* Chicago: University of Chicago Press, 1962.

Laderman, Carol. "Symbolic and Empirical Reality: A New Approach to the Analysis of Food Avoidances." *American Ethnologust* 3 (1981):468–493.

———. *Wives and Midwives.* Berkeley: University of California Press, 1983.

———. "Destructive Heat and Cooling Prayer: Malay Humoralism in Pregnancy, Childbirth and the Postpartum Period." *Social Science and Medicine* 25 (4 [1987]):357–366.

Laird, Carobeth. *The Chemehuevis.* Banning, Calif.: Malki Museum Press, 1976.

Lakoff, George. *Women, Fire and Dangerous Things.* Chicago: University of Chicago Press, 1987.

Lame Deer (John Fire) with Richard Erdoes. *Lame Deer, Seeker of Visions.* New York: Simon and Schuster, 1972.

Langdon, Steven. "Technology, Ecology and Economy: Fishing Systems in Southeast Alaska." Ph.D. diss. Stanford University, 1977.

———. "Comparative Tlingit and Haida Adaptation to the West Coast of the Prince of Wales Archipelago." Vol. 18, *Ethnology* (1979) 102–119.

———. "Alaskan Native Self-regulation of Subsistence Resources: Traditional Practices and Emerging Institutions." Paper presented at the annual meeting of the American Anthropological Association, 1985.

Langer, Ellen. *The Psychology of Control.* Beverly Hills: Sage, 1983.

Lansing, J. Stephen. "Balinese 'Water Temples' and the Management of Irrigation." *American Anthropologist* 89 (1987):326–341.

———. *Priests and Programmers.* Princeton: Princeton University Press, 1991.

Lansing, J. Stephen, and James N. Kramer. "Emergent Properties of Balinese Water Temple Networks: Coadaptation on a Rugged Fitness Landscape." *American Anthropologist* 95 (1993):97–114.

Lau, D. *Mencius.* Harmondsworth, Sussex: Pelican, 1970.

Lave, Jean. *Cognition in Practice.* Cambridge: Cambridge University Press, 1988.

Lazarus, Richard. *Emotion and Adaptation.* New York: Oxford University Press, 1991.

Leakey, Richard, and Roger Lewin. *Origins Reconsidered.* New York: Doubleday, 1992.

Lee, Rance. "Perceptions and Uses of Chinese Medicine among the Chinese of Hong Kong." *Culture, Medicine and Psychiatry* 4 (1980):345–375.

Legeza, Laszlo. *Tao Magic.* New York: Random House, 1975.

Lehr, Jay, ed. *Rational Readings on Environmental Issues.* New York: Van Nostrand Reinhold, 1992.

Leopold, Aldo. *A Sand County Almanac*. New York: Oxford University Press, 1949.

Lepofsky, Dana, Nancy J. Turner, and Harriet V. Kuhnlein. "Determining the Availability of Traditional Wild Plant Foods: An Example of Nuxalk Foods, Bella Coola, British Columbia." *Ecology of Food and Nutrition* 16 (1985):223–241.

Lerner, Melvin. *Belief in a Just World: A Fundamental Delusion*. New York: Plenum, 1980.

Leslie, Charles, and Allan Young, eds. *Paths to Asian Medical Knowledge*. Berkeley: University of California Press, 1992.

Lévi-Strauss, Claude. *La Pensée sauvage*. Paris: Plon, 1962.

———. *Mythologiques*. Paris: Plon, 1964–1971.

———. *The Way of Masks*. Seattle: University of Washington Press, 1982.

Lewis, Henry. *Patterns of Indian Burning in California*. Socorro, New Mex.: Ballena Press, 1973.

———. "Indian Fires of Spring." *Natural History* 89 (1980):76–77, 82–83.

Lewis, Martin. *Green Delusions: An Environmentalist Critique of Radical Environmentalism*. Durham: Duke University Press, 1992.

Lewis, Thomas. "Cloaked in a Wise Disguise." *National Wildlife* (Oct.–Nov. 1992):4–8.

Libecap, Gary. *Contracting for Property Rights*. Cambridge: Cambridge University Press, 1989.

Limbaugh, Rush. *The Way Things Ought to Be*. New York: Pocket Books, 1992.

Lip, Evelyn. *Feng-Shui: A Layman's Guide to Chinese Feng-Shui*. Singapore: Heian, 1979.

Liu, Frank, and Liu Yan Mau. *Chinese Medical Terminology*. Hong Kong: Commercial Press, 1980.

Lopez, Kevin Lee. "Returning to Fields." *American Indian Culture and Research Journal* 16 (1992):165–174.

Lovejoy, Owen. "The Origin of Man." *Science* 211 (44 [1981]):341–350.

Lu, Henry. *Chinese System of Food Cures*. New York: Sterling Publishing Co, 1986.

Ludwig, Donald, Ray Hilborn, and Carl Walters. "Uncertainty, Resource Exploitation, and Conservation: Lessons from History." *Science* 223 (1993):17–18.

Lutz, Catherine. *Unnatural Emotions*. Chicago: University of Chicago Press, 1988.

Lynch, Kevin. *The Image of the City*. Cambridge, Mass.: M.I.T. Press, 1960.

McCabe, J. Terrence. "Turkana Pastoralism: A Case against the Tragedy of the Commons." *Human Ecology* 8 (1990):81–104.

McCabe, J. Terrence, Scott Perkin, and Claire Schofield. "Can Conservation and Development be Coupled among Pastoral People? An Examination of the Maasai of the Ngorongoro Conservation Area, Tanzania." *Human Organization* 51 (1992):353–366.

McCay, Bonnie, and James Acheson, eds. *The Question of the Commons*. Tucson: University of Arizona Press, 1987.

McClellan, Catherine. *My Old People Say*. Ottawa: National Museums of Canada, 1975.

McDaniel, Jay B. *Of Gods and Pelicans: A Theology of Reverence for Life*. Louisville: Westminster/John Knox Press, 1989.

———. *Earth, Sky, Gods and Mortals: Developing an Ecological Spirituality*. Mystic, Conn.: Twenty-Third Publications, 1990.

McEvoy, Arthur. *The Fisherman's Problem*. Cambridge: Cambridge University Press, 1986.

McHarg, Ian. *Design with Nature*. Garden City, NY: Natural History Press, 1969.

McKean, Margaret. "Success on the Commons." *Journal of Theoretical Politics* 4 (1992) 247–281.

McNeary, Stephen A. "Image and Illusion in Tsimshian Mythology." In *The Tsimshian and Their Neighbors of the North Pacific Coast,* ed. Jay Miller and Carol Eastman, 3–15. Seattle: University of Washington Press, 1984.

McNeill, J. R. The Mountains of the Mediterranean World. Cambridge: Cambridge University Press, 1992.

Maas Colli, Hilaria. Transmición cultural: Chemax, Yucatán. Thesis, licenciada, antropologia social, Universidad Autónima de Yucatán, 1983.

Malinowski, Bronislaw. *Argonauts of the Western Pacific*. New York: Dutton, 1922.

———. *Myth in Primitive Psychology*. New York: W. W. Norton, 1926.

———. *Coral Gardens and Their Magic*. New York: American Book Co., 1935.

———. *A Scientific Theory of Culture*. Raleigh: University of North Carolina Press, 1944.

———. *Magic, Science and Religion*. Garden City: Doubleday, 1948.

Mallory, Walter H. *China, Land of Famine*. New York: American Geographical Society, Special Publication no. 6, 1926.

Marchak, Patricia. "What Happens When Common Property Becomes Uncommon?" *BC Studies* 80 (1989):3–23.

Marks, Robert. *Rural Revolution in South China*. Madison: University of Wisconsin Press, 1984.

Marten, Gerald, ed. *Traditional Agriculture in Southeast Asia*. Honolulu: East-West Center, 1986.

Martin, Calvin. *Keepers of the Game*. Berkeley: University of California Press, 1978.

Martin, Paul S. "Pleistocene Overkill: The Global Model." In *Quarternary Extinctions,* ed. Paul Martin and R. Klein, 354–403. Tucson: University of Arizona Press, 1984.

Maslow, Abraham. *Motivation and Personality*. 2d ed. New York: Harper and Row, 1970.

Maud, Ralph. *A Guide to B.C. Indian Myth and Legend*. Vancouver: Talonbooks, 1982.

Meilleur, Brien. "Forest and the Polynesian Adaptation." In *Tropical Deforestation: The Human Dimension,* ed. L. Sponsel, T. Headland, and R. Bailey. Cambridge: Cambridge University Press, 1992.

Merchant, Carolyn. *Ecological Revolutions*. Chapel Hill: University of North Carolina Press, 1989.

———. *Radical Ecology*. London: Routledge, 1992.

Merleau-Ponty, M. *La Structure du Comportement*. Paris: Presses Universitaires de France, 1960.

———. *The Phenomenology of Perception*. Trans. Colin Smith. New York: Humanities Press, 1962.

————. *Signs*. Trans. John McCleary. Chicago: Northwestern University Press, 1964.

Mesquita, Batja, and Nico H. Frijda. "Cultural Variations in Emotions: A Review." *Psychological Bulletin* 112 (1992):179–204.

Mikesell, Marvin. *Northern Morocco: A Cultural Geography*. Berkeley: University of California Press, 1961.

Mills, C. Wright. *The Sociological Imagination*. New York: Oxford University Press, 1959.

Mischel, Walter. "On the Predictability of Behavior and the Structure of Personality." In *Personality and the Prediction of Behavior*, ed. Robert A. Zucker et al., 269–305. New York: Academic Press.

Morales Valderrama, Carmen. *Ocupación y subrevivencia campesina en la zona citrica de Yucatán*. Mexico City: INAH, 1987.

Morrell, Mike. *The Gitksan and Wet'suwet'en Fishery in the Skeena River System*. Hazelton, B.C.: Gitksan-Wet'suwet'en Tribal Council, 1985.

Murdock, George. *Our Primitive Contemporaries*. New York: Dutton, 1934.

Murphy, Earl. *Governing Nature*. Chicago: Quadrangle Books, 1967.

Myers, Isabel Briggs. *Gifts Differing*. Palo Alto: Consulting Psychologists Press, 1980.

Nabhan, Gary P., et al. "Papago Influences on Habitat and Biotic Diversity: Quitovac Oasis Ethnoecology." *Journal of Ethnobiology* 2 (1982):1224–1243.

Nabhan, Gary P., and Stephen Trimble. *The Geography of Childhood: Why Children Need Wild Places*. Boston: Beacon Press, 1994.

Needham, Joseph. "Review of *Ideas* and *Pharmaceutics*, by Paul Unschuld." *American Ethnologist* 15 (1 [1988]):182–183.

Neihardt, John. *Black Elk Speaks*. New York: William Morrow, 1932.

Neisser, Ulric. *Cognition and Reality*. San Francisco: Freeman, 1976.

Nelson, Richard K. *Hunters of the Northern Forest*. Chicago: University of Chicago Press, 1973.

————. "A Conservation Ethic and Environment: The Koyukon of Alaska." In *Resource Managers*, ed. Nancy Williams and Eugene Hunn, 211–228. Boulder, Colo.: Westview Press, 1982.

————. *Make Prayers to the Raven*. Chicago: University of Chicago Press, 1983.

Netting, Robert. *Balancing on an Alp*. Cambridge: Cambridge University Press, 1981.

————. *Cultural Ecology*. 2d ed. Prospect Heights, Ill.: Waveland Press, 1986.

Nisbett, Richard, and Ross, Lee. *Human Inference*. Englewood Cliffs, N.J.: Prentice-Hall, 1980.

North, Douglass. 1990. *Institutions, Institutional Change and Economic Performance*. Cambridge: Cambridge University Press, 1990.

Oberg, Kalervo. 1973. *The Social Economy of the Tlingit Indians*. Seattle: University of Washington Press, 1973.

Orr, David W. "For the Love of Life." *Conservation Biology* 6 (1992):486–487.

Ortiz de Montellano, Bernard. "Empirical Aztec Medicine." *Science* 188 (1975):215–220.

Ortony, Andrew, Gerald Clore, and Allan Collins. *The Cognitive Structure of Emotions*. Cambridge: Cambridge University Press, 1988.

Ostrom, Elinor. *Governing the Commons*. Cambridge: Cambridge University Press, 1990.

Overholt, Th. W., and J. Baird Callicott, eds. *Clothed-in Fur and Other Tales: An Introduction to an Ojibwa Worldview*. Washington: University Press of America, 1982.

Painter, Muriel. *With Good Heart*. Tucson: University of Arizona Press, 1985.

Parfit, Derek. *Reasons and Persons*. 1984. Corrected reprint, Oxford: Oxford University Press, 1989.

Pearce, David, and R. Kerry Turner. *Economics of Natural Resources and the Environment*. Baltimore: Johns Hopkins University Press, 1990.

Peraza Lopez, and Maria Elena. "Patrones alimenticios en Ichmul, Yucatán." Thesis, Facultad de Antropología y Historia, Universidad Autónima de Yucatán, 1986.

Perez Toro, Augusto. "La agricultura milpera de los Mayas de Yucatán." In Gobierno de Yucatán: Enciclopedia Yucatanese, 173–204. Mérida: Gobierno de Yucatán, 1977.

Perrings, Charles. *Economy and Environment*. Cambridge: Cambridge University Press, 1987.

Pettitt, George. *Primitive Education in North America*. Berkeley: University of California Press, 1946.

Pielou, E. C. *After the Ice Age*. Chicago: University of Chicago Press, 1991.

Pillsbury, Barbara. "Doing the Month." Paper presented at the annual meeting of the American Anthropological Association, 1976.

Pinkerton, Evelyn, ed. *Cooperative Management of Local Fisheries: New Directions for Improved Management and Community Development*. Vancouver: University of British Columbia Press, 1989.

Ponting, Clive. *A Green History of the World*. New York: Penguin, 1991.

Poole, William. "Neither Wise nor Well." *Sierra* (Nov.–Dec. 1992):59–61, 88–93.

Porkert, Manfred. *Theoretical Foundations of Chinese Medicine*. Cambridge, Mass.: M.I.T. Press, 1974.

Posey, Darrell. "Reply to Parker." *American Anthropologist* 92 (1992):441–443.

Putnam, Robert D. *Making Democracy Work: Civic Traditions in Modern Italy*. Princeton: Princeton University Press, 1992.

Radin, Paul. "The Winnebago Tribe." Bureau of American Ethnology Annual Report for 1915–1916, 33–560. Washington, D.C., 1923.

———. *Primitive Religion* 1937. Reprint, New York: Dover, 1957.

Rapoport, Amos. *House Form and Culture*. Englewood Cliffs, N.J.: Prentice-Hall, 1969.

Rappaport, Roy A. "The Sacred in Human Evolution." *Annual Review of Ecology and Systematics* 2 (1971):23–44.

———. *Ecology, Meaning and Religion*. Richmond, Calif.: North Atlantic Books, 1979.

———. *Pigs for the Ancestors*. 2d ed. New Haven: Yale University Press, 1984.

Read, Bernard. "Chinese Materia Medica: Animal Drugs." *Peking Natural History Bulletin* 5 (4 [1931]):37–80, 6 (1 [1931]):1–102.

Reichel-Dolmatoff, Gerardo. *Amazonian Cosmos*. Chicago: University of Chicago Press, 1971.

———. "Cosmology as Ecological Analysis: A View from the Rain Forest." *Man* 11 (1976):307–316.

Repetto, Robert. "Deforestation in the Tropics." *Scientific American* (April 1990):36–42.

———. "Accounting for Environmental Assets." *Scientific American* (June 1992):94–100.

Richards, Audrey. *Hunger and Work in a Savage Tribe.* London: Routledge, Kegan Paul, 1932.

———. *Land, Labour and Diet in Northern Rhodesia.* London: Oxford University Press, 1939.

Richardson, Allan. "Control of Productive Resources on the Northwest Coast of North America." In *Resource Managers,* ed. Nancy Williams and Eugene Hunn, 93–112. Boulder, Colo.: Westview Press, 1982.

Rico-Gray, Victor, et al. "Species Composition, Similarity, and Structure of Mayan Homegardens in Tixpeual and Tixcacaltuyub, Yucatán, Mexico." *Economic Botany* 44 (1992):470–487.

Ridington, Robin. "Technology, World View, and Adaptive Strategy in a Northern Hunting Society." *Canadian Review of Sociology and Anthropology* 19 (4 [1982]): 469–481.

Ridington, Robin. *Little Bit Know Something.* Iowa City, IA: University of Iowa Press, 1990.

Ridley, Matt, and Boi S. Low. "Can Selfishness Save the Environment?" *Atlantic Monthly* (Sept. 1993):76–86.

Rifkin, Jeremy. *Beyond Beef.* New York: Dutton, 1992

Riskind, John H., and James E. Maddux. "Loomingness, Helplessness, and Fearfulness: An Integration of HarmLooming and Self-Efficacy Models of Fear." *Journal of Social and Clinical Psychology* 12 (1993):73–89.

Robarchek, Clayton. "Primitive Warfare and the Ratomorphic Image of Mankind." *American Anthropologist* 91 (1989):903–920.

Rogers, Carl. *On Becoming a Person.* Boston: Houghton Mifflin, 1961.

Rogoff, Barbara, and Jean Lave. *Everyday Cognition.* Cambridge, Mass.: Harvard University Press, 1984.

Rolston, Holmes, III. *Environmental Ethics.* Philadelphia: Temple University Press, 1988.

Rosales Gonzales, Margarita. *Oxcutzcab, Yucatán, 1900–1960.* Mexico City: INAH, 1988.

Rosenberg, Alexander. *Economics—Mathematical Politics or Science of Diminishing Returns?* Chicago: University of Chicago Press, 1992.

Rosenblum, Mort, and Doug Williamson. *Squandering Eden.* New York: Harcourt Brace Jovanovich, 1987.

Rossabi, Morris. *Khubilai Khan.* Berkeley: University of California Press, 1989.

Rossbach, Sarah. *Feng Shui: The Chinese Art of Placement.* New York: E. P. Dutton, 1983.

Ruddle, Kenneth, and Tomoya Akimichi, eds. *Maritime Institutions in the Western Pacific.* Osaka: National Museum of Ethnology. Senri Ethnological Studies no. 17, 1984.

Ruddle, Kenneth, and Ray Chesterfield. *Education for Food Production in the Orinoco Delta*. Berkeley: University of California Press, 1977.

Ruddle, Kenneth, and Zhong Gongfu. *Integrated Agriculture-Aquaculture in South China*. Cambridge: Cambridge University Press, 1988.

Rudofsky, Bernard. *Architecture without Architects*. New York: Museum of Modern Art, 1965.

Safina, Carl. "Bluefin Tuna in the West Atlantic: Negligent Management and the Making of an Endangered Species." *Environmental Conservation* 7 (1993):229–238.

Sahlins, Marshall. *Tribesmen*. Englewood Cliffs, N.J.: Prentice-Hall, 1968.

——. *Culture and Practical Reason*. Chicago: University of Chicago Press, 1976.

Salisbury, Richard E. *A Homeland for the Cree*. Kingston and Montreal: McGill-Queens University Press.

Samuelsson, Kurt. *Religion and Economic Action*. Trans. Geoffrey French. 1961. Reprint, New York: Harper and Row, 1961.

Schiele, Linda, and David Freidel. *A Forest of Kings*. New York: William Morrow, 1990.

Schippert, Kristofer. 1978. "The Taoist Body." *History of Religion* 17 (3–4 [1978]):355–386.

Schueler, Donald G. "Southern Exposure." *Sierra* (Nov.–Dec. 1992):42–49, 76.

Schulz, Richard. "Some Life and Death Consequences of Perceived Control." In *Cognition and Social Behavior,* ed. John S. Carroll and John W. Payne, 135–153. New York: Academic Press, 1976.

Schwartz, Theodore, Geoffrey M. White, and Catherine A. Lutz, eds. *New Directions in Psychological Anthropology*. Cambridge: Cambridge University Press, 1992.

Science 260 (25 June 1993):1883–1909. "Environment and the Economy."

Scientific American (Nov. 1993.):41–57. "Debate: Does Free Trade Harm the Environment?"

Scott, James. *The Moral Economy of the Peasant*. New Haven: Yale University Press, 1976.

——. *Weapons of the Weak*. New Haven: Yale University Press, 1985.

Seaman, Gary. "The Material Soul." Paper presented at the annual meeting of the Association for Asian Studies, 1987.

Sen, Amartya. "The Economics of Life and Death." *Scientific American* (May 1993):40–47.

Sharp, Henry S. "Giant Fish, Giant Otters, and Dinosaurs: 'Apparently Irrational Beliefs' in a Chipewyan Community." *American Ethnologist* 14 (1987):226–235.

Shipek, Florence. *Pushed into the Rocks*. Lincoln: University of Nebraska Press, 1987.

Shrader-Frechette, K. S. *Risk and Rationality*. Berkeley: University of California Press, 1991.

Simon, Herbert. *Models of Man*. New York: Wiley, 1957.

Simon, Julian. *The Ultimate Resource*. Princeton: Princeton University Press, 1981.

Singleton, Sara, and Michael Taylor. "Common Property, Collective Action and Community." *Journal of Theoretical Politics* 4 (1992):309–324.

Skinner, Stephen. *The Living Earth Manual of Feng-Shui*. London: Routledge, Kegan Paul, 1982.

Smil, Vaclav. *The Bad Earth*. Armonk, N.Y.: M. E. Sharpe, 1984.

Smith, E., and D. L. Medin. *Categories and Concepts*. Cambridge, Mass.: Harvard University Press, 1981.

Smith, Eric Alden. "Risk and Uncertainty in the 'Original Affluent Society': Evolutionary Ecology of Resource-sharing and Land Tenure." In *Hunters and Gatherers: History, Evolution and Social Change,* ed., Tim Ingold, David Riches, and James Woodburn, 221–251 New York: Berg, 1988.

———. *Inujjuamiut Foraging Strategies.* Seattle: University of Washington Press, 1991.

———. "Whatever Happened to Ecological Anthropology?" Paper presented at the annual convention of the American Anthropological Association, 1992.

Sproat, Gilbert Malcolm. *The Nootka: Scenes and Studies of Savage Life,* ed. Charles Lillard. Victoria: Sono Nis Press, 1987.

Stein, Rolf. *The World in Miniature.* Stanford: Stanford University Press, 1990.

Stevenson, Glenn G. *Common Property Economics: A General Theory and Land Use Applications.* Cambridge: Cambridge University Press, 1991.

Stevenson, Harold W., Chuansheng Chen, and Shin-Ying Lee. "Mathematics Achievement of Chinese, Japanese, and American Children: Ten Years Later." *Science* 259 (1993):53–58.

Stuart, James. "Maize Use by Rural Mesoamerican Households." *Human Organization* 49 (1990):135–139.

Sullivan, Paul. *Unfinished Conversations.* Berkeley: University of California Press, 1989.

Suttles, Wayne. "The Economic Life of the Coast Salish of Haro and Rosario Straits." Ph.D. diss., University of Washington, 1951.

———. *Coast Salish Essays.* Vancouver: Talonbooks and Seattle: University of Washington Press, 1987.

Swanton, John. *Haida Myths and Texts: Skidegate Dialect.* Washington, D.C.: Bureau of American Ethnology, Bulletin no. 29, 1905.

———. *Social Conditions, Beliefs, and Linguistic Relationships of the Tlingit Indians.* Washington, D.C.: Bureau of American Ethnology, Annual Report no. 26, 391–486.

———. *Tlingit Myths and Texts.* Washington, D.C.: Bureau of American Ethnology, Bulletin no. 39.

Swezey, Sean, and Robert F. Heizer. "Ritual Management of Salmonid Fish Resources in California." *Journal of California Anthropology* 4 (1977):6–29.

Tanner, Adrian. *Bringing Home Animals.* London: C. Hurst and Co, 1979.

Taylor, Shelley. *Positive Illusions.* New York: Basic Books, 1989.

Thaler, Richard H. *The Winner's Curse.* Princeton: Princeton University Press, 1992.

Thompson, E. P. *The Making of the English Working Class.* 1963. Reprint, New York: Vintage, 1966.

Thompson, Lucy. *To the American Indian.* Eureka, Calif.: Lucy Thompson, 1916.

Thurow, Lester. *The Zero-Sum Society.* New York: Basic Books, 1980.

Tiger, Lionel. *Optimism.* New York: Simon and Schuster, 1979.

Tisdell, Clem. *Environmental Economics: Policies for Environmental Management and Sustainable Development.* Brookfield, Vt: Edward Elgar, 1992.

Toledo, Victor. "What Is Ethnoecology?" *Ethnoecologia* 1 (1992):5–21.

Topley, M. "Chinese Traditional Ideas and the Treatment of Disease: Two Examples from Hong Kong." *Man* 5 (1970):421–437.

Totman, Conrad. *The Green Archipelago: Forestry in Preindustrial Japan.* Berkeley: University of California Press, 1989.

Tuchman, Barbara. *The March of Folly.* New York: Knopf, 1984.

Turnbull, Colin. *The Mountain People.* New York: Simon and Schuster, 1972.

Unschuld, Paul. *Medicine in China: A History of Ideas.* Berkeley: University of California Press, 1985.

———. *Medicine in China: A History of Pharmaceutics.* Berkeley: University of California Press, 1986.

———. *Medicine in China: Nan-Ching: The Classic of Difficult Issues.* Berkeley: University of California Press, 1986.

———. "Illness and Health in Chinese Medicine." Paper presented at the annual conference of the Association for Asian Studies, 1987. Boston, MA

Vecsey, Christopher, and R. Venables. *American Indian Environments.* Syracuse: Syracuse University Press, 1980.

Villa Rojas, Alfonso. *The Maya of East Central Quintana Roo.* Washington, D.C.: Carnegie Foundation, 1945.

Vygotsky, Lev S. *Mind and Society.* Cambridge, Mass.: Harvard University Press, 1978.

Walens, Stanley. *Feasting with Cannibals.* Princeton: Princeton University Press, 1981.

Walters, Derek. *Feng-Shui: The Chinese Art of Designing a Harmonious Environment.* New York: Simon and Schuster, 1988.

———. *The Feng Shui Handbook.* London: HarperCollins, 1991.

Warner, Lloyd. *American Life: Dream and Reality.* 2d ed. Chicago: University of Chicago Press, 1962.

Weber, Max. *The Protestant Ethic and the Spirit of Capitalism.* Trans. Talcott Parsons. 1905. Reprint, New York: Scribners, 1958.

———. *The Sociology of Religion.* Trans. Ephraim Fischoff. 1922. Reprint, Boston: Beacon Press, 1963.

Weckmann, Luis. *The Medieval Heritage of Mexico.* Trans. Frances M. Lopez-Morillas. New York: Fordham University Press, 1992.

Weeks, Priscilla. "The State vs. the People: Strategies of Two Texas Communities." Paper, presented at the annual convention of the American Anthropological Association, 1992. San Francisco

Weinstein, Neil. "Optimistic Biases about Personal Risks." *Science* 246 (1989):1232–1233.

Weller, Robert P. *Unities and Diversities in Chinese Religion.* Seattle: University of Washington Press, 1987.

Weltfish, Gene. *The Lost Universe.* New York: Basic Books, 1965.

Werner, Emmy, and Ruth Smith. *Vulnerable but Invincible.* New York: McGraw-Hill, 1982.

Wilk, Richard. *Household Ecology.* Tucson: University of Arizona Press, 1991.

Wilken, Gene. *Good Farmers.* Berkeley: University of California Press, 1987.

Williams, Nancy, and Eugene Hunn. *Resource Managers.* Boulder, Colo.: Westview Press, 1982.

Williams, Ted. "Taking Back the Range." *Audubon* (Jan.–Feb. 1993):28–33.

Willis, Paul. *Learning to Labor.* New York: Columbia University Press, 1981.

Wilson, E. H. *On Human Nature.* Cambridge, Mass.: Harvard University Press, 1978.

Wilson, Gilbert. *Agriculture of the Hidatsa Indians: An Indian Interpretation.* Minneapolis: University of Minnesota, Studies in the Social Sciences, no. 9, 1917.

Wright, Angus. *The Death of Ramon Gonzalez.* Austin: University of Texas Press, 1991.

Yim, Denise. *Maori Ideology and Religion: 2000 Years of Ecological Success.* Ms., 1992.

Yoon, Hong-Key. *Geomantic Relationships between Culture and Nature in Korea.* Taipei: Orient Cultural Service, 1976.

Young, John. *Business and Sentiment in a Chinese Market Town.* Taipei: Orient Cultural Service, 1974.

Zajonc, Robert. "Feeling and Thinking: Preferences Need No Inferences." *American Psychologist* 35 (1980):151–175.

Zozayong. *Diamond Mountain.* 2 vols. Seoul: Emille Museum, 1975.

Index

Abstraction: dangers of in classification, 49

Acceptable risk: how calculated, 109

Action: from moral and practical factors acting in concert, 156

Actions: not culture, result in changes, 129

Acton, Lord: on power, 117

Adults: rarely religious converts, 164

Aggression: and culture, 95

Aimslie, George: on human tendency to value immediate over distant, 115

Al-Biruni: on protection of cow in India, 129

Alar, 125

Albigensian Crusade, 166

Alienation: and resource mismanagement, 120

Allergies: Chinese views of, 37

Alternative spiritual traditions: and environmentalism, 180

"Altruistic" acts, 108

Amazon rainforests: local peoples of have no conservation traditions, 168

America: as homeland of conservation science and center of nutritional research, 178

American patriotism: as secular religion, 162

Americans: view of of illness as invasion, 41

Americas: pre-Columbian civilizations of and hot/cold system, 37

Analogic thinking: characteristics of, 49; in Chinese philosophical thought, 49

Analogy: Chinese conception of, 49; in Chinese philosophy, 49

Anderson, Terry and Donald Leal: on "free-market environmentalism," 139–40

Anderson, Barbara: on "naturalistic" and "personalistic" medicine, 50

Anderson, M. L.: on cancer, 47

Animals: avenge selves on humans in Gitksan belief, 63–64; belief in powers of by peoples of northern Northwest Coast, 58; bonding of with humans in American subarctic, 56–57; and "Doctrine of Signatures," 45; humanization of, 71; seen as living in humanlike societies by Native Americans, 57; in mythology of Northwest Coast peoples, 60; nature of relations of with humans among Northwest Coast peoples, 63; as part of human community, 57; of secular/social world among Northwest Coast peoples, 61

Antisocial behavior: predictable from environment, 92; theory of, 94–95

"Aphrodisiacs": and supplementing foods, 46

Apples: apple scare of the 1980s, 125

Aral Sea Catastrophe, 5

Araucanian Indians: and potato varieties, 148

Archetypal ideas, 103

Astrology: as world-wide belief system, 103

Authoritarian polities: effects on environment of, 136

"Back to the land" movement, 180

Bacon, Francis: on "idols," 104

"Bad" behavior, 93; behavior and brain damage, 93

"Bad" science: and the environment, 143

"Bad" things: as externals, 50

Baker, Hugh: on lineage conflict and graves, 24

"Balance": in Chinese medicine, 34; Chinese terminology for, 35; and harmony in China (conception of, 41; and the environment, 42; why picked as overarching symbol system, 42); of heating and cooling foods, 36; nature of in Chinese medicine, 35; as social function, and food, 35; in views, 125; between *yin* and *yang*, 36

Balance-and-harmony rhetoric: and other forms of Chinese medicine, 40

"Balanced diet": as seen by Americans, 41

Bali: water regulation of, 164, 167

Bandura, Albert: on human need to negotiate self-efficacy, 52; on human need for a sense of effectiveness, 118; on psychological and physical importance of perceived control, 43

Banyan, 20

Bark strips: use of by Native American peoples, 54

Barkow, Jerome H., Leda Cosmides, and John Tooby: on human intelligence, 119

Basic human needs: classification of, 86–88; limitations of, 49; nature, 49

Bateson, Gregory, viii

Baumeister, Roy and Steven Scher: on feeling good and self-destructive behavior, 115; on acting to prevent reality checks, 118

Bear: demand for gall in East Asian medicine, and extermination of bear 26, 126; gall of used in Chinese medicine, 128

Beavers: benefits to environment from, 137; craze for fur of and long-term environmental impact, 130; overexploited in nineteenth century, 126

Beck, Aaron: cognitive therapy of, 116

Beekeeping: importance of among Maya, 76

Behavior: not simply emotion or "rational self-interest," 98: some is learned, 93: towards environment, as function of general overall socialization, 96

Belief: contrasted with knowledge by emotional involvement, 161; does not mean dogmatism, 161; emotional investment in, 161

Belief systems, 11; how and why accepted, 124; nature and basis of, 11

Beliefs about resources: how do they become accepted as canon?, 123; and feed back from the real world, 124

Bellah, Robert: on moral and ethical changes, 159; on need for a return to a more "communitarian" universe, 147; on new community institutions, 98

Benedict, Ruth: views of on China, 42

Bhopal, 156

Bias: as learned, logic driven, 121

"Big business," 97

"Big government," 97

Big governments: problems of, 139

Bigots: behavior of, 95

Biological functionalism, 170

Bioregionalism, 180

Biotic management: as practiced today, 172

Biotic resource management: importance of daily experience for, 125

Bird-watching: impact upon environment of in United States, 130

Bloating and flatulence-causing foods: in Chinese medicine, 47–48

Bodley, John: on who pay the costs of resource overuse, 138

Bourdieu Pierre: and "distinction," 116; on how tightly structured human thought is, 132; and J. Passeron, on education as reproducing society, 133

Bowen, William: on issue of control in Chinese medicine, 51

Brains: as food, and "Doctrine of Signatures," 45

Brecht, Bertold: on importance of food, 106

Brightman, Robert: on Rock Cree resource management, 56; on white influence on resource management of Rock Cree, 56

Buddhism: in China, 166; and philosophical realism, 50

Buffalo, 158–59

Bullard, Robert: on toxic waste disposal in the United States, 138

"Bullheads": mythology of, 62

Bureaucratic state: and rise of naturalistic Chinese medicine, 51

Bureau of Land Management: holdings of, devastated, 150; and livestock industry, 158

California Indians: and environment, 126

Cancer: Chinese views of, 47

Cancún: foci of encroaching Spanish-speaking world for Maya, 82

Cantonese folk culture: character of, difference from elite culture, 39

Cantonese of Hong Kong: values assigned to specific foods by, 36–37

Cantonese (language): ian, "person," "individual in society," 42

Casseroles or soups: and supplementing, 44

Castle Peak Bay, Hong Kong: role of balance and harmony in local medicine of, 36; Chinese medicine of, and coin-rubbing, moxibustion, 39; and feng-shui, 15; herbal medicine, exercise, massage and physical therapy of, 39; medicine of, 35; belief in potency of crustacean parasite of giant grouper of, 46

Cattle-raising: in Latin America and deforestation, 154

Cattle: artificially favored, 158

Cedar tree: sacredness to Native American peoples and taking of bark strips, 54

Central control of environment: problem of, 136

Ceremonies and rituals: character of, 163

Cernea, Michael: on "social variables" lying at the structural core of environmental problems, 124

Ch'achaac, 83

"Cheaters": detection of by cooperators and se lection against, 92; and "nonreciprocation," 92;

"Cheating": and religion, 165

Ch'i, 46; augmentation of, 32; role in "balance," 35; and Chinese analogic logic, 49; in Chinese landscape painting, 17; circulation of and *feng-shui*, 19; flow and manipulation of, 31–32; flow of and organs, 35; flow of as common denominator, 18–19; flow of in Chinese medicine and in landscape planning, 16; harmonization of, 39; in Hong Kong, 34; and tree worship, 20; associated with weirdness, 46; and worshipped objects, things, 20–21; *See also* Chinese language (terms)

Chaac gods: of Maya, 84

Cheng, Libin: on poisonous combinations, 47

Chernobyl, 156; disaster, 5

Chicken: soup, and *pu p'in*, "supplementing," 44; soup, how made in China, 44; stewed with vinegar, 44

Chief Seattle: spurious elements in speeches, 56

Children: and key moral choices, 165

Chiloe Island: potato varieties of, 148

China: accelerated environmental decline of under Communists, 26; and breakdown of *feng-shui*, 25; Ch'ing Dynasty (bureaucratic rule of, 52; few doctors and bureaucrats during, 52; gynecology of, 51; Chou Dynasty: (court dietitians of, 30; and Systems Theory, 36; demonic medicine of, 32); experience of similar to USSR in mismanaging the environment, 136; most famines of in north, 132; feeding large population key historical problem of, 30; Han Dynasty (Confucianism of, 32; medical texts of, 30, 34; philosophical debates during, 32); long history of systemization of information about nutrition in, 28; Kweichow Province of, and eating of pangolin, 46; "land of famine" 30; large population, lack of cropland of, 30; Sung Dynasty, history of Chinese medicine during, 32

Chinese and Greek philosophy, 49

Chinese cooking: and medicinal effects of foods, "balance," 38

Chinese cosmology: dominate role of flow of *ch'i* and *feng-shui* in, 18

Chinese culture: behavioral distinctions in between worshiping and planning, 18

Chinese folk belief: and environmental choice, 9

Chinese folk medicine: as "empowering" ideology, 43

Chinese ginkgo tree: saved from extinction, 131

Chinese herbal remedies: and poison, 47

Chinese "humoral theory": and Western humoral medicine, 32

Chinese landscape painting: aesthetic experience of and *ch'i*, 17; and *feng-shui*, 16–17

Chinese language (terms): *ch'i*, 16, 31; *ch'ing*, "cleansing," 32, 48; *ch'ing-pu-liang*, "cleansing, supplementing and cooling," 38; *chung*, "the median," 35; *fan*, "boiled rice," 36; *feng-shui*, 16; *ho-p'ing*, "harmony and balance," 35–36; *hsiao*, "dispelling, clearing away," 48; *kan-ch'ing*, "sentiment," explained, 40; *kuan-hsi*, "mutual goodwill," 40; *lien-ho*, "cooperation," 42; *min*, "face," 42; *p'ing*, "balance," 35; *p'ing-an*, "balance and secu rity," 35; *pou pan*, "supplementing things," 43 (*see also pu p'in*); *pu*, "augment," 32; *pu p'in* ("supplementing" or "patching," 38; "supplementing things," 43–4); *shan-shui hua*, "mountain-and-water pictures," 16–17; *tu* ("poisonous or poison-potentiating," or "dangerously strong in potentially harmful force," 32; "poisonous," "poison potentiating," 46); *tun* ("steaming process," and supplementing, 44; "steaming process," described, 44); *wu shih*, "male and female shaman," 38; *yang* and *yin*, 31

Chinese materia medica: and environment, 127–28

Chinese medicine: as accommodating in meth odology and discourse, 53; as accommodation between ideology and experience, 30; to be analyzed in own terms, 127; application of by elite and broad masses, 51; and assertion of individualism, 43; connected with social system through concept of "balance," 43; danger in translating concepts of, 52; different language of, 52; fivefold correspondence doctrine of, and Hong Kong villagers, 40; history of, 30–33; humans in as total persons confront animals, plants, and minerals with medicinal functions, 28; as holistic, somatizing, naturalistic, individually localized, 50; humoral system of, 34; lack of distinction in between food and medicine, 28; organs of, 35; as practiced in Hong Kong, 40; (similarity of to other systems, 34); rational and irrational contradictions in, 102; as system for incorporating truths into a plausible logical structure, 28; storehouse of knowledge or system? 33; as tradition, 30; various rhetorics of, 40

Chinese nutritional therapy, 28–53; compared to western, 33; Hong Kong variant of, 34; logic of based upon empirical knowledge base, 29; major errors of, 33; parallels elsewhere, 30; strengthening, "cleansing," and poisons in, 43; as theoretical system, 48–49

Chinese people: in comparison to Japanese and Americans, 42

Chinese politics: and medicine, 39

Chinese site planning: and *feng-shui*, 15–16

Chinese spirit mediums: prescribe herbal and dietary medicine, 39; *see also* shaman

Chinese traditional landscape science: similarity of to Chinese traditional medicine, 16

Chou Li: possible Han origins of material, 30

Christianity: differing views within on environmental management in modern United States, 168

Chuang Chou: on "useless tree," 20

Chunhuhub, 73, 74; description, 74; *ejido*, 74–75; as proof of effectiveness of Maya environmental strategies, 82; recent problems of, 80

Civilizations: rise and fall of and environmental misuse, 99

Classic Maya civilization: fall of, war, and ecological damage of, 128; *see also* Maya

"Cleansing": and "dispelling" foods, 32; characteristics of, 48; as contrasted to strengthening and poison-potentiating foods, 48

Code: and institutions, enforcing conservation and resource mechanism, 177

Cognition: involves emotional reactions, 115; the "unpleasant" in, 115

Coin-rubbing: described, 39

"Cold" cognition: definition of, 50

"Cold" rationality, assumed in social sciences, 88–89

Colli, Hilaria Maas: on how Mayas learn their culture, 80

Comaroff, Jean: on ideology and passive resistance, 43

"Cormorant and the bittern," 168

Command-and-control strategies: for "saving" the environment, 134

Common pastures, 149

Common pool resource: explained, 148

Common property: management groups for, 152; management of, 148; and vestment in smaller user groups, 153; as management, 151; problem of managing resources of, 151

"Common sense": based upon cross-cultural similarities in the perception of nature, 119

Communal morality: problems of, 165

Communitarian universe, 147

Community: when overstressed, disunited, 153; and socialization, 153; solidarity in, importance for conservation, 151

Commuting, 6

Competition: implications of, 158; types of, 158

Complex political ideologies, 98

Conservation, 6; of animals and plants, as burning, emotional, personal issue, 64; cannot be looked at in isolation, 159; as a cause, 184; dependent upon solidarity and the ability of people to work together 122; dilemmas of, 183; ideologies of, not found in all traditional societies, 167; inseparable from economic equity, 179; and justice and security, 179; made a part of a religiously sanctioned ethical code, 11; must be rationally planned, 160; must be taught directly, 184; nature of, 184; absolute necessity of for the survival of humanity, 184; among Northwest Coast peoples (evidence for, 67; examples, 66; was ideology a factor? 66; taught through powerful religious and social documents, 62–63); about people, not about resources, 123; as political issue, 160; and resource management (and the problem of social breakdown, 90; requires moral code and social institutions, 177); what is? 184

Conservationists: must expand appeal beyond economic logic, 118; need to appeal to fear as well as love, 184

Consumption, 147; of beef as preferred meat in American diet, 131; reasons for, 154

Control: in Chinese traditional medicine, 50; and history of Chinese medicine, 51; as individual matter in China, 52; with regard to the environment, 120

Conventional morality, and daily experience, 165

"Cool" cognition: explained, 112; type mistakes, 112

Cooperation: as "empowering" factor, 122; and game theory, 144; how does it become good or bad? 182

Coping strategies, 116; of hurt people, implications for environment, 120

Cosmides, Leda: on the handling of probabilities by people, 114

Cost/benefit accounting: problems of, 139

Costa Rica: professional squatters destroy protected lands in, 133

Costs of production: all those benefiting must pay, 181

"Counterfactual" beliefs, vii

Crary, Mary Elizabeth, 23

Cult of dead: in China and *feng-shui*, 23

Cultivated lands: different attitudes towards in China and West, 22

Cultural beliefs, 126

Cultural consistency, 122

Cultural constructed knowledge, 143

Cultural constructionist view, 102–3

Cultural ecology, 29, 169

Cultural relativism: limitations of, definition, 127; should not constrain other views, 127

Culture, 123–34; as feedback system, 125; function of in finding solutions, 105; as institutionalizer, 145; institutionalizes (as generalization, 143; mistakes, 122, 123; sensible, corrective views, 123); keeps people in line, 122; and nature, boundary between and boundary between human and animal, 57; not straitjacket or unchanging body of tradition, 129; as provider of institutions, 116; result of countless human decisions, 129; as selector, 132; as way out of the limits set by information processing, 123

Currier, Richard: on the concept of "balance," 35; on medical and social harmony, 40; and social order, 40

Cycles: as described by Ibn Khaldun not inevitable, 146; *see also* Ibn Khaldun

Damaged tissue: and supplementing, 44

DDT: environmental dangers of, 183

Death: as due to individually controllable causes in the United States, 53

Decision makers: number of important, 152

Decisions: reasons why not based on "practical reason," 8

"Deep ecologists" and "spiritual" ecologists: areas of interest of, 175

Deer antlers in velvet: as supplementing food, 46

Demand-driven systems, 29

Demand-driven structure: problem of, 150

Democracy: gives poor a voice but power to majority, 141

Demons: in Chinese medicine, 104

Deontological and assertoric ethics, 161

Depleted *ch'i*: and supplementing, 44

Depletion of commons, 149

Depression: and accurate self-perception, 115; and "learned helplessness," 120; and self-destruction, 115

Destruction: of nature as a divine mission, 168; of a species or an ecosystem, 182

Destructiveness: and environmental mismanagement, 94

"Development," 147

"Deviance": as straightforward personality comparison, 96

DeWalt, Billie: on combining local knowledge with outside ideas, 127

Dialectics, 125

Diet therapy: major form of medicine in Castle Peak Bay, 39

Direct knowledge: theory that replaced poetic systems of symbol, metaphor, and dream when lacking, 102

"Disenchantments": according to Max Weber, 164; *see also* Weber Max

Dispassionate rationality: unobtainable for humans, 112

"Dispelling" foods: characteristics of, 48

Dispersed cost: explained, 138

Displacement: and projection of failings, 121

Diversity: of human ability and personality, impact on environment, 96

"Doctrine of Signatures": and supplementing foods, 45

Dog: beliefs concerning, 58

"Doing the month," 45

Dos Aguadas: and rain-making ritual, 83

Douglas, Mary, 46

Dracunculus vulgaris, "dragons," 104

Dramatic rocks: and *ch'i*, 21

Drucker, Peter, 7

Dryzek, John: on institutional arrangements and success in dealing with ecological issues, 142; on moral suasion, alternatives, 142–43; on Rational Choice Theory and the environment, 108

Duck and deer management: in United States, 167

Dum or *dam*, 44

Durkheim, Emile: on religion, 55, 162

Each-we dilemmas, 7

Earthquakes: and *ch'i*, 21

Eastern European governments: and ecological crisis, 5

Ecological crisis: interpretations of, 3–4; simple choice as solution to, 5–6

Ecological knowledge: taught by myth, 66

Ecological management of "traditional societies": scientific issues of and human emotion and motivation, 5; views on, 13

Ecological morality: definition of, 179; and theory, 155

Ecological rationality: according to Dryzek, 142

Ecologically and economically successful development: examples, 147

Ecologically rational institutions: need for, according to Dryzek, 142

Ecology, 5; cognitive and emotional sides to, viii; and people, not experts, 169

Economic accounting methods: changes needed in, 147–48

Economic arguments: limits of, 182

Economic benefits: of conservation, often undervalued, 148; greater from resource use through more efficient technology, 180

Economic calculus: meaning of, 106

Economic determinalists: theories criticized, 119

Economic self-interest: in United States elections, 97

Economic theory: value of practical application of, 155

Economically "rational" behavior, 176

Economics: and culture, nature of interaction, 131; nature of, as compared to politics, 5

Economists: limitations of views, 175

Ecosystems: normally dynamic and diverse, 180

Edible birds' nests: as supplementing food in China, 46

Education: changing roles of, 164; and freedom of opportunity, 181; to involve people directly in environments, 179; of young in environmentalism, 184; of younger generation in resource management strategies, environmental knowledge, morality, and cultural rules, 69

Educational strategies: current, 179

Ehrenfeld, David: on people loving their plants and animals, 172

Eight Trigrams: in *feng-shui*, 22

Eisenhower, Dwight, D., 98

Ejido: 76–77; and forest management, 77

Elite ideology: functions of, 41

Elite views, 102; *vs.* those of the "stupid masses," 102

Elster, Jon, 8; on people "making the best of things," 116; on social norms and facilitation of action, 133

Emergent phenomena: culturally coded knowledge systems as, 129

Emotion, 89; economy of love and hate, 183; resource management must be structured to take it into account, 175; role of in decision making, 112; runs through all human experience, 112; as social bond through love, 92

Emotional appeals and over-optimism: prevent rational thought, 110

Emotionality and emotionality-based choice: as factor preventing compromise and problem solving, 8

Empirical bases: for "useful error," 9

Empirical knowledge: and Chinese traditional cosmology, 16

Empirical observation: combined with creative inference and explanation, 104

Empirical observations: role of in classifica tion, 49

"Empowering," 122

"Enchanted" views of reality, 178

Encoding: of emotional and personal material about animals and plants, 72

Endangered species: exterminated for small local profits, 137

Enemy: denigrated and satanized, 122

Enforcement: varieties of in communities in contrast to command-and-control systems, 152

Enlightenment: and view of reason as rare thing, 110

Environment: higher-level representations of, and religion, 172; and popular attitudes, 66, 164; structure of imposed on by humans, 12

Environmental behavior: how selected for, 91–92

Environmental destruction: not especially due to capitalism, 100

Environmental ethic: minimum for detailed, 173

Environmental ethics: 162

Environmental experience: need to pool, 127

Environmental management: debate about, 13; need of for simple ethical code, a religious or other system to involve emotionally, 162; need to document actual systems of, 127; real problem of is damage done before the inefficient weeded out, 150; and society, social values, viii; systems of need not be religions, 162

Environmental mismanagement: benefits for some in, but costs passed on, 136

Environmental misperceptions: the general process that lies behind, 102

Environmental policy: much founded on mistakes and half-truths, 101 Environmental politics: contradictions of, 160

Environmental problems: as due to a mix of reasons and passions, 9; how do people cope with? 88; and trade off between short- and long-term interests, 4–5

Environmental spirituality, 96

Environmentalists: "are Chicken Littles," 164; as repository of all vileness, 121; as scapegoats, blamed for loss of logging jobs in the Pacific Northwest, 121

Environments: exploited by societies to satisfy social and "intangible" as well as physical needs, 91

Erosion of genetic resources: fought by government fiat, 184

Error: even in the most rigorous science, 101; explanations for, 9

Escape, 153

Ethical codes, 169; need to be applied strictly and widely, 90; as strictly enforced characteristic of functional societies, 90; where to find, 169

Ethicists: schemes of and disagreement over, 161

Ethics: modern reviews of, 161

Ethnic hatred: and destruction of environment, 120

Ethnobiology, 169

Ethnoecology: according to Victor Toledo, 160–61

European medicine: emphasis on surgery contrasted to Chinese, 31

Existential reality: seen as process focus in Chinese philosophy, 49

Experience: as corrective, 125

"Externalities," 85, 158, 181; and the disenfranchised, 138; need to eliminate, 181; pollution and waste treated as such and passed on to the powerless, 138

Extremism, 121

Fascism: and depression of 1930s, 146

Facts: different ways of interpreting and Chinese folk belief, 15–16

Factual knowledge: why not considered in ecological management, 12

Failure: course of predictable, 178; roots of, 177–78

Failures: and scientific views, 178

"Fairness," 178

False views: why do people hold them? 101

Fan "boiled rice": as ideal category in Chinese food, 36; see also Chinese language (terms): fan

Farm subsidies: leading to overcultivation, 157; and small farm, 157

Fear: based upon helplessness, 120

Feng-shui, 15–27, 174; and acupuncture, 16; arcane language of, 23; based in classical Chinese cosmology modified by common experience, 26; breakdown of in urban Orient, 25; changing evaluations of, 17; as Chinese folk belief system, 18; and Chinese science and art relating to landscape, 18; in comparison to medical ideology, 24; and conflict, 24; "Cutting the dragon's pulse" in, 15; and direction of winds, 20; ecological explanation of, 25; and emotional response to landscape, 16–17; and empirical observation, 18; experts, varying faith of users in, 23; and geomancy, 18; and good environmental management, 176–77; good feng-shui, 19; "Green Dragon" in, 19; and interface of science and religion, 26; and interior design, 22; and local politics, 24; lore of and religion, 17; means for local people to assert control over lives, 24; as medicine of gigantic presences, 16; merging with religion of, and environment, 26; as motivator of communities to follow guide lines, 25; not predictable by social functions, 25; and planning of offices and public places, 22–23; rules of, 22; scope of, 16; similarity of to Chinese medicine, 39; and site drainage, 20; social significance of, 24; as strategy (to control ch'i, 16); which works, 16; as superstitition, 17; as system for managing interaction of spirits and people, 17; and trees, 20; in United States, 23; and water supply, 19; "White Tiger" in, 19

Ficus microphylla, 20

Field biologists: and subjects, 172

Final demand: culture determined, 85; and "externalities," 85; nature of, 85

First impressions: incomplete or wrong, 125

Firth, Raymond, 11

Fisheries: management of, 167

Fitzgerald, Edward, 3

Five elements: definition of, 31; nature of in China, 31; as new system in early China, 31

Five Sacred Mountains: institutionalized worship of in China, 20

Flow of ch'i: and good and ill fortune according to feng-shui, 18

Flying lizards: as supplementing food in China, 46

Folk beliefs: as combinations of truth and inaccuracy, 101

Folk concepts of leadership and friendship: in China, 42

Folk science, traditional systems: practical value of, 101

Folk wisdom, 101

Food: codings, basis of in Hong Kong, 37; consumption (as driver of food production, 29; logic of in China, and popular views about resources, 29); an end in itself, contrasted to money, 86; and health, Chinese views of, 28; products produced and sold in China due to medicinal properties, 29; system, and fisheries, 29

Foods: classification of as *tu* and non-*tu* by Chinese, 47; coding of, as heating or cooling or wet, dry, 36; as cures for disease in Hong Kong, 37; that are less supplementing, 46; rules for grouping of by Chinese, 48

Forest destruction: for rangeland, 78

Forests: sources of damage in, 157

Formal law codes and police: found in civilizations, 91

Foster, George, 40; on "image of limited good," 144; on "naturalistic" and "personalistic" medicine, 50

Foucault: on medical discourses as discourses about control, 51

Fox and grapes: story of, 104

France: 1993 elections in, and "green" parties, neo-Fascists, 97–98

Fraser River, 67

Free enterprise: contrasted to government regulation, 159; and environment, 158;

Free market: approaches in to environmental management, 139; environmentalism in, 139–40; explained, 139; no government has allowed a real free market to exist, 141

French Revolution: state cult of, 162

Frontier societies: and "externalities," participants in, able to escape from pollution problems, 138

Fruit-growing: as basis for Maya prosperity and survival, 80

Fundamental attribution error: in human behavior, 114

Fundamentalist and hierarchic religious establishments, 180

Fungi: important as supplementing foods, 44

Fur trade era, 158

Furth, Charlotte: on Ch'ing Dynasty gynecology, 51

Future benefits: sacrificed for tiniest of current returns, 137

Games: absorb people's lives, 146; differences in the eye of the beholder, 144; various kinds of, explained, and resource management, 143

General economic development: does not lead to conservation, 184

Generalization, chunking of data and inference, 49

Genetic varieties: importance of for Maya agriculture, 75–76

Genitalia as food: and "Doctrine of Signatures," 45–46

Germany: and social morality, 161

"Germs:" and American view of illness, 41

Gigerenzer, Gert: on probabilities and probability errors, 114

Gilmore, Melvin: on Indian attitudes towards the environment, contrasted with European, 169; on religion and biological knowledge, 171

Ginseng: and "Doctrine of Signatures," 45; most famous of supplementing herbs, 44

Gitksan, 63

Goals: assumed to be short-term and narrow, 100

Gogeet, "bogeyman": belief in among Anglo-Canadians, 59

"Good," 52; and cognition, 115

"Good" and "evil influences," 18

"Good" person: in China, and harmony, 40

"Goody-goodies," 90

Gore, Al, viii; on a moral code, 182; on who pay the costs of resource overuse, 138

Gould, Richard: on learning of myth by children and myth environmental content, 69

Government: coercive role of limited and dangerous in environmental management, 177; control, government special favors, lead to disaster, 158; and ecological crisis, 5, 158; as institution of recourse in environmental mat ters, 139; and religious belief in Japan, 12; role of in resource management, 140–41; too soft-hearted, 139

"Grassroots" power, 139

Graves: and *feng-shui*, 23; fortunate and unfortunate sites for, 24

Great Plains, 183

Groot, J. J. M. de: on *feng-shui*, 17

Guided democracy: according to Martin Lewis, 158

Habermas: on ordinary social morality, 161

Habitus: a persistent collection of ideas and preferences according to Bourdieu, 132

Haida language (terms): *gagixit*, "person changed into a land otter," 59

Haida of Queen Charlotte Islands: desperateness of economic plight of, and resource management, 67; social organization of, 65

Halibut fishing: among Native American peoples of the northern Northwest Coast, 58; and shamanic curing and bewitching, 58

Hall, Edward, 18

Haly, Richard: on worldview of Nahuatl of Mexico, 170

"Happiness," 178; possibly confused with vengeance or escapism, 183

Hardin, Garrett, 7; on the "Tragedy of the Commons," 95

Harmony, 26; in Chinese life, 39; in Chinese society, 35

Harris, Chief Kenneth: on vengeful animals attacking humans, 63

Harris, Marvin: on materialist concerns, 129; on protection of cow in India, 129

Hate: due to cheating or any threat menacing group integrity, 92

Health: and control, 43

Heat and cooling: 30; in foods, a belief independently invented in various places, 103; more important in Chinese medicine than wetting- drying, 36

Heating, cooling, wetting, drying, and neutral qualities in foods and medicine: theory of first fully developed by T'ao Hung-ching, 32

Helping behavior: as general solution to all human problems, 181

Herbal medicine: handmaiden of nutrition in China, 30; major form of medicine in Castle Peak Bay, 39

"Heretics," 163

Heuristic thinking, 26

Hierarchic societies: focus on harmony of and elite ideology, 41

Higher level management: role of in modern resource management, 134

Hilsdale, Karin: on danger of Chinese medicine losing paradigm, 53; on need to preserve framework of Chinese medicine in West, 53

"Hits": in Positive Illusion Theory, 118

Ho-p'ing, "harmony and balance," 35; *see also* Chinese language (terms): *ho-p'ing*

Hobbes, Thomas: negativist view of human behavior of, 93; and social breakdown, 146; views not so Hobbesian, 93–94; on "war of each against all," 95; "warre" of, 149; (dynamics, and community breakdown, 95; as lack of institutionalized order, 93; most often found in autocratic states, 95); on "warre," and ethnic and ideological rat fight, 120

Hofling, Charles: on "Lords of Animals," 77

Hong Kong, 9, 15; and "cleansing" and "dispelling" foods, 48; free market economic system of, 141; and lineage conflict, 24; orientation of houses and villages in, 21; universal reliance on *feng-shui* experts in, 23; villagers lack interest in some concepts of Chinese medicine, 40

Hot and cold: as generator of special characteristics of the Chinese medical system, 52; in Hong Kong, 34

Hopes: adjustment of to fit realistic expectations, and environmental crisis, 8

"Hot" cognition: as distinct from "cold," 50; explained, 112

Hot/cold belief system: in world cultures, 37

Households: and ecological problems, compared to firms, communities, 153

Human: what does it mean to be? 105

Human abilities, 183

Human action: and rational calculus of need, 105

Human actions: explanations for, 85–99

Human choice: and ecological problems, vii; role of emotion in, vii

Human error: psychological findings on, 101

Human evolution, and group size, 153

Human information processing: characteristics of and ecological management, 12; and institutions, 135; problem of, vii; theories of, 103

Human motivation, 123

Human nature: negativist view of, explained, 93; *tabula rasa* view of, 93

Human needs: satisfied by drawing on the environment, 88

Human political choices: realities of, 155

Human social world: extension of to include animals, 63

Human society: requires many human gifts and abilities when well run, 96; what it must accomplish to succeed, 177

Human successes and mistakes: interpretation of and Rational Choice Theory, 101

Human survival: depends upon education in eco logical morality, 179

Human thought: how tightly structured? 132

Human wants: as culture-bound and contingent, 86

Humans: as basically "good," 92; basic needs of not confined to humans, 88; imperfect planners, 175; inborn needs of, and reproduction, 86; make mistakes, have positive illusions, cheat, 177; have natural tendency to cooperate, are social beings, 92; do not act in their rational self-interest, 175; not perfect information processors, 114–15; not rational, 108; not solely creatures of emotion, 175; prone to act emotionally rather than sensibly, 176; when well-socialized, 90

Hume, David, 8–9; says "bad" people use inverted moral scale, 93; and everyday experience as guide to morals, 92; on family as source and basic model of society, 94; on history of negativist view of human behavior, 93; on "self-interested" behavior, "altruistic" acts, 108

Humoral medicine: in West, 50

Humoral theory, 32

Hurt and anger: in environmental discourse, 121

Hutterite colonies: size and stability of, 153

Ibn Khaldun: on cycles of dynastic rise and fall, 145–46

Idea of "mind" divorced from body: alien to China, 42

Ideal society: one in which people have a chance to realize differing potentials and work together, 96

Ideological regulation: without real religious sanctions in Japan, 167

Ideology: and actual management practices, how related, 72; of "balance," biological benefits of in China, 41; as higher-order intergrative device, 72; as key element, 72; as validator (of psychological healing system, 72; of the ritual management of resources among Northwest Coast peoples, 72)

"Idols," 104

Illness: considered as due to malevolent and vengeful entities in Africa, Oceanesia, 50; and landscape, offending the spirits in China 39; seen as natural by Chinese of Hong Kong, 50; as viewed by Cantonese of Hong Kong, 50

Image of limited good: in peasant societies, 40

Imperial China: fewness of government officials in, and control, 52

Imperial Valley, California: ecological problems of, 5

Improvements in life: more heavily weighted by humans, 114

Inaccurate beliefs, 9

India: why cow protected? 129

Individual variation, 96

Individuality: value placed on in Castle Peak Bay, 43

Individuals: the actors in culture, 129; need to motivate to conserve, 177

Inference: erroneous from valid observation and Chinese folk belief, 9

Infinitesimal-effect problem, 7

Information about environment: abundance of, 12

Information processing, 100–22; and behavior towards environment, 110–11; biases in, 139

Information: basis of problem solving, 7; need for as much as possible, 179; need for perfect information to make decisions, 109; does not help in "each-we dilemmas," 7

Inquisitions, 166; rooted in religious contradiction, 166

"Insider" accounts, 170; contrasted with "outsider," 170

"Insiders," 171

Instinct: does not determine environmental behavior, 91

Institutions: as defined by Douglass North, 135; as defined by others, 135; exist for a purpose, 135; new institutions needed to stop damage, pay transaction costs, 137–38; to provide solutions, 154; and resource management, 135–59; set up to protect forests, 157; and success at ecological management, 135

Intelligence, 91; situational and interactive, 113

Interconnection of cosmos, individual and community: in China, 39

International free trade: arguments about, 140

Interpretive anthropology, 102

Inuit hunting: interpretation of, 129–30

"Invisible Hand": concept, 139; difficulty of in practice, 140

IQ: one-factor intelligence replaced by other views, 96

Irrational taste: with favorable impact on the environment, 130

Irrationality, 85; and inability to evaluate alternative means, 111

Isolated individuals: problem of, 116

Jacobs, Lynn: on banning grazing on public land, 157

Japan: conservation of forests and fisheries in under Tokugawa, 167

Jefferson, Thomas, 157, 179

Jobs and environment: trade-off between 13

Jonaitis, Aldona: on magical animals as anomalous beings, 61; on Tlingit animal lore, 60

Judeo-Christian tradition, 168

Judson, Sheldon: on soil erosion in core areas of Roman Empire, 129

Jung, Carl: on "archetypal ideas," 103

Justice: does not guarantee good resource management, 184

Kafka, Franz: on unpredictable, uncontrollable situations, 87–88

Kagan, Spencer: on cultural differences in children playing games, 145

Kahnemann, D., Paul Slovic, and Amos Tversky team: flawed research methodology of, 114

KAka': Tlingit story of, 59

Katzie Salish of the lower Fraser River: beliefs regarding sturgeon of, 57–58

Kenyatta, Jomo: as producer of an "insider" ethnography, 170

Keynes, John Maynard, 7; view of, "In the long run we are all dead," 7

Killing only for food: among Mayas, 73

Kleinman, Arthur: and "somatization," 42; on somatization and "mind," 50

Knowledge: basis for making a difficult landscape yield food, 79; collection of as an institution, 143 more important the realm of, the more distortion by wishful thinking, 124

Korea: orientation of houses in, 21

Kottak, Conrad and Alberto Costa: on importance of enlightened cooperation between international agencies and local peoples, 128

Kronenfeld, David: on the handling of probabilities by people, 114

Kwakiutl language (terms): numaym, "descent group owning and managing resources," 65

Kwakiutl. See Kwakwaka'wakw

Kwakwaka'wakw, 65; social organization of, 65

Lack of genetic diversity: and environmental disaster, 148

Lack of sensitivity: problem of for environmentalists, 13

Laderman, Carol, 37, 47

Laguna, Frederica de: on land otters and Tlingit beliefs regarding, 59; on Tlingit moral teachings, 62

Laird, Carobeth: on learning of myth by children and myth environmental content, 69

Land: as world of spirit forces in Chinese folk belief, 17

Land otter, 55; beliefs associated with among Tlingit and shamanism, 63; beliefs regarding among Native American Peoples of the northern Northwest Coast, 58–59; giver of power to the Tlingit, 72; among Northwest Coast peoples, 60–61; soul stealer according to Northwest Coast peoples, 55; stories about on Northwest Coast, 59

Langer, Ellen: on "empowerment," efficacy, 120; on psychological and physical importance of perceived control, 43

Language: as example of arbitrary convention, 133

Lansing, Stephen: on religion as supplier of cultural and emotional involvement to motivate, 163–64; on water regulation in Bali, 167

Large groups: involved in common-property management, 153

Large old trees: worship of in China, 20

"Law and order": absorbs resources, 138

Law of the Sea Treaty, 149

Leaders: may become more unrealistic with age, 117

"Learned helplessness," 116, 120

Lehr, Jay: advocates uncontrolled capitalist development, 110; and "rational" calculus put to emotional needs, 109

Lele people, 46

Lerner, Melvin: on people believing the world is more fair and just than it is, 118

Lévi-Strauss, Claude: concept of bicoleur, 132; on human information processing, 103; on opposition of "culture" and "nature," 57

Lewis, Martin, 13; and debate between romanticizers of the primitive and attackers of the savage, 204n.11; wants government-guided economics shifted to favoring conservation, 158

Li Ki: abundant information about food in, 30

Licorice: use of in Chinese medicine to harmonize, 38

"Little community": no more in modern world, 98

Livelihood: key role of in environmental debate, 13

Liver as food: and "Doctrine of Signatures," 45

"Living in a sacred manner," 81

Logging, 6

Logical extrapolations for conventional wisdom: in ecological management, 12

Long Valley Creek in northeastern California: damage due to destruction of beavers, 137

Long-term beliefs: and long-range consequences, 10

Long-term interests: tendency to value immediate over, 4

Long-term wide-flung costs and benefits: problem of calculating, 110

"Lords of the Animals," 77

"Lords of the Forest," 77

Loss of ceremonies: and destruction of conservationist worldview, 83; means loss of cultural integrity and pride, 82

Love: as early-warning system, 183; for the world, 182; necessary for broad environmental strategy, 183

Ludwig, Donald, 5

Lungs as food: and "Doctrine of Signatures," 45

Lutz, Catherine: on *tabula rasa* view of human nature, 93

MacHarg, Ian, 25

Macrocosm and microcosm: equation of in *feng-shui*, 19

Magical animals: among Northwest Coast peoples, 60

Maintenance of a "balance" of qualities: in Chinese medicine of Hong Kong, 34

Maize: basis of Maya agriculture in the Yucatán, 76

Malinowski: role of in anthropology, 170

Malnutrition: single most important cause of death in China, 30

Management: how achieved by culture and society through institutions, 133; based in costs and benefits, 180; as a social choice, 133; of space, as cultural universal, 18; strategies of and human feelings, 13

Managing and venerating the landscape: lack of distinction between among Chinese, 18

Maoris of New Zealand: conservation ethic of, 124; and extermination of moas, 124; learning from experience of, 124

Market rationality: contrasted to "ecological rationality," 142

Marsh, Charles: and "conservation," 6

Martin, Calvin: and debate between romanticizers of the primitive and attackers of the savage, 204n.11

Martin, Katherine Gould: on poisonous combinations, 47

Martin, Paul S.: and debate between romanticizers of the primitive and attackers of the savage, 204n.11

Marx and Engels: and wishful thinking, 125

Maslow, Abraham: on basic human needs, 86

Mass-media worldviews: as religion, 162

Materialist concerns: do not determine ecological belief systems, 129

Maud, Ralph: on the use of myths as teaching devices in Northwest Coast cultures, 69

Maximization of utility: and "rationality," 106

Maximizing our inclusive fitness, 86

Maya, 73–84; agriculture (and knowledge of resource base, 78; working with nature rather than against it, 76; of Chunhuhub, compared to European infield-outfield farming, 75); agricultural strategy of (best suited to landscape, 79; high investment of in labor and learning, 79); agricultural system of and environment, 77; breakdown of old order among, 82; at Chunhuhub, agriculture of, 75; of Chunhuhub, crops, 75; and the crisis of the present, 80; ceremonies of (and agriculture, 81; purpose, 81–82; teaching function of and agriculture, 82); civilization (collapse of, causes for, and possible Maya responses to, 79; and constraints of environment, 79; decline of to a lower level of complexity, 128); communal landholding of, 76–77; competing housing styles among, 73; cosmos and life of, relationship with agriculture, 81; description of culture, 74; diet, 76; farming cycle of, and ceremonialization, 81; forest (management of, contrasted to cattle-raising, 154; use of, 77); future of, and conservation ideology 83; gender issues among, 80; lack of artificial separation between religion and daily life among, 82; Maize God of, 81; myth of and agriculture (maize), 81; past and present compared, 74; population pressure among and Maya agriculture, forestry, 77; productivity and sustainability of fields of, 75; of central Quintana Roo, history, 74; a record of successes and failures, 128; religion of, and conservation, 82; ritual sacrifice and feasting among, and agriculture, 81; ritual of for "feeding the field," 10; sacred ceiba tree of, 84; shifting agriculture among, 75; subsistence agriculture of, does not mean poverty, 76; success of and environmental management, 128; theme of vengeful animals among, 64; traditional education of in conservation, 81; traditional religion of, and Christianity, 81

Maya language (terms): *ch'achaac*, "calling the rain gods," 81; *chachalacas*, "pheasantlike native bird," 81; *col*, "outfields," 75; *ha'abin*, "name of local tree," 83; *hanlicol*, "feeding the field," 10, 81; *hetzmek*, 81; *hmen*, "one who knows," 83; *koben*, "hearth and tortilla-making area," 81; *maaya*, the Maya, 74; *maayab*, "Maya land," 74; *pachpakal*, "assorted vegetable, fruit, and root crops," 75; *pom*, "tree that is a source of incense," 84; *yum il ba'alche'ob*, "Lords of the Animals," 77; *yuntziloob*, "Lords of the Forest," 77

McDuck, Scrooge, 86

McEvoy, Arthur, 5; on attitudes towards resource bases, 154; on comparative fisheries management, 148–49

McNeill, J. R.: on environmental changes in Mediterranean mountains, 124

Means and ends: problem of, 107

Means-ends, 112

Meat: supplementing, 44

Medical foodways: adverse environmental impact of in China, 29; influence of on Chinese food production, 29; past importance of in preserving species, in promoting agricultural diversity, 29

Medicinal herbs: grown or gathered by Maya of Chunhuhub, 75

Medicine: goal of in Chinese view, 39

Medicines: qualities of in China, 38

Medieval European bestiaries, 104

Merchant, Carolyn: on rational individualism as product of capitalism, 100

Mérida: focus of encroaching Spanish-speaking world for Maya, 82

Mexican and American children: cultural differences of, 145

Microeconomics: real behavior different than, 112

Microhabitat: importance of in Maya agriculture, 76

Milpa: guardian spirits of, 81

Milpas: similarity of to natural burns, 76

Mind: and overriding, crosscutting, and integrating survival needs, 88; not separate in Chinese view, 50

Minimalist communities: and religion, 163

"Minority rights": rooted in religion and civil morality, 141

"Misses": in positive illusion theory, 118

Mistakes: how do people make them? 101

Modern resource management: influences on, 172

Modernization, 80; as destructive force among Maya, 82; and ecological and social devastation, 147

Money: as a counter in a game, 86; as means to what we want, 86

Monocropping: problems of, 180

Moral behavior: according to Hume, 8–9

Moral code: for environmental action, 179–80; fundamental tenets needed in, 181; type needed, 182

Moral codes: cannot be based on emotion only, or practical reason, 161; construction of, 166; criticism of, 90; must be believed, 161; never final, 181; not enough, 182; and Social Contracts, 96; and "Wrong," 89

Moral "crusade," 95

Moral ecology, 163

Moral suasion, importance of in change, 155

Moral systems: needed to encourage long-term, wide-flung self-interest, 108

Morality: basis of, 180; changes in and world environmental problems, 155; as society in process, 181

"Morals," 89

Most useful error, 9

Mother's grave: importance of in China, 24

Motivation, 161; an emotional matter, 123

Mountains: sacredness of in rural China, 20

Moxibustion, 39

Multiple abilities: as measure of intelligence, 96

"Multiple use," 150

Murphy, Earl, 7; on one group enjoying benefits but passing on costs, 136

Mutual accommodation: problem of, 13

Mutual respect: necessary for cosociation of humans and nonhumans among Northwest Coast peoples, 63

Mutual-aid relationships: of humans and nonhumans among Northwest Coast peoples, 63

Myth: of abundance masks limited food resources of most Northwest Coast peoples, 67–68; of American small farm, 157; of conservationist Indian, 56; and folktale, and environmental education of young, 69; of the

(Myth, *continued*)
"Invisible Hand" weeding out inefficient ranchers, 150; "of the savage," 102

Nahuatl of Mexico, 170, 173
Narrow self-interest: and environmental mismanagement, 94
National Commission on the Environment: on tax restructuring and ending subsidies, 177
National Forests: incentives for unrestricted use, 158; and logging, 157; managed worse than private forest land, 158; purpose of, 158
Native American environmental management strategies: and white man, 126
Native American peoples: good environmental management strategies of, 126; of Northwest Coast (animal lore of), 55; characterization of cultures, societies, 55; compared to Chinese, 55; nature of belief in "land otter," 55
"Native" ethnography, 171
Natural environment: need to define as part of our personal community, 173
Natural forces: according to Chinese folk belief, 16
Natural forest: and Maya gardens, 76
"Naturalistic" and "personalistic" medicine, 50; not meaningful to Castle Peak Bay Chinese, 39
"Nature," 168
Near East: civilizations of, failure and ecological factors, 129; overirrigation in, 168
Near Eastern peoples: overgrazing among before rise of cities, 127
Needham, Joseph: on Chinese medicine as storehouse of knowledge, 33
Negative-sum game: played by a whole country, 145
Negative-sum games, 143; political game, 97
Negativist view: and absolutism, 94; and anti-environmentalists, 94; widely held today: why does it sell? 94
Nelson, Richard: on Kaska, and white influence on resource management of, 56
Neo-Confucianism, 42
Neo-Hobbesian sociobiologists: postulate a vicious society, 94
Neutral point: in the humoral system, and "balance," 36
"Neutrality": in heating, cooling, wet or dry system, 36
New Age: religions, 96; spiritualists, 166

New Territories of Hong Kong: and breakdown of *feng-shui*, 25; changes taking place in, 34; Chinese medicine of, 35; Chinese nutritional therapy of, 33; concept of "balance" in medicine of, 34; conservatism of people of, 33–34
Nisbett, Richard and Lee Ross team: flawed research methodology of, 114; on the tendency to support wild games, 117
Nonhuman powers: and involvement with natural resources among Northwest Coast peoples, 66
Nootka. *See* Nuu-chah-nulth of Vancouver Island
"Normal" personalities: variation among, 96
"Normality": as personality comparison, 96
North Sea herring fisheries, 6
North, Douglass: purpose of institutions to lower translation costs, 135
Northwest Coast Native Americans. *See* Northwest Coast of North America: Indians of, peoples of
Northwest Coast of North America: conservation of peoples of, 68; forests of, 54; Indians of (belief that objects and things of nature are persons, 113; relationships of with nonhuman beings, 66; views on natural and healing power, 41); myth of abundance of, 67–68; Native American (art of, 60–61; myths of, and environmental resources, 62; peoples of and fishing, 55; management strategies, 126); peoples of (apologize to tree, plant, or animal for taking, 64; descent groups owners and man agers of most resources among 65; relationships with animals, 62; view of animals contrasted with modern American, 71); religion of peoples of, and environmental management, 176
Northwest United States: extreme forest problems of, 157
Nourishment of health, 52
"Nourishment of life," 43; and Cantonese of Hong Kong, 50
Nutrition: head of medical specialties in China, 30
Nuu-Chah-Nulth language (terms): *mamalni*, "floating-house people," 57
Nuu-Chah-Nulth of Vancouver Island: attitude of towards animals, 62; kinship, social or ganization of, and resources, 65; viewed first white men as salmon in human form, 57

Octopus, *Octopus* spp.: associated by peoples of northern Northwest Coast with important powers, 58; role of in Northwest Coast mythology, 60

Old Testament: ecological teachings of, 168

Older medical traditions: survival of in China and in the West, 32–33

Open society: according to Dryzek, 142

Operators competing for a resources: problem of, 150

Opponents: seen as repository of all vileness, 121

Oppression: as factor in underdevelopment, 176

Optimism: and environmental damage, 164

Oranges: main Maya cash crop, 76

Orans, Martin: on Indian nonviolence and protection of cow, 129

Orr, David 5; on "cold" rationality, 113; on people loving their plants and animals, 172

Orr, Robert: on the need for emotion in text books, 133

Ostrom, Elinor: case studies of failed management, 152; on needs of decent resource management, 151–52; on perfect rationality, 152; on poor regulation and cheating, 151; on public and private regulation, 151; on people interested in consuming to satisfy physical needs, 154

Otters: basis of mythology of, 61; in life and mythology, 61

"Outsider" accounts, 171; and "insider" literature, 171; and "insider" views, 170

"Outsider" literature of ethnobiology and cultural ecology, 170

Overarching high-level systems, 49

Overarching symbol systems, 41–42; why one chosen over others, 42

Overarching, all-connecting symbols or values: importance of in China, 41

Overconfidence: and leadership, 117

Overfishing: character of, 136

Overgeneralization: problem of, 113

Overgrazing: and low fees, 157

Oversimplification and emotional distortion: role in ecological crisis, 5

Overspecialization: decouples from a broad ecological view, 125

Ownership: and management of resources by descent groups among Northwest Coast peoples, 65; of resources among Northwest Coast peoples, 65

Oystercatcher, *Haemotopus bachmani*: associated by Native American peoples of northern Northwest Coast with important powers, 58; role in Northwest Coast Native American mythology, 60

Pangolin: and *ch'i*, 49; magically powerful among Lele people, 46; scales used in Chinese medicine, 128; as supplementing food in China, 46

Panicking: as response to stress, 96

Paper recycling, 6

Parfit, Derek 7, 181; on Present-Aim Theory, 161

Pariah groups: not always defined by religion, 141; and religion, 141

Passenger pigeon, 158

Passion: and reason, dichotomy between, 9; role of in decision making, 8–9

Pedraza, Jesus Salinas: and native ethnography, 170–71

People: as brilliant approximators, 178

Perceived control, 87

Pereira, Gilberto Balan: on Maya medicine, 75

Perfect information: problem of in an imperfect world, 111

Perfect relationship with the environment: no group has, 127

Personal decisions: most "rational" and "sensible," 8

Pests: consumption of by Mayas as part of agricultural system, 76

Phenomenologists, 125; criticized, 119; mistaken views of, 112

Phlogiston Theory, 104

Physical survival needs of human beings, 86

Pinkerton, Evelyn: on people interested in consuming to satisfy physical needs, 154

Plants: and "Doctrine of Signatures," 45; mountains, rocks, and even weather phenomena regarded as persons by Northwest Coast peoples, 57

Platycodon, 127–28

Players: psyches of, and perceived nature of a game, 144

Poaching: as indication of social breakdown, 90–91

Poisonous combinations: according to Chinese, 47; how handled, "Using poison to drive out poison," 47; outside of China, 47; *See also Tu* foods

Poisonous meats: according to Chinese, 47

Political apathy: and helplessness, 120

"Politicians," 113

Politics: 120–21, 183; character of, 160; as competition between groups, 5; about conflicts and emotion, 13; and emotion, 5, 113; and environment, 172; and hurt people, 120; and other belief systems, 160

Polynesian language (terms): *kapu*, 11; *tabu*, 11

Polynesians: resource management of, 11

Pork: displaced by beef in American diet, 131

Porkert , Manfred, 31

"Positive" feedback: not all positive in effects, 125

Positive Illusion Theory: better than Rational Choice Theory, 118; problems as a theory, 118

Positive illusions, 4; as important cause of hu man failure, 119; and rational self-interest, 175; and resource overuse, 117; and thinking best of one's own reference group, 121

Positive-sum games, 143; and scientists, 95

Post hoc, ergo propter hoc arguments: as plausible mistake, 103

Postmodern views: inadequacy of, 102

Postmodernists, 125

Potlaches: and wasting of resources, 68

Poultry: supplementing, 44

Power: and Chinese medicine, 51

"Power-animal": and fear of witchcraft among Tlingit, 63

Practical reason, 8, 170; and survival of species, 8

Practical, applied sciences: emphasized in China, 52

Prejudices and preconceptions: role of in misunderstanding, 112

Present satisfaction and future benefit: the problem of, 110

Present-Aim Theory, 161

"Primitive": views of, 170

"Primitives," 168; as happy children of nature, 126; as natural ecologists, 126

Prisoner's dilemma, 7, 143

Pritchard, John: on Haisla when resources were short, 67

Private ownership: and problem of overgrazing, 149

Privatization: as remedy for common-pool prob lems, 149; makes "tragedy of commons" worse, 149

Probabilities: problem humans have in calculating, 113–14

Problem solving: different, possibly opposed interests involved, 107; optimally, difficulty of, 107;

Proper living: in a comparative context, 41

"Property," 148; problem of, 181

Prosocial behavior: genetic basis of, 92; rule of, 92

Protected land: problems of, 133

Psychological problems, 42

Psychological pressures: and mismanagement of resources, 96

Psychological strategies: promoting sound ecological management, 10

Psychological uses of the wild: in West and among Northwest Coast societies, 71

Pu foods, 45

Pu p'in, "supplementing things": use of herbs and food as part of, 44; *See also* Supplementing

Pu. See Supplementing

Public ideology: of resource management and wise use among Northwest Coast peoples, 65–66

Public opinion: enforces regulations and management schemes, 91

Public vs. private: and personal social functions among Northwest Coast Native Americans, 61

Pure science: lack of in China, 52

Puritanism, 166; and conservation movement, 166

"Pursuit of happiness," 183

Qualities of objects: superficial and basic, 49

Queen Charlotte Islands: beliefs in 57, 59; Haida of, 67

Quintana Roo, 73–74; deserts of, 77–78

Raccoon dogs: as supplementing food in China, 46

Radin, Paul: on Winnebago religion, 172

Rainforest: and rational economists, 110

Rainforests: saving, 180

Ranches: the well- and the badly-managed, 150

Rapid population growth: destructive of regulation systems, 149

Rappaport, Roy: on religion, 160; on religion as a carrier wave for ecological knowledge, 171; on religion as coder of ecological knowledge, 111; and view that ecological knowledge is coded as religious knowledge, 27

"Rat choice people," 108

"Rat choices," 109

Rational acts, 107

Rational behavior: economists' models for assume perfect knowledge, 111

Rational Choice Theory, 107–9; explained, 100; problem of rigid application of, 111

Rational economists: and nuclear power, 110
Rational ethics: problem of, 165
Rational ideas: and anti-environmentalism, 109
Rational individualism, and capitalist world, 100
Rational self-interest, 89, 98
Rational solutions, 112
Rational thinker: acts only if sure, 109
Rational thinking, 85, 172, 176; and Puritanism, 166
Rational thought, 112; and environmentalism, 109; definition of cannot be decided by rational calculus, 109
Rationality: according to economists, 108; definitions of, 105–6; general claims of, and environmental disaster, 110; and institutions, 153; problems with defining, 109
Raven, *Corvus corax*: associated by Native American peoples of northern Northwest Coast with important powers, 58; role in Northwest Coast Native American mythology, 60; special position of in among Northwest Coast Native American art, 61
Reaganomics, 145
Real costs of production: and "externalities," 181
"Real games," 143
Real-world situations: and cooperation or competition, 145
Real-world cognition: and decision making, bases for, 112
Reality: as counter to mistaken impressions, 125
Reason: an aid to reach goals set by instinct and emotions, 12
Rebellion: social manipulation of, 133
Reciprocation: evolutionary importance of, 92
Relations: of "empowerment," among animals and humans, 57; of production and social superstructure, according to Marx, 124
Religion: activity, must involve sharing of moral and emotional foundations of society, 163; and ambiguity, 163; association of with good resource management, 166; based on a sacred book, symbolic rituals of, 163; bigotry in and environmentalism, 180; and children, 164; deals directly with human emotion and suffering, 161; and direct emotional involvement with natural resources among Northwest Coast peoples, 66; and economic behavior, 162; educational role of, 172; environmentalism does not need, 180; and generalized philosophy and cosmology, 163; how it "sells" a code, 162; involves (community in sanctions, 165; emotion in

moral codes, 161; emotions, the community and has non-logical approach, 111); keeps adults because of community, rituals, and symbols, 164; key element in convincing people to manage environment in some way, 167; lack of word for in Chinese, 18; and landscape, among Native American peoples, 54; and linking of ethical codes, 168; as manipulation of good, 20; many ends served by, 162; may be excuse for abuse of power, 141; not code or system but a general term, 162; no equation of one religion and one moral code, 163; not necessary for an environmental ethic, 173; not the same everywhere, 172; possible negative role of, 141; provider of a moral argument and an institution, 141; and positive illusions, 164; provides (poor with ideology of resistance, 141; rules against shortsightedness, 164); and resource management and wise use, among Northwest Coast peoples, 66; role of (in modern Western societies, 171; in traditional societies, 160); serves to bind emotional appeals to codes for living, 163; and technical philosophy, 161; used in traditional societies to sanction management strategies, 160; also used to sanction environmental destruction, 168; whole religion not necessary, rather a minimum of basic points, 98; why stronger than common sense as coder of ecological knowledge, 111; and worldview and resource management strategies, 167
Religions, 162; do not need to "represent the community," as seen by Emile Durkheim, 162; how do they sell moral codes? 161
Religious construction of sanctions: not necessary for effective conservation management, 167
Religious diversity: according to St. Paul, 163
Religious leaders: will be remembered longer than philosophers, 161
Religious "reforms," 166
Renaissance: and science, 143
Reproduction: as "bad" word, 122; as key cultural issue, 122
Resistance: in a constrained Chinese society, 42
Resource base: varying attitudes towards, 154
Resource management: common themes of in various cultures and belief systems, 11; how can it assert self in a Hobbesian world?, 98; need to look at all institutions of a society to comprehend, 130; and religious representation

(Resource management, *continued*)
of, 55; as religion, 11; role of local
communities in, 134; rules for, 146–47
Resource use: as the real problem, 123
Resources: and an actual community, 151;
conscious management of for long-term use in
North America, 68; importance of knowing
value of, 142; saved because people take as end
in themselves, 131
"Reverence for nature," 81
Revitalization movement, 90
Rhinoceros horn: as supplementing food in
China, 46; used in Chinese medicine, 128
Rhinos: exterminated for medicinal horn, 29
Rice agriculture in south China: 131; reasons for
rise of, 131; success of, 132
Ridington, Robert: on Beaver Indians and spirit
power, 64; on religion used to sanction
conservation, teach, 55
"Rights": for plants and animals, 182
River otter, *Lutra canadensis*. *See also* land otter
River otter *Lutra canadensis*: associated by Native
American peoples of northern Northwest
Coast with important powers, 58
Rizvi, Najma: on food beliefs and medical
practices in India, 43–44
Rocks and rock formations: worship of in China,
20
Roman Empire: environmental damage during,
124
Romanticizers of the primitive and attackers of
the savage: debate between, 203–4n.11
Rosenberg, Alexander: on "relationship between
beliefs, desires and behavior," 107
Rossabi, Morris: on Kublai Khan, 117
Rules: of conduct towards plants and animals
among Northwest Coast peoples, 64;
enforcement of, according to Ostrom, 152;
general and specific, how maintained, 151;
limiting use of environmental resources,
among Canadian and Alaskan Native cultures,
56; of resource manage ment, 133
Ruddle, Kenneth and Ray Chesterfield: on
education of younger generation in food
production, 69

Sacred books: "canonical" and poetical, 163
Sacred groves, 11; and preservation of old forest
types, 12
Sacred tree: world-wide belief in, 103
Safina, Carl: on destruction of bluefin tuna
resource, 149

Sahlins, Marshall: on "practical reason," 171
Saint Paul, 163
Salish: concept of spirit guardian among, 64;
guardian spirits of, 72; kinship, social
organization of, 65
Salmon: mythology of among Northwest Coast
Native Americans, 57
San Marino, California: and *feng-shui*, 23
Santa Ana River: damage due to destruction of
beavers, 137; improved by action of beavers,
130
Scapegoat: role played by, 159; weaker group as,
122
Scapegoating, 121; and breakdown in
conservation and resource management,
96–97
Schultz, Richard: on human need to cope, 43
Science: and absolute truth, viii; in all societies,
143; nature of, viii; role of observation in, viii
Sciences: differences, 143
Sea cucumbers: as supplementing food in China,
46
Sea otter: overexploited in the nineteenth
century, 126
Seaman, Gary, 16
Secular humanism, 162
Secular religions, 167
Security: basis of work, 178
"Self": and "want," 161
Self-actualization: and Maslow, 86
Self-defensive-anger: and failure, 177
Self-efficacy, 87; major area for positive illusions,
118
Self-interest: problem of extreme, 94; material
and economic, and emotion, 97
Self-interested behavior, 108
"Selfish greed:" blamed for resource depletion,
126
Selfishness and violence: associated with the
breakdown of a complex society, 95
Shaman: activities of and association with herbal
medicine in China, 38; of Hong Kong, and
natural causes for illness, 51; and land otters on
Northwest Coast, 59–60
Shamanism: among peoples of the northern
Northwest Coast, 58; and corollaries of,
69–71
Short and long term interests: in ecological crisis,
6
Shrader-Frechette, K. S.: on the rational person
ensuring against future disaster, 109; vis-à-vis
Leh, 110

Simon, Herbert: influence of theories of, 111; on using imperfect information, 111

Simon, Julian: on environmentalist received wisdom, 183

Simple societies: most regulated by moral codes, 5

Simplification of world: need for among humans, 114

Singleton, Sara and Michael Taylor: critical of Ostrom, 152; on strong communities, 152

Skeena River, 67

Small farm: as virtuous, 157

Smil, Vaclav: on breakdown of traditional ecological management in China, 26

Smith, Adam: on mercantilism, 141

Smith, Eric Alden: applies materialist calculus to Inuit hunters of northern Canada, 129–30; on materialist concerns, 129

Smith, Page: on power, 117

Sociability: entails need for a social system, 89

Social breakdown: environmental impact of, 136

Social codes and institutions promoting ecological management, 10

Social goals, pursued once the need for food and shelter met, 86

Social harmony: and Chinese politics, 38–39; connection with shaman in China, 38

Social inequality: and injustice, victimization, 138

Social life: and need for control, 89

Social mechanisms: and resource pressure, 126

Social morality, 161; bases, character of, 161

Social needs: and emotion, 89; only indirectly involved with the environment, 120

Social order vs. autonomy: problems in resource management due to conflict between, 89

Social policies: and game theory, 144

Social pressures: nature of, influence, 132

Social science theories: limitations of, 155

Social systems and institutions: and environment, 124

Social variables, 124

Social Contract, 89, 94; no solution in Hobbes' "war of each against all," 95

Societies: and cultures, 123; problem of too weakly organized, 136; unjust or ethnically polarized and environmental management, 138

Society: cemented by arbitrary convention according to Elster, 133; and control, a partial contradiction, 178; degeneration of into ethnic or ideological rat fight, and conservation, 120

Sociobiology, 91, 108

Soil Conservation Service: worked by persuading, 149

Soil erosion in the United States: problem of, 149, responses to, 184

Solutions to world ecological crisis: must have psychological as well as economic dimensions, 14

"Somatization," 42

"Song": power from spirits, 64

"Sour Grapes": problem of, 8

South America: small populations of groups and conservation, 127

South Korea: and breakdown of *feng-shui*, 25

South Mexico: needs of local people rank above survival of species, 134

South Wind: in mythology of Haida, 57

Southern Yucatán: deserts of, 77–78

Soviet Communism, as religion, 162

Soviet planners: as rational economists, 110

Spanish Inquisition, 166

Spanish language (terms): *ejido*, "communally owned tract of usable land: history," 74; *milpas*, "outfields," 75; Yucatán, etymology of, 74

Species and ecosystems: must not be sacrificed to the economic system, 182

Spiritual "empowerment": by creatures, among university-educated Native Americans, 72

Spirituality: revival of, 173

Sport, Mrs. Mable: on protection of fish, 61–62

Springs, points in the sea: magical properties of in China, 20

Spiritual medicine: major form of medicine in Castle Peak Bay, 39

Sproat, Gilbert Malcom: on planting of salmon eggs in streams by Nuu-Chah-Nulth, 66–67

Stable preferences: assumed by economists, 111

Stress: and control, 51–52

Strict rules: in resource management, 140–41

Strong communities: do not guarantee sane resource use, 184

Strong social code: importance of for people to recognize long-term interests, 176

Structuralist and structural-functionalist theories: divorced from practice, 155

"Stupid masses," 102

Suboptimizing, 116

Subsidies: and American myth, 158; as major problem area, 148; problems created by, 150; and uneconomic behavior, 158;

Success: and emotion, 178; foundations for, 178

Successful environmental practices: foundation for, 134

Suicide: and "rational" choice, 107–8

Sullivan, Paul: on Maya, 74

Supplementing foods: application, nutritional qualities of, 44–45; characteristics of, 44; examples, applications of, 44–45; gently heating in China, 44; not all rational in system of, 45; and poison, according to Chinese, 47; slow cooking of in China, 44; as strange and uncanny, 46; the stranger the more powerful, 46

Supplication: and ch'i, 21

Swanton, John: recorded conservationist morals of Haida, 62

Swiftlets: exterminated as medicine, 29

Switzerland: regulation of grazing land in, 150

Syllogistic logic, 49

Systems: of factual knowledge, 103–4; linking science and public morality, 26;

Systems Theory: and China, 36

T'ao Hung-ching: and Chinese medical classics, 32; in later Chinese medicine, 32–33

Taboo, 11

Taiwan: and brown sugar, 48; and "cleansing" and "dispelling" foods, 48

Tanner, Adrian: and debate between romanticizers of the Primitive and attackers of the Savage, 204n.11; on bringing home animals, 57

Tao, 18

Tax breaks: and environmental problems, 157

Taylor, Shelly: on belief that humans act in their economic self-interest, 117; on achievement and self-image, 118; on human need for a sense of effectiveness, 118; on Positive Illusion Theory predicting racism and prejudice, 118; on rules of Positive Illusion Theory, 118; should we make people more positively self-deluding? 119

Teaching: and improving performance, 114

Technical philosophy, 161

Television, 182

Thaler, Richard: on the limited ability to calculate optima, 106–7

Theory: role of in science, viii; divorced from practice, 155

"Think globally, act locally," 180

Thinking and emotion: as characterized by Chinese, 50

Third World: source of environmental problems of, 156

Thompson, E. P.: on working class, 43

Thoreau, H. D.; coiner of word "ecology," 5

Threat or stress: and irrationality, 153

Three Mile Island, 5

Thurow, Lester: on the United States as a "zero-sum society," 144

Tiger, Lionel: on instinctive distortion of perceptions, 117

Tit for Tat Program, 144–45

Tlingit language (terms): kucdaga, "person changed into a land otter," 59; shluch, "power bundle," "medicine pouch," 60

Tobacco production: heavily subsidized, 157

Tokugawa Shogunate: conservation policies of, 167

Toledo, Victor: on "ethnoecology," 160

Totem poles, 61

Tradition: and change, 10

Traditional China: difficulty of enforcing rational planning in, 25; ecological management in, problems of, 26; life in terms of constrainment in, 42

Traditional Chinese folk medical system, 43

Traditional Chinese foreign policy, 47

Traditional Chinese society: view of natural and supernatural, belief and secular knowledge, 18

Traditional culture systems: valuing of, 165

Traditional cultures: and learning, 124

Traditional ethical and religious teachings: and conservation, 163

Traditional peoples: disagreements about conservationist nature of, 128

Traditional resource management: among Canadian and Alaskan Native cultures, 56; goal is actual personal and emotional involvement with landscape and nonhuman inhabitants, 174

Traditional societies: beneficial aspects of seemingly irrational behavior in, 9; moral teachings of and environment, 174; as societies which have come to terms with environments, 173; and solutions to environmental problems, 10; values of experiences of and ecological management, 10

Traditional worldviews, 10; not unchanging, 10

Tragedy of the Commons, 7, 77, 177; averted by Maya religion, 82; avoided by some, 154–55; in fisheries, beaver trapping, 136–37; and Hobbes' "state of warre," 93

Transaction costs: of environmental damage, who pays? 137

Tropical forests: destruction of for pastures, 126

Tropical rainforests: cut to support cattle, 137

"Truth": in classification, 49

Tsimshian: social organization of, 65

Tu foods: characteristics, 46–47

Tung Chung-shu: and the new medical system of Han, 32

Turnbull, Colin: on Ik and social breakdown, 90

Udall, Stuart, 98

Uncastrated male poultry: and cancer according to Chinese, 47; explanation of poison in, according to Chinese, 47

Unfettered freedom: American experience of, 158

Union Carbide, 156–57

"Union with nature," 10

United States: anti-environmental movement in, 176; as antithesis of traditional China or Northwest Coast, 156; changes in and game theory, 144; changing political landscape in, 98; could have done much worse, 156; elections since 1980, 97; and environmental movement, 156; environmental catastrophes of, 157; old errors sell well in, 102: position in world of, 156; problems of agricultural system of, 157; problems of, not unique, 176; rise of networks, support groups, work groups, special interest groups in, 98; social morality of, 161; success in protecting environment in, 156; voting power of western states of, 158

"Unity (or harmony): with nature," 180

Unregulated private enterprise: and environmental disaster, 158

Unschuld, Paul, 34; on change to "personalistic" emphasis by Chinese medicine, 50; on Chinese medicine as system, 33; on many varieties of Chinese medical tradition, 39; on a naturalistic Chinese medicine, 51

Urban design: in traditional China, 25

Urban life, decoupled from experience with ecological reality, 125

USSR: antienvironmentalism of, 156; failures in environmental management of, 136; successor states of, 156

Utility, 106; and altruism, hurting others, 108

Venerated spots: in *feng-shui*, 20

Vitamins: importance in superiority of Western nutritional medicine, 33

Votes "against," 97

"Voting: against everything," 159; one's fear, 97

Vultures: as supplementing food in China, 46

Wang Ch'ung: and rationalism, 32

Wastes: all returned to soil by Mayas, 76

Water: pollution, 6; problem of in a Maya land, 79; quality, political issues associated with, 7

"Way of life": problem when protected, 157

Ways of reaching: choice between, 85

Weak: importance of rights for, 142; resistance strategies of, 141

Wealth: in *feng-shui*, 22; transfer of from poorer to richer in United States, 97

Weber, Max: on "disenchantment" with the world, 168; on "disenchantments," 164; on emotion displacing rational calculation, 135

Weinstein, Neil: on lack of realism about personal risks, 117

Western medicine: compared to Chinese, 34; as practiced in Castle Peak Bay, 39

Western philosophical realism: rejected by Chinese, 49–50

White influence: on Native American cultures of Northwest Coast, 56

Whooping cranes: saved by international treaty and local suasion, 134

Wild gambles: do not pay off, 117

Wild man: varieties of, 57

Wild meat: more supplementing than tame, 44

Willis, Paul: on English working-class youth, 132–33

Wine: and "Doctrine of Signatures," 45

Wise use advocates: and extremists, 121

Wise Use Agenda, 13–14

Wishful reinterpretation of perception: to suit illusion, 4

Wishful thinking and positive illusion: and world ecological crisis, 4

Wolfthorn berries: in Chinese folk belief, nutritional values of, 9

Womb: symbolism of in *feng-shui*, 19

Working "for money": but not for money itself, 86

World environmental problem: and human emotions, 176

World environmental problems: and the wishful reinterpretation, 4

World religions: and symbols, 163

Worldview: animals in among Northwest Coast peoples, 71; and learning, 10; of Northwest Coast peoples, in myth and ritual, 72; sources of distortion in, 71

Worship: and *feng-shui* mutually supporting in China, 27; and *feng-shui*, two different ways of

(Worship, *continued*)
 observing facts and principles, 27; of trees and
 rocks in China, 20

Yang and *yin*: character of, 31; in Hong Kong, 34;
 as new system in early China, 31
Young, John: on Yun Long in Hong Kong, 40

Yucatec language, 74

Zajonc, Robert: on connection of stimulus and
 emotion, 89; on importance of emotion in
 human thinking, 52
Zero-sum game: and politics, 95
Zero-sum games, 143